This Is The Day

Dorothy Eaton Watts

This book is published in collaboration
with the Youth Department as an enrichment of
the Morning Watch devotional plan.

Review and Herald Publishing Association
Washington, D.C. 20012

Copyright © 1982 by
Review and Herald Publishing Association

Editor: Bobbie Jane Van Dolson
Cover Design: Howard Bullard, Jr.

Library of Congress Cataloging in Publication Data

Watts, Dorothy Eaton, 1937-
    This is the day.

    Includes index.
    Summary: A collection of devotional readings for every day of the
year, each recalling an event from the recent or remote past which took
place on that date.
    1. Youth—Prayer-books and devotions—English.
2. Children—Prayer-books and devotions—English.
3. Devotional calendars—Seventh-day Adventists.
[1. Prayer books and devotions. 2. Devotional calendars
—Seventh-day Adventists] I. Title.
BV4850.W32   242'.2   82-613
ISBN 0-8280-0145-6   AACR2

Printed in U.S.A.

For my mother,
ESTEL EATON
Who taught me to count each new day
God gives as a day of
opportunity and challenge.

THIS IS THE DAY!

This is the day when many exciting things happened in the long ago. Out of the many incidents of history that actually took place on this day in other years, one has been chosen as the basis for each day's reading. Each story emphasizes something important that young people need to do on this day, in 1983.

This is the day to love, laugh, sing, share, and grow. It is a day to praise the Lord. It is a time when we can count our many blessings.

This is the day to decide to follow Jesus. It is a day to choose between the right and the wrong. It is a day to confess our sins and make things right.

This is the day when we should study our Bibles as never before. It is a day to draw closer to God through prayer and meditation.

This is the day that we must make certain of what we believe and where we stand in the great battle between good and evil that is going on in this world.

This is the day to get ready for Jesus to come. It is a day to witness to others. It is a day to share our faith.

This is the day of opportunity for God's youth. We are never sure about tomorrow. Yesterday is gone. Today, this day, is all that we have.

"This is the day which the Lord hath made; we will rejoice and be glad in it" (Ps. 118:24).

ABOUT THE AUTHOR

Bird watching, cycling, and hiking are leisure time activities of this year's author. A lover of animals, she has had a variety of pets, including a python and three monkeys.

Mrs. Watts grew up in the hills of southern Ohio and attended Mount Vernon Academy, Columbia Union College, and Andrews University. She and her pastor-evangelist husband worked in Western Canada before accepting a call to India, where they have served for sixteen years. While her husband traveled as president of South India Union and later as Ministerial secretary of the Southern Asia Division, Mrs. Watts kept busy rearing a family of three adopted children, two boys and a girl. At various times she worked as a secretary, teacher, principal, and Home and Family Service director.

She was the first director of Sunshine Orphanage, a home for abandoned babies, which began in a bedroom of her home. She also directed the Adventist Child Care Agency, where she coordinated the sponsorship of 5,000 orphans and needy children.

Mrs. Watts has written stories for *Primary Treasure, Guide, Insight,* and *Adventist Review.* She is the author of *Who Is God?* a guide for teachers of kindergarten Bible in mission day schools.

MIDNIGHT CALL

I heard the voice of the Lord, saying, Whom shall I send, and who will go for us? Then said I, Here am I; send me. Isaiah 6:8.

"What is it?" asked Ida. "Can I do something to help you?" The light of her oil lamp revealed the tense features of one of the town's leading men.

"Oh, yes! I desperately need your help for my wife. She is a lovely girl, only 14, and she is dying in childbirth. Since you have come from America, I thought you might help."

"Oh, I'm so sorry!" Ida sympathized with the young Indian. "It is my father you want. He's the doctor. I'll call him."

"Never!" exclaimed the distraught husband, barring the passageway. "No men besides those of her own family have ever seen my wife. *You* must come."

"But I'm not a doctor. I'm not even a nurse. I can't do anything. Surely you'll let me call my father to save her life."

"No!" replied the young man. "That is impossible. Won't you come?"

Sadly Ida shook her head, then watched him turn away and go out into the night. Twice more before morning men came on similar errands, begging her to help their young wives who were dying in childbirth. Twice more she had to tell anxious husbands that she could do nothing and watch them turn away without medical aid because their religious convictions would not allow a man to attend their wives. Early morning brought the news that all three young women had died.

Before breakfast that day Ida walked into her parents' bedroom and announced, "I'm going to America to study to be a doctor so that I can come back here and help the women of India."

On January 1, 1900, Dr. Ida Scudder, now a physician, stepped off the boat at Madras, ready to fulfill her promise. Today, Christian Medical College, Vellore, stands as a memorial to Ida's dedication. Hundreds of doctors and nurses are trained there to serve the people of India.

God had a plan for young Ida Scudder's life. He called her to service that dark night so long ago. He has a plan for your life, too. Perhaps 1983 will be the year when God will reveal that plan. How will you respond?

MOTHER BICKERDYKE'S BONFIRE

His word was in mine heart as a burning fire. Jeremiah 20:9.

New Year's Day, 1864, was miserably cold. For more than a week sleet and wind had beat against the hospital tents where lay more than two thousand casualties from the Civil War Battle of Lookout Mountain. Mother Mary Ann Bickerdyke had kept the soldiers warm by building a large bonfire, but now, as the thermometer touched zero, the supply of logs ran out. It was already late afternoon, and in desperation Mrs. Bickerdyke hurried off to find the doctor in charge before he left for headquarters.

"The logs are all gone," she panted, when she finally caught up with him. "Better send out a chopping party before it gets any later."

Looking up at the darkening sky, the doctor replied, "It's too late now. You'll just have to manage until tomorrow." He turned, mounted his horse, and galloped off to his warm room in Chattanooga.

Mrs. Bickerdyke was furious. She stood there in the road and shook her fist at him. When he was out of sight she walked the half mile to the nearest camp, where she persuaded a group of soldiers to accompany her to the hospital.

After giving the men a hot drink, she ordered them to tear out a line of log fortifications that was near the hospital and put the wood on the fire. Destroying military property without orders was a serious crime, but many of the men had been cared for by Mrs. Bickerdyke when they were ill. Besides, they knew that no one ever said No to this courageous woman from Illinois. They tore out the logs, chopped them, and piled them on the fire.

Hundreds of lives were saved that night because Mrs. Bickerdyke kept the fire burning.

God has a similar task for you today. He needs youth who are on fire for Jesus Christ. He needs boys and girls whose hearts are aglow with His love and truth. If the faith of Jesus is burning in your heart you will radiate warmth and blessing wherever you go. Many from the cold world around you will be attracted to the glow of your fire and will thus find hope and salvation.

Make sure you keep the fire burning in your heart this year.

THE LEPERS' FRIEND

Even so faith, if it hath not works, is dead, being alone. James 2:17.

Molokai, one of the Hawaiian Islands, has a pleasant climate, shady palms, sandy beaches, rugged mountains, fantastic scenery. It is also known as the "Friendly Island" because of the courtesy its people show to visitors. Sounds like a perfect place for a holiday, doesn't it? However, few tourists visit this tropical paradise, for Molokai is a leper colony. It was made famous by the sacrifice of Joseph Damien.

Joseph was born in Belgium to devout Catholic parents on January 3, 1840. How proud they were the day he decided to become a priest! Little did they realize the special place God had for their son.

Not long after his ordination Joseph heard of the hundreds of lepers on the island of Molokai. "All are hungry, ragged, forsaken," his church leaders told him. "Their only friendship is that which misery invents for itself. We must send someone to take the hope of Christ to them." Joseph volunteered.

When he arrived on Molokai and saw the ugliness of the lepers' disfigured faces and crippled limbs, he turned away. He chose to live apart in a little hut of his own, cooking his own meals, and washing his own clothes. No leper was allowed in his home. He went to chapel and preached; but his words had no effect.

One day Joseph realized that talking was not enough. The love of Christ must be demonstrated. "How," he asked himself, "can I help them if I try to avoid them?"

Joseph began to mingle with the lepers. He helped them build better houses. He bathed their sores and dressed their wounds. He helped dig wells and secured clothing and food for them. He truly became one with them, for Joseph Damien died a leper. However, before his death he had the joy of seeing all the people on the island accept Christ.

There are people in your community who are just as sad and lonely as were the lepers of Molokai. They are waiting for someone to give a demonstration of faith in the way that Joseph Damien did, by being a friend.

Are you ready to put your faith into action today? Try being a friend. It's fun!

11

EXPECTING THE IMPOSSIBLE

For with God nothing shall be impossible. Luke 1:37.

The thermometers in Battle Creek registered 10 degrees below zero the Monday morning of January 4, 1875. It was a good day to stay at home and sit around the fire.

However, at about ten o'clock in the morning, scores of warmly-dressed people could be seen hurrying along snow-packed Washington Avenue toward the highest point in town. There stood the three-story brick building that would be dedicated as the first Seventh-day Adventist college.

Spirits were high as friends greeted one another and climbed the stairs to the chapel. Enthusiasm had been building for several months. The dedication was a fitting climax to a month-long ministerial institute that had been held for nearly 150 denominational workers from several States.

Adding to the excitement of the day was the presence of Ellen G. White. Many in the crowd knew of the miracle that made it possible for her to take part in the dedication ceremony. During the institute meetings she had become so ill that the doctors feared she would not live. The afternoon before the dedication her husband had knelt by her side, along with Elders Uriah Smith and Joseph Waggoner, begging God to spare her life.

As they knelt Sister White began to pray in a hoarse whisper. Two or three minutes later her voice rang out loud and clear, "Glory to God!" She was in vision.

With those present at the dedication she shared the picture God had given her of a worldwide publishing work. To that small group of believers such a task must have seemed impossible. At that time they had only one press printing in one language.

Today the Seventh-day Adventist Church has 50 publishing houses printing gospel literature in 182 languages, illustrating the fact that nothing is impossible with God.

Are there impossibilities in your life? Do you have a loved one who seems to care nothing about Jesus and whose conversion seems out of the question? Are you thinking it impossible that you will ever have enough money to go away to school to prepare for God's service? Whatever the problems are that perplex you today, do not give up. God can do the impossible!

THE PEANUT MAN

I can do all things through Christ which strengtheneth me. Philippians 4:13.

George Washington Carver, known as the Peanut Man, stood up to face a tired group of Congressmen in Washington, D.C. The lawmakers had heard many speakers that day. Some breathed a sigh of relief that Dr. Carver was the last. They hoped he wouldn't go over the allotted ten minutes.

On the table Dr. Carver placed the boxes he had brought. Out of them he pulled ink, oil, dyes, plastics, cheese, paints, candy, soap, and dozens of other things he had made from peanuts.

For two hours he kept the men spellbound as he talked about the more than three hundred products he had produced. He explained how explosives, animal feed, cosmetics, and medicines could be manufactured from this lowly legume.

"Amazing!" the men whispered to one another. "Unbelievable!"

Just as amazing as the products Dr. Carver had produced from the peanut was what God had made of his life. He was born a slave on a Missouri farm and no one expected that he would be more than a common worker. Yet when he died on January 5, 1943, he was internationally famous. He had been awarded many medals and eighteen schools were named after him. Congress had even designated a special day in his honor.

These achievements were possible because young George Carver believed that with Christ helping him he could do "all things." He taught himself to read. At the age of 14 he went to school for the first time, walking eight miles.

He didn't have money to pay for a college education, but he saw no reason why this could not be included in the "all things" that were possible through Christ. God had supplied the opportunity; would He not also give the means for him to make use of it? George Washington Carver enrolled in school with only ten cents in his pocket; but God saw him through.

Do you have a handicap? Is there some obstacle in your way to success? Do you feel that you are unfortunate?

God can help you just as He did young George Carver. In His strength you, too, can succeed. Aim high and see what God will do.

PUNY TEEDIE

And in every work that he began, . . . he did it with all his heart, and prospered. 2 Chronicles 31:21.

"I just don't know what we can do about Teedie," sighed Mrs. Roosevelt. "Sometimes it seems he can hardly breathe."

It was a real problem for the robust Roosevelts. Teedie, as they affectionately called puny little Theodore, had asthma so bad that it did at times seem that he would quit breathing altogether. There were other problems, too. One day when Theodore was playing with some friends, the boys began reading the words on a nearby billboard. Theodore not only could not read the words; he couldn't even see the giant letters. From that time on, his round face was adorned with big glasses.

When Theodore was 12, his father told him frankly that if he were to have a sharp mind, he would have to develop a strong body. So Theodore began working on that project. He hiked, swam, and played in the out of doors as much as possible. And before long he was on the way to becoming a strong athlete.

His mind developed too. Folks began to hear about Theodore Roosevelt, who was now called Teddy by crowds of affectionate people. When his picture was taken holding a small bear cub, a toy manufacturer commenced making little stuffed cubs, which were called then and forevermore teddy bears.

Teddy Roosevelt was the youngest man ever to become President of the United States. During his terms of service the Panama Canal was begun. President Roosevelt became concerned about the giant business trusts in which one man would control an entire industry and thousands of lives. He worked hard to break up these monopolies.

He was very active in conservation, doing all in his power to preserve the natural beauties of our land.

At the time of his death on January 6, 1919, puny little Teedie Roosevelt was known as a rough-and-ready champion of the people. He was one of the four Presidents chosen to be immortalized by the giant sculpture on Mount Rushmore.

What a wonderful lesson he has left with us. There is no excuse for anyone, particularly a Christian, not to improve himself or herself. God has given to every person a measure of strength, a talent of some kind, or a special gift. He leaves it with each of us to increase it to His honor and glory.

LONG-DISTANCE CALL

And it shall come to pass, that before they call, I will answer; and while they are yet speaking, I will hear. Isaiah 65:24.

It was on this day, January 7, 1927, that the first trans-Atlantic radio-telephone conversation took place between New York and London.

Today, by the use of superhigh frequency radio waves called microwaves, your telephone is linked to telephones in 190 countries of the world. One microwave route can carry 23,000 telephone conversations at the same time.

Think for a moment how marvelous this is. What if your voice had to travel at the speed of sound, 740 miles per hour? It would take four hours for your first Hello to travel from New York to San Francisco. At that rate how long would it take a message to travel from London to Sydney or from Tokyo to Paris? Yet, by microwaves your Hello reaches its destination in a fraction of a second.

Even more wonderful than the radio-telephone is your prayer link with heaven. Faster than the speed of sound, faster than a microwave, your cry for help travels to the throne of God. Your whispered prayer for forgiveness hurdles past unnumbered worlds in the winking of an eye and instantaneously the answer comes back, "Forgiven."

The miracle of communication with heaven came forcefully to me one night when I was trying to make telephone connections from my home in Jackson, Ohio, to my husband in Bangalore, India.

After a half-hour wait, telephone connections were made with his number, but no one answered. It was urgent that I contact him. What was I to do?

I knelt there beside the phone and began to tell God all about it. I asked Him to bring my husband to the phone so that I could talk to him.

I was still praying when the phone rang less than five minutes later. It was my husband. Knowing nothing of my attempt to reach him, he had been impressed to phone me. While I was still praying, God had answered my prayer.

You can make a long-distance call to the throne of God at any time. The line will always be open. He will always be there. He will hear and answer your prayer in the best way.

15

NEEDLESS BATTLE

The way of peace have they not known. Romans 3:17.

"The British are coming! The British are coming!"

The cry of warning echoed through the streets of New Orleans on the morning of January 8, 1815. Fear gripped the hearts of the people, some of whom fled with their valuables. Others stayed to guard their homes, but all wondered, "Will our beautiful city be destroyed?"

"Over my dead body!" promised General Andrew Jackson as he put his men to work fortifying the city. Bales of cotton were rolled out of the warehouses and used to make bastions for the attack.

When one of the cotton merchants discovered that his warehouse had been broken into, he rushed over to Jackson's quarters shouting, "The soldiers have taken my cotton. They have no right to do that. It is my property."

"Since this is your property, sir, it is your business to defend it," said General Jackson, thrusting a gun into the merchant's hands. "Get into the ranks."

Sir Edward Pakenham marched his eight thousand soldiers straight toward the bales of cotton, and some two thousand men were killed or wounded in fifteen minutes, all of them needlessly.

The two generals did not know that two weeks earlier the Treaty of Ghent had been signed and the United States and Great Britain were at peace. The war was over and the Battle of New Orleans need not have been fought. Hundreds died because the message did not get through.

When Jesus died on the cross He signed the peace treaty for our souls. From that moment man could be free if he believed. From that moment there was no need to fight. From that moment peace was possible.

Still, millions continue with the battle. Every day people die without knowing that there is peace. How much longer will souls be lost because the message of Heaven's peace did not get through?

They must get the message! With your help it can go through. "With such an army of workers as our youth, rightly trained, might furnish, how soon the message of a crucified, risen, and soon-coming Saviour might be carried to the whole world!"—*Education,* p. 271.

MURDER IN THE JUNGLE

Go ye into all the world, and preach the gospel to every creature. Mark 16:15.

On January 9, 1956, people all over the world picked up their newspapers to read the shocking headlines:

"Five Missionaries Missing:

Believed Killed by Auca Spears"

Six days earlier five young men had landed their small plane in Auca Indian territory in the dense Ecuadorian jungle. They set up camp beside the Curaray River and waited for the Aucas, one of the most primitive tribes left on earth. They knew they were taking a risk; but somehow the gospel must be preached to every creature and that command surely included the Aucas of Ecuador.

After three days of waiting, three Indians came. For the first time civilized man made personal contact with this savage tribe. The men radioed to their base: "This is a great day for the advance of the gospel in Ecuador!"

The Aucas left, but two days later they returned with six others. As they were approaching the camp one of the men radioed the news: "Pray for us. This *is* the day! Will contact you next at four-thirty."

At the appointed hour anxious wives sat beside their radio receivers waiting for the report that never came. Later, a search party found the men dead beside their plane.

The sacrifice of these young men was not in vain. Their bravery in the face of death eventually made it possible for others to go and live with these people, learn their language, and translate the Bible for them.

The very men who had killed the missionaries later wept as they realized why the five men had been so eager to enter their territory.

"I did not do well. That was before I knew God," said one of the Aucas.

There are still many people who do not know God. Millions have never heard the gospel of Jesus Christ.

God is calling for brave young Christians who will take up the challenge. He is looking for consecrated youth who will take the message of God's love to every creature. He needs you!

TRUE FREEDOM

If the Son therefore shall make you free, ye shall be free indeed. John 8:36.

"What do you think of Tom Paine's new book?"

"Well, it *is* only common sense that America should be independent; only common sense that men should rule themselves; only common sense that all men should be free."

This conversation might have taken place some two hundred years ago. The first copies of the book, *Common Sense,* came off the press on January 10, 1776. It gave a clear statement of why the colonists wanted their own country. It helped the people understand why they were fighting, and helped unite the thirteen colonies in a common cause that finally won. Since then scores of countries have become free.

But are we, wherever we may live, really free? We may vote for the leaders of our country, but we are still subject to a King. Every person chooses one of two masters for his or her life: Lucifer, Prince of Darkness, or Jesus, Prince of Peace.

"Serve me," Lucifer promises, "and you will have freedom. You can go to the movies, drink, and smoke. You don't have to follow all those silly rules."

Those who choose this king eventually discover that they are in chains. Take Alec, for instance.

"I was 17, and in my pocket was my first bought package of cigarettes. I knew exactly what I was doing. Or did I?

"Did I really know? Did I know then, that by now I would be hooked so bad on the habit that all thoughts of quitting would have been abandoned, and that keeping down to a pack a day would be such an ordeal? Did I know that by now more than 1,500 of my hard-earned dollars would have been burned up and left in ash trays? Did I know, at 17, that I would be waking each morning to a mouth with the taste of a ditchdigger's glove, accompanied by a cough that comes all the way from the stomach?" *

"No, I didn't know," says Alec. "Had I known, what a difference it might have made!"

Today, like Alec, you must choose between two masters for your life. Which one will it be?

---

*Creeping Madness (Review and Herald Pub. Assn.), pp. 139, 140.

18

A PLACE FOR YOU

I have redeemed thee, I have called thee by thy name; thou art mine. Isaiah 43:1.

Fifteen-year-old Alexander stood in the tropical sunset of his West Indies home and dreamed of the future. Tomorrow he would sail for America and adventure! He would show the people of this small island a thing or two. He would become someone important. He would take his place in the world.

Born on January 11, 1757, Alexander Hamilton had a hard life. His father went bankrupt and left the family. His mother died when he was small. For several years he worked as a clerk in his uncle's counting house. Now his big chance had come. He was going to America to study law.

Soon after he arrived in New York, the Revolutionary War began. Alexander left school to join the American army. One day the young captain of artillery was working hard digging an embankment when he felt that someone was watching him. He looked up to see General George Washington.

"I have been watching you for some time, Alexander," the commander said. "I like the thorough way that you do every task assigned to you. I want you to be my assistant."

Alexander did such a good job that he was promoted to lieutenant colonel. When Washington became President of the United States, he chose Alexander Hamilton to be secretary of the Treasury.

Like 15-year-old Alexander, you, too, dream about your future. What will it be like? Can you picture yourself as a doctor, engineer, pilot, or college president?

Right now you may not know what you want to be, but of this much you can be certain: God is watching you. He knows your name and your talents. He takes notice of the way you fulfill the small duties that come your way. He has a plan for your life.

"Not more surely is the place prepared for us in the heavenly mansions than is the special place designated on earth where we are to work for God."—*Christ's Object Lessons,* p. 327.

One day the heavenly Commander will come to you and say, "Betty, Mac [or whatever your name is], I want *you* to work for Me." Will you be ready to fill that place?

WHAT DR. BROWN MISSED

When the word of the prophet shall come to pass, then shall the prophet be known, that the Lord hath truly sent him. Jeremiah 28:9.

"Dr. Brown, come quickly! Mrs. White is in vision."

Dr. Brown hurried to the Seventh-day Adventist church in Parkville, Michigan. The atmosphere was tense as he strode down the aisle to the platform where Mrs. White was sitting.

The doctor stepped to her side and began to examine her. He believed that Ellen White was a spiritualist medium and he had declared that he could control her vision if he were given the opportunity. Today was his chance!

He had barely begun the examination when he began shaking like an aspen leaf. His face was pale as death.

"Will the doctor report her condition?" asked Elder White.

"She does not breathe," replied Dr. Brown as he left the platform and headed for the door.

"Go back and do as you promised! Bring that woman out of vision," challenged someone at the door. Without answering, the doctor grasped the door knob and tried to pull the door open. Some of the men crowded around him.

"What is it, Doctor?" they questioned.

"God only knows; let me out of here."

It was too bad he didn't stay, for when Mrs. White came out of vision she had some dramatic news to give, news of the bitter struggle that would soon take place in the Civil War. South Carolina had already seceded from the Union but no one expected war. All thought the trouble would blow over.

During the vision, Mrs. White rose to her feet and said, "I have just been shown that . . . there will be a most terrible war. . . . There are those in this house who will lose sons in that war."

Three months later the war began at Fort Sumter. At least ten people who heard Mrs. White speak on January 12, 1861, lost sons in the fighting that followed.

One of the tests of a true prophet is that his or her predictions must come to pass.

Does Ellen G. White pass the test? The vision that she had in Parkville has convinced many that she was indeed a prophet of God.

Dr. Brown missed the best proof of all.

20

RESCUE AT YUBA GAP

Lo, this is our God; we have waited for him, and he will save us. Isaiah 25:9.

On this day in 1952, the streamliner *City of San Francisco* left Donner Summit and headed down the mountain. The 226 passengers expected to reach their destination by early afternoon. Three days later they were still on the mountain, trapped by the worst blizzard the high Sierras had experienced in a hundred years.

At Yuba Gap the train slowed to a crawl, stopped, backed up and tried again to plow its way through the gigantic drifts. At last the diesel came to a halt and refused to move.

The conductor announced to the passengers that a snow plow was on its way and they would be in San Francisco by nightfall. By evening they were still in the midst of the shrieking blizzard.

Soon the trapped people began to grow more and more concerned. Food was gone. The storage batteries went dead. The boilers ran out of water. The situation seemed hopeless. Imagine yourself sitting in complete darkness with snow drifting all around you, feeling that you had been forgotten.

But the people trapped in the train at Yuba Gap were not forgotten. Skiers reached them with emergency rations. A relief train, traveling at the speed of one mile an hour, was on its way with help. Another snowplow had started out. Finally, on the morning of the fourth day the weary passengers saw the smoke of the relief train. A shout of joy passed from car to car. Deliverance had come!

Our old world is like that train. As it has been slowly moving through the centuries, the snowdrifts of sin and wickedness have been piling up. The storm rages around us. Wars, hatred, famine, disease, and troubles of all kinds have us trapped. Statesmen and scientists say that something must happen soon or this old world is lost. There seems to be no hope for this cold, forgotten planet.

But, wait! What is this? Echoes from a hill called Calvary reach our ears: "For God so loved the world, that he gave his only begotten Son, that whosoever believeth in him should not perish, but have everlasting life" (John 3:16).

There is hope—and more good news from heaven: "Behold, I come quickly" (Rev. 3:11).

21

IN HIS STEPS

For even hereunto were ye called: because Christ also suffered for us, leaving us an example, that ye should follow his steps. 1 Peter 2:21.

What is your definition of a Christian? Is it one who goes to church each week, does nothing bad, and enjoys himself surrounded by friends who believe the same as he?

Albert Schweitzer, born on this day in 1875, had a much better idea of what it means to be a Christian. He believed that a Christian must imitate Christ, live His life, and follow in His steps. For Albert Schweitzer those footsteps led to Africa.

"We can't believe it! Are you actually resigning as principal of St. Thomas College to go to Africa?" Albert's friends asked. "There is no one in Europe who knows more about Bach than you. You are in demand for organ concerts everywhere. Surely you aren't giving all this up!"

It was true that in the thirty years since Albert's birth in a village in Upper Alsace, Germany, he had accomplished a great deal. He had become an internationally famous philosopher, musician, clergyman, and writer. Now, he had just resigned his job and informed his friends of his plan to study to be a doctor so that he could go to Africa.

"I want to be a doctor so that I might be able to work without having to talk," explained Dr. Schweitzer. "I want to show people love, not just tell them about it."

Dr. Schweitzer spent more than fifty years in Lambaréné, Africa, giving a demonstration of Christ's love. He built a hospital and leper colony and went humbly about his business of helping the people and walking in the footsteps of Jesus.

Would you like to walk in the footsteps of Jesus? You need not go to Africa or some far-off island of the sea. You can find His footprints in the place where you live.

You can "find His footprints beside the sickbed, in the hovels of poverty, in the crowded alleys of the great cities, and in every place where there are human hearts in need of consolation."— *The Ministry of Healing,* p. 106.

His footprints might lead next door or just down the street. Can you say today, "I will follow Thee"?

A STONE SPEAKS

I tell you that, if these should hold their peace, the stones would immediately cry out. Luke 19:40.

The year was 1799. The place was Rosetta, Egypt. Mr. Boussard, an officer in Napoleon's engineering corps, was digging a trench four miles north of town. Suddenly, he noticed a large piece of black stone sticking out of the mud. Thinking it might be some ancient tablet, he bent down to examine it more closely. There were strange markings carved in the stone and Engineer Boussard felt sure the scholars accompanying Napoleon would be interested in it.

The next time he went to headquarters he carried with him the large black stone with its carved inscriptions in Greek and two forms of ancient Egyptian. This was not an easy task! Imagine a solid rectangular stone three feet nine inches high by two feet four and one-half inches wide and eleven inches thick.

Scholars studied more than twenty years before they understood what it said. First they had to translate the Greek part. Next, they picked out the names of people and places in the Greek portion and found the same names in the picture-writing section. Little by little the hieroglyphics began to have meaning. Once people could read this ancient Egyptian writing they could learn much about what life was like in Egypt during the time of Joseph and Moses. This did a lot to help people believe the stories of the Bible.

If you ever go to London, be sure to visit the British Museum. More than a quarter of a billion people have passed through this famous institution since it opened on January 15, 1759. It is a huge place and you couldn't begin to see everything in one day. Be certain, however, to visit the Department of Egyptian antiquities and see the Rosetta Stone.

To all those who would listen, the Rosetta Stone has cried out: "The Bible is true! Because of me, men can now read the Egyptian language as it was in the days of the ancient Pharaohs. I have unlocked the secrets of the past. I have helped prove that the Bible stories are true."

Since that long-ago discovery on the banks of the Nile, many other stones with inscriptions have been found. All of them have indicated, with the Rosetta Stone, that God's Word is true.

LENNIE WAS DECEIVED

Wine is a mocker, strong drink is raging: and whosoever is deceived thereby is not wise. Proverbs 20:1.

During the late 1800s Christian women of America joined together to fight liquor. Working through churches and schools, they rallied enough support to take their battle to Washington, D.C. There they demanded a law prohibiting the manufacture and sale of alcoholic beverages.

The Eighteenth Amendment became law on January 16, 1920. Saloons were closed and members of the Women's Christian Temperance Union rejoiced. Naturally, the manufacturers of liquor were not happy. Neither were the bartenders and drinkers. Thirteen years later the law was repealed.

Today beer, wine, whisky, and gin are available almost everywhere. Parents stock their refrigerators with their favorite brands and teen-agers follow their example. The result is broken lives, broken homes, misery, and death.

Ask Jerry Rogers. He can tell you about Lennie.

It happened the night of the high school party. Some of the students, including Lennie, brought liquor. Lennie had a brand-new Thunderbird, and later he took Jerry out to the car and pulled a bottle of whiskey from under the seat. Lennie took a few swallows, and offered it to his friend.

"No, thanks, I don't drink," Jerry replied.

Later that night he was glad he had been wise enough to say No. He was sitting in a doughnut shop drinking hot chocolate when he heard the shriek of sirens and knew instinctively that Lennie must have had trouble.

Leaving his drink half finished, Jerry hurried to his car and followed the wailing sound of the ambulance. He hadn't gone far before he saw the flashing red light of the highway patrol. Then he saw the ambulance whiz past him on its way to the county hospital.

Within a hundred feet of the accident Jerry stopped and got out of his car. Slowly he approached the wreck. It was Lennie's Thunderbird all right. He had rolled it and the shiny metal was smashed flat. Jerry felt sure no one could have come out of that car alive.

Shattered glass and crimson blood covered the ground. In the middle of the mess lay a broken whiskey bottle.

DILIGENT BEN

Seest thou a man diligent in his business? he shall stand before kings. Proverbs 22:29.

What do we mean by *diligent?* The dictionary says that a diligent person is hardworking and industrious. He is painstaking in his efforts to do a good job. He gives careful attention to the details of his work so that it is done to the best of his ability. He is the kind of person who can work without supervision. He does his best whether or not someone is looking.

The Bible says that diligent young people will stand before kings. They will be successful in life. Joseph and Daniel were diligent youths whose faithfulness won for them a place in the king's court.

Ben Franklin was another young man of whom it could be said that he was diligent in his business. Born in Boston on this day in 1706, he became famous on both sides of the Atlantic as a scientist, writer, statesman, and diplomat. He was as much at home with the kings of Europe as he was with the farmers of New England.

One of his neighbors wrote about him: "The industry of that Franklin is superior to anything I ever saw. . . . I see him still at work when I go home from the club; and he is at work again before his neighbors are out of bed." *

Ben was the fifteenth child and youngest son in a family of seventeen. Two years of schooling were all his parents could afford to give him. Yet, by making use of spare moments he taught himself algebra, geometry, navigation, grammar, logic, and science, becoming one of the best-educated men of his time.

If you want to build a successful life, diligence is one of the stones you must put into the foundation now. When you faithfully perform the tasks assigned to you, however dull they may be, you are receiving a training that will fit you for a position of trust and usefulness later on.

Mrs. White puts it this way: "In the faithful performance of the simple duties of the home, boys and girls lay the foundation for mental, moral, and spiritual excellence."—*Messages to Young People,* p. 212.

In other words, be diligent; it pays!

---

* *World Book Encyclopedia* (Field Enterprises Educational Corporation, Chicago, 1973), vol. 7, p. 413.

AS GOOD SOLDIERS

Thou therefore endure hardness, as a good soldier of Jesus Christ. 2 Timothy 2:3.

God loves us and wants us to be happy. However, it is also true that in this world of sin we will have suffering and trouble.

God expects us to bear these burdens bravely instead of whining and complaining. After all, this world is not a parade ground, but a battlefield. We are called upon to endure hardness as good soldiers.

Capt. Robert Scott knew what it was to endure hardness. He and four companions began their journey to the South Pole with Siberian ponies and Yukon huskies. The ponies couldn't walk in the snow and had to be shot. The dogs went wild. Determined to reach the Pole, Scott and his men harnessed themselves to the sledge and struggled on for fourteen days.

On January 18, 1912, they reached their goal, only to discover that Capt. Roald Amundsen, of Norway, had been there first. In his diary that day Captain Scott wrote: "This is an awful place and terrible enough for us to have labored to it without the reward. . . . Well, it is something to have got here. Now for the run home and a desperate struggle."

Temperatures dropped to $-40°$ F. Wind whipped the snow around them at thirty-five miles per hour. Two men died, but Scott and his two companions pressed on. Stinging blasts coated their faces with ice. Fingers and feet were frozen. At last they came within eleven miles of a depot of buried supplies. They could make it in one day and they had supplies left for two.

That night a blizzard tore across the plateau of ice where they were camped. For twelve days it raged about them so savagely that it cut ridges in the ice. No one could face such a storm and live. The three men were trapped. Supplies ran out.

Eight months later a search party found the dead explorers. Under Scott's body was a letter that said, "I do not regret this journey, which has shown that Englishmen can endure hardships."

Sometimes we, too, face struggle, difficulty, and disappointment. With Christ's help it is possible for us to endure any difficulty without complaint. We can bear our burdens bravely and be counted as good soldiers of Jesus Christ.

POWER REVOLUTION

Power belongeth unto God. Psalm 62:11.

Matthew Boulton was showing James Boswell, the famous biographer through his new foundry at Birmingham, England. Turning to his guest, Mr. Boulton said, "I sell here, sir, what all the world desires."

"And what is that?" asked Mr. Boswell.

"Power," came the answer.

For that Mr. Boulton had his partner, James Watt, to thank, for it was he who made the steam engine practical and invented a double-acting rotative engine. For the first time steam power was made available to run all kinds of machines.

Wind, water, and muscle were the only known sources of power when James Watt entered the world on January 19, 1736, in Greenock, Scotland. By the time he died in 1819, the world was a different place. His inventions had resulted in the factory system. The use of a new kind of power brought about the industrial revolution. In one man's short lifetime the world changed.

The power that belongs to God can also change the world. Following the reception of the Holy Spirit on the Day of Pentecost, great power accompanied the preaching and witness of the Christians. Thousands were converted. People flocked into the church. The early Christians turned their world upside down. In one generation the world changed.

Before Jesus comes there is going to be another power revolution. Young people are going to yield themselves to God completely. The Holy Spirit will then come into their lives, bringing them great power.

Where these youths were weak and overcome by temptation, they will become strong to resist the devil. Where they were afraid to speak up and witness to their friends and classmates, they will become bold. They will join hands with other Spirit-filled youth to take God's message to all the world in one generation.

Why not make this the day when you let Jesus come and fill you with His Holy Spirit? The power you receive will change your world.

FOR SUCH A TIME

Who knoweth whether thou art come to the kingdom for such a time as this? Esther 4:14.

Thousands of spectators were gathered on Capitol Hill the cold, clear morning of Inauguration Day, January 20, 1961. Some had been there all night in 22 degree weather in order to assure themselves a good look at the thirty-fifth President of the United States as he rode up Pennsylvania Avenue.

Three thousand servicemen had worked all night to remove eight inches of snow that had fallen the day before. As the hour of noon approached, all was in readiness.

The sun was glittering bright as the ceremony began. Bareheaded in spite of the cold, John F. Kennedy removed his overcoat and stepped to the lectern.

Conversation in the crowd stopped as he placed his left hand on the open Bible, raised his right hand and repeated after Chief Justice Earl Warren: "I do solemnly swear that I will faithfully execute the office of President of the United States."

Millions of people around the world were stirred as they heard him say: "In the long history of the world, only a few generations have been granted the role of defending freedom in its hour of maximum danger. I do not shrink from this responsibility—I welcome it. I do not believe that any of us would exchange places with any other people or any other generation."

Suddenly people were glad to be living at such a moment, glad for the challenge to sacrifice and devotion given by this youthful President: "My fellow Americans: ask not what your country can do for you—ask what you can do for your country. My fellow citizens of the world: ask not what America will do for you, but what together we can do for the freedom of man."

To Seventh-day Adventist youth these words hold an even greater challenge. Yours may be the generation that witnesses the final dramatic scenes of this world's history. It is in your hands to finish the task and usher in Christ's kingdom of glory and true freedom of man.

What an hour to be alive! What a privilege is yours!

SOMEONE HELPED LIFT

For he shall give his angels charge over thee, to keep thee in all thy ways. Psalm 91:11.

The Karachi-bound passenger express was doing sixty miles an hour on the morning of January 21, 1954. Rounding a curve the engineer saw the danger too late to avoid disaster. The express plowed straight into a derailed oil freighter. Within four minutes the smashed cars were ablaze, with more than one hundred people trapped inside.

Pastor A. F. Jesson was asleep in an upper berth of the third car from the engine when the initial crash occurred. He awakened to find himself pinned under his bunk. He felt what he thought was water flowing over him up to his waist. Actually this was diesel oil from the wrecked tanker. Pastor Jesson pushed against his bunk and was able to get free.

Flames from the oil tanker were already forty feet high and the winter wind was blowing them in the direction of Pastor Jesson's compartment. Just then he heard screams for help. One of his traveling companions was trapped under three feet of wreckage.

After trying to lift the planks, Pastor Jesson called for help. By now the fire was at their car and the helper fled.

"Don't leave me to die!" the trapped man pleaded.

Pastor Jesson sent a cry to God for help, then he bent down to make one more effort.

"Someone lifted with me," Pastor Jesson said, "and we were able to set the man free."

Pastor Jesson looked around for the man who had helped, but no one was there.

Although Pastor Jesson and the man he had rescued were now surrounded by flames, their oil-soaked trousers did not catch fire. Hand in hand the two men ran from the blazing compartment.

"You saved my life!" said the grateful man.

"Thank the Lord," said Pastor Jesson, looking back at the burning train. "Without Him we would not have come out alive."

Excusing himself, Pastor Jesson then went behind a grove of cactus to praise the Lord for his miraculous deliverance. Not only was he alive, but he had not a cut or a bruise anywhere.

29

TRY THE EXPERIMENT

O taste and see that the Lord is good. Psalm 34:8.

"Tomorrow I will collect your science notebooks," Mr. Burke announced. "Make sure today's experiment is included."

"There goes my evening!" groaned Barbara on the way out of class. "I like the experiments, but I hate writing them up."

"Me, too," sympathized Ellen. "There is so much to write. I don't see why we have to do all that."

"I wonder who invented all those experiments in the first place," complained Barbara.

"I don't know," replied Ellen, "probably some science teacher."

Wrong. It was a government officer in London four hundred years ago. Francis Bacon, born on this day in 1561, was one of the earliest and most influential champions of the experimental method of solving problems.

Bacon believed that most scientific knowledge of the Middle Ages was false because people did not explore the facts. He wrote that man could discover truth only through experimentation and careful observation. He insisted that certain steps must be followed before a logical conclusion could be reached. He helped prepare the way for today's scientific laboratory procedures.

Modern man does not want to accept something for a fact unless it is tested and proved. That is why many young people have given up on God. They say, "How can you prove that there is a God?"

The answer is simple: experiment!

No, you cannot put God in a test tube and analyze Him in the laboratory. However, you can prove Him in your own life. That is what He wants you to do: "Taste and see."

Listening to others tell what they have done will not convince you. You must do the experiment yourself.

Here is the experiment: There are more than three thousand promises in God's Word. Read your Bible carefully, looking for them. When you find one that fits your need, write it down. Then ask God to do for you what He has clearly said He will do. Watch to see what happens.

Your answered prayers will be proof enough that God is there.

RIGHT COURSE

In all thy ways acknowledge him, and he shall direct thy paths. Proverbs 3:6.

Elizabeth sat alone in the guestroom of a friend's house in North Carolina and thought of home. The ten-day journey from Ohio by carriage had been tiring. Two brothers had come with her, but tomorrow they would leave. Already she was homesick.

Whatever made her think she could be a doctor? No other woman had ever done it. What if she failed?

Tears streamed down Elizabeth's cheeks as she tried to decide whether to stay or go back home. Lifting her eyes to the dark sky she cried, "Please, dear God, show me what to do!"

"Then suddenly an answer came," she later wrote in her diary. "A brilliant light of hope and peace instantly filled my soul. . . . The terror fled away, my joy came back, a deep conviction came to me that my life was accepted, that I should be helped and guided. A peace as to the rightness of my course settled down in my mind that was never afterwards destroyed."

Elizabeth buckled down to a stiff program of learning Greek, studying borrowed medical books, and giving music lessons.

However, when she applied for medical school, no one wanted her. Imagine a girl studying to be a doctor!

Then one day she sat down to open the reply to her twenty-ninth application and could hardly believe her eyes.

"Look!" she cried. "They want me!"

Actually, Geneva Medical School of Western New York did not want Elizabeth either. The professors there decided to let the students vote on her admission. One vote would keep her out. For some reason the rowdy young men thought it would be a great joke to have a girl in class. They voted unanimously to accept her.

By the time Elizabeth Blackwell was graduated on January 23, 1849, she had made friends with the professors as well as the students. The first woman physician had come through with honors!

God kept His promise to Elizabeth and He will do the same for you. Put your life completely in His hands as Elizabeth did that night so long ago. Ask Him to direct your paths. He will show you the way to go, and He will be with you all the way.

BETTER THAN GOLD

The judgments of the Lord are true and righteous altogether. More to be desired are they than gold, yea, than much fine gold. Psalm 19:9, 10.

James Marshall rushed into John Sutter's private rooms and stretched out his hands. "Look!" he whispered, excitedly.

"Gold!" exclaimed Sutter in a hushed voice. "Where did you find it?"

"At the sawmill," replied Marshall.

This news, whispered at Sutter's Fort on January 24, 1848, was soon on everyone's tongue. From around the world gold seekers arrived by ship, horseback, and covered wagon to seek their fortunes. The California gold rush was on! The lure of gold brought nearly 100,000 prospectors to California during the first twelve months. Accommodation was so scarce and gold so plentiful that a tumbledown shack rented for 100 dollars a week and a copy of an old New York newspaper sold for a dollar.

Men lived recklessly and fought over claims. Far from civilization, bedraggled prospectors with tattered clothes and scrubby beards roamed over the Sierras behind their mules, hoping to strike it rich. Day after day they panned in the streams, looking for those precious nuggets that would bring them a fortune.

Across the continent another search was in progress—a search for something far better than gold. A group of about fifty "prospectors" met at Albert Belden's farm near Middletown, Connecticut, to begin their digging. Led in their search by Capt. Joseph Bates and James White, the people dug deeply into the Word of God, comparing scripture with scripture, until they had in their possession the precious nuggets of truth. By the time the first forty-niners reached San Francisco, the early Adventists had already mined their treasure of truth.

The California gold rush came to an end long ago, but the search for truth goes on and on, for the Bible is a mine that is never exhausted.

Around the world thousands are still discovering the gold of God's Word. For the precious nuggets of salvation—such as the Sabbath, and the second coming of Jesus—they are willing to risk all. For them the truths of the Bible are "more to be desired . . . than gold." Have you made this discovery?

THE BEST LAID PLANS

For that ye ought to say, if the Lord will, we shall live, and do this, or that. James 4:15.

Robert Burns, the national poet of Scotland, learned early how difficult it is to make plans for the future.

He was born on this day in 1759 in a humble two-room cottage on the River Doon. The son of a farmer, he grew up knowing the meaning of struggle and fruitless dreams. Twice the family moved to a new location hoping to improve their circumstances.

Then Mr. Burns died and Robert, the eldest son, had to take over the farm. Gone were his dreams of an education and an easier living. At the age of 16 he described his life as "the cheerless gloom of a hermit and the unceasing toil of a galley slave."

Robert wanted very much to go to school but there was no time for that. He did learn to read, and then proceeded to educate himself. He often ate his meals with a book in one hand. He carried books in his pockets so that he could study while driving the cart.

Robert whistled Scottish folk melodies while following his plow and soon came up with original poems to fit the tunes. You have probably sung one of them, "Auld Lang Syne."

Perhaps he was thinking of his own disappointed ambitions when he wrote the poem "To a Mouse." In it he expresses the thought that the best-laid plans of mice and men often go astray.

This may be true of mice and men; but it is not true of God, who says, "I have spoken it, I will also bring it to pass; I have purposed it, I will also do it" (Isa. 46:11).

God has a purpose for your life and His plans are sure.

"In His loving care and interest for us, often He who understands us better than we understand ourselves refuses to permit us selfishly to seek the gratification of our own ambition. He does not permit us to pass by the homely but sacred duties that lie next us. Often these duties afford the very training essential to prepare us for a higher work. Often our plans fail that God's plans for us may succeed."—*The Ministry of Healing*, p. 473.

Ask God to work out His will in your life today, even if it means that *your* plans may all fail.

AS HIGH AS THE HEAVENS

For as the heavens are higher than the earth, so are my ways higher than your ways, and my thoughts than your thoughts. Isaiah 55:9.

In the late 1700s, British jails were crowded with debtors and political prisoners. Judges continued to sentence people to leave England, though there was no place to send them since the American Revolutionary War. A solution had to be found.

Joseph Banks, a member of Cook's expedition, felt that Australia was ideally suited for the establishment of a prison. Escape would be almost impossible. The natives did not appear hostile. The climate was mild and there was enough land to support the people. Timber and fuel were plentiful.

So it was that Capt. Arthur Phillip was given charge of some seven hundred convicts and sent with a marine guard to New South Wales, Australia. They later moved to Port Jackson and what Phillip called "the finest harbour in the world." On January 26, 1788, the English prisoners set foot on their new homeland. Later, free settlers arrived and with the help of enforced labor, the settlement of Sydney took shape.

Members of the British Parliament thought they had established a prison colony. Little did they realize the greater plans God had for Australia. This island continent was destined to become an important center for the spreading of the Adventist message throughout Asia and the Pacific.

Almost one hundred years after the settlement of Sydney, Adventist missionaries arrived at the same port. Since that small beginning thousands have sailed away from that beautiful harbor to take the message to India, Africa, and the islands of the Pacific.

The first Seventh-day Adventist union conference was organized in Australia, setting the pattern for the world church. Avondale College developed under the guidance of Ellen White and became a model for Christian schools in many lands. Australia has also led the way in the development of a health food industry.

How thrilling to realize that God is silently working out His higher purposes for men and nations. Parliaments, princes, and prisoners are all in His hands. You are there, too, and His purpose for your life is as high as the heavens.

THE TIME OF TROUBLE

And there shall be a time of trouble, such as never was since there was a nation . . . : and at that time thy people shall be delivered. Daniel 12:1.

A boy of about 7 darted into a courtyard. Yelizaveta Sharypina noticed and decided to investigate. She watched the child go to a pile of frozen garbage and begin digging with a small stick.

"What are you doing here?" Yelizaveta demanded.

"I'm looking for something for my sister Lena to eat," the boy answered.

Actually, everyone in the Russian city of Leningrad was searching for food. There was scarcely a cat, dog, or rat left.

In the Leningrad Museum of History you can see the torn pages of the diary of 11-year-old Tanya Savecheva. One by one she records the starvation deaths of six family members. The last entry reads: "All died. Only Tanya remains." Soon she was gone, too.

More than a million people perished during the nine hundred horror-filled days of the siege of Leningrad. This is more than ten times the number who died when the city of Hiroshima was atom bombed.

Then, at eight o'clock in the evening of January 27, 1944, the few living skeletons left in the city looked up to see a cascade of golden arrows over the great dome of St. Isaac's Cathedral. A flaming stream of red, white, and blue rockets lit the sky over the battered city. A 324-gun salute marked the liberation of Leningrad.

As dreadful as those days were, they cannot compare with the time of trouble just before Jesus comes. But at the darkest hour, the people who are waiting for His return look up to see a rainbow shining with glory from the throne of God. The sun appears at midnight. The earth quakes and the heavens open. The waiting throng see a hand holding God's law. Then, like the voice of thunder, comes the announcement of the day and hour of Christ's return.

In the east there appears a small black cloud about the size of a man's hand. It comes nearer and nearer until Jesus can be seen surrounded by all the angels of heaven. A mighty trumpet sounds. The graves are opened. The liberation of Planet Earth is a reality.

A LETTER DID IT

He that regardeth reproof is prudent. Proverbs 15:5.

It was nearly nine o'clock on the morning of January 28, 1872. With a sigh, Elder J. N. Loughborough closed the door of his room in San Francisco and set out for the church.

He had spent most of the previous night in prayer for his friend and fellow evangelist, M. E. Cornell. Now he was on his way to a meeting where disciplinary action had to be taken against Brother Cornell. Elder Loughborough had tried to get him to see his mistake, but Cornell insisted on his right to do as he pleased. Now Loughborough feared a split in the church over the problem.

As Elder Loughborough reached the sidewalk he was surprised to find Brother Cornell there weeping.

"I am not going to the meeting," he said.

"Not going to the meeting? But it concerns your case," remonstrated Elder Loughborough.

"I know," replied Cornell, "but I am all wrong. Here is a letter of confession I have written. Please read it to the church."

"What has caused this change in you?" questioned Loughborough.

"I went to the post office last night," explained Cornell. "There was a letter from Sister White written from Battle Creek. Read this. Tell the church I accept it as a testimony from God and I repent."

When Mrs. White's letter was read to the church, the people were amazed that it should have come when it did. No one had informed her about the problem.

On January 18, Mrs. White awakened with an impression that she must write out a testimony and mail it to Brother Cornell immediately. Before breakfast she sent her son Edson to the post office with the letter and he made sure it was put in the mailbag. Nine days later it reached San Francisco, just when it was needed.

Brother Cornell accepted the reproof and was able to claim the promise of 1 John 1:9: "If we confess our sins, he is faithful and just to forgive us our sins."

Brother Cornell was a wise man to accept the reproof for his wrong course. I hope today you will be just as wise.

THE FAMILY CAR

But thou, O Daniel, shut up the words, and seal the book, even to the time of the end: many shall run to and fro, and knowledge shall be increased. Daniel 12:4.

The increase of knowledge in the past two hundred years has been astounding. Take, for instance, the field of transportation. At the beginning of the nineteenth century man traveled much the same as he had for thousands of years—by foot or horse-drawn vehicles. Sailing ships took many weeks to cross the ocean.

During the middle of the last century a dramatic change occurred. Steamships and railways greatly increased the speed of travel. Then came the automobile.

Karl Benz, of Germany, was a pioneer in making a successful car. Imagine that you were there on the day that he pushed that first model out of his workshop. Carefully he seated himself and started the engine. There was a clatter and a bang and the wheels began to turn. His wife ran alongside clapping her hands and shouting above the noise, "You've done it, Karl. You've done it!" After twelve years of experimentation Benz had produced an internal-combustion engine that actually moved a vehicle.

A few months later during a public demonstration a series of explosions made the crowd jump with fright as the carriage lurched forward. There were screams as they watched it rush out of control, throwing Karl and his wife to the ground before it crashed against a stone wall.

On January 29, 1886, Karl Benz was awarded a patent for the first automobile. The machine reached the amazing speed of seven and two-tenths miles per hour! This was too much for the alarmed city officials of Mannheim, Germany. A speed limit of three and one-half miles per hour was enforced within the city limits.

What would those people think if they could see the speeds at which cars race along the freeways in 1983?

The family car has become a necessity. There are more than 200 million of them in the world today. The average distance driven per car is ten thousand miles per year. That is a lot of running to and fro.

Could this be part of what Daniel saw in vision? Could this be one of the signs that Jesus is coming soon?

LOVE YOUR ENEMIES

Love your enemies, bless them that curse you, do good to them that hate you, and pray for them which despitefully use you, and persecute you. Matthew 5:44.

Sometimes even our friends are hard to love, so it is certainly not an easy thing to love our enemies. How can we wish good for the one who wishes us ill? To do something nice for one who hates you is really hard; yet we are supposed to pray for those who work against us, making our lives unhappy.

Jesus Christ was One who was able to do this perfectly. When He was hanging on the cross, suffering agony for your sins and mine, He thought to pray for His persecutors. "Father, forgive them," He said, "for they know not what they do."

Mahatma Gandhi was a man with the same spirit. In 1947 someone tried to kill him with a homemade bomb. After the incident Gandhi said, "No one should look down upon the misguided youth who threw the bomb. He probably looks upon me as an enemy of Hinduism." He asked his followers to pray for the young man. Had Gandhi lived he would have had the same attitude toward his assassin in 1948.

Just after five o'clock on the afternoon of January 30, 1948, Mahatma Gandhi walked to the prayer ground, where five hundred people waited. The crowd stood as he approached and pressed closer to get a better glimpse of the little man dressed in the simple white loincloth and sandals. Touching his palms lightly together in the traditional greeting, Gandhi smiled and moved toward the wooden platform on which he usually sat.

A high-ranking Brahman moved quickly through the crowd to the front row. As Gandhi came near the man bowed, then, reaching into the pocket of his khaki jacket, he withdrew a pistol and fired three shots.

"Oh, God," Gandhi whispered and fell to the ground, dead.

Two hours later Prime Minister Jawaharlal Nehru, went on the air to plead with the citizens of India to face the tragedy in the spirit of Gandhi. He suggested prayers in place of violence.

Unlike Mahatma Gandhi, most of us do not have enemies who threaten our lives. Our enemies are the kind that annoy and make life unpleasant. And these are the people we are asked to love. Will you try?

SAFE BEHIND THE SHIELD

He is a shield unto them that put their trust in him. Proverbs 30:5.

Before astronauts were allowed to risk their lives in space, several unmanned satellites were put into orbit to gain information about conditions space travelers would have to face. One of the most valuable of these was Explorer I, launched from Cape Canaveral on January 31, 1958. Under the direction of Dr. James A. Van Allen the satellite carried eighteen pounds of special instruments. Some of these were to measure space radiation.

Scientists were surprised to learn that there is a concentrated belt of charged particles trapped in the magnetic field of the earth. Named the Van Allen radiation belt after their discoverer, this belt posed a real problem for manned space flights. The electrical particles produced dangerous X-rays when they came in contact with a satellite.

Scientists tried to find special insulation materials for the heat shield that would protect man from radiation so high that exposure to it would mean certain death. Experiments finally produced a combination of materials that have reduced the radiation effects of the Van Allen belt to that of a dental X-ray.

Although it is reasonably safe to send men into space today, there are still risks. Man in space must depend entirely on his ship. Success depends on whether or not it operates perfectly. The human space traveler cannot leave his craft for long; for in it are the vital supplies of oxygen and food. It is his link with ground control and his protection against the hazards of the flight. Behind its heat shield he can penetrate the Van Allen radiation belt and return safely to earth.

Spiritual exploration works in a similar way. Everything depends on the adequacy of our spiritual spacecraft. We will be safe from the deadly radiation of sin only as we abide in Jesus. Our vital oxygen supply is prayer and the Bible is our inexhaustible source of food. By staying close to Jesus, we will maintain our communication link with heaven. His companionship will shield us from the heat of Satan's temptations.

Abiding in Christ through prayer, Bible study, and songs of praise, we have hope. There we are safe behind the shield.

THE MESSAGE OF THE TELESCOPE

Lift up your eyes on high, and behold who hath created these things. Isaiah 40:26.

Have you ever tried to count the stars? With luck you may reach 5,119, the number ancient star gazers placed on their maps of the heavens. Sky photographs made with modern giant telescopes reveal millions of stars where your naked eye can see but one.

Go out tonight and look for the constellation Orion. In the small area of the sky where it is located, three hundred other stars may be seen. On photographs taken with the 200-inch telescope on Mount Palomar, 6 million are visible!

If you should ever be in San Diego, California, visit the observatory on nearby Mount Palomar. You will stand in awe at the sight of the 500-ton telescope that needs a building twelve stories high to enclose it.

The lens itself weighs twenty tons and took fifteen years to make. Several months were needed just to prepare the giant ceramic mold into which was poured molten glass heated to 2,700 degrees Fahrenheit. The liquid glass was kept at high temperatures for eleven months, the temperature being lowered one or two degrees each day. Finally the glass reached room temperature and was ready for grinding and polishing. This task took more than eleven years. At last it was ready to fit into the telescope on Mount Palomar.

On the clear night of February 1, 1949, the telescope was focused on the constellation Coma Berenices near the north pole of the Milky Way and for the first time man could see 6 billion trillion miles away.

Since that day, many men have used this telescope to lift their eyes on high. Through its powerful eye they have seen the Creator's handiwork magnified forty thousand times. The sight leaves no doubt as to the existence of a creator God.

"He called himself an atheist, There is no God, said he;
God is a dream of hopeful fools adrift on a sunless sea.
Thus did he speak in thoughtless vein until at the close
　of day,
He looked up through a telescope, and knelt him down
　to pray."

James Warnack, Los Angeles *Times.*

A TWELVE-TALENT BOY

Well done, thou good and faithful servant: thou hast been faithful over a few things, I will make thee ruler over many things. Matthew 25:21.

"Fritz, come here this minute!" Father's voice broke into the lively game of cops and robbers in the back yard.

"Why, Father?" Fritz asked, hoping to gain a few more minutes of play.

"It is time to practice." Father's voice was firm and Fritz knew he would have to go. Reluctantly he left his friends and followed his father into the house. It wasn't that Fritz didn't enjoy playing the violin; he did. But he would much rather play with his friends than practice the scales, which he hated.

"Not again, Father," he would complain after the umpteenth time through the scale of A minor.

"Yes. Again, until you can do it perfectly. Your ability will never improve without hard work."

Fritz Kreisler was born on February 2, 1875, into the family of a physician in Vienna, Austria. His father was his earliest teacher. At the age of 7 the boy gave his first concert. He was then allowed to attend the Vienna Conservatory even though the minimum age for admission was 14. At 10 he was graduated with a gold medal. He then won more honors in Paris. At 13 he gave his first concert in the United States.

Like the man in the parable, Fritz not only increased the talent he had but all through life gained new talents and abilities.

By 12 he was an accomplished pianist. He learned to paint when he was in his teens. He became a well-known composer, writing more than two hundred pieces. He learned to read eight different languages.

What about you? What are you doing with the talents God has given you?

"The youth need to be impressed with the truth that their endowments are not their own. Strength, time, intellect, are but lent treasures. They belong to God, and it should be the resolve of every youth to put them to the highest use."—*Education,* p. 57.

Is that your resolve? If it is, like Fritz, you will see your talents grow, and one day you will hear the Master say, "Well done."

WHY, MOTHER, WHY?

Bless them which persecute you. Romans 12:14.

"Dog! Jew!"

It was not the first time 10-year-old Felix had heard such words since his birth in Germany on February 3, 1809; but it hurt more this time because of the circumstances.

The day before he had played the piano at a very important concert. Everyone remarked about how well he had done. His parents were proud of him. The audience was enthusiastic. Newspapers reported nothing but praise. People had been dropping by the house all day saying what a fine young man he was.

No wonder Felix was happy that afternoon as he went skipping down the street. He was still floating on air from his first big success. Then he met one of the young princes from the royal house of Germany who shouted those cruel words.

It was too much! Tears sprang to the boy's eyes and he ran home to his mother's warm arms with the question, "Why, Mother, why?"

On another occasion Felix and his sister were walking quietly down a street when suddenly they were surrounded by a gang of ragged urchins who pelted them with stones and sticks.

"Why, Mother, why? What did we do?"

And the mother must have replied as many others have done, "Nothing, my children. They are angry because you are different. Pay no attention. They don't know any better. You must do as Jesus said. Return good for evil. Bless them that persecute you. Work hard and show the world what you can do. Make them ashamed of the way they have acted."

Felix did just that. By the age of 9 he was playing the piano publicly. At 11 he was keeping beautifully-made copies of all his original compositions. One of these, his G Minor Sonata, is still played today.

Because he was reared in a Christian home, Felix tried to follow the command of Jesus. As a result, Felix Mendelssohn grew up to become one of the best loved men in all Europe and his music is enjoyed by people of many lands.

Has someone called you bad names? Cursing them will make you feel worse. Instead, do something good for them today and see what happens. You may be surprised at the results.

HUMAN GUINEA PIGS

Beloved, I wish above all things that thou mayest prosper and be in health. 3 John 2.

The convicts marched into the dining hall at Mississippi State Penitentiary. With a hearty breakfast, all except twelve of the prisoners began another day. For those twelve men February 4, 1915, was the beginning of a ten-week experiment in which they were to be human guinea pigs. Their diet would be restricted to starch and sugar. For them there would be no milk, eggs, whole grains, vegetables, or any food containing Vitamin B.

Dr. Joseph Goldberger, of the United States Public Health Service, had been experimenting with animals for some time. He was now convinced that pellagra, a disease common in the Southern United States, was caused by a diet consisting chiefly of starch.

The governor of Mississippi assisted Dr. Goldberger in finding people for the experiment by offering a pardon to those prisoners who took part.

Of the twelve who began the experiment, six became ill with pellagra within a few weeks. They grew tired and nervous. Their skin became rough and sensitive to the sun. Their stomachs were upset. Had they continued with the experiment they might have become insane and died.

By risking their lives, these twelve unknown men did much to help people live more healthfully. They helped prove that foods rich in Vitamin B are necessary for good health.

When God created man He wanted him to be happy and healthy. Therefore, He gave instructions as to what we should eat to maintain good health. God gave a diet of fruits, grains, nuts, and vegetables. Had man followed this plan, there would be no pellagra nor many of the other deficiency diseases in the world today.

You see, health does not come by chance. It is not something you can win in a lottery. Health comes as a result of obeying the natural laws of living that God has given us.

As you study in school you will learn more about these laws. The Bible and the Spirit of Prophecy also outline some of them.

God wants us to enjoy life without sickness. He wants us to cooperate with Him by obeying His health laws.

INTO THE WILDERNESS

Render therefore unto Caesar the things which are Caesar's; and unto God the things that are God's. Matthew 22:21.

"Roger! Roger! Wake up!" There was urgency in Mrs. William's voice as she tried to arouse her sick husband.

"What is it? What is wrong?"

"A band of armed men is on its way from Boston to arrest you and send you back to England. Friends have brought word. You must leave immediately!"

In spite of his illness, Roger Williams got out of bed and dressed. Saying goodbye to his wife and small daughters, he stepped out into the darkness of the New England blizzard.

For fourteen weeks Roger Williams wandered in the wilderness. At times his only shelter was a hollow tree. He got his food where and when he could. At last he found his way to a friendly Indian village, where he was made welcome.

Somewhere on that journey Roger Williams celebrated the fifth anniversary of his arrival in the New World. On February 5, 1631, he and his bride of one year stepped onto the shores of their new home, hoping to find freedom to worship God.

However, they were disappointed to find that people who had fled Europe to escape religious persecution, had set up a similar church-state where dissenters were persecuted. The court would allow no one to vote who was not a member of the church. The civil rulers felt it their duty to enforce all commands of the Bible.

"No," Roger Williams protested. "People must be free to worship God or not, as they choose. God is a God of love. He will accept only voluntary allegiance. The government and the church should be kept separate. No one should be forced to follow any religion."

Because Roger Williams believed that man should "render therefore unto Caesar the things which are Caesar's; and unto God the things that are God's," he was forced to flee that cold winter night.

We know the time is coming when Christians will have to flee into the wilderness for safety. What will you do when a law is passed forbidding you to buy or sell unless you honor Sunday as the Sabbath? Why not decide today that you will be true to God and His Word, regardless of the cost?

44

WHERE HAS GRANDPA GONE?

His breath goeth forth, he returneth to his earth; in that very day his thoughts perish. Psalm 146:4.

On this day in 1952, Princess Elizabeth of England and the Duke of Edinburgh were relaxing at a forest lodge in Sagana, Kenya, when they heard the news that Elizabeth's father, King George VI, was dead. Canceling their plans to tour Australia and New Zealand the royal couple flew home immediately.

Meanwhile, the maids who were looking after Prince Charles and Princess Ann at Sandringham were doing their best to keep the news from the children. However, Prince Charles was quick to notice that the maids had been crying.

"Why is everyone so sad?" he wanted to know.

"Grandpa has gone away," one of the maids replied.

But somehow that didn't seem something to cry about. The king was always going off somewhere. Why should everyone cry so just because Grandpa had gone on a trip? There must be some other reason and the little prince was determined to find out what it was. He would ask Granny and she would tell him.

His grandmother, the queen, came into the nursery and gathered the small prince into her arms. He looked intently into her tear-stained face and knew that something was wrong.

"Granny," asked Prince Charles, "where has Grandpa gone?"

But his grandmother was silent. How could she explain death to such a small child?

Many sad children have been told, "Grandpa has gone to heaven," or "Grandpa has gone to be with Jesus." But are those words true?

Where *did* King George go? He went where all of us will eventually go if time should last. He stopped breathing. His heart stopped beating. He began his long sleep in the grave.

What a beautiful thought to know that our grandpas and grandmas are simply sleeping until Jesus comes.

They can't feel any more pain. They can't look down and see all the troubles their grandchildren are having. They can't come back as ghosts to frighten us at night.

They will know nothing until the trumpet sounds. Then the voice of Jesus will call forth from their graves those who loved the Lord. At the Second Coming we will see our dear ones again.

POVERTY AND PROMISES

I have been young, and now am old; yet have I not seen the righteous forsaken, nor his seed begging bread. Psalm 37:25.

"What is going to happen to us, Mother?" questioned Charles. "How are we going to live without father?"

The 10-year-old boy found it difficult to swallow the porridge his mother set before him. He kept looking across the table at his dad's empty chair. How long would he be in prison? His father was a good, kind man. His only crime was poverty. He had gone to prison for his unpaid debts.

"Do you think we will have to beg?" Charles asked.

Putting her arm around her boy, Mrs. Dickens gave him a squeeze and tried hard not to let her own anxiety show. "No, Charles. God will help us. We must have faith in His promises."

And, of course, mother was right. God did help them. At first Charles went to the pawnshop with a few pieces of household furniture to get money for their food. Then the day came when he had to sell all ten of his books. Writing about this experience later, he said, "When I sold my books, I thought my heart would break."

When there was nothing left to sell, Charles went looking for work. He got a job in a shoe factory pasting labels on bottles of blacking. It was hard work and the hours were long. The warehouse where he worked was dirty and rat-infested. But with the $1.50 per week that he earned he was able to support the family until father was released.

With Mr. Dickens home things got better. Charles attended school and then got a job as a lawyer's assistant. In the evenings he began to write stories.

Although he soon became quite well off financially, he never forgot those years of poverty and how God had helped his family. Those experiences helped him write *David Copperfield* and fifteen other well-known books.

After the Bible and the works of William Shakespeare, the books of Charles Dickens, who was born on this day in 1812, have sold more copies than those of any other author.

God kept His promises. He supplied the needs of the Dickens family long ago in England. He will supply your needs, too, if you will ask Him.

PRETENDING TO WIN

But they ... went backward, and not forward. Jeremiah 7:24.

Dr. Harry Miller wanted to go home for a furlough in America after his first term as a missionary doctor in China. Remembering how seasick he had been while crossing the Pacific Ocean, he was determined to find another way home.

He planned to go through Manchuria to Russia and then across the Trans-Siberian Railway to St. Petersburg. From there he would cross Europe and the Atlantic Ocean.

The only problem was that a war was in progress. On February 8, 1904, Japanese ships attacked Russian ships at Port Arthur. The Russo-Japanese war was being fought in Manchuria, the country through which Dr. Miller wished to pass.

Everyone thought Russia to be the stronger power. However, each day the Russian army lost ground to the Japanese.

The Czar began sending urgent messages to Kuropatkin, the commander in chief of the Russian forces in Manchuria, requesting news about the state of the war. Not wishing to say he was losing, Kuropatkin sent back the message, "We are just leading the Japanese on."

Again the Czar sent a message asking for the true picture of how things were going in Manchuria. Again the reply was given: "We are just leading the Japanese on."

By this time the Russian forces had "led" the Japanese almost to Siberia. Finally, the Czar realized that the Russian Army was actually retreating. He sent back the message: "I pray you, my dear Kuropatkin, please do not lead them on to St. Petersburg."

By the time Dr. Miller was ready for his journey the war was over. Japan won and Kuropatkin could no longer pretend he was winning when he was losing.

How is it in your battle with sin? Are you trying to fool your friends into thinking you are winning when you are actually losing? Are you going backward in your Christian experience instead of forward?

Do not retreat any longer. Turn. Advance. Surrender your life to Jesus Christ. Let Him fight the battle for you. With Him in command you will surely win. You will no longer need to pretend.

47

OUT OF THE FIRE

Is not this a brand plucked out of the fire? Zechariah 3:2.

Five-year-old John awoke near midnight on February 9, 1709, to find his room as light as day. Poking his head through the curtains that enclosed his bed, he saw red fingers of flame racing across the ceiling. He jumped out to call his mother, but the door was already a mass of flames. Going to the window he climbed onto a chair and looked out. In the light of the burning house he saw the upturned faces of his neighbors.

"Daddy, help me!" John called out into the cold night.

Mr. Wesley was behind the house with his wife collecting the other seven children when he heard John's call. He ran inside, but the staircase was in full blaze. He tried to force his way up through the flames, using a pair of trousers to protect his head, but the fury of the blaze beat him back.

Meanwhile, one of the men in the crowd ran forward and helped another man up to the window where John stood crying. The stranger's face frightened John and he ran toward the door. The whole room was now on fire. Even the bed and curtains were burning. In desperation the child ran back to the window and leaped into the man's arms. At that moment the roof crashed in.

John's father kissed him over and over again to make sure he was really safe. Then calling to the onlookers he said, "Come, neighbors, let us kneel down: let us give thanks to God! He has given me all my eight children: let the house go, I am rich enough."

When John Wesley grew up, the burning room became a symbol to him of a perishing world. He pictured each human being surrounded with the flames of sin and death. He was determined that he who had been rescued from the burning house at midnight would give himself to pluck others from a more terrible fire. Soon he was preaching throughout the countryside and thousands listening to him preach in the open air in the villages of England were convicted of their sins.

What about you? Are you not also a brand plucked out of the fire for a purpose? Aren't you thankful for what Jesus has done for you? Won't you ask God to help you save someone else?

THE CAPTURE OF A POPE

We have also a more sure word of prophecy; whereunto ye do well that ye take heed. 2 Peter 1:19.

"Vive la République Romaine!"

"The French have come! They are camped just outside the walls."

The arrival of General Berthier and his 18,000 French troops was the topic of conversation throughout Rome on February 10, 1798. The soldiers seemed to be making themselves comfortable. When would they enter the city?

Eighty-year-old Pope Pius VI shut himself up in the Vatican. He had heard about the terrible things that happened in France. Religion was outlawed. God was declared dead. The priests had gone in exile, and a bounty was offered for their heads. Property belonging to the Catholic Church had been taken by the government.

The pope had done all he could to stop the destruction of the church in France. Because of this, he knew that he was the reason for the arrival of the soldiers. The French were demanding the life of the pope.

Day and night the pope knelt at the altar, pleading for Heaven's protection. But his prayers were in vain, for God had decreed that the hour had come for the power of the pope to be taken away.

Daniel and John had prophesied that the authority of the pope would be supreme for 1260 years. The papacy had gained both temporal and spiritual authority in A.D. 538. The 1260 years were finished. The prophecy must be fulfilled.

Five days later General Berthier was escorted to the capital in triumph. The people proclaimed the Roman Republic. Soldiers were sent to the Vatican to demand the pope's surrender. He refused, so they dragged him from the altar and took him as a prisoner. The prophecy was fulfilled on time.

This very clear fulfillment of the 1260-year prophecy gives us assurance that God's Word is true. It shows that God is still in control. It is evidence that He still rules and that all things come to pass according to His will. Parliaments and kings can go no further than what God allows for the working out of His purposes for this world.

THE FASTEST OPERATOR

Whatsoever thy hand findeth to do, do it with thy might.
Ecclesiastes 9:10.

"I would like to see Mr. George F. Milliken, please."

The receptionist took one look at the speaker and decided the superintendent of Western Union was too busy to see him.

"Do you have an appointment?"

"Not exactly, but he sent word I should come for an interview."

The receptionist went to speak to the boss. "There's a young country bumpkin out there from Port Huron. Thomas Edison."

"Yes, yes. Send him in." Mr. Milliken remembered the neat handwriting on Thomas' application. If the young man could take messages off the wire the same way, he would surely hire him.

The door opened and closed. For a long moment Mr. Milliken said nothing. His eyes took in the uncombed hair, patched clothing, and torn shoes. How could such an unkempt boy write so neatly? Finally he said, "Come back at five-thirty. I'll try you out."

At the appointed hour Thomas took his place at the table. The other operators stopped working to watch the fun. They had wired the fastest operator in New York to send an 800-word report at top speed. They were expecting Thomas to look foolish.

Tom picked up a pile of blanks, gripped his pen and signaled, "Ready!" The message began pouring in faster and faster. Tom's fingers flew just as quickly. The grins on the operators' faces turned into looks of amazement. The "country bumpkin" was actually keeping ahead of the message.

Thomas was hired and proclaimed the fastest operator in the Western Union service. How had it happened?

Thomas had the habit of putting everything he had into the job at hand. Back in Port Huron, when he had been given a chance to learn telegraphy, he was so much in earnest that he practiced eighteen hours a day until he mastered the skill.

Thomas Edison, who was born on this day in 1847, believed our text. Anything he found to do, he did it with his might. The same attitude helped him to invent the electric light bulb and many other useful things. Why not take Ecclesiastes 9:10 as your motto, too?

A TALE OF TWO BOYS

Choose you this day whom ye will serve; . . . but as for me and my house, we will serve the Lord. Joshua 24:15.

February 12, 1809, is the birthday of two boys who helped to change the world. One was born in Shrewsbury, England, the son of a wealthy physician. The other gave his first cry in a log cabin on the Kentucky frontier.

The English boy was graduated from Cambridge. The American boy had a total of one year of schooling.

At the age of 22 both struck out on their own. The first, Charles Darwin, sailed as a naturalist with a British expedition aboard the HMS *Beagle.* The five-year voyage took him to South America, the Galapagos Islands, and New Zealand.

The other youth, Abraham Lincoln, took a journey of twenty miles to New Salem, Illinois, where he got a job as a clerk in a general store. He spent his evenings reading the Bible, literature, and law.

In 1859 Darwin published his famous book, *On the Origin of Species.* It claimed that all living things had evolved over billions of years. Man was told he descended from apes. The book was a bombshell in a world where most people still believed that God had made the earth in six days. Because of this book millions lost faith in the Bible.

A few months after the publication of Darwin's book, Abraham Lincoln was elected President of the United States. Then the Civil War began. Many a night Lincoln was on his knees pleading with God to save his country. He kept his Bible on his desk and often turned to it for counsel.

In one of his speeches Lincoln stated, "It [the Bible] is the best gift God has given to men." Another time he said, "Take all of this Book upon reason that you can, and the balance on faith, and you will live and die a happier man."

Two boys were born on this day in 1809. In their youth they made important choices. One's choice destroyed the faith of millions. The other's choice built the faith of a nation.

You, too, have choices to make today. The results of those choices may be just as far reaching as those of Darwin and Lincoln. Your future happiness and eternal destiny depend on the choices you make now. You must choose today whom you will serve. I pray that it might be the Lord Jesus Christ.

51

A PROPHET'S LAST DAYS

Bear ye one another's burdens. Galatians 6:2.

The doctor bent over the bed of the frail, elderly woman and carefully examined her. There was a break in the left hip. At the age of 87 it could not be expected to heal.

After giving directions for her care, the doctor returned to St. Helena Sanitarium on the hill above Elmshaven where he had been on duty when called that Sabbath morning, February 13, 1915, to attend to Mrs. Ellen White.

Sister White had fallen while entering her study. Her niece, May Walling, had been nearby. She helped her aunt from the floor to the bed where she was lying when the doctor came. There she remained until her death five months later.

If you had been living near Elmshaven then I am sure you would have enjoyed spending an afternoon with Grandma White.

Even though ill, she was always cheerful and happy. No doubt she would have asked you to read to her from the Bible that lay open on the table beside her bed. Perhaps you would have helped make her more comfortable so that she could see the spring flowers from her big bay window. If you had volunteered to sing, she might have requested "There's a Land That Is Fairer Than Day" or "There Is Sunlight on the Hilltop."

If you had asked her how she felt about her situation, she might have told you as she did others: "My courage is grounded in my Saviour. My work is nearly ended. Looking over the past, I do not feel the least mite of despondency or discouragement."—*Life Sketches,* p. 443. Visiting those who are shut in can be a very rewarding experience. Older people particularly appreciate talking to young people and hearing them sing. Can you think of some elderly persons that you could visit today and help to bear their burdens? Perhaps you could take them some flowers or fruit or a picture you have drawn. Read something worthwhile to them. Sing some of their favorite hymns. Ask them to talk about their lives.

I'm sure it will make them happy. You will be surprised to discover how happy it will make you, too.

This would be a good day to do what our text says, "Bear ye one another's burdens."

BE MY VALENTINE

My son, give me thine heart. Proverbs 23:26.

This is the day of hearts—paper hearts, lace hearts, satin hearts, cookie hearts, chocolate hearts, and bright red candy hearts. People in many countries send greeting cards shaped like hearts to their friends and loved ones. It is a day for friendship and love.

February 14 is called Saint Valentine's Day because it is the feast day of two men named Valentine who were martyred in the second century for their faith in Jesus Christ.

One Valentine was taken, about A.D. 270, to the Palatine Hill near the site of an altar to Juno, where his head was cut off. He was a priest who was killed because he gave shelter to persecuted Christians.

The other Valentine died three years later about sixty miles from Rome. He was a Christian missionary who was sentenced to death for converting a Roman family to Christianity.

February 15 was the Roman feast of Lupercalia, a lovers' festival for young people in honor of the pagan gods Juno and Pan. Juno was the goddess of love and marriage, and Pan was the god of nature. Boys and girls drew partners and exchanged gifts with each other.

By A.D. 496 Christianity was the popular religion in Rome. Hoping to please the people, the church leaders tried to give some Christian meaning to the heathen festivals. They changed the Feast of Lupercalia to coincide with Saint Valentine's Day on February 14.

From now on, when you think of Valentine's Day I hope you will remember the two martyrs who were willing to sacrifice their lives for Christ.

Jesus is calling you, too, to give all you are and have to help spread His message of love. He asks you to be His "Valentine." He says, "My son, give me thine heart." "My daughter, give me thine heart."

Will you respond as Lowell Mason did and say:
"Take my heart, O Father take it,
Make and keep it all Thine own;
Let Thy Spirit melt and break it,
This proud heart of sin and stone."

INTERNATIONAL HARVESTERS

The harvest truly is plenteous, but the labourers are few. Matthew 9:37.

Imagine for a moment that it is June in Kansas. The temperature is ninety degrees in the shade, but it doesn't bother you, for you are high above the heat, in a two-seater plane. Below you rippling fields of wheat stretch like a golden ocean. At intervals you pass tall grain elevators that will soon be full.

To the left you notice two red dots. Circling and dipping lower, you see them as toy combines knifing straight rows through the fields of wheat, cutting and threshing the grain as they go. Flying still lower, you see the word *McCormick* painted in white letters on the red machines.

Cyrus Hall McCormick, born on February 15, 1809, loved to work in his father's machine shop in Virginia. It wasn't long before he was trying to help his father to give the world an automatic grain reaper.

Although his father failed to reach this goal, Cyrus built on his father's knowledge and succeeded. In 1831 he demonstrated the first successful reaper, a machine that was drawn by a single horse. He continued to improve his invention and his company grew. Today it is known as the International Harvester Company and is one of the largest manufacturing concerns in the world. Because of McCormick's invention one man can harvest enough wheat to feed thousands of people.

Before the automatic reaper, harvest was slow and difficult. With sickles and scythes one man could handle only a few acres. Today the average farm in Kansas is 544 acres. Some wheat farms are much larger, so big that they are measured in square-mile pieces called *sections*. Each section has 640 acres. Farms of one or two sections are common.

In one of His parables Jesus represented the world as a wide harvest field. International harvesters are needed to go out and bring in the people of all nations for His kingdom.

Laborers are few. Our church is small. God needs young people who will be McCormicks for Him, inventing new ways to reap the harvest of the world quickly so that Jesus can come.

Will you join God's "International Harvester Company" today? Your help is needed!

TRAPPED IN THE CAVE

Beloved, if God so loved us, we ought also to love one another.
1 John 4:11.

On January 30, 1925, Floyd Collins decided to investigate a sand cave on the Estes farm in central Kentucky. He found the entrance in a deep ravine, under an overhanging rock. Floyd crawled in and disappeared into the blackness.

He hadn't come out by the next morning so the Estes' 17-year-old son went to check. Floyd was trapped with his foot wedged into a crack in the wall of a narrow tunnel and a large rock was on top of his leg. Early efforts to free him were fruitless.

Newspapers and radio carried the news of Floyd's plight to the whole country. Reporters flocked to the spot. The Red Cross arrived with a trained rescue team. Money, equipment, and telegrams began to pour in. People all over America were praying for the rescue of Floyd Collins. Nothing seemed to help.

Finally, a 55-foot shaft was dug straight down to within a few feet of the helpless man. Then a tunnel was carefully picked out of the rock. Shortly after noon on February 16 the rescue team reached Floyd, but it was too late.

During the funeral service Pastor Roy Biser said, "No other incident within memory has brought so many prayers from the brotherhood of man for one fellow man."

It was true. Thousands of dollars had been spent. Hundreds of men had worked in vain for more than two weeks to rescue one man. Was it worth it?

"The value of a soul—who can estimate? Would you know its worth, go to Gethsemane, and there watch with Christ through those hours of anguish, when He sweat as it were great drops of blood. Look upon the Saviour uplifted on the cross. . . . Look upon the wounded head, the pierced side, the marred feet. Remember that Christ risked all. For our redemption, heaven itself was imperiled. At the foot of the cross, remembering that for one sinner Christ would have laid down His life, you may estimate the value of a soul."—*Christ's Object Lessons*, p. 196.

All about us are young people trapped in sin. Someone must rescue them. There is not much time. One boy or one girl is worth all the effort you can muster. Will you join the rescue team? Tomorrow may be too late.

FOUND: THE TRUE CHURCH

The dragon was wroth with the woman, and went to make war with the remnant of her seed, which keep the commandments of God, and have the testimony of Jesus Christ. Revelation 12:17.

"Margaret, I am certain that the seventh day is the Sabbath of the Lord and that God wants us to keep it holy," Louis Rondeau spoke with conviction.

"Yes," agreed his wife. "But I don't know any church that keeps Saturday, do you?"

"No, but there must be one, and God will lead us to it."

One day Louis felt impressed to take the phone book and go down the list of ministers in the yellow pages and ask them to help him. Picking out a name he dialed the number.

"Hello. This is Louis Rondeau. My wife and I are looking for the church that keeps all the commandments of God, including the seventh-day Sabbath. Do you know of such a church?"

No, the minister didn't. After several more calls, Louis was given the name of Peter Uniat, pastor of the Seventh-day Adventist Church.

Louis phoned immediately. In his home, Elder Uniat picked up the receiver to hear a man's voice say, "I am looking for a church that keeps the seventh day holy. Can you help me?"

"Yes," Elder Uniat replied. "I surely can."

Studies were soon arranged and Louis and Margaret were thrilled with the beauty of the message that was unfolded before them. Every piece of truth harmonized with the whole. Here indeed was the church for which they had been searching.

On Sabbath, February 17, 1973, Louis and Margaret were baptized in the Edmonton South church and they walked out of the water as members of God's remnant church.

Louis and Margaret didn't have to search any longer. They had found God's remnant people. They had found the church that keeps all the commandments of God, including the seventh-day Sabbath. They had found the church of Revelation 12:17.

What about you? Have you been baptized yet? Have you made your decision to join God's remnant church? If not, there is no better time to decide than right now. Why not phone your pastor and tell him that you want to join the baptismal class? He will be happy to help you.

THE MYSTERIOUS SAMSON

All ye are brethren. Matthew 23:8.

It was almost midnight on February 18, 1952. Charlie Jones, a black man from Houston, Texas, was on his way home when he noticed the flashing lights of a patrol car. He stopped to see whether he could help.

A fourteen-wheel truck-trailer had smashed into an oak tree. The trailer was piled up onto the cab, crushing the roof and trapping the driver, Roy Gaby, between the steering wheel and seat. Roy's feet were caught between the brake and clutch pedals and flames were crawling along the floor mat and licking at his shoes.

A wrecker and a truck were quickly chained to the cab but were unable to budge it. The fire department was on its way with cutting torches, but they would be too late to save the driver.

Charlie Jones walked over to the wreck and with his bare hands tore the door from its hinges. He pulled out the flaming mat and reached in and straightened the steering wheel. He pushed the brake pedal and clutch apart to free Roy's feet. Then he crawled into the cab beside the driver and began pushing his 220 pounds upward against the crumpled roof. He pushed until the metal gave way and the man was pulled free.

All eyes were on the rescued man and no one noticed Charlie Jones quietly leave the scene. The next day the whole city was wondering about the mysterious "Samson." Not even Charlie's wife knew what he had done. When he was finally discovered, he was asked to tell how he had been able to do what three trucks and a wrecker could not accomplish.

"A man don't know what he can do until another man is hurting," said Charlie.

One interesting thing about this story is that it happened during Brotherhood Week, when people were being reminded that all men are brothers regardless of race, religion, or culture. This black man's rescue of his white brother was a dramatic demonstration of brotherhood and love.

This is the kind of love that you and I need—a love that reaches across all barriers and unites us in the family of God.

"By this shall all men know that ye are my disciples, if ye have love one to another" (John 13:35).

CHANGING THE CENTER

If any man will come after me, let him deny himself, and take up his cross daily, and follow me. Luke 9:23.

On February 19, 1473, a boy was born in Torún, Poland, who became one of the few men of whom it can be said, "He changed the world."

When Nicolaus Copernicus went to school he learned what boys had been learning about the universe for 1,300 years: The earth was flat, stationary, and the center around which all heavenly bodies moved. Was it not plain to see that the sun came up every morning and went down every evening? Heaven was up and hell was down and man, the center of everything, was in between.

Nicolaus did not see it that way. After much study he was convinced that the earth was rotating on its axis as did all the other planets. Not only that, he believed that the sun, not the earth, was the center around which the planets revolved.

His writings were banned as dangerous to religion and some who taught his ideas were burned at the stake.

Today few believe that the earth is flat. Most take it for granted that the earth rotates on its axis. However, there are still some people who seem to think that they are the center of the universe. This is the type of person who must have his own way at all times. Every activity must revolve around him.

Such a person is determined to watch a certain television program regardless of what others want. He must have a new outfit whether or not others in the family get what they need. He doesn't want to play a certain game, so why should others play it? If he is not the center of attraction, he pouts or causes trouble.

Speaking of children, Mrs. Ellen White says, "Parents should teach them lessons of self-denial and never treat them in such a way as to make them think they are the center, and that everything revolves about them."—*Child Guidance,* p. 132.

Have you learned to deny self for the happiness of others? Perhaps you need to move the center of your life from self to Jesus, the Sun of Righteousness. Then other people will find their rightful place in your universe. This is what self-denial is all about, changing the center of our lives.

Another way to spell self-denial is J-O-Y: Jesus first, Others second, Yourself last.

THE COUNTDOWN

So likewise ye, when ye shall see all these things, know that it is near, even at the doors. Matthew 24:33.

"Ten, nine, eight, seven . . ." Thousands held their breath as Lt. Col. John Glenn counted down the seconds to blast off on the clear morning of February 20, 1962. ". . . Six, five, four, three, two, one, zero. Lift off. The clock is operating. We're on our way."

By television, millions watched the giant Atlas rocket carry the spacecraft *Friendship 7* into the light blue sky above Cape Canaveral, Florida. For the first time an American was going to orbit the earth.

From a height of 100 miles John Glenn radioed: "Oh, that view is tremendous!"

John Glenn's thrilling journey into space lasted for four hours and fifty-six minutes. He circled the earth three times, traveling at a speed of more than 16,000 miles per hour. He crossed the continents of Africa, Australia, and North America.

Joshua saw the sun stand still; but for John Glenn it seemed to speed up. During his five-hour flight he saw three sunsets and experienced three nights. The stars seemed like diamonds on black velvet. The gulf stream was a ribbon of blue in the darker waters of the Atlantic.

As wonderful as all of this was, it is nothing compared to the seven-day space flight you and I are going to take to reach heaven.

The countdown has already begun. Ten—the great Lisbon Earthquake of 1755. Nine—the Dark Day of May 19, 1780. Eight—the falling of the stars on November 12-13, 1833. Seven—wars and rumors of wars. Six—famines in China, India, and Africa. Five—strange diseases. Four—earthquakes in many different places. Three—the rise of spiritualism and the occult. Two—Sunday laws. One—the gospel into all the world.

Speaking of this time, the prophet Joel prophesied, "The day of the Lord is near."

Jesus said, "When ye shall see all these things, know that it is near, even at the doors."

Zero hour is approaching. It is almost time for lift-off. We'll soon be on our way. Are you ready?

FROM DARKNESS TO LIGHT

The entrance of thy words giveth light. Psalm 119:130.

"Lead kindly Light, amid the encircling gloom,
    Lead Thou me on;
The night is dark, and I am far from home;
    Lead Thou me on.
Keep Thou my feet; I do not ask to see
The distant scene; one step's enough for me."

John Henry Newman, whose birthday is today, wrote this hymn while traveling from Palermo to Marseilles by sailing ship. In the Straits of Bonifazio between the islands of Sardinia and Corsica, they came to an area where there was no wind for several days and the ship was unable to proceed. It was during this lull in the voyage that homesick Mr. Newman wrote this testimony of how he came from darkness into light.

In his early teens John Newman doubted God and the Bible. He had a strong will and was quite sure he could run his own life without help. Thus he walked alone in the darkness.

At the age of 15, however, John yielded to the Holy Spirit. He turned his life over to God and asked Him to lead. From that day onward John walked in the sunshine.

John Newman had been like Christian in the book *Pilgrim's Progress*. At one time Christian was a prisoner in Doubting Castle where lived the Giant Despair, but he discovered a key called Promise that opened the door. He used it to let himself out into the sunshine and light of trust in God. John Henry Newman used this same key to escape the darkness of his doubts.

In February, 1983, young people are still tempted to doubt. Darkness closes around them. A mother dies of cancer. A friend is hopelessly crippled in a car accident. A respected leader leaves the church. Why does God allow such things to happen? they wonder. Life doesn't make sense and gloom encircles them. They need to use the key called Promise.

Should you find yourself doubting God's love, open your Bible and begin to read. Ask the Holy Spirit to guide you to the sunshine. He will give you a promise that will open the door that leads from darkness to light.

ANGEL PROTECTION

The angel of the Lord encampeth round about them that fear him, and delivereth them. Psalm 34:7.

"If you baptize her, I will kill you!" threatened the postmaster of a small town in Haiti.

He was referring to his former sweetheart, who was determined to be baptized. She had attended Adventist meetings and knew that she must follow what she had heard.

On February 22, 1913, people came from many miles around to witness the baptismal service. They fully expected to see the missionary killed.

As the service was about to begin, armed men hired by the postmaster marched up to the baptismal site and took their places along the waterfront. The postmaster stationed himself near a large rock where he could see everything.

After a few songs the woman stepped forward into the water and made her way to the pastor. The missionary lifted his hand above her head. "I now baptize you in the name of the Father, Son, and Holy Spirit. Amen." Gently he lowered her into the water and brought her up again. It was over and not one shot had been fired.

For some reason the postmaster never gave the order to fire. The pastor and the woman baptized were certain their guardian angels had been there that day protecting them.

The postmaster himself was so impressed by the experience that he, too, began Bible studies and was later baptized.

Perhaps you cannot point to such a definite incident in your life when you were certain the angels protected you. Nevertheless, your guardian angel is always by your side. When you get to heaven he will have many exciting stories of deliverance to tell you.

"From what dangers, seen and unseen, we have been preserved through the interposition of angels, we shall never know, until in the light of eternity we see the providences of God. Then we shall know that the whole family of heaven was interested in the family here below, and that messengers from the throne of God attended our steps from day to day."—*The Desire of Ages,* p. 240.

As you go to school today try to imagine your angel by your side. Throughout this day you will not be alone.

I WILL BE THAT MAN

Have ye received the Holy Ghost since ye believed? Acts 19:2.

Charles Hall sat in his chemistry class and listened as Professor Jewett lectured on aluminum.

"This metal is more precious than gold," the teacher said. "Napoleon III, Emperor of France, had a set of aluminum spoons and forks that he used for his most honored guests. Yet, aluminum could become a most useful metal if someone could find a cheap way of producing it. It is light and easily shaped. It is strong, rustproof, and does not tarnish. It is a good conductor of electricity and is artistic in appearance. The man who discovers a cheap way of unlocking aluminum from its ore will benefit the world."

"I will be that man!" Charles whispered.

Immediately he set up a small laboratory in his father's woodshed. Assisted by his sister, Julie, he experimented with a number of methods, none of which worked. Then one day he decided to try electrolysis. He would find a liquid that could dissolve the aluminum ore. Then he would pass an electric current through the solution.

On February 23, 1886, Charles melted some cryolite-alumina mixture. He attached some wires to the carbon crucible and threw the switch. After allowing the current to flow through the red hot mixture for several hours, he turned it off and allowed it to cool. Breaking open the now solid mass, he found shiny lumps of aluminum.

Electrolysis is still used to extract aluminum. As a result of Charles Martin Hall's discovery, aluminum is now one of the most useful of metals. It is used in thousands of items from gum wrappers to airplane construction.

Do you want to be really useful in this world? Let the rich current of the Holy Spirit flow through your life. Just as electricity purifies aluminum, so the Holy Spirit will purify you. Through His power sin will be separated out of your life. Only then can you be used of God to fill a place of usefulness.

Listen to this! "There is no limit to the usefulness of one who, by putting self aside, makes room for the working of the Holy Spirit upon his heart, and lives a life wholly consecrated to God."—*The Desire of Ages,* pp. 250, 251.

Will you be such a one?

AN HONEST AD

Who hath woe? who hath sorrow? . . . who hath wounds without cause? who hath redness of eyes? They that tarry long at the wine. Proverbs 23:29, 30.

On February 24, 1886, the people of Boise, Idaho, opened their newspapers to read the following advertisement for a bar owned by James Lawrence:

"Friends and neighbors, having just opened a commodious shop for the sale of liquid fire, I embrace this opportunity of informing you that I have commenced the business of making drunkards, paupers, and beggars for the sober, industrious, and respectable portion of the community to support.

"I shall deal in familiar spirits which will incite men to deeds of riot, robbery, and bloodshed, and by so doing, diminish the comfort, augment the expenses and endanger the welfare of the community.

"I will furnish an article that will increase accidents, multiply the number of distressing diseases, and render those which are harmless incurable.

"I will cause many of the rising generation to grow up in ignorance and prove a burden and a nuisance to the nation. I will cause mothers to forget their offspring, and cruelty to take the place of love."

If this advertisement is true, and it is, then why do so many people drink? Perhaps the main reason young people drink is that they don't want to be "different." But what is wrong with being different?

Van Cliburn didn't mind being different. At the height of his piano career he said, "I have found that social acceptance does not depend on drinking, nor does it enhance one's esteem either professionally or socially. In fact, people the world over respect one for refusing to drink."

Another reason young people drink is to prove they are grown up. Nancy Anne Fleming, a Miss America winner, didn't agree with that idea. She said, "I think there is nothing quite so pathetic as a teen-ager who thinks he must drink to gain recognition as an adult. Actually, he is proving how inadequate he is to face the problems and decisions of a mature person."

Ask God today for strength to be different. He will give you the maturity you need to resist those things that are harmful.

63

A HUMBLE SPIRIT

Better it is to be of an humble spirit with the lowly, than to divide the spoil with the proud. Proverbs 16:19.

The life of José de San Martin, who was born on this day in 1778, is an illustration of today's text.

Born in Argentina, José went to school in Spain. There he fought as an officer in the army. When he heard that the Spanish colonies in South America were fighting for independence, he decided to go and help. Once there he was given command of the revolutionary army.

In the winter of 1817, José led his soldiers across the snowcovered Andes Mountains and surprised the Spanish. As a result, he could easily have been the leader of the new nation, Chile, but he left the honor to others and went to help Peru.

Soon Peru was also proclaimed a free country. San Martin was appointed the Protector of Peru and the leader of the nation. However, others wanted this position. Rather than fight over the spoils, he chose to give up his position in favor of another.

Back in Argentina, José found the same struggle for power taking place. Unselfish and humble in spirit, he refused to take part in it. Although San Martin probably did more than any other man for the cause of independence in Argentina, Chile, and Peru he turned his back on the spoils and went off to Europe to live a life of seclusion.

John the Baptist had the same kind of spirit. For a while he was the most popular person in the land. Although crowds of excited people flocked to hear him, he did not seek honor or power. When his disciples brought news of the rising popularity of his cousin, Jesus, John did not strive to keep first place. Humbly he said, "He must increase, but I must decrease."

What a happy place our homes would be if each member would be humble in spirit, putting others before himself.

What a difference it would make in school if each student would let Jesus come into his heart and remove all self-seeking and pride. If all were humble in spirit like San Martin and John the Baptist, there would be no pushing for first place in line. There would be no fights for the teacher to settle. There would be no quarreling over swings and balls.

Let us pray today for a humble spirit.

A MILLIONAIRE AT THIRTY

For what shall it profit a man, if he shall gain the whole world, and lose his own soul? Mark 8:36.

Jesus told a story about a rich man whose land produced such an abundant harvest that his barns were not large enough to store all the grain. So he made plans to tear down the old buildings and make new ones to hoard his wealth.

"Ah!" he sighed. "I have enough to last the rest of my life. Now I can stop working and have a good time."

That night he died. Others ate his food, lived on his property, spent his money. Jesus said that man was a fool.

People today act in the same foolish way. Take, for instance, the story of Briton Hadden.

Mr. Hadden, together with Henry R. Luce, originated the popular news magazine *Time*. His goal was to become a millionaire by the age of 30.

In New York, Mr. Hadden pursued his goal with enthusiasm. The pressure of work caused him to spend most of his time at his desk. If he was to become a millionaire, he had no time to exercise, sleep, and eat normal meals. He worked late, then stayed up even later attending parties. He dined and danced, confident that his dream would soon be realized.

Then one day he got a sore throat. The infection worsened, and he was rushed to the hospital. While there, Henry Luce brought him the good news that he had reached his goal; he was a millionaire! Briton Hadden achieved his dream on time; but he was too sick to enjoy the money. On February 26, 1929, he died, leaving it all to someone else.

How much better it would have been if Briton Hadden had taken the time to eat, sleep, exercise, and live a balanced life. How much better it would have been if he had taken time to know God and to help his fellow men.

Here is a problem in mathematics for you to solve. On the first line put everything you could possibly desire in this world: power, fame, wealth, a Cadillac, a Mercedes-Benz, a yacht, a private plane, a house on the lake, a cabin in the mountains, a mansion in the city, expensive furniture, and fabulous clothes—anything that appeals to you. From your total subtract: Jesus, salvation, and eternal life. What is your remainder?

BLOOD TRANSFUSION

In whom we have redemption through his blood. Ephesians 1:7.

This is the birthday of Henry Wadsworth Longfellow, the popular American poet of a hundred years ago. Few people living today have heard about the tragedy that kept him from enjoying his success to the full.

His wife, Frances, whom he loved very dearly, died while still quite young. This is how it happened.

On that particular day Frances had some packages to mail. It was necessary to seal them first with sealing wax, so taking the red stick of wax she held it over a flame to melt it. In the process her dress touched the fire and immediately she was ablaze.

"Help!" she cried. "Henry, help me! I'm on fire!"

Mr. Longfellow ran to her aid and beat out the flames but Frances had been burned very badly. The doctors didn't know what to do and she died as a result of the burns, leaving Henry Wadsworth Longfellow a very lonely man.

Had it happened a hundred years later Frances would have been rushed to the hospital in an ambulance. There she would have been given blood tranfusions that might have saved her life. But in the mid-1800s no one had heard of such things. There was no knowledge of shock, or plasma, or other aspects of medicine that are so well known today.

Plasma is the straw colored liquid part of the blood. It is plasma that you see under blisters when you are burned. When a lot of this vital fluid leaks out of the body, the blood pressure goes down and the injured person goes into a state of shock. If something isn't done, death will result.

We have all been burned by sin. This puts us in a state of spiritual shock, as it were. If we stay in this condition we will surely die. We must have a "blood transfusion." Our only hope is the blood of Jesus.

Will you accept the life that He offers you today? He hung upon the cruel cross and gave His blood that you might live. The blood that flowed from His head, His hands, and His feet was for you. He loves you and wants you to live now and forever. Through His blood you can be saved.

AT THE CROSSROADS

Come and follow me. Matthew 19:21.

I wonder what that is all about, Wilfred thought as he passed the huge tent. I think I'll go inside and see.

A man was praying on a platform at the front of the crowded tent. The congregation stood with bowed heads, but the people seemed to be getting restless. It was evident the prayer had continued for a long time and was going to be much longer.

Wilfred was about to leave when one of the kneeling men on the platform stood up. Stepping forward he said, "Let us sing a hymn while our brother finishes his prayer."

Wilfred liked that! He decided to stay and hear what that man had to say.

Wilfred Grenfell stood at the crossroads that night. If he chose one road he would no doubt become a fashionable doctor in London. Perhaps he would become wealthy and famous, with a life of luxury and ease.

But the speaker, Dwight L. Moody, showed Wilfred another road. At its beginning stood Jesus, saying, "Come, follow Me." The young man knew that if he traveled that road he could never be just an ordinary doctor. He would have to make his life, like that of Jesus, one of service to others.

Wilfred Grenfell chose to follow Jesus. After graduation from London University he became a physician on a mission ship that served the fishermen of the North Sea. Later he went with a hospital ship to Newfoundland and Labrador. He then spent the rest of his life as a missionary doctor in Labrador.

Sir Wilfred Grenfell, who was born on this day in 1865, never regretted the decision he made the night he heard Dwight L. Moody preach.

Toward the end of his life he wrote: "If there is one thing about which I never have any question, it is that the decision to endeavor to follow Christ does for men what nothing else can do."

Today you might be standing at the crossroads of your life. There are two roads you can take. At the beginning of one stands Jesus. "Come," He says, "and follow Me." Which road will you choose?

CAROLE'S CRY

This poor man cried, and the Lord heard him, and saved him out of all his troubles. Psalm 34:6.

It was two o'clock the morning of Wednesday, March 1, 1972. Carole Taylor had been trapped under her car for two hours. The engine was still running and the rear wheels were spinning. The weight of the car was pressing hard on her hips. Her legs were burning from the heat of the exhaust, while her upper body was freezing. A light snow was falling on her upturned face.

On her way home from Montreal General Hospital where she was a secretary, Carole realized she had forgotten something. Turning down a side street, she tried to find a shortcut. Instead, she lost her way, ending up on a dead-end street in an isolated factory area.

Carole tried to turn the car around, but it became stuck in the snow. Realizing she could wait all night for help in such an isolated spot, she decided to try something her brother had told her about.

She put the car in reverse, pulled out the choke, left the door open and tried to push it out of the rut. The car began to move. Carole ran ahead so she could jump into the driver's seat, but her boots slipped and she fell flat. The left rear wheel ran over her legs and stopped.

Carole knew that if help came at all, it would be from God. And so she prayed, really prayed for the first time in her life. When the situation seemed hopeless, she heard a car coming down the desolate road. It stopped nearby and with relief Carole looked up into the faces of two policemen standing over her.

Later she learned that the officers had been patrolling the area for more than a week but had never before turned into the road where she lay trapped. There was no reason for them to do so that night either.

"I had no intention of patrolling that unused stretch," Officer Wooley explained. "As I reached it, though, I just turned in without thinking."

What caused him to take that turn? Was it chance? Carole believes with all her heart that God sent help in answer to her prayer. Carole cried to God; He heard her and delivered her out of her trouble. He will hear you, too, this day and always.

SAVED BY AN EAGLE

Forgetting those things which are behind, and reaching forth unto those things which are before, I press toward the mark. Philippians 3:13, 14.

Sam stood on the deck of the riverboat and stared at the dark water below. The muddy, turbulent stream seemed a reflection of his own disturbed soul.

What is the use of living? he questioned himself. Everything is finished. My wife has deserted me. My career is gone. I have betrayed the trust of the people. I have no future.

At that moment, when Sam was ready to jump to his death, an eagle flew out of the Tennessee wilderness and swooped close to the deck where he was standing. Then, screaming, it flew west into the sun.

Immediately Sam felt better. Closing his eyes he could still see the dark bird soaring into the blazing sun. Why had the eagle come at that decisive moment in his life? Could it be that he did have a future after all?

The man facing the sunset that spring day was Sam Houston, who later helped win independence for Texas. He served as president of the Republic of Texas and later, when it became a part of the United States, he became governor.

Today, March 2, is celebrated as Texas Independence Day in honor of Sam Houston, who was born on this day in 1793.

Like Sam, many young people face times of discouragement. They find it hard to live down the mistakes of their past.

Take Andy, for instance. During his eighth-grade year he fooled around too much and failed. His friends went away to academy and left him behind. Andy felt like giving up, but he tried again and succeeded.

Then there was Joyce, a lively girl who got in with the wrong crowd. She did a lot of things she shouldn't have done and felt ashamed to attend church because everyone knew. Satan told her it was no use, but she asked God to forgive her past and He helped her to have a happy life again.

Sometimes you may also feel like giving up because of what you have done. Please don't. Turn your back on the past and face the Son. Jesus still loves you. He can give you the strength you need today. He can help you forget the past. He can set your steps in a new direction.

FINGERPRINTS

Behold, what manner of love the Father hath bestowed upon us, that we should be called the sons of God. 1 John 3:1.

One by one the men pressed their ink-blackened fingers onto the white card containing their name and number. The prisoners of Sing Sing Prison in Ossining, New York, were making history. It was May 3, 1903, and for the first time a penal institution was making a file of the prisoners' fingerprints. This later became a part of the master file kept by the Federal Bureau of Investigation in Washington, D.C.

Today there are more than 200 million fingerprints on record in the FBI Identification Division. This file is used to help identify criminals and missing persons. Each year more than 1,500 dead bodies are identified through fingerprints. In one year more than 15,000 criminals are arrested with the help of fingerprints.

Take the case of the great train robbery of 1963, the biggest cash robbery of all time. With the help of fingerprints left on a kitchen window, a bathtub, and a beer can, the twelve participants were eventually caught and sentenced to a total of 291 years in jail.

With fingerprints there can be no case of mistaken identity. Even identical twins have different fingerprints. No two fingerprints have yet been found to be the same. Therefore, they are the surest way to establish a person's identity.

The uniqueness of your fingerprint is one way in which God shows that you are someone special. The Bible says that even the hairs of your head are numbered. Then why not the lines, whorls, arches, and loops of your thumb? There is nothing about you that He does not know.

"He knows each individual by name, and cares for each as if there were not another upon the earth for whom He gave His beloved Son."—*The Ministry of Healing,* p. 229.

God made you unique, and He loves and cares for you as an individual. So precious are you that Jesus would have come to die for you even if you were the only sinner in the world.

God made you different from everyone else. He wants you to recognize yourself as a person who is special in His sight. You are His child, whom He loves very much.

WHERE WILL YOU BE?

And when the thousand years are expired, Satan shall be loosed out of his prison. And shall go out to deceive the nations. Revelation 20:7, 8.

The fingers of King Louis trembled as he tried to open the envelope. Smoothing out the paper, he read its message and turned pale.

For a few moments on March 4, 1815, the king of France sat with his head in his hands. At last he raised his face and spoke to one of his government ministers. "Do you know what it says?"

"No, sir."

"Napoleon has escaped from exile. He is marching toward Paris. We have a revolution on our hands."

A few days later Napoleon rode triumphantly into the city. For 100 days he ruled France, until his defeat at Waterloo.

This story reminds me of Lucifer. Like Napoleon, he lost his position of honor and was sent into exile. Instead of being banished to an island in the Mediterranean, Satan went to a small planet on the outer edges of the universe. For one thousand years following the second coming of Jesus, he will be imprisoned on this earth. Like Napoleon, he will be planning his return to the city where he once lived.

At the end of the one thousand years Jesus will return to the earth. The wicked dead will be raised to see the Holy City descend. When Satan sees this vast throng of people he gains courage. Using the mighty military leaders of all ages, he marshalls the wicked into companies and divisions and announces an attack on the city of God.

I can imagine this vast army moving across the earth led by such leaders as Hitler and Alexander the Great. They surround the city, and with their combined military genius success seems certain.

Suddenly, the wicked throngs are transfixed by sights in and above the city. The throne of God appears and Christ is crowned King. The books of record are opened and a cross appears above the throne. The history of sin and sinners unfolds above the city like a giant movie. The army falls to its knees. Fire falls from heaven and Satan and his host are no more.

Where will you be on that day? Will you be inside the city with King Jesus or outside with Lucifer? The choice is yours.

FEAR EPIDEMIC

Let not your heart be troubled: ye believe in God, believe also in me. John 14:1.

Have you ever been afraid, really afraid? I'm not talking about the momentary fear of a barking dog, looking over a cliff, or speaking in public.

I'm talking about a fear that lives with you night and day—a fear that your world is going to fall apart.

Some circumstances that cause this kind of fear are the loss of a parent through death or divorce, the fear of failure in school or a relationship, and the loss of ability to lead a normal life because of a crippling disease or accident.

Grown-ups sometimes face this fear when they can't get work to support their family or when they think they are going to lose their home and savings. Many people had this kind of fear in 1933.

Twelve million people were out of work. How would they feed their children? Those who had jobs, many of them working for only 10 cents an hour, were afraid they would lose them. Those who had money in the bank were afraid the banks would go broke, so they asked for their money back. Frightened people withdrew one billion dollars in two weeks.

President Franklin D. Roosevelt knew he would have to do something to stop this epidemic of fear. On March 5 he announced that all banks would close for three days. Then he talked to the people about the problem of fear.

He admonished the people not to be afraid. They would not lose their money. He promised to help them get jobs. "The only thing we have to fear is fear itself," he said in his first inaugural address.

President Roosevelt went on to explain how fear paralyzes us. It confuses the mind so that a person can neither think properly nor act wisely.

When we face scary situations, it is hard not to be afraid, but if we know Jesus we can conquer our fears. Isn't that what Jesus is trying to tell us in today's memory verse? "Don't be afraid. Trust me. Everything will work out."

THE FAITHFUL WATCHDOG

If ye love me, keep my commandments. John 14:15.

We don't know his name. We don't even know what breed of dog he was. But we do know that he lived on North Main Street on the Island of Chincoteague, off the coast of Virginia. We do know that he loved his master and was obedient to his commands.

On Tuesday, March 6, 1962, a storm raged along the Atlantic Coast of North America. Winds of hurricane force destroyed hundreds of homes and businesses.

When the rain stopped and the wind died down a reporter from the Washington *Star* went over to Chincoteague to inspect the damage. He found that the island was one of the hardest hit of all places along the path of the storm. As he walked down North Main Street he saw that nothing remained of this once busy thoroughfare but a jumbled mass of boards, pipes, bricks, and stones. All was a picture of desolation.

Suddenly, the reporter stopped and stared. There in the middle of the rubbish heap that had once been his master's home, sat a watchdog on guard. The reporter snapped a picture of the obedient animal and it was published in the *Star*.

This pet's faithfulness to duty gives us an example of what it means to "stand for the right though the heavens fall." The watchdog loved his master, and regardless of what happened he watched his home and protected it from intruders.

God needs boys and girls who will stand firmly for right. Joseph was that kind of boy. When his brothers sold him as a slave his whole world seemed to collapse around him. Nevertheless, regardless of the circumstances, Joseph determined to be obedient to the God he loved.

When Joseph was tempted by his master's wife to do what he knew to be wrong, he bravely replied, "How can I do this great wickedness and sin against God?" Even when put into prison he remained loyal and obedient to his God.

Have you made Jesus Christ the Master of your heart and life? Won't you determine today to love Him and keep all of His commandments? Will you pledge yourself this day to obey Him no matter what happens?

MARY JONES'S BIBLE

Search the scriptures; for in them ye think ye have eternal life: and they are they which testify of me. John 5:39.

Bibles were scarce in Wales in 1794. The available few were so expensive that only the wealthy could afford one. The Jones family was poor, but that did not stop Mary from searching the Scriptures.

One day she walked two miles to a neighbor's home and timidly asked, "Please, may I read your Bible for just a little while?"

"Of course, my child," the farmer's wife replied. "Come in." She led Mary into the best room of the house where the Bible sat in a place of honor. Then she quietly slipped out leaving the girl alone with a Bible for the first time in her life.

Breathless with excitement, Mary lifted the cloth and placed it on the table beside her. With trembling hands she opened the large book. By chance it fell open to John 5. There she read the words of Jesus, "Search the scriptures."

"I will! I will!" she cried. "Oh, if only I had a Bible of my own!"

Six years later Mary walked barefoot twenty-eight miles to the town of Bala, where Welsh Bibles were for sale. In her pocket was the money she had saved. She went straight to the home of Pastor Thomas Charles, who had the only copies then available.

"I am very sorry," Pastor Charles explained. "All of the Bibles I have are already reserved."

Mary couldn't believe it! She began to cry as if her heart would break. As Mr. Charles saw her grief, tears filled his eyes, too.

"You shall have a Bible," he said, handing her one of his reserved copies.

Two years later Mr. Charles told Mary's story in London and pleaded for a society to be formed to print and circulate Welsh Bibles.

"Why for Wales only?" someone else suggested. "Why not for the whole world?"

So it was, because of Mary's desire for a Bible, that the British and Foreign Bible Society was formed on March 7, 1804. Today most people can get a Bible in their own language. Surely you have one. Will you not determine to read it more faithfully?

A BRIDGE TO GOD

I am the way, the truth, and the life. John 14:6.

Leaning against the iron railing at Niagara Falls, Canada, I looked across the deep gorge to the American side. To my right was the Horseshoe Falls and to my left, overhanging branches framing the scene in picture-postcard beauty, was Rainbow Bridge, arching over the whirling rapids below.

Standing there, I thought of the twelve other bridges that had been built across that gorge. One of the most interesting was constructed by Charles Ellet and John Augustus Roebling.

Mr. Roebling believed that ropes strong enough to hold motor traffic could be made of steel wire. Using this idea he built the first railway suspension bridge across the Niagara Gorge. The 825-foot bridge had two decks. The lower one was a 15-foot wide highway. The upper deck was a 25-foot wide railway track.

On March 8, 1855, a breathless crowd stood on each side of the gorge to watch the first train cross the bridge. The spectators cheered as the locomotive and cars safely reached the other side. For forty-two years trains crossed that bridge until it was finally replaced by a new arch span.

For me that scene at Niagara brought back memories of Sabbath school in the small-town church of my childhood. In those days the teachers got help from a magazine called *The Sabbath School Worker*. The lessons were sometimes illustrated by cartoons depicting the main theme of the lesson. One such picture was a scene similar to the one at Niagara Gorge.

On one side of the drawing was man; on the other side was God. The rapids of sin separated the two, but spanning the gorge was a bridge in the shape of a cross. On the bridge was written the words of today's text: "I am the way."

In the beginning God and man enjoyed daily fellowship. God came into the garden in the cool of the day to walk and talk with Adam and Eve.

Then something happened to separate man from God. Adam sinned and there came a great gulf between him and his Creator. But at the appointed time, Jesus came, lived a perfect life, and died on the cross. In doing this He built a bridge from man to God. Will you cross that bridge today?

ARMOR OF IRON

Put on the whole armour of God, that ye may be able to stand against the wiles of the devil. Ephesians 6:11.

At about one o'clock the afternoon of March 8, 1862, officers aboard two Union sailing ships noticed a strange-looking vessel steaming down the Elizabeth River in their direction.

It was the *Merrimac,* a Confederate ironclad ship. To construct it, Southern engineers had cut a regular wooden ship down to the water line. On the new deck they built a rectangular box of wood and covered the whole thing with metal plating.

Although the Union ships, the *Congress* and the *Cumberland* had eighty guns between them to the *Merrimac's* ten, they were no match for the ironclad ship.

The next morning, March 9, the *Merrimac* headed toward the Northern ship *Minnesota,* hoping to repeat the victory of the day before. Then the Southern pilot saw another ironclad ship coming in his direction. It was the Northern ship *Monitor.*

The two ironclads seemed evenly matched. But just after noon a shot from the *Merrimac* found its way into the sight hole of the pilot's house on the *Monitor* and blinded the commanding officer. The *Monitor* was forced to withdraw and the battle was over. This battle of March 9, 1862, marked the beginning of a new type of naval warfare.

No modern navy would think of sending wooden ships into battle. Sometimes Christians are not as careful of their defenses and go unprotected to fight the enemy.

Read Ephesians 6:10-17. Notice how many parts of the Christian's armor refer to the Bible. Your best weapons of defense in the battle against evil are verses of Scripture.

David knew where his armor was. He said, "Thy word have I hid in mine heart, that I might not sin against thee."

Jesus protected himself with the armor of the Word. When Satan tempted Him, Jesus met him with, "It is written."

You, too, can be successful in your battle with the devil. Put on the armor of God each day. Spend time in prayer and Bible study. Hurriedly reading the Morning Watch is not enough. Think about the meaning of what you read. Memorize the Bible verse. By so doing you will be putting on an armor of iron that will keep you safe from temptation.

IT COULDN'T BE DONE

And nothing shall be impossible unto you. Matthew 17:20.

"It cannot be done," the scientists argued. "You cannot send a continuous vibration of human speech over a stop-and-start current of electricity."

"Then I will make a continuous current of electricity," Alec replied.

"That is not possible!"

"I know that it can be done," Alec insisted. "I am going to find a way to do it."

Working in the attic of the house where he lived, he set up a jumble of wires, batteries, and tuning forks and began his experiments.

"If he had known anything about electricity," a scientist wrote later, "he would never have invented the telephone."

But Alexander Graham Bell didn't know very much about electricity. He had a dream and he worked to make it a reality. He thought that if he could take a piece of steel and vibrate it in front of the pole of an electromagnet, he would get the kind of current he wanted.

Everyone said it was impossible, but on March 7, 1876, just after his twenty-ninth birthday, Alexander Graham Bell received his first patent for the telephone.

Three days later, on March 10, he spoke the famous words, "Mr. Watson, come here. I want you!" He had done the impossible.

In my scrapbook is a poem by Edgar Guest called "It Couldn't Be Done." I wonder whether the poet had Alexander Graham Bell in mind when he wrote:

"Somebody said that it couldn't be done,
But he with a chuckle replied
That 'maybe it couldn't,' but he would be one
Who wouldn't say so till he'd tried.
So he buckled right in with the trace of a grin
On his face. If he worried he hid it.
He started to sing as he tackled the thing
That couldn't be done, and he did it."

God needs boys and girls who are willing to attempt the impossible for Him. This is the day to decide to be such a worker for God.

I WILL RETURN

I will come again, and receive you unto myself; that where I am, there ye may be also. John 14:3.

During World War II, Bataan Peninsula became the center of an intense struggle between the allied United States and Filipino troops and the much greater Japanese forces.

In the thick of the battle, on March 11, 1942, General Douglas MacArthur, United States Army Commander for the Far East, was ordered by President Roosevelt to leave the Philippines. He was to go to Australia to take command of all Allied troops in the Southwest Pacific. MacArthur left immediately aboard a Navy torpedo boat.

That night was a dark one indeed for the soldiers left behind. Without their leader, they feared surrender. However, MacArthur left a promise to cheer them: "I shall return!"

A few weeks later the United States and Filipino forces surrendered. About 75,000 Americans and Filipinos were put in prisoner-of-war camps. Through the bitter days that followed, the prisoners cheered one another with General MacArthur's promise. Two and one half years later the General did return to recapture the peninsula and set the prisoners free.

On a long-ago day another group of disheartened men gathered around their departing General. Before leaving He promised, "I will come again." Just as General MacArthur kept his word, so Jesus will return, as He has promised, to set earth's prisoners free.

I would love to be living on that day, wouldn't you? Imagine what it will mean for those chained in dark dungeons awaiting their execution. Imagine the joy of those hiding in caves and mountain fortresses!

At that midnight hour, when it seems that God's people will be destroyed by evil men, Jesus will return. The angry multitude will be stopped by a dense blackness that covers the earth. Their shouts will die away and they will stand in silence before a most beautiful rainbow. "Shining in glory from the throne of God," it "spans the heavens and seems to encircle each praying company."—*The Great Controversy*, p. 636.

Then God's people will hear a clear, sweet voice saying, "Look up." Behind the rainbow the black clouds will roll apart. They will see Jesus coming in the clouds of heaven.

78

REACHING THE IDEALS

Wherewithal shall a young man cleanse his way? by taking heed thereto according to thy word. Psalm 119:9.

Today is the birthday of the Girl Scouts in the United States and this week is being celebrated as Girl Scout Week. On this day in 1912 the first troop meeting was held in Savannah, Georgia, in the home of Mrs. Julliette Gordon Low.

The Girl Scouts and Boy Scouts are similar to the Pathfinder Club. Members learn ideals of character and patriotism. They work hard to earn badges in such areas as first aid, nature, cooking, swimming, hospitality, and world understanding.

Girl Scouts are expected to be trustworthy, loyal, helpful, friendly, courteous, kind to animals, obedient, cheerful, thrifty, and clean in thought, word, and deed.

These high ideals are also expected of members of Adventist Pathfinder Clubs. The main difference between Pathfinder Clubs and Scout Troops is the emphasis on God's Word.

Scout leaders hold up the ideals and urge their young people to reach them. Pathfinder leaders not only support the standard of conduct, but they show the method of accomplishment.

Bible study is included as a part of a Pathfinder's training. Why? Because the Bible is the tool God uses to transform our characters and make us what we ought to be. There is power in the study of God's Word. It "quickens the physical, mental, and spiritual powers, and directs the life into right channels."—*The Ministry of Healing,* p. 458.

How can a boy or girl be clean in thought, word, and deed? "By taking heed thereto according to thy word."

The young person who makes the Bible his guide will not go wrong. It will lead him to be truthful, loyal, and helpful. It will teach him how to be obedient, cheerful, and courteous. It will help him reach his ideals.

Is there an active Pathfinder Club in your church? Do you belong to it? Working and learning with other members can help to make you a better person.

If your church does not have a Pathfinder Club, perhaps you can help to get one started. If your church is too small maybe you can join together with a nearby church to get something going. Discuss it with your parents, pastor, and youth leader. Pray about it and see what happens.

THE RUNAWAY TRAIN

Behold, how great a matter a little fire kindleth. James 3:5.

On Friday, March 13, 1959, a train ran away killing one man and injuring twenty others.

It all began in the middle of the afternoon at the Tumwater switchyards two miles south of Olympia, Washington. The switching crew uncoupled fifteen cars from the locomotive and placed them on a siding for Olympia. The remainder of the cars were pulled into the Olympia Brewing Company yard. For some reason no one thought to set the hand brakes on the fifteen cars.

At about five forty-two p.m. the fifteen cars began to move. Soon nearly two million pounds of steel and wood were rolling down the track at a mile a minute, headed for the back of the Fourth Avenue Station.

At approximately 5:45 P.M. the runaway train crashed through the steel bumper guard at the end of the line. It tore through the concrete platform and into the brick wall of the station then charged through the station and out the opposite wall into the street. It plowed into the Sta-Well Health Store and came to rest in a tangled mass of brick, lumber, and health-food tins.

Some of the cars were slammed into other shops. Others overturned in the street. Behind the station still others lay in a jumbled mass of steel and wires. The railroad telegrapher was dead.

What a lot of damage was done within a few minutes—all because someone forgot to put on the brakes. Even one small block beneath the wheels could have prevented the tragedy. One small mistake took the life of one man, wounded twenty others, and did thousands of dollars' worth of damage to at least eight buildings.

It only takes a little worm to spoil an apple. A small mistake may ruin a life. It only takes a little word to wreck a friendship. One match can set a forest on fire.

"Never underrate the importance of little things. Little things supply the actual discipline of life. It is by them that the soul is trained that it may grow into the likeness of Christ, or bear the likeness of evil."—*Messages to Young People,* p. 202.

Little things are important. Therefore, let us watch the little things in our lives today.

THE SCHOOLHOUSE VISION

And they shall fight against thee; but they shall not prevail against thee; for I am with thee, saith the Lord, to deliver thee. Jeremiah 1:19.

On March 13 and 14, 1858, forty new Adventists gathered in the community schoolhouse at Lovett's Grove, Ohio, to hear Elder and Mrs. James White speak.

The Whites planned to return to Michigan on Sunday afternoon, March 14, but Elder White was asked to stay to conduct the funeral service of a young man from the community.

The one-room building was not big enough to hold all who came for the service. Some stood around the open windows to hear the sermon. When her husband was finished, Mrs. White stood up to give her testimony of faith in the coming of Christ.

After speaking a few sentences she received a vision that lasted for two hours. During this time she was given many scenes of the great controversy between Christ and Satan. She was instructed to write out the vision, but she was was warned that it would not be easy, for Satan would do his best to keep the story from being written.

On the train back to Michigan, Mrs. White made plans to do as the angel had instructed her. However, upon arriving at the home of Mr. and Mrs. E. R. Palmer, she was stricken with paralysis. For several weeks following the attack Mrs. White was very weak. Sometimes she could write only a page a day and then she would have to rest for three days.

Later God revealed to her that Satan had tried to kill her so that she could not write out the vision. At that time angels were sent to rescue her from Satan's power.

The book which resulted is *The Great Controversy*. The last three chapters are particularly interesting for young people. These chapters give a detailed account of what is going to happen just before Jesus comes. They tell about the difficulties God's followers will face at the end of time. They describe the marvelous deliverance of His people. There is a description of the one thousand years in heaven and the third coming of Jesus.

Knowing about these events in advance should help you to get ready to face them. Perhaps your family would like to join you in reading the final chapters of *The Great Controversy* for worship. Today would be a good day to start.

A TEEN-AGER'S DISCOVERY

All scripture is given by inspiration of God. 2 Timothy 3:16.

John Trever went to work as usual the morning of March 15, 1948. At his desk in the American School of Oriental Research in Jerusalem he looked over the morning's mail and found the letter he had been expecting. It bore the return address of William F. Albright, a well-known archeologist. Carefully opening the letter, Mr. Trever read and reread its contents.

"Good!" Mr. Tever exulted. "He agrees with me. Those scrolls are ancient."

This was putting it mildly. The letter actually said, "It is the greatest manuscript discovery of modern times."

What did Mr. Albright mean? What was so great about a bunch of dusty old leather and papyrus scrolls? Who discovered them? How? Where?

One day in 1947 Mohammed the Wolf, a 15-year-old shepherd boy, was looking for a lost goat on the cliffs near the northeast corner of the Dead Sea. Spotting a circular hole that might lead to a cave in the cliff, Mohammed threw a stone inside. There was a sound of crashing pottery. Scrambling through the hole the boy found several leather scrolls wrapped in dusty linen.

Taking his find to Bethlehem, Mohammed sold it to some merchants. Five of the scrolls were later received by the American School of Oriental Research where John Trever worked. One of these was the complete book of Isaiah copied out by Jewish scholars about the time of Christ.

Before the discovery of the Dead Sea scrolls, the oldest copy of the Bible known to be in existence had been made about A.D. 1000. Many people were asking, "How can we know the Bible we now have is accurate? Perhaps so many mistakes have been made that we can no longer believe what it says."

The Dead Sea scrolls prove that the Bible is the same as it was two thousand years ago. We can see how God has protected His Word through the centuries. Without a doubt we can accept the Bible as right and true. No wonder Mr. Albright called the teen-age shepherd boy's find "the greatest manuscript discovery of modern times." Now, as never before, we can believe that the Bible is really what it claims to be, the inspired Word of God.

TREASURE FOR THE KING

They shall be mine, saith the Lord of hosts, in that day when I make up my jewels. Malachi 3:17.

You and I are God's jewels. We are His special treasure. So precious are we to Him that He came all the way from heaven to earth to make sure we could shine in His kingdom throughout eternity.

The search for treasure has always fascinated young people. One such search began in 1519 when Ferdinand Magellan set sail from Seville, Spain, with five small ships and 234 men to look for a new route to India and her treasures of gold, ivory, silk, spices, and jewels. The ships traveled west to the coast of Brazil, around the tip of South America, and across the Pacific Ocean in search of treasure for the king of Spain.

On March 16, 1521, Magellan landed on the island of Cebu in the Philippines. The Spaniards set up a makeshift altar on shore and conducted mass. Curious Filipinos gathered around. Within a few weeks 800 natives had accepted Christianity and were baptized as Roman Catholics. Shortly after this Magellan and some of the crew were killed in a battle while helping their new friends.

One of Magellan's ships, the *Victoria,* returned to Spain with the remaining men. It was the first ship to go completely around the world.

Although the sailors did not bring back the wealth of gold and jewels that they had sought, they had news of a different kind of treasure—people who were willing to leave their pagan ways to worship the true and living God. Soon Roman Catholic missionaries were on their way to the Philippines to gather these jewels.

Almost four hundred years later Seventh-day Adventists went to the Philippines to begin looking for the special treasure of men, women, boys, and girls who would be ready for Christ's coming. The search for souls still continues in the Philippines and around the world. It is the greatest treasure hunt of the ages.

If you search you might find such treasure in your own neighborhood. You can be an adventurer, as was Ferdinand Magellan, seeking treasure for your King.

THE GLORY OF THE LORD

And they shall see the Son of man coming in the clouds of heaven with power and great glory. Matthew 24:30.

What will the glory of the Lord be like? Paul speaks of "the brightness of his coming" in 2 Thessalonians 2:8. Peter describes it like this: "The heavens shall pass away with a great noise, and the elements shall melt with fervent heat" (2 Peter 3:10).

Probably the nearest thing to such glory that man has seen is the explosion of an atom bomb. Only those who are prepared can look at such brightness and live.

On the morning of March 17, 1953, hundreds of reporters gathered on a small hill outside Yucca Flats, Nevada. They had come to see one of the greatest atomic blasts ever witnessed by man.

Each man had in his hands a pair of thick, dark glasses that he must wear while watching the explosion. One of the newsmen put his glasses on ahead of time and waved his hand directly in front of the lens. He could see nothing.

The time came when all were instructed to put on their glasses and stand ready. Moments later a terrific explosion sent a deafening roar across the barren earth. A blinding flash of light and a brilliant, mushroom-shaped cloud filled the sky.

When it was over, the men rushed to Las Vegas to send their stories to their hometown papers. After the news had been dispatched, a group of reporters gathered together to discuss what they had seen.

"What headline will your report have?" someone asked.

"Hell Bomb Biggest Yet," one suggested.

"Atom Blast Rips Nevada Skies" said another. One by one the reporters gave their ideas until there was only one man left.

"And what will your editor label your story?" someone asked the remaining journalist.

"Gentlemen," he said after a long pause. "I think, if my editor is wise, he will write: 'Mine eyes have seen the glory of the coming of the Lord.'"

Are you prepared to look at the brightness of Christ's glory? Are you ready for Jesus to come? Today is given that you might prepare. What are you doing to get ready?

THE PRIME MOVER

But ye shall receive power, after that the Holy Ghost is come upon you: and ye shall be witnesses unto me. Acts 1:8.

"Ron! You're home!" I exclaimed as my husband hugged me after an itinerary in South India. "How did you get here so soon? I wasn't expecting you for another three hours."

"They have dieselized the *Island Express,*" he explained. "We can now leave later and arrive earlier."

For my husband's early arrival I must thank Rudolf Diesel, a German mechanical engineer whose birthday is today. Born in Paris in 1858, he attended school in Munich, Germany.

One day at the close of a class the professor remarked, "And so, gentlemen, we must conclude that, considering the great amount of fuel required, existing prime movers produce relative small power."

Rudolf's life was shaped by those words. He decided to make a better prime mover. He developed an internal combustion engine that used oil instead of gasoline as a fuel and did away with the need for a carburetor and spark plugs. Because the diesel engine was so simple, cheap, and efficient, it revolutionized transportation. Today diesel engines are used in tractors, trucks, buses, trains, ships, and some cars.

The discovery Rudolf Diesel made in the physical world is one that you and I need to make in the spiritual world. The question Rudolf asked himself that day in Munich is one that we also need to ask.

What is the "prime mover" in our lives? What kind of power do we need in order to fulfill Christ's command to take the gospel into all the world? The answer lies in our text for today. "Ye shall receive power, after that the Holy Ghost is come upon you."

This is the power that revolutionized the lives of the disciples. In one generation the gospel was carried to the then-known world. The same thing is going to happen in the last generation before Jesus comes. Young people will be filled with power and will go forth to witness to their neighbors and friends.

Would you like to see this happen in your lifetime? Will you not then determine today to let the Holy Spirit be the "prime mover" in your life?

THE OUTSTRETCHED HANDS

And I, if I be lifted up from the earth, will draw all men unto me. John 12:32.

Twelve-year-old David had been going to church ever since he could remember. Sunday after Sunday he had trudged the three miles behind his father without question. Going to church, like attending family worship, was not something to be questioned; it was something to be done.

One misty morning the walk across the Scottish moors seemed endless and for the first time David felt rebellious. He didn't want to sit in a gloomy church while the minister preached a long, boring sermon. He wanted to be out in the fields and meadows chasing colts.

Church that Sunday was no different from any other Sunday. The sermon was monotonous. As David looked around the stone walls for some diversion, his eyes were drawn to a picture he had seen countless times before.

It was a picture of a smiling Jesus with outstretched hands. A crowd of people pressed toward Him. David looked at the individuals in that crowd. Some were sick. Others were crippled. As the boy continued to stare at the picture he felt as if he were part of the group moving closer and closer to Jesus.

"Christ who loves all people, who loves everyone, needs you and your hands to minister to others," David heard the pastor say. At that moment young David knew that God was calling him.

That afternoon on the way home David lengthened his strides to catch up with his father. "Father," he said as he came abreast, "am I too young to join the church?"

"No, my lad," Neil Livingstone answered. "Not in years, but you are in knowledge. One of the elders must instruct you first."

So it was that David Livingstone, born on this day in 1813, responded to the magnetic power of the Saviour. That day he set his heart and feet to follow the Man of the outstretched hands. That decision led him to Africa to become one of the world's best-known missionaries and explorers.

Will you, too, respond to the outstretched hands of Jesus? He is calling you. He needs you and your hands today.

FOOLISH WISE MAN

*Professing themselves to be wise, they became fools. Romans
1:22.*

"Where can Isaac be now?" Mrs. Newton wondered aloud one
evening at chore time.

"Isaac! Oh, Isaac!" she called time and again. She looked in
the various corners of the house and barn where her son might
be hiding.

"Here I am," Isaac answered from a corner of the hayloft.
Putting aside his book, he went to help his mother. However,
Isaac spent so much time reading that Mrs. Newton decided to
hire a helper and let him prepare for Cambridge University. He
was a student for the rest of his life, learning all he could about
the universe.

Shortly before his death on March 20, 1727, he wrote: "I seem
to have been only like a boy playing on the seashore . . . whilst
the great ocean of truth lay all undiscovered before me."

Isaac Newton discovered the color spectrum. He constructed
the first reflecting telescope. He invented a new kind of
mathematics called calculus. Perhaps you have heard the story
about the falling apple and Sir Isaac Newton's theory of gravity.
Because of these discoveries, he is often called the Father of
Modern Science.

Not only was Newton a diligent student of science, he was
also an earnest student of the Bible. As he studied prophecy he
became convinced that new methods of transportation would be
developed that would allow men to travel at the speed of more
than fifty miles an hour.

Voltaire, the infidel, ridiculed him. "Now look at that mighty
mind of Newton's who discovered gravity and told us such
marvels for us all to admire—when he became an old man . . . he
began to study that book called the Bible. And it seems that, in
order to credit its fabulous nonsense, we must believe that the
knowledge of mankind will be so increased that we shall be able
to travel at the rate of fifty miles an hour."

I wonder what Mr. Voltaire would say if he could spend an
hour on the Los Angeles Freeway? I wonder what he would say
about airplanes and space shuttles?

Voltaire is a good illustration of today's text.

SAVED BY HOPE

Looking for the blessed hope, and the glorious appearing of the great God and our Saviour Jesus Christ. Titus 2:13.

Twenty-three-year-old Stein Gabrielson stood on the deck of the Norwegian freighter *Norse Variant* and watched the coast of Virginia recede. It was Wednesday evening, March 21, 1973. With luck they should reach Glasgow with their load of coal in a few days. But the coal never got to Glasgow. The next morning a hurricane tore the ship apart.

"The life rafts! Throw them overboard and jump after them," Captain Hansen bellowed above the shrieking winds. As he spoke a giant wave descended on the ship, forcing it beneath the water.

The suction of the sinking vessel pulled Stein under. As the pull weakened he struggled to the surface, where he was tossed about like a cork.

Miraculously, a lifeboat floated by and Stein climbed in. One hundred-mile-an-hour winds and fifty-foot waves made survival seem impossible. Stein hoped the Coast Guard would find him in a few hours.

A giant killer wave ripped the craft into a thousand pieces and once more Stein was dumped into the wild Atlantic. He managed to swim to another lifeboat and again began to hope for rescue.

By Saturday morning Stein was exhausted. He had been without sleep for two full days. He wanted to rest but the hope of rescue kept him awake until Sunday morning when help finally came. He had been without food, water, or sleep for seventy hours. He had struggled alone against wind, waves, freezing temperatures, and driving sleet. It seemed impossible that anyone could have survived, but Stein did. He was saved by hope.

In the time of trouble that is to come upon this world before Jesus returns you will have an experience similar to Stein's. Survival will seem impossible. Huge waves of doubt will sweep over you. "Are all my sins confessed and forgiven?" you will ask yourself. "Will I be saved?" In that hour you will be saved from discouragement by faith in God's promises and the hope of His coming. The promises you learn now will buoy you up.

THE GUN WOULDN'T WORK

No weapon that is formed against thee shall prosper. Isaiah 54:17.

"Give me ten bullets or I'll kill you!" Cristobal Torres warned, lurching up to the counter, where Brother Mincho, the shopkeeper, stood.

Two more armed men stepped into the doorway, blocking the escape route. Pastors Westphal, Maxson, Camarena, and Pajon looked on helplessly as the bandit moved closer to Brother Mincho.

"Mincho, if you give me bullets I'll go away," Cristobal promised. Brother Mincho obediently went into the back of the store and brought out six cartridges. Cristobal loaded his pistol, but he did not leave. Instead he demanded money and more bullets.

Pastor Westphal was becoming concerned about his wife, who had gone birdwatching in the nearby jungle. Pushing Cristobal aside he made for the door. But Cristobal grabbed him roughly by the shirt, pressed the gun against Pastor Westphal's back, and pulled the trigger.

Brother Pajon closed his eyes and waited for the sounds of the gunfire and Brother Westphal's body falling to the floor. But there was no such sound. Three times Cristobal pulled the trigger, but nothing happened!

Just then Cristobal's horse began to prance nervously, and Cristobal went outside to scold the man who was holding it. The five men escaped quickly through the back door.

Five Seventh-day Adventist Christians felt the icy breath of death that March 22 in the jungle of Chiapas in southern Mexico. Surely the angels were there to deliver them.

In the trying days before Jesus comes you may be in a similar position. Do not be afraid. God will help you.

Speaking about the time when the death decree has gone out and Sabbathkeepers are to be destroyed, Mrs. White writes: "But none can pass the mighty guardians stationed about every faithful soul. Some are assailed in their flight from the cities and villages; but the swords raised against them break and fall powerless as a straw. Others are defended by angels in the form of men of war."—*The Great Controversy, p.* 631.

HALLELUJAH!

Praise ye the Lord. O give thanks unto the Lord; for he is good: for his mercy endureth for ever. Psalm 106:1.

"Hallelujah! Hallelujah! Hallelujah! Hallelujah!
For the Lord God omnipotent reigneth!"

On March 23, 1743, the majestic music of the "Hallelujah Chorus" filled the hall where Londoners had come to hear the performance of George Frederic Handel's new oratorio, *The Messiah*. In the audience was King George II of England.

Thrilled by the music, the monarch reverently stood to his feet, acknowledging Jesus Christ as the King of kings and the Lord of lords. He remained standing during the entire rendition.

Seeing King George stand, the audience rose and stood at reverent attention. From that day to this audiences always stand when Handel's "Hallelujah Chorus" is performed.

The words of this chorus are found in the description of a heavenly praise service in Revelation 19:6. "And I heard as it were the voice . . . of mighty thunderings, saying, Alleluia: for the Lord God omnipotent reigneth."

When at last the history of this sinful world comes to an end I want to be among the great choir of redeemed ones who sing this song before the throne of God, don't you? Imagine the glorious music of a choir composed of thousands upon thousands of the saved from all ages! If we want to sing Hallelujahs then, perhaps we should practice them now.

Hallelujah is a Hebrew word meaning "Praise ye Jehovah" and it is written in our Bibles as "Praise ye the Lord."

Take a few moments to look up Psalms 104, 105, and 106. Can you find the "Hallelujah" at the end of each psalm? Look at Psalms 111, 112, and 113. How does each one begin? Yes, with "Praise ye the Lord."

Read through these six Hallelujah psalms and you will find many gifts for which we should praise the Lord: protection, answered prayers, guidance, comfort in sorrow, salvation, guardian angels, beauties of nature, mercy, forgiveness, strength, and food.

We can also praise Him for family, friends, homes, school, cars, health, a free country in which to live, freedom to worship God, and, oh, so many more things! Praise ye the Lord!

IT IS A MIRACLE!

Therefore if any man be in Christ, he is a new creature: old things are passed away; behold, all things are become new. 2 Corinthians 5:17.

"I can't hold her long, lads," the captain of the British bomber announced. "You'll have to jump!"

Nicholas Alkemade, the rear gunner, opened the door behind him to get his parachute and looked into a blazing inferno. It was too late. His parachute was on fire!

Death seemed certain to the 21-year-old sergeant that night of March 24, 1944. Should he burn or jump? He jumped.

The next thing Nicholas knew he was lying in a pile of heavy underbrush covered with snow. Above him stars twinkled through thick fir branches. He hurt all over, but he was alive!

German soldiers found Nicholas a few hours later. When the commander had verified the story, he exclaimed: "Gentlemen! A miracle—no less!"

Yes, it was a miracle that Nicholas Alkemade was alive. He had fallen 18,000 feet, reaching a speed of about 122 miles per hour by the time he hit the earth. He had many injuries, but most of them had been sustained while he was still in the plane.

What is a miracle? Webster's Dictionary defines it as "an extraordinary event brought about by superhuman agency." Nicholas would agree. When he awoke in the brush pile, the first thing he did was to look up to the stars and thank God for his life.

Life itself is a miracle, but an even greater miracle is the new life we can find in Christ. Just as miraculous as the birth of a baby is the new birth that makes us sons and daughters of God.

Think of the transformation in the life of Saul, the killer, into Paul, the apostle. Was that not a miracle, "an extraordinary event brought about by superhuman agency"? There was no way that Paul could have done that for himself. It had to be a miracle of the grace of God.

This miracle of love and grace can be yours, too. God can transform your life. He can give you a new experience. He can take away old habits and hurts and in their place give you peace and radiant joy. The miracle He offers will cleanse you from sin and make you the person you have always wanted to be.

91

LOOK TO JESUS

Look unto me, and be ye saved, all the ends of the earth. Isaiah 45:22.

On March 25, 1861, Charles Haddon Spurgeon, age 26, preached his first sermon in the London Metropolitan Tabernacle. It had been built by his New Park Street congregation to handle the large crowds that came to hear him speak. On one occasion 23,654 people attended one of his meetings.

How did it happen that Charles Spurgeon became such a powerful preacher? I believe that he would not have been the great preacher he was had it not been for something that happened when he was 15.

At the age of 10 Charles began to go through a period of terrible mental struggle. He became very discouraged because of his sinfulness. As he thought of the horrors of punishment he expected to endure in hell, he was overcome with fear. Over and over again he had heard that all men are headed for the lake of fire and that in His mercy, God looks down and picks out a few here and there to be saved. For the rest there is no hope. The thought that God may not have chosen him filled Charles with such horror that he could not sleep.

On Sunday night, January 6, 1850, the struggle came to an end. Charles had planned to attend a certain church, but a fierce storm was raging and he went down a side street to a Primitive Methodist church instead. The preacher was absent and a layman was taking the service. His text was Isaiah 45:22: "Look unto me, and be ye saved, all the ends of the earth."

After about ten minutes the lay preacher noticed the discouraged expression on Charles's face. He cried out, "Young man, you're in trouble! Look to Jesus Christ! Look! Look! Look!"

Charles did look to Jesus that night, and the burden of his guilt rolled away. Having experienced the joy of salvation, he decided to spend his life inviting men and women to look to the Saviour. In the open air, in vacant barns, in theaters, and in church, he preached the message of salvation by faith.

Do you sometimes feel like young Charles? Do your sins press upon you, making you feel hopeless? Young friend, look to Jesus! See Him on the cross. He died for you. He loves you and wants to save you. Accept that love today.

RAY'S VICTORY

Lord, who shall abide in thy tabernacle? . . . He that . . .
speaketh the truth in his heart. Psalm 15:1, 2.

The National Hockey League game between the Chicago Black Hawks and the New York Rangers on March 26, 1969, was what hockey players call a "nothing" game. The Black Hawks were in sixth place in the league and nothing that happened that night could upset the Rangers' lead.

However, something did happen that was more important than the winning or losing of the game.

The Black Hawks were in the Rangers' end of the rink. Stan Mikita was behind the net. The puck went out to defenseman Ray McKay, standing near the blue line. He got a clear shot. Stan Mikita skated around front and stuck out his stick just in time to deflect the puck between the Ranger goalie's legs.

"Goal scored by Ray McKay for the first National Hockey League goal of his career," the announcer told the crowd. There was a roar of approval from the stands.

The applause sounded good to Ray, but he knew it was not rightfully his. Many would have let it pass and accepted the goal as theirs. After all, who would know the difference? But Ray was a boy who "spoke the truth in his heart." After all, God knew and he knew, and he would have to live with himself.

With the shouts of approval still sounding across the ice, Ray skated over to Stan Mikita and said, "You tipped in that goal, didn't you?"

"Yes," nodded Stan.

"It wasn't my goal," Ray then told the officials. "Stan Mikita tipped it in."

The change was made and announced and the "nothing" game continued. Ray McKay lost his goal, but he scored a victory in the game of life.

God expects truthfulness from us even in the smallest matters. No matter how tiny a lie is, it is big enough to keep a person out of heaven. Ask God today to give you the kind of victory Ray McKay had. Ask Him to help you to tell the truth even when it means a loss to you. Ask Him to make you a person who speaks the truth in his heart.

THE SEVENTH TIME

A just man falleth seven times, and riseth up again. Proverbs 24:16.

The spider let go its hold on the ceiling of the hut and dropped, spinning a silken thread behind it. The man lying on the cot below watched the spider try to jump to the next beam. It missed and hung for a moment in space before climbing back up its line to the starting point.

Again the spider jumped, pulling the thread behind it. Again it missed the beam and dropped to a vertical position. Once more it climbed back up the thread.

Fascinated, the man on the bed watched the spider try to reach the rafter six times and fail. On the seventh time it succeeded.

"That spider is a lot like me," the young man mused. "I have tried six times to free Scotland from English rule. Six times I have failed. But I will try again. The spider has taught me a lesson."

The man lying on the cot was Robert Bruce. On March 27, 1306, he had been crowned king of Scotland. From that day his defeats began, for King Edward I of England sent soldiers to overcome him. Time after time Robert Bruce was defeated. It was while in hiding, feeling like giving up the struggle, that he saw the spider and took heart. He rallied his soldiers and won the battle. Victory was his because he did not give up.

What if the Israelites had marched only six times around the walls of Jericho? Would they have had the victory?

What if Naaman had walked out of the River Jordan after dipping only six times? Would he have been healed?

Perhaps you have tried and failed many times to overcome an evil habit. Satan knows your weak points. Again and again he has defeated you and you feel that there is no use trying any longer.

It is at such times that you must have faith in God's promises. You may fall, but God can help you to rise again. Jesus has promised to forgive and cleanse you. He has promised strength. He has promised power to overcome. You must not give up. You must try and try again! Victory lies ahead for you!

A LIFE-AND-DEATH MATTER

Blessed are they that do his commandments, that they may have right to the tree of life. Revelation 22:14.

There are times when life depends on obedience. March 28, 1954, was one of those days.

It was almost seven o'clock in the morning. The British troopship *Empire Windrush* was headed home through the Mediterranean with about 1,500 people on board returning from the Far East. Suddenly an explosion rocked the ship. Within moments the midsection was ablaze.

Colonel Robert Scott, troop commander, grabbed a megaphone and announced, "We are going to abandon ship. Stand fast on deck. Wait until you are assigned a boat."

The men stood in rank upon the deck while the lifeboats were filled with women, children, and invalids. When the boats were loaded, 300 men still stood on deck. At this time, kegs, planks, and deck chairs were thrown overboard. Then Colonel Scott gave his orders: "Remove outer clothes and shoes and go overside, but do not swim to a lifeboat."

Every man obeyed. If just one had disobeyed more would surely have followed and many lives might have been lost. Because the men obeyed their commander, there was no panic. Within two hours four rescue ships had saved all 1,500.

Obedience to God's commands is also a life-and-death matter. Can you think of some examples from the Bible? Adam and Eve disobeyed and lost a world. Lot's wife disobeyed and became a pillar of salt. Achan disobeyed and perished. Saul disobeyed and lost his kingdom. Ananias and Sapphira disobeyed and lost their lives.

On the other hand, Naaman obeyed and was cured of leprosy. Shadrach, Meshach, and Abednego obeyed and were delivered from the fiery furnace. Rahab obeyed and saved her family. Elijah obeyed and was taken to heaven. Joseph obeyed and saved a nation from famine. Abraham obeyed and God led him to the Promised Land. Moses obeyed and delivered a multitude from slavery. Jesus obeyed and saved a world.

The way of disobedience leads to eternal death. The path of obedience leads to eternal life. Which way will you go?

TRY THE SPIRITS

Believe not every spirit, but try the spirits whether they are of God: because many false prophets are gone out into the world. 1 John 4:1.

"The Seventh-day Adventist Church cannot be the true church," Abraham insisted.

"Why do you say that?" the Adventist pastor asked. "You believe the Sabbath message, I know."

"Yes, I do believe that Christians should keep the Sabbath. I cannot help but accept all the doctrines of your church because they are based on the words of Scripture. However, there is one thing missing."

"What is that?" asked the pastor.

"You do not speak in tongues," Abraham explained.

Soon afterward Brother Abraham, who lives in India, attended a funeral in a pagan village in the high ranges of Kerala. During the service some of the people began to shout and fall to the floor. Unknown syllables came from their lips as they lay in a sort of trance. Abraham was shocked! Surely God wouldn't give the Holy Spirit to these heathen people; but yet he had seen the same manifestations in Christian churches.

For the first time Abraham realized that speaking in tongues could not be used as a basis to judge the truthfulness of a message. Only the Word of God is a safe guide. Abraham was baptized and is now a Seventh-day Adventist worker.

Adventist ministers became the subject of a prayer meeting at Riverside, California, on March 29, 1972. A group of businessmen pledged $2,500 to take the message of the gift of tongues to all the ministers of the Seventh-day Adventist Church. They made a plan to send each pastor a magazine giving accounts of miracles and speaking in tongues.

This propaganda had no effect on Pastor Abraham. He knows from experience that the spirits of devils can also work miracles. He has learned to test the spirits.

Speaking in tongues is popular among Christians today. Many who believe in this are preaching in Christ's name and working miracles. If you would distinguish the true from the false you must not look to the outward signs, but rather test all teachings by the Word of God.

THEY SAW THE LIGHT

I am the light of the world: he that followeth me shall not walk in darkness, but shall have the light of life. John 8:12.

It was seven-thirty on Friday morning, March 30, 1906. The stable guard was sweeping the passageway at level 306 in Pit Number 2 of a coal mine near Mericourt, France. At the end of the passageway was the door to Pit Number 3, where Europe's worst mining disaster had taken place on March 10. An explosion of unknown origin had released deadly gases and set fire to the mine. One thousand and ninety-nine miners had been killed.

As the guard neared the padlocked door he thought he heard knocking. He stopped to listen. Yes, there it was again, only much louder. Then the door gave way and thirteen men burst through. Their gaunt faces, though caked with blood and black with coal dust, wore smiles of wonder and joy as they stood in the light. For twenty days and twenty nights they had groped their way along the maze of tunnels in the dark mine, searching for a way out. Without food or water, the weakened men were about ready to lie down and die when they reached a bend in the tunnel and saw the light. It was only a tiny gleam, but it was enough.

Light—how beautiful it is! But millions in this world are in darkness just as black as that experienced by the thirteen miners. Millions bow down to gods of wood and stone, having never heard of Jesus Christ, the Light of the world.

While traveling in India, my husband stopped to talk with some young men beside the road. "Have you ever heard of Jesus Christ?" he asked.

"Nobody by that name lives around here," they responded.

Briefly he told the story of Jesus. As it began to dawn on the young men that Someone had actually loved them enough to die for them, their faces lit up. "Send us a teacher," they begged. "We could love a God like that." Their darkened hearts had seen the Light and they were willing to follow.

Thousands of villages in India still sit in darkness. There are millions of people in China and the islands of the sea who have never heard of Jesus. Who will take the Light to them?

God has "called you out of darkness into his marvellous light" of a knowledge of Jesus Christ. What are you doing to share this light with others?

REACHING THE TOP

For many are called, but few are chosen. Matthew 22:14.

We stood on the Champ de Mars in Paris and looked up at the gigantic capital "A" formed in steel.

"Shall we walk up or take the elevator?" Father asked.

"How many steps are there?" questioned David.

"One thousand five hundred and eighty-five."

"I'm taking the elevator," Grandma decided, and the rest of the family agreed. We rode to the top of the 984-foot Eiffel Tower and enjoyed a magnificent view of the city.

At the very top, inaccessible to tourists, is the spot where the last rivet was hammered home. The next day, March 31, 1889, the first people climbed the tower. About fifty started out but only twenty reached the top. The flag of France was raised and a twenty-one-gun salute celebrated the completion of the tower.

The journey to heaven is something like reaching the top of the Eiffel Tower, only there are no elevators to make it easy. We all have to go the same way, step by step overcoming sin with the help of the Holy Spirit and rising to new heights in our Christian experience.

Many people start out to climb the Eiffel Tower but never reach the top. Their legs begin to ache and they become short of breath. Some decide a heart attack is imminent if they proceed. Others feel it isn't worth the effort. They turn and go back down.

It is like that in the Christian life. Many young people decide for Christ, are baptized, and begin the climb to heaven. But to reach the top takes effort. They must stretch their spiritual muscles and keep going no matter what trials or discouragements come their way.

If someone were to offer these climbers an elevator entrance to heaven they would gladly go, but they are not willing to struggle against their sinful desires. They follow the easy way. They turn around and go down—to destruction.

"Many are called, but few are chosen." Many begin the climb but few reach the top. Many are baptized but few will be saved. Many have their names on the church books who will not see inside the city of God.

What about you? Will you determine today to reach the top?

APRIL FOOLS

See then that ye walk circumspectly, not as fools. Ephesians 5:15.

The story is told about an April Fools' joke played in London 123 years ago. During the last week of March, invitations were sent to many of the city's prominent citizens. It read: "Tower of London. Admit bearer and friend to view the annual ceremony of Washing the White Lions on Sunday, April 1, 1860. Admittance at the White Gate." Many carriages drove around Tower Hill that day looking for a white gate that wasn't there.

The custom of April Fools' Day probably began about 400 years ago when Pope Gregory brought out a new calendar making January 1 the beginning of the year. Until then March 21 had been the start of New Year's celebrations that ended on April 1. After the calendar was changed, some people still held on to the old festivities at that time of year. These people were called April Fools.

Gradually the day became one for making people look foolish. Unsuspecting folks have been sent on futile errands to bring back hens' teeth, pigeons' milk, or sweet vinegar. They have looked in the mirror for smudges that did not exist, or answered the doorbell to find no one there.

However, today is not the only day when fools are about. Perhaps you have met headstrong people who will not take advice. "The way of a fool is right in his own eyes" (Prov. 12:15).

Proverbs 14:9 tells about the fool who makes a "mock at sin." "Oh, come on," such say, "do it this once. A little fun can't hurt you."

The blind fool is mentioned by Jesus in Matthew 23:17. This is the person who doesn't see himself as he really is.

The worst fool is he who is unprepared. Jesus told a story about a rich man who was so busy building barns and saving for future good times that he neglected getting ready to meet God. Jesus said, "Thou fool, this night thy soul shall be required of thee" (Luke 12:20).

Foolish people do not think things through. They fall for the devil's jokes. They really believe his lies. When it is too late they wake up to the fact that they have been tricked.

Wise young people will be on their guard every day, for they know that Satan does not confine his tricks to April 1.

THE FOURTH MAN

God is our refuge and strength, a very present help in trouble. Psalm 46:1.

It happened during World War I. Commander H. G. Stoker and two friends escaped from a prison camp in central Turkey. They planned to move southeast toward the coast where they hoped to be rescued.

On April 2, 1916, the eleventh night of their journey, they reached the most difficult part. Then a strange thing happened.

The men were walking in single file fifteen paces apart with Commander Stoker at the rear. Suddenly, he became aware that a fourth figure was following them. When the men stopped to rest, the stranger did not join them but remained in the shadows. As soon as they resumed their march, he took his place, never speaking, but seeming very interested in their welfare.

Did Commander Stoker imagine this presence or had the fourth man really been there? The next morning he told the others about the experience. They, too, had noticed the stranger and wondered where he had gone. "He seemed to be encouraging us," one remarked.

The next night the stranger stayed with the men again. During this time they covered twice the usual distance and escaped capture at one of the most carefully watched points on their route.

Who was the fourth man?

Did Jesus accompany these men through the dangerous mountains, just as He walked with the three Hebrews in the fiery furnace? Was it their imagination, or was the fourth man an angel sent to encourage them? Could we have a similar experience?

"He who walked with the Hebrew worthies in the fiery furnace will be with His followers wherever they are. His abiding presence will comfort and sustain. In the midst of the time of trouble—trouble such as has not been since there was a nation—His chosen ones will stand unmoved. Satan with all the hosts of evil cannot destroy the weakest of God's saints. Angels that excel in strength will protect them."—*Prophets and Kings*, p. 513.

HALO ROUND THE SABBATH

Remember the sabbath day, to keep it holy. Exodus 20:8.

It was Sabbath, April 3, 1847. Outside the home of Stockbridge Howland in Topsham, Maine, birds sang, sap flowed, and pussy willows bloomed.

Inside, the warmth of spring was reflected in the hearts of the Adventists gathered there for a weekend of Bible study. Some, like James and Ellen White, were Sabbathkeepers; others were undecided.

"We felt an unusual spirit of prayer," wrote Ellen White in her book *Early Writings*. "As we prayed the Holy Ghost fell upon us. We were very happy."—Page 32.

Suddenly, 19-year-old Ellen shouted, "Glory! Glory!" All knew that she was having a vision.

Later she reported being carried by an angel to the Holy City and right into the heavenly sanctuary. He led her through the Holy Place to the veil at the other end where Jesus stood waiting for her.

Ellen's guide took her inside the Most Holy Place where she saw a golden ark with angels at each end looking down into the ark where lay two tables of stone folded together like a book. She watched as Jesus opened them.

"I saw the ten commandments written on them with the finger of God," Ellen said. "On one table were four, and on the other six. The four on the first table shone brighter than the other six. But the fourth, the Sabbath commandment, shone above them all. . . . A halo of glory was all around it."—Pages 32, 33.

Why do you think the fourth Commandment was surrounded by a halo? Doesn't it show how very important the Sabbath is to God? He wants to be sure that we do not forget it.

Today is a good time to begin to "remember the sabbath day." Plan now so that all your work is done before sunset on Friday. Be sure your shoes are repaired and polished. Hem your dress. Sew on that missing button. Plan ahead what you will do on Sabbath afternoon.

If we will remember God's day all week, there will be less confusion when it comes. If we keep a halo around the Sabbath every day, then we will surely have a glorious day when it arrives.

MARTIN'S DESIRE

Teach me to do thy will; for thou art my God. Psalm 143:10.

"Bill's mother says I can't play at their house anymore. Why?" Six-year-old Martin searched his mother's face for an answer.

"Come sit down and I will tell you," Mrs. King replied. "It is because you are black and Bill is white."

She told the little boy about the slave ships that went to Africa and brought the first Negroes to America. She described their hard lives. She told him about the Civil War and Abraham Lincoln's setting the slaves free. She explained that even though black people were no longer slaves, they usually didn't mix with white people. Where Martin's family lived, the blacks and whites went to separate schools and used different public rest rooms. They sat in different sections of buses and theaters.

"But that isn't fair," Martin protested.

"No," his mother agreed. "But that's how it is. Someday it will change."

As Martin grew older he experienced a series of insults that made him more aware of how other black people were suffering. Gradually there grew within him a desire to do something to make the change come soon.

In the blacks' struggle for equal rights in America, Martin Luther King, Jr. found what he believed was God's will for his life. To this cause he dedicated his all. That commitment led to his death by an assassin's bullet on the evening of April 4, 1968.

The day before his death Martin said, "I would like to live a long life. But I'm not concerned about that now. I just want to do God's will."

The desire to do God's will is a worthwhile ambition for young people today. What a noble aim—to do God's will regardless of the consequences!

There is a need for such brave men and women in the world today, men and women who "do not fear to call sin by its right name, . . . who will stand for the right though the heavens fall."

God needs boys and girls with the courage and commitment of Martin Luther King, Jr. He needs young people who are not afraid to pray David's prayer: "Teach me to do thy will." He needs youth who will follow where He leads, however dangerous that path may be.

THE WALLET'S TESTIMONY

But seek ye first the kingdom of God, and his righteousness;
and all these things shall be added unto you. Matthew 6:33.

Peter opened his worn, brown leather billfold and studied the contents. There were three clippings of soccer games in which he had been the goalkeeper, a few calling cards, two picture post cards of Scotland, various letters of recommendation, and enough money to buy his food for two weeks.

Peter had left his steady job at a machine shop in Scotland, had said goodbye to family and friends, and had come to the United States because he believed this was what God wanted him to do.

When Peter stepped off the ship in New York on April 5, 1927, he didn't know how God would provide; but he was sure that God would. The young man couldn't foresee the wonderful way his heavenly Father would open doors of opportunity for him; but he did believe his mother's parting words.

"Don't forget your verse, my laddie, 'Seek ye first the kingdom of God, and his righteousness; and all these things shall be added unto you.' Long ago I put you in the Lord's hands, and I won't be taking you away now. He will take care of you. Don't worry."

God did take care of Peter. He helped the young man to find suitable work. He impressed businessmen to back him for two years in the seminary. Once a department store called for Peter to come and pick out a suit that someone had paid for on his behalf. All through the depression years of the 1930s there was money enough in his brown wallet to see him through.

Eventually, Peter Marshall became a minister in Washington, D.C., and chaplain of the United States Senate.

Once in a sermon Peter said: "I can testify that through faith in God, through prayer and trust . . . my every need has been supplied."

God will supply all your needs, too, if you will put your trust in Him. Jesus has promised that if we will make the seeking of God and His righteousness our first goal in life, trusting Him for all our needs, He will never let us down. If we will meet the conditions, God will fulfill His word.

God is as real as your pocketbook. He will supply your every need. You can safely put your trust in Him.

NINETY NORTH

And ye shall seek me, and find me, when ye shall search for me with all your heart. Jeremiah 29:13.

Wild winds roared across the endless stretch of Arctic ice and tore at a lone cabin half buried in the snow. Inside, an American explorer lay alone on a cot. He had not walked since his feet had frozen three months before. The pain seemed unbearable. Would he have to give up his dream of reaching the North Pole?

Again he tried to stand on his swollen feet, but the pain caused him to fall back onto the bed. Then, leaning over, he wrote on the nearest wall, "I shall find a way or make one. Robert E. Peary."

Peary's one goal in life was to reach the North Pole. He pushed ahead through years of dreadful hardships that would have devastated most men. Whatever obstacles he met in the wild, white world of the North, he overcame.

At ten o'clock on April 6, 1909, Robert E. Peary took out his sextant and measured the altitude of the sun. Finishing his calculations, he shouted to his fellow explorer, Matthew Henson, "Matt, oh, Matt! Ninety north!" Peary was the first man to stand on the spot from which all directions are south.

As soon as possible he telegraphed his wife: "Have made good at last. I have the Pole."

Robert E. Peary found what he was seeking because he put his whole heart into the search. If he had been making plans to look for sunken treasure in the Caribbean at the same time he was searching for the North Pole he would probably have been unsuccessful in both ventures.

It is one of the laws of life that scattered efforts accomplish little. So, if you are really serious about finding God, then you must put your whole heart into the search. Halfhearted attempts at Bible reading now and again will not accomplish it. Once a year at camp is not enough. It must be a daily search.

"I would give anything to have a faith like Jan's," Dave said. But he was not willing to put forth the effort in daily prayer and Bible study to make such faith a reality. He was not willing to commit his entire life to the search.

Do you really want to know God? Is this the one aim and purpose of your life? If it is, and you put your whole heart into the search, you will surely find Him.

THE DARKEST DAY

He was wounded for our transgressions, he was bruised for our iniquities: . . . and with his stripes we are healed. Isaiah 53:5.

For many who watched, it was the most unforgettable day of their lives. For the central figure in the drama it was a day of agony, horror—and victory. To the Man's friends it was a day of sorrow and despair. For the Roman soldiers it was a long day that had begun in the early hours of that Friday morning when they were sent to the Garden of Gethsemane to arrest the Man.

Now the darkest day of earth's history was nearly over. The Man hung on a cross between two thieves. His weeping mother stood nearby. The soldiers played a game of chance for His coat as the crowd settled themselves on the rocks of Golgotha to watch Him die.

The Man's flesh was raw from the beatings He had received. Blood flowed from His wounded head. Pain wracked His body. He was thirsty. His quivering lips formed the words, "My God, my God, why hast thou forsaken me?" (Matt. 27:46).

"He saved others; himself he cannot save. Let Christ the King of Israel descend now from the cross, that we may see and believe," his enemies jeered (Mark 15:31, 32).

Christ could have come down from the cross. He didn't have to suffer and die on that cruel tree. He didn't have to endure the torture and the shame.

He stayed there for you. He was punished that you might go free. He suffered that you might be saved. He died that you might live.

We are not certain that April 7, A.D. 30 is the correct date of Christ's death. Some scholars think so. Others think it was April 27, A.D. 31. But whether it happend today or another day doesn't really matter. The important thing is that it *did* happen. Jesus did die—and He did it for you. Why? Because He loves you.

How such love is possible we will never fully comprehend. We can only agree with Isaac Watts who wrote:

> "Were the whole realm of nature mine,
> That were a tribute far too small;
> Love so amazing, so divine,
> Demands my life, my soul, my all."

THE FOUNTAIN OF YOUTH

The water that I shall give him shall be in him a well of water springing up into everlasting life. John 4:14.

"We have found a marvelous fountain of water. Old people who drink this water are made young. Young people who drink it never grow old."

Ponce de León, governor of Puerto Rico, was interested. "Where is this wonderful fountain?" he asked.

"It is on the island of Bimini."

"But where is Bimini?" No one seemed to know. So Ponce de León set out by ship to find it for himself. Soon he saw the coastline of Florida and landed near what is now St. Augustine. On April 8, 1513, he took possession of the land in the name of the Spanish king.

Eagerly de León searched for the miraculous fountain. He explored many miles of coastline. He drank from every spring he came upon, hoping to find the magic water, but he was disappointed.

Would you like to discover such a fountain? How great it would be to drink and never be troubled by gray hair, false teeth, or wrinkled skin. What a joy to be forever young!

"Impossible!" you say. "There is no fountain of youth. It is only a fairy tale."

Wrong! There is a fountain of life-giving water. Ponce de León looked in the wrong place.

Jesus spoke of it as He sat by Jacob's well. He startled the Samaritan woman by saying: "Whosoever drinketh of this water shall thirst again: but whosoever drinketh of the water that I shall give him shall never thirst; but the water that I shall give him shall be in him a well of water springing up into everlasting life" (John 4:13, 14).

Everlasting life and eternal youth are yours for the asking. It is yours if you accept Jesus as your Saviour. When He comes into your heart He brings with Him the water of life.

If you drink now of this water you can have the assurance that someday soon Jesus will come to take you to a land where you will never grow old, where there will be no pain, sickness, false teeth, or wrinkles. It will be a land of eternal youth, happiness, and joy.

Won't you drink of the water of life today?

MR. MCCLEAN'S SURPRISE

Yield yourselves unto God, . . . and your members as instruments of righteousness unto God. Romans 6:13.

Appomattox Court House in 1865 was a sleepy Virginia village consisting of a few houses, a store, an empty jail, and the courthouse. Near the courthouse stood the red-brick home of Wilmer McClean.

On Sunday morning, April 9, Mr. McClean was walking along the road near the courthouse when five men on horseback approached him.

"We are here on behalf of General Lee. An important discussion is about to take place and we need a house. Do you know of one?"

"My house is just up the road a piece," Mr. McClean offered. "I guess it's about the best around here."

"Thank you. Will you conduct us there, please?"

So it was that General Robert E. Lee and General Ulysses S. Grant sat down in the McClean living room to discuss the surrender of the Southern forces that would end the American Civil War.

What a story Wilmer McClean had to tell his grandchildren! How thrilling to know that he had a small part in the surrender!

A greater General than Lee or Grant is begging entrance into your home and heart today. He wants to put an end to your struggle with sin. Jesus Christ would like to negotiate a surrender in your heart. Will you let Him in?

Maybe you are asking, "'How am I to make the surrender of myself to God?' You desire to give yourself to Him, but you are weak in moral power, in slavery to doubt, and controlled by the habits of your life of sin. . . . You cannot control your thoughts, your impulses, your affections. . . . What you need to understand is the true force of the will. This is the governing power in the nature of man, the power of decision, or of choice. . . . You cannot change your heart, you cannot of yourself give to God its affections; but you can *choose* to serve Him."—*Love Unlimited,* p. 47.

Your situation is similar to that of Mr. McClean at Appomattox Court House. He couldn't end the war, but he could open his home and allow the surrender to take place. You can do the same today.

JUST LIKE A TREE

And he shall be like a tree planted by the rivers of water. Psalm 1:3.

"Just like a tree planted by the waters, I shall not be moved" are the words of a chorus that we sometimes sing. However, all Christians are not like that. Not everyone stands firm and immovable as a tree.

Some people are easily influenced by others. When their friends go to a church program, they go. When their friends go to the movies, they follow. They may go along to a Friday night ballgame, because they don't have the courage to stand for what they know is right.

Why is it that all of us do not stand firm as a tree planted by the rivers of water? Ellen White says it is because we do not take time for daily meditation and prayer.

Does the psalmist agree? Open your Bible and read all of Psalm 1 to find out.

David says that the person who is like a tree loves the Word of God. He likes to read it and think on it day and night. Such a person is like a tree that is set deep in the earth, sending down its roots to an ever-flowing stream. The Christian who is able to stand firm and unmoved is the one who is planted deep in the Word of God. Every day he receives strength from the waters of salvation.

Today is the anniversary of the first Arbor Day, celebrated April 10, 1872, in Nebraska. Now, every State except Alaska and most Provinces of Canada celebrate this day. It comes at different times in different places, but wherever it is observed, trees are planted. On this day schoolchildren are encouraged to plant trees and then to carefully tend them.

The Aztecs had a custom of planting a tree whenever a child was born. Maybe we should plant a tree each time a child of God is born. This might be an interesting addition to the baptismal service.

The newly baptized person could be asked to protect and tend his tree. As he became aware of the needs of the tree, perhaps he would understand better his own spiritual need for nourishment and growth. He might be reminded of what God intends him to be: just like a tree.

A DIFFERENT KIND OF COURAGE

But I say unto you, That ye resist not evil: but whosoever shall smite thee on thy right cheek, turn to him the other also. Matthew 5:39.

"Do you have the guts not to fight back?" asked Branch Rickey, president of the Brooklyn Dodgers.

"Mr. Rickey," Jackie Robinson replied, "are you looking for a man who is afraid to fight back?"

"I'm looking for a ballplayer," Mr. Rickey answered, "with guts enough *not* to fight back. I know you're a good baseball player. What I don't know is whether you can play the game no matter what happens. It's going to take a lot of courage to be the first black man to play in a major league. Some people aren't going to like it."

When Jackie Robinson entered professional baseball in 1945, the only teams he could play on were those in the Negro leagues. He was playing for the Kansas City Monarchs when Branch Rickey discovered him. Mr. Rickey decided that Jackie was the player he had been looking for to help break through the prejudice that marred America's favorite sport. However, the man who would do this must be courageous enough to take slights, even from his teammates.

Because Jackie had that kind of courage, on April 11, 1947, he signed a contract with the Brooklyn Dodgers and his name is now registered in the Baseball Hall of Fame. How was such courage possible?

In his autobiography, *Breakthrough to the Big League,* Jackie refers many times to the enabling power of God in his life. He also gives credit to the faith and prayers of his mother.

Soon after Jackie's birth, Mrs. Robinson held him in her arms, and looking around at the poverty of their home in Cairo, Georgia, said, "Bless you, boy. For you to survive all this God will have to keep His eye on you."

Many times when the going was hard Jackie felt God's eye upon him. By God's grace he received strength to control himself when he wanted to strike back.

God's eye is on you too. He will help you to turn the other cheek. He will give you self-control. He will give you the courage not to fight back.

GOD'S COSMONAUTS

Then we which are alive and remain shall be caught up together with them in the clouds, to meet the Lord in the air: and so shall we ever be with the Lord. 1 Thessalonians 4:17.

Everyone knows that Yuri A. Gagarin was the first man in space when he orbited the earth on April 12, 1961.

Or was he? Could others have escaped the gravitational pull of Planet Earth before him? Is it possible that someone sailed the universe before the Russian cosmonaut? Yes. There were at least three.

Can you guess this riddle? Who was the oldest man who ever lived, yet he died before his father? The answer is Methusaleh. He lived 969 years but his father, Enoch, only lived 365. Yet Methusaleh died before his father, because Enoch did not die. "He was not," Moses said, "for God took him." In one of Ellen White's visions, she saw Enoch on a planet with seven moons. When asked if that place was his home, he responded that he lived in the New Jerusalem and had only come there for a visit.

Moses also made the journey from earth to heaven. Think of the incredible speed, greater than the speed of light, at which he must have traveled! What a lot of planets and stars he must have passed en route. Moses would have been translated as was Enoch, we are told, but was denied this privilege because of his sin of anger in hitting the rock. So he died, was buried on Mount Nebo by angels, and was resurrected by Christ to become the second cosmonaut.

No one saw Enoch or Moses leave Planet Earth. One person saw Elijah translated. Elisha said that it looked as though a chariot of fire with horses of fire came and took his master away. Although fifty men went looking for Elijah, they could not find him because he was already untold miles out into space.

You and I have the opportunity of becoming cosmonauts, too. Whether we live or die, when Jesus comes we will be caught up in the clouds together for a seven-day journey through space to our heavenly home. I wonder whether we will make any stops on the way and what beautiful and exciting things we will see.

Then we will stand on the sea of glass before the gates of the Holy City. Jesus and the angels will be there to welcome us. What a happy time that will be! Our songs of joy will make heaven's arches ring.

THE PURSUIT OF HAPPINESS

Happy shalt thou be, and it shall be well with thee. Psalm 128:2.

Those with a birthday today share it with Thomas Jefferson, the third President of the United States and the author of the Declaration of Independence. In it he wrote: "We hold these Truths to be self-evident, that all Men are created equal, that they are endowed by their Creator with certain unalienable Rights, that among these are Life, Liberty, and the Pursuit of Happiness."

Happiness is sought by all, but found by few. Is there any sure way of finding it?

"Tell us how to be happy," a small girl from the Boston slums once asked Alice Freeman Palmer. In response Alice gave the following rules:

1. Commit to memory something nice every day—a pretty poem, or a Bible verse. Learn something you'd be glad to remember if you went blind.

2. Look for something pretty every day—a leaf, a cloud, a flower. Search for beauty and loveliness all around you.

3. Do some service for somebody every day. Find someone else you can make happy.

Harry McLean, a Canadian multimillionaire, used to travel across the country passing out one-hundred-dollar bills. His reason: "To get happiness out of life, you must put happiness in."

An editor wrote to a minister asking the question, "What things have you done in your life that have brought you the greatest pleasure and happiness?"

"What I have done for the good of other people," the minister replied.

"A word of cheer, an act of kindness, would go far to lighten the burdens that are resting heavily upon weary shoulders. It is in unselfish ministry that true happiness is found."—*Testimonies,* vol. 7, p. 50.

Jesus, then, must have been the happiest Man who ever lived because no one else has brought so much joy to others. Wherever He went He spread sunshine and cheer.

If you follow His example you surely will find happiness and lasting joy.

UNKIND WORDS

Let the words of my mouth, and the meditation of my heart, be acceptable in thy sight, O Lord, my strength, and my redeemer. Psalm 19:14.

Shortly after ten o'clock on the night of April 14, 1865, John Wilkes Booth opened the door of the Presidential box at Ford's Theater in Washington, D.C. Taking careful aim at Abraham Lincoln's head, he fired one shot and leaped to the stage. Waving a dagger he cried: "Thus ever to tyrants!" and disappeared through a back door.

President Lincoln was carried to a neighboring house, where he lay unconscious, surrounded by his family and high Government officials. When he died at seven twenty-two the next morning, Secretary of War Edwin Stanton, rose from the bedside where he had been kneeling and pulled down the window blind. Turning to look at the silent face on the pillow, he said, "Now he belongs to the ages."

In those moments of sorrow old quarrels were forgotten and Mr. Stanton said, "There lies the greatest ruler of men the world has ever seen."

Mr. Stanton had been one of Abraham Lincoln's political enemies. That day he must have regretted the unkind things he had said about the President. Once he had called Mr. Lincoln a "low, cunning clown" and the "original gorilla."

As Mr. Stanton stood at the President's casket he must have wished that he could recall all the cruel words he had spoken, but it was too late.

Will Carleton expressed in poetry this feeling of regret we all experience for hasty words spoken:

Boys flying kites haul in their white-winged birds,
You can't do that when you're flying words. . . .
Thoughts unexpressed sometimes fall back dead,
But God Himself can't kill them once they're said.

So that you may be spared a similar experience, why not pray David's prayer daily: "Let the words of my mouth, and the meditation of my heart, be acceptable in thy sight, O Lord, my strength, and my redeemer."

Jesus can give you the victory over a cruel tongue. Only He can write the law of love in your heart and give you a mouth that speaks only kind words.

THE UNSINKABLE SHIP

Whoso putteth his trust in the Lord shall be safe. Proverbs 29:25.

The *Titanic*, eleven stories high and four city blocks long, was the biggest ship afloat in 1912. She was also the safest, with sixteen watertight compartments surrounding the superstructure, any four of which could be flooded and the ship remain afloat. In case of damage to any of these compartments the captain could seal off the rest of the ship by pushing a button.

In spite of all these features, the *Titanic* lasted only five days. Shortly before midnight on April 14, she struck an iceberg. On April 15, within two and one-half hours of the accident the "safest" ship man had ever made lay two miles beneath the surface of the Atlantic Ocean, taking more than 1,500 people to their death.

Among those drowned were some of the richest men in the world. John Jacob Astor, worth $150 million, owned a spacious mansion with eighteen cars in the garage. Harry Widener was the son of the wealthiest man in Philadelphia. Isidor Straus was a member of Congress and a Presidential advisor. Benjamin Guggenheim owned many mines and factories.

However, when tragedy struck there was only one thing that made the difference between life and death. It was not *who* the people were, but *where* they were that counted.

So it will be when you face death. It matters not whether it comes now or later and who you are will not be important. You might be a preacher's son or a doctor's daughter, but that will not count. Your father may be on the school board or on the conference committee, but that will not help.

The deciding question will be, "Where are you?" If you are standing with the world and its pleasures, then you will go down with the sinking ship. But if you have placed yourself on the lifeboat—if you have accepted Christ's offer of salvation—then you will be saved.

Many young people are caught up in the music, movies, and merriment of the world. They don't know the ship is sinking.

Turn your back on the world and accept safety in Jesus Christ today. Tomorrow may be too late. Put your trust in the Lord and be safe. Get in the lifeboat.

BY FAITH ALONE

For by grace are ye saved through faith; and that not of yourselves: it is the gift of God: not of works, lest any man should boast. Ephesians 2:8, 9.

In the spring of 1521 all Germany was talking about three pamphlets written by Martin Luther. These books denounced the Roman Catholic system of indulgences whereby a person could receive a "sure" entrance into heaven by the payment of money for the building of St. Peter's Church in Rome. They declared that faith alone, not money or good works, saves a man.

At this time Emperor Charles V called a council of princes and priests to meet at Worms, Germany. War was brewing and the king feared he would not get Rome's support if Martin Luther was allowed to continue preaching and writing. The council summoned Luther to come to Worms and publicly admit his errors.

On April 16, as the reformer neared Worms, he received a message that he should return to Wittenberg as it was not safe for him to enter the city.

"Though there were as many devils in Worms as there are tiles on the roofs, I will go there," answered Luther.

A band of knights rode out to escort him safely into the city. More than 2,000 people surrounded his carriage, craning their necks to see the man who dared defy a pope.

The next day, dressed in simple monk's attire, Luther stood before the Emperor, princes, nobles, and clergy. On a table nearby was a collection of his books.

"Are these your books?" asked one of the officials. "And will you retract them?"

Martin Luther admitted they were his books but requested time to prepare his answer to the second question. On April 18 he bravely faced the council and said, "My conscience is captive to the Word of God. I cannot and I will not recant anything, for to go against my conscience is neither right nor safe. God help me. Here I stand. I can do no other."

This moment was a turning point in history—the beginning of the Protestant Reformation.

Seventh-day Adventists are Protestants. With Martin Luther we agree that the Bible, not tradition, must be the basis of all our teaching and practice.

THE PRIVATE'S QUESTION

For the wages of sin is death; but the gift of God is eternal life through Jesus Christ our Lord. Romans 6:23.

It happened in Assam in 1944. During the Battle of Kohima Ridge, a scratch force of British and Indian troops held off an entire division of enemy soldiers for two weeks.

By the night of April 17, the allies were hemmed into a space of 350 square yards. It was hardly possible for a shell to burst in such a small area without its killing someone. The situation was desperate. The last ditch had been dug. The enemy was only 200 yards away. Death for all seemed certain.

That night Col. H. U. Richards and a very young private stood duty outside the command post. Each seemed to be deep in thought. Finally the private broke the silence.

"Sir, may I ask you a question?"

"Of course. What is it?"

"When we die, sir, is that the end or do we go on?"

When death stares a person in the face, he wants this question answered above all others.

Millions of people in Asia say, "Yes, you will live forever, but in a different form. A good farmer might come back as a wealthy merchant. A bad man might return as a snake or a rat."

In Christian lands millions proclaim: "Yes, you will live forever. The good man goes to heaven when he dies. The bad man goes to hell to burn eternally."

In Catholic lands multitudes more declare, "There is a place somewhere between heaven and hell where you can suffer for your sins and still have a chance to reach heaven."

Still others believe that the souls of our ancestors come back and live in the trees and flowers.

Will everyone live forever? What does the Bible teach? Only God has immortality; however, eternal life is a gift that He will share with certain people. Those who receive Jesus as their Saviour possess this gift.

If you accept Jesus as your Saviour, He will take you to live with Him for always when he comes the second time. If you have accepted His sacrifice for you, the gift of eternal life is yours. If you haven't made that decision, do it today.

HEARING GOD'S VOICE

And thine ears shall hear a word behind thee, saying, This is the way, walk ye in it. Isaiah 30:21.

Ten-year-old Maybelle awoke at five-fifteen the morning of April 18, 1906. She could hear screams and the windows of the boarding school where she stayed rattled and broke. Furniture bounced back and forth across the room.

"My first thought was that I was having a terrible nightmare and I tried to go to sleep again," remembers Maybelle Billington. But it was not a dream. The great San Francisco earthquake was in progress.

"Get dressed, girls!" the matron shouted. In the confusion Maybelle tried to stuff her nightgown into her stockings. All the while the two-story brick building shook violently. The bewildered girls dressed and stumbled into line at the head of a wide stairway.

"Come down quickly and march along the hall to the vacant lot across the street," the matron commanded.

The frightened children clutched one another's hands and began to descend the trembling stairs.

Suddenly the matron screamed, "Do not come down! Stay where you are!"

Moments later the entire front wall of the building fell out across the street. If the girls had gone outside they would have been killed.

"God impressed me to change my orders," the matron told the girls later.

Sometimes God does speak to people telling them, "Do this" or "Don't do that." Why don't more of us hear His voice?

God is just as willing to talk to us as He was to speak to Maybelle's matron. He speaks in many ways: through nature, the circumstances of life, and the Bible.

Try going to some quiet spot just to be alone with God, to think, and to listen for His voice. As you watch the clouds floating by on the horizon or look at the waves rolling up to the shore, God somehow seems closer. Then read your Bible for a while and take time to listen to what He is saying to you.

God wants to speak to you today. Will you be listening?

UNSUNG HEROES

A book of remembrance was written before him for them that feared the Lord, and that thought upon his name. Malachi 3:16.

Listen, my children, and you shall hear
Of the midnight ride of Paul Revere,
On the eighteenth of April, in Seventy-five;
Hardly a man is now alive
Who remembers that famous day and year.

These lines by Henry Wadsworth Longfellow have helped make Paul Revere famous. His deed, which took place during the late night hours of April 18 and the early morning hours of April 19, is recorded in the history books. His statue stands in Boston. Every educated American has heard of Revere's twelve-mile ride to warn Minutemen of the approaching British.

Few know the names of Israel Bissell and Sybil Luddington, although both outrode Paul Revere in taking the same message. Bissell, a 23-year-old postrider, left Watertown, Massachusetts on the night of April 19. Using a relay of horses he rode day and night for four days to take the message to the Continental Congress meeting in Philadelphia.

Two years later Sybil Luddington, 16-year-old daughter of a colonel, rode all night to round up her father's troops for the defense of Danbury, Connecticut.

While a statue, a poem, and history books commemorate Paul Revere's ride, Israel Bissell and Sybil Luddington sleep, forgotten in New England graves.

How like life this is! Many good deeds and noble acts go unremembered. There are many unsung heroes.

Have you felt bad at times because no one noticed the good things you did? Have you been discouraged because someone who did a lot less than you got the credit?

Your family and friends may not notice, but God does. He will not forget what you do for Him and the good of others.

Today's verse says that God has a book of remembrance. Psalm 112:6 states that we will be in "everlasting remembrance" before God. History books and statues will someday be destroyed, but what God records in His book will be remembered forever. That's where I would like my good deeds recorded, wouldn't you?

THE BEST WEAPON

Charity never faileth. 1 Corinthians 13:8.

Twenty-nine years ago today Mr. and Mrs. Einar Mickelson left California for a remote interior valley of Dutch New Guinea to live with the Danis, a recently discovered primitive tribe of sixty thousand people.

"I wouldn't go into that valley with anything less than a regiment of soldiers," a Dutch official told Einar.

On the map in the government office, the word "Uncontrolled" was written across the area where the Danis lived. The people were described as crafty, cruel, treacherous, and vindictive.

"Understand, you are on your own." a government officer warned as he gave the necessary permission for the Mickelsons to enter the forbidding valley.

"I believe the love of Christ can change hearts and lives," Mr. Mickelson replied.

Taking no weapon but love, the Mickelsons went to live among the Danis. They gave medicine when the people of the tribe were sick. They invited them to their home and shared garden produce with them. They took part in the Dani festivals and funerals, telling wherever possible the story of Jesus, the One who loved them enough to die for them.

Within three years the power of love had worked such a transformation among these people that the government declared the area civilized enough for a post to be opened and an airstrip to be built. What an army could not do, the Mickelsons accomplished through love. Love is the Christian's best weapon.

Sue learned that one day when she came in from recess in tears. "What's wrong?" her teacher asked.

"All the girls are against me," she sobbed. "I hate them!"

"It isn't any fun having enemies," her teacher sympathized. "Why don't you get rid of them?"

"I wish I could," said Sue. "But I don't know how."

"The best way to get rid of enemies," her teacher explained, "is to make them your friends. Find ways to be nice to those girls. Share a treat or help them with an assignment."

A few days later Sue greeted her teacher, all smiles. "It worked," she said. "We are friends now!"

Do you have people problems? Try love. It never fails.

ICE PAN ADVENTURE

Yet the Lord will command his lovingkindness in the daytime, and in the night his song shall be with me. Psalm 42:8.

Spring comes late in northern Newfoundland. The ground was covered with snow the morning of April 21, 1908, and the inlets were still frozen over.

Dr. Wilfred Grenfell decided to use his sledge and dog team to visit a critically ill man sixty miles away.

The ice appeared to be solid and the wind was blowing toward land so he took a shortcut across one of the inlets. However, when the crossing was almost made, the wind changed. The ice began to break up and drift out to sea.

Dr. Grenfell cut the traces of his team, releasing the dogs from the sledge just before it sank to the bottom of the ocean. He and the dogs were then able to scramble onto a small ice pan floating by.

After the sun set, the wind rose and temperatures dropped to below freezing. In order to keep warm, Dr. Grenfell killed three of his dogs and used their skins as protection against the icy wind. In the morning he made a pole by using their frozen legs tied together. On the top he tied his shirt for a flag. Some seal hunters noticed the flag and rescued him.

In his autobiography, Dr. Grenfell tells how in the dark, lonesome hours on the ice pan the words of an old hymn kept running through his head, giving courage and strength.

"My God, my Father, while I stray
Far from my home on life's rough way,
Oh, help me from my heart to say,
Thy will be done."

After that Dr. Grenfell said he felt quite ready to live or die according as God saw best.

Often in times of darkness and despair Christians have found hope and strength in song. Remember how Paul and Silas were able to sing at midnight in the dark prison cell?

God has not promised that the Christian life will always be easy. There will be dark nights of perplexity. You may feel at times like Wilfred Grenfell, adrift on an ice pan with no help at hand. At such times God will not forsake you. He will give you a song in the night.

THE GREAT LAND RUSH

In my Father's house are many mansions. John 14:2.

It is almost noon on April 22, 1889. There is much excitement along the border of the Oklahoma territory. At twelve o'clock today all those who want land will be allowed to cross the boundary and stake out their claim. Fifty thousand homesteaders are now gathered there.

Soldiers mounted on horses patrol the border to keep out "sooners," people who want to sneak in early to get the best claims. Everyone must have an equal chance.

Some people have been camping for days to assure their place in the lineup. Now the campfires are out; the tents folded and put away. Drivers are checking and rechecking their teams to make sure everything is ready.

Fifteen trains of the Atchison, Topeka, and Santa Fe Railway steam up to the border, crowded with people. The overflow cling to the sides and sit on top. These latecomers will have to literally run on their own two feet to stake out their claims.

The day is warm and bright. As noon approaches, horses and wagons of all descriptions form an unbroken line to the horizon in either direction. Shouting and laughter die away and the border is the quietest it has been for many days. Horses stamp the ground, impatient to be going. The crowd seems to be holding its breath, awaiting the signal.

A sharp report splits the air. The race is on!

Today another race is on. Noon hour is approaching. Soon Jesus will come. The trumpet will sound and all those who are ready and waiting will be whisked across the borders of time and space to their heavenly home.

There can be no "sooners." All of us have an equal chance. Those who meet the conditions of surrender to Christ will receive title to a mansion. We will be like homesteaders in a new land. Only we won't have to build our houses of sod as the Oklahoma settlers did.

God has something much better for us. Read about it in Revelation 21 and 22. The beauty of that home is beyond our imagining. Will you be ready and waiting when the trumpet sounds and Jesus comes to take you there?

THE TOWN THAT DISAPPEARED

Seek ye the Lord, all ye meek of the earth, which have wrought his judgment; seek righteousness, seek meekness: it may be ye shall be hid in the day of the Lord's anger. Zephaniah 2:3.

On the night of April 23, 1971, residents of Saint-Jean-Vianney, Quebec, heard a loud thump under their houses.

The people were not aware that beneath them the earth was slowly dissolving and flowing away. The ground in this area of Canada is composed of clay with pockets of sand. Recent heavy rains and a quick rise in temperature had produced a fast thaw, oversaturating the sand pockets with moisture and liquefying the soil. The people of Saint-Jean-Vianney had only twelve more days before their town would disappear.

By the night of May 4 the earth had dissolved to a depth of nearly one hundred feet, making a river of liquefied clay flowing to the Saguenay River three miles away. It took with it thirty-eight houses and thirty-one lives.

Survivors remembered a number of strange happenings. Cracks had appeared in the city streets. Two driveways had settled about five inches. One man painted his house in the fall and by spring it had settled nearly eight inches. People heard water flowing beneath their houses. Then came the thump of April 23. Too late they understood the meaning of the signs.

Like the residents of Saint-Jean-Vianney, many will be caught unaware when Jesus comes. Islands and mountains will disappear. Cities will be leveled and the wicked will be destroyed.

To those who understand Bible prophecy this will be no surprise, for they have seen God's warnings in earth, sea, and sky. Ask your parents or teacher to help you make a list of these signs. Then you will realize how near is the end.

When the heavens are rolled back as a scroll and we see Jesus coming with ten thousand times ten thousand angels, it will be too late to confess our sins and make wrongs right.

Today is the time to come to Jesus. We must get ready now, while we still have opportunity. One day soon beautiful homes and magnificent skyscrapers will crumble and fall. Schools and churches will be no more. Our only safety will be in Jesus. We must seek Him today if we would be saved then.

UNIDENTIFIED FLYING OBJECTS

For they are the spirits of devils, working miracles, which go forth unto the kings of the earth and of the whole world, to gather them to the battle of the great day of God Almighty. Revelation 16:14.

On April 24, 1969, Helio Augier, a Brazilian businessman, was riding home on his motorcycle. Near Piata he seemed to automatically stop. A silvery disc hovered low over the road before him. Quickly Helio took out his camera and snapped three shots of the object. While doing so he felt a strange pressure in his head. Within a few seconds he lost consciousness.

A cruising police car found Helio slumped over his motorbike. At first the officers laughed at his story. To test it they developed the film. Their laughter turned to shock when they saw the photographs.

Unidentified flying objects (UFOs) have been sighted and recorded all over the world. In the United States, the Air Force set up a two-year study for analysis of UFO sightings. They were able to prove that some were the result of misinterpretation of ordinary objects such as weather balloons and fast jet fighter planes. Others proved to be hoaxes. But for some there was no feasible explanation.

Some would have us believe that these are spacecraft from other planets. Is it possible that beings from outer space mingle with people of Planet Earth and help guide our affairs?

The Bible tells us that after God created this planet there was war in heaven. Satan and the rebellious angels were cast out into this earth. Since then Satan has been clever enough to use miraculous methods to reach men's minds.

John saw that just before Jesus comes Satan would work all sorts of miracles to deceive men and women.

Let us not be taken in by flying saucers or any other miraculous occurrence. Let us be wise and test all such phenomena by the Word of God. Only then can we be sure and safe.

We are living in a period of time when we can no longer trust our senses. Our eyes and ears may deceive us. Our only safe course is to accept what the Word of God says. Today we need to study as never before so that we will not be fooled.

WIRELESS COMMUNICATION

I cried unto the Lord with my voice, and he heard me out of his holy hill. Psalm 3:4.

In 1983 we think nothing of turning on the television and watching games or wars in far-off places. You can carry a transistor to a picnic and listen to a symphony concert from London or pick up the phone and talk with a friend in Tokyo.

When Guglielmo Marconi was born on this day in 1874 there was no radar, radio, telephone, television, or communication satellite.

While still in his teens, Marconi read about the experiments of Heinrich Hertz and his discovery of electromagnetic waves. "I believe it is possible to use those waves to send signals and even voices through the air," Marconi declared. By the time he was 28 he had sent a message across the Atlantic Ocean without wires.

Ships at sea began to use the wireless method to communicate with one another and with lighthouses along the shore. The value of the wireless for emergencies was first illustrated on April 28, 1899. A ship was sinking off the English coast. It used its wireless set to send an SOS. Help arrived in time to save all on board. Since then countless lives have been saved because of Marconi's invention, which led to the development of other means of communication such as radio, television, and radar.

We don't need wires today to talk to someone in Peking or Portugal. Neither do we need wires to talk with Heaven. We can transmit an instant SOS across the universe to the throne of God.

When David was fleeing from Absalom he composed Psalm 3, in which we find today's verse. In that darkest hour David cried out to God for help. And wonder of wonders, the great God of heaven heard and answered him!

> "If radio's slim fingers can pluck a melody
> From night—and toss it over a continent or sea;
> If the petalled white notes of a violin
> Are blown across the mountains or the city's din;
> If songs, like crimson roses, are culled from thin blue air—
> Why should mortals wonder if God hears prayer?"
> —Ethel Romig Fuller

SPARROWS AND YOU

Fear ye not therefore, ye are of more value than many sparrows. Matthew 10:31.

Today is the birthday of John James Audubon, a bird artist. He published a book of his drawings called *Birds of America.* Maybe you have seen an Audubon wildlife film. Or perhaps you have taken part in a study of the conservation of soil, water, plants, and wildlife sponsored by the Audubon Society, which was named for him.

As a small boy John was playing in the garden one day when he heard a little sound coming from the rose bushes by the gate.

Kneeling down he peered under the long, thorny branches. Way back under the bush he saw a tiny brown ball of fluff. Ever so carefully he reached through the thorns and picked up the baby bird.

"Poor lost little thing," John said. "You must have fallen out of your nest. Don't worry, I'll put you back so your mother can find you."

But though he searched carefully, he could not find the nest.

"You could make a place for it in a candy box," his mother suggested. "You can use bits of cotton batting like I use to make my quilts. Then you can try to feed it."

John soon had a cozy nest for the tiny bird, but the little thing sat in one corner with its eyes closed and refused to eat. By evening it was dead.

John ran sobbing to his mother. She wiped his tears away and held him close to her. Then she reached over and picked up the Bible from a nearby table.

"Listen," she said, "I want to read you something. 'Are not five sparrows sold for two farthings, and not one of them is forgotten before God?'"

That verse made John feel better; and it has a message for us, too. If not even one little sparrow can fall to the ground without God's noticing it, do you think anything can happen to you without His knowing and caring? He sees each time you fall. He hears each time you cry. Nothing that happens to you is too small for Him to notice.

God loves and cares for the sparrows—and you, too.

"WHAT HATH GOD WROUGHT!"

Every good gift and every perfect gift is from above, and cometh down from the Father of lights, with whom is no variableness, neither shadow of turning. James 1:17.

A distinguished group of men, many of them officials of the United States Government, gathered in the Supreme Court chamber. They were there to witness the first official test of a telegraph line between Washington, D.C., and Baltimore.

Had $30,000 been spent for nothing? Was it possible that written words could actually be transmitted through wires?

The inventor, Samuel F. B. Morse, whose birthday is today, seated himself at the sending device. Slowly he tapped out the message in code.

"Dot, dash, dash, dash, space, dot, dot, dot, dot, space, dot, dash, space, dash, space, dot, dot, dot, dot, space . . ."

At the Baltimore railroad station, Alfred Vail received the message and returned it to Washington. The waiting men heard the clicks of the receiver proclaim, "What hath God wrought!"

Later, speaking at a banquet given in his honor, Mr. Morse said, "If not a sparrow falls to the ground without a definite purpose in the plans of Infinite Wisdom, can the creation of an instrument so vitally affecting the interests of the whole human race have an origin less humble than the Father of every good and perfect gift? I am sure I have the sympathy of such an assembly as is here gathered together, if in all humility, and in the sincerity of a grateful heart, I use the words of Inspiration in ascribing honor and praise to Him whom first of all and most of all it is preeminently due. 'Not unto us, not unto us, but to God be all the glory'—not, what hath man, but, 'What hath God wrought!'"

It is a rare individual who recognizes God as the giver of his or her talents. Most people are like Nebuchadnezzar, who proudly said, "Is not this great Babylon, that *I* have built?" (Dan. 4:30). We have the tendency, when we do something well, to be proud and think, See what I have done! Everyone must now recognize what an important person I am.

How much better to be like Samuel F. B. Morse and acknowledge God as the source of every good thing that we do.

Let us pray today, "Lord, make me humble. Help me to praise and honor You in everything I do."

NO OXYGEN!

Pray without ceasing. 1 Thessalonians 5:17.

At an altitude of 25,000 feet, Russell Laba was freezing, semiconscious, lost, and rapidly running out of fuel.

On Thursday, April 28, 1977, Mr. Laba was flying a Cessna 310 from Winnepeg to Vancouver. Near the Saskatchewan-Alberta border the heating system of the plane stopped working and his oxygen supply failed.

Gradually, hypoxia, or oxygen starvation, crept over him. He felt lightheaded and his reflexes slowed down. Soon his fingernails turned blue. He tried to contact the Calgary airport, but there was no response so he set his controls on automatic pilot and drifted into semiconsciousness.

As he described it later, the feeling was pleasant. He could hear the radio conversations, but didn't realize they were about him. He seemed unaware of his now-perilous position.

Death for Russ Laba was sure unless help could be found. Fortunately, an Air Canada flight was nearby. The pilot managed to break through Mr. Laba's stupor enough to direct him to a lower altitude, where oxygen began to revive him. Then another Cessna 310 came to his rescue and led him to the nearest airport.

In those frantic moments when Russ Laba was trying to respond to the radio directions to lower his altitude, he found each breath a great effort. He said later that at the time he thought, Man does not live from day to day or even from meal to meal. He lives from breath to breath.

Ellen White must have had this idea in mind when she wrote, "Prayer is the breath of the soul."—*Gospel Workers,* p. 254.

Without prayer, spiritual hypoxia occurs. It comes on so gradually you do not know that you are in danger. Your spiritual reflexes slow down. You may even feel quite happy with your life. Sin no longer seems so wrong. Before you know it, you are off course.

"The darkness of the evil one encloses those who neglect to pray. The whispered temptations of the enemy entice them to sin; and it is all because they do not make use of the privileges that God has given them in the divine appointment of prayer."—*Steps to Christ,* p. 94.

THE BIG SPENDER

For a man's life consisteth not in the abundance of the things which he possesseth. Luke 12:15.

Would you like to have an allowance of $140,000 a week? That would give you $14 for every minute.

William Randolph Hearst, Sr., had that much money. He was the richest newspaper publisher in the world. Born to the wife of a wealthy mine owner on April 29, 1863, he inherited more than sixteen million dollars. Then he worked hard for sixty years to get more!

It's a good thing Hearst had plenty of money because he was a big spender. He bought 240,000 acres of land in California on which to build four lavish castles. His ocean-side frontage stretched for fifty miles along the Pacific Coast. There he placed herds of zebras, buffaloes, giraffes, and kangaroos. He collected thousands of exotic birds. He had lions, tigers, and elephants in his private zoo.

Mr. Hearst brought shiploads of art treasures from all over the world. He even bought entire castles. These were torn down, then each stone was labeled, packed, and shipped to America where the structure was rebuilt on his estate. He collected so many things, from cuckoo clocks to Egyptian mummies, that he had to have a huge warehouse to hold them all and twenty employees to take care of them.

When Mr. Hearst wanted something, he got it. He once paid $22,000 to move a tree that was blocking his view of the ocean, rather than have it cut down.

But there were some things his money couldn't buy—things such as health, happiness, and life itself. So concerned was Mr. Hearst about dying that he never permitted anyone to talk about death in his presence. If he could have purchased life for a million dollars or so a year, he would be alive today. But he died in 1951 and has returned to dust, the same as any poor man.

You see, money isn't everything. There is more to life than paychecks, cars, yachts, airplanes, and beautiful houses.

Focus your attention on Jesus and service to Him. Only a right relationship with God can bring you real satisfaction and make your life worthwhile. Only He can give you those things that money cannot buy. Only He can give you a life that will never end.

127

HITLER'S CHOICE

I have chosen the way of truth. Psalm 119:30.

"Once to every man and nation
Comes the moment to decide,
In the strife of truth with falsehood,
For the good or evil side."

James Russell Lowell was right when he wrote those words. If only we knew when that golden moment is to come in our lives, how carefully we would weigh the consequences!

Adolf Hitler is an example of where a choice can lead. As a boy he sang in the church choir and contemplated becoming a priest. When he was a man he made light of religion and spread death across Europe.

Somewhere between the boy and the man a choice was made. That choice was for evil and led to his destruction.

On April 30, 1945, Hitler said goodbye to his closest friends, then went to his suite in an underground bomb shelter and shot himself. At the same time his wife took poison.

Somewhere, sometime in his youth, Adolf Hitler stood at the crossroads and chose the wrong road. One path led to happiness, satisfaction, and a life of usefulness. The other led to hatred, disappointment, and death.

We are not robots. God made us with the ability to think. We can choose right or wrong. We can eat healthful foods or refuse to eat them. We can smoke or refrain from smoking. We can accept drugs or we can reject them. We can attend movies or we can stay away. We can follow truth or we can follow error. The choice is ours.

God does not prevent us from making wrong choices, unless we specifically ask Him to do so. In the asking our choice is made for truth.

"When you rise in the morning, do you feel your helplessness, and your need of strength from God? and do you humbly, heartily make known your wants to your heavenly Father? If so, angels mark your prayers, and . . . when you are in danger of unconsciously doing wrong, and exerting an influence which will lead others to do wrong, your guardian angel will be by your side . . . choosing your words for you, and influencing your actions."—*Messages to Young People,* p. 90.

128

HE DIED PRAYING

The love of Christ constraineth us. 2 Corinthians 5:14.

It was still dark on Thursday morning, May 1, 1873. The shimmering stars looked down on the African village of Ilala. Among the circle of huts was a temporary one made two days earlier to house Dr. David Livingstone, who was sick with fever.

Just before daybreak the night boy ran to call the servants, Susi and Chuma. They hurried to the doorway and peered inside. In the flickering light of a candle, they could see Dr. Livingstone kneeling beside his bed, his head buried in his hands before an open Bible. At first they hesitated to go in. Then one of them stepped quietly to his side and touched his cheek. It was cold. Their beloved master was dead!

Why did David Livingstone turn his back on the prospects of fame and fortune in London and go to work in the swamps of equatorial Africa? What compelled him to forsake home and friends for a lonely life as an explorer and missionary? It was the love of Christ and the knowledge that millions were dying without that love.

One day while he was still in medical training, Livingstone had heard Robert Moffat tell about his experiences in Africa. "I have seen in the morning sun the smoke of a thousand villages where no missionary has ever been," Mr. Moffat had said. "People are dying there like cattle upon a thousand hills, dying without ever hearing the name of the wonderful Master."

Livingstone determined then to enter the unexplored areas of Africa with the message of Christ's love. It was this love that drove him farther and farther into the dense jungles with medicine and a message of hope. This same love sent him to his knees to plead for the conversion of men and women whose minds were darkened by sin and devil worship.

The love of Jesus is the strongest force in the world. It is a compelling power that will send you out to share the Gospel with others. It is a holding power that will keep you on the path of right and duty. It is a controlling power, shaping your life and making it worthwhile.

Accept God's mighty love for you today. Let it control your life. Let it drive you to your knees in prayer for yourself and your friends. Let it send you out to share.

CAUGHT AT LAST

Be sure your sin will find you out. Numbers 32:23.

There was nothing unusual about Willie Sutton's childhood. His family lived in a modest two-family frame house on High Street in Brooklyn. His father was a blacksmith. The family appeared to be a happy one, going to church together, and coming home to Mom's special dinner.

Willie's mother often sent him to the corner store to buy groceries. One day he slipped a few things into his pocket when the clerk wasn't looking. He did this several more times.

The next step was to visit the store at night. He climbed in the back window and helped himself to the money in the cash register. No one suspected Willie Sutton.

As he grew older he found it easier to rob a bank than to work. He went from city to city, pulling off a bigger robbery each time. Occasionally he was caught and put in jail, but each time he escaped and continued his life of crime.

Then one day the game was over. Someone spotted Willie on the New York subway and reported to the police. As a result, on May 2, 1952, Willie Sutton stood before the judge of Queens County Court in New York City and heard him say, "The sentence of the court is that the prisoner be confined in a state prison for a period of not less than thirty years."

Fed up with the wasted years of his life, Willie Sutton wrote his autobiography. He knew that some boys would look on him as a hero. They would think that because he got away with crime many times, they too could escape. He wanted to warn them where the path would lead. He said, "I studied robbery the way an honest man studies law or accounting. I made a science out of crime. And yet I lost!"

Those who break the law always lose. Someday their sins will find them out. Sooner or later the day of reckoning will come; for all must appear before the judgment bar of God.

Have you tried to hide something you have done? Before that day of judgment, why not confess it and receive pardon? If you have stolen something, return it or make plans to pay for it. Ask God to keep you from following in the footsteps of Willie Sutton.

THE OPEN DOOR

It is better to trust in the Lord than to put confidence in man.
Psalm 118:8.

Additional buildings were needed for Avondale College, but there was no money. The Australian mission president, A. G. Daniells, went to lumbermen, plasterers, and plumbers and asked them to give supplies and labor on credit. He promised to pay as soon as an expected check arrived from the General Conference the first week of May.

May came and the mail boat arrived. There was a letter, but no check! The church in America was having troubles of its own and the brethren suggested that building plans be stopped.

It was too late for that. What was Elder Daniells to do? Putting his trust in the Lord, he went out under a eucalyptus tree and cried to God for help. He stayed there all night until, in the early hours of May 3, 1899, assurance came to him that God would provide the needed funds. Soon after breakfast Elder Daniells left for the city, confident he would find the money.

The next morning he read Daniel 6:16 for worship. The words "He will deliver thee" seemed to stand out in bold letters on the page. This gave him added faith to believe that God would supply the money to deliver the school from embarrassment. Along the margin he wrote, "7:30 a.m. 5/4/99."

At four o'clock that afternoon, Daniells and a friend walked past a certain bank. Although it was an hour after closing time, the door was slightly open. The two men walked in, to the great surprise of the banker.

"How did you get in?" he demanded.

"The door was open and we just walked in," the men replied.

The banker was positive that he had bolted the door and hooked the chain. Yet, here were two men standing in front of him. "What do you want?" he asked.

It didn't take Elder Daniells long to explain their needs. By five o'clock he had £300 in his hands.

That night Elder Daniells again opened his Bible to Daniel 6:16 and wrote beside it: "Fulfilled, 5:00 p.m. 5/4/99."

Sometimes people in whom we trust let us down. The church may fail us as it did Elder Daniells. Our friends may not always keep their promises. But Jesus never fails. His promises are sure. You can count on Him.

SEND YOUR FEARS FLYING

There is no fear in love; but perfect love casteth out fear. 1 John 4:18

It was almost sunset on Friday, May 4, 1973. Eight-year-old Terry Jesko sat in the tractor cab with his father, watching him work the controls. Behind the tractor they pulled a planter and a rod weeder. The weeder was a knifelike device attached in front of the planter and was used to cut down weeds and grass.

Mr. Jesko slowed the tractor down and told Terry to steer while he checked the seed boxes. As he climbed back into the cab, his foot slipped and he fell under the wheel and was drawn into the weeder blade.

Terry had seen his father start up the steps then disappear. Frightened, the boy tried to think what to do. He must stop the tractor. He had never done it before but he had watched his dad. He must try. He put one small foot on the brake and the other on the clutch and the tractor stopped.

Terry jumped out and saw his father trapped beneath the weeder. Hurrying back into the cab, he grabbed the power lift lever and raised the implements off the ground. He rushed back to his unconscious father, but couldn't budge him. He must get help. He ran over to the truck and started the motor. Somehow he reached home. Mother was gone. What should he do? He would telephone the operator and call Uncle Pete. Quickly he dialed. "My father needs help," the boy called into the mouthpiece. Soon an ambulance carrying Terry's dad was on its way to the hospital.

That night the doctor let Terry see his father for one minute. "You did exactly the right thing, son," the grateful man whispered. "You saved my life."

"I was so scared," said Terry through his tears.

Of course he was scared; but love for his dad overcame that fear and enabled Terry to rescue him.

Your friends who do not know Jesus are in a similar position to that of Terry's father. They are trapped under a load of sin.

"I'm so scared," you may be saying. "What if they laugh?"

It is only natural to be frightened; but genuine love for Christ and your friends will send your fears flying and give you courage to witness for Jesus.

MEDAL OF HONOR

For them that honour me I will honour. 1 Samuel 2:30.

"Doss, you are the only medic available. They need help on the ridge," said Capt. Frank Vernon. "I know it is Saturday, but people die on Saturdays, too."

Corp. Desmond T. Doss was studying his Sabbath school lesson when he was called on that morning of May 5, 1945. "I'll go," he responded.

Along with members of the 77th Division, Desmond climbed the rope ladder up a steep cliff to the top of Hill 187 in Okinawa. There he participated in what has been called "the biggest and bloodiest of all Pacific battles." Before it was over the platoon had to retreat. Fifty-five men got back down the ladder, leaving 100 wounded and dying at the top of the ridge.

"Where is Doss?" the lieutenant asked.

"Still up on the ridge," someone replied. Looking up, they saw the medic tying rope around a wounded man.

"Come on down, Doss," the captain ordered.

Instead of obeying, Desmond carefully lowered the soldier over the cliff. Under heavy enemy fire he went back again and again, until he had rescued at least seventy-five men. Only then did he slide down the rope himself.

For this act of bravery, Desmond T. Doss was awarded the Congressional Medal of Honor, the highest award the United States Government can give.

Many people have asked, "What made you so brave?"

The answer was, "During all the time I was in the Army my source of strength was found in daily study of the Bible and in prayer. I did more praying overseas than in all my life before. When I talked with God, I seemed to lose all sense of fear. That is the only way I can account for anything like bravery on my part."

It was not easy for Desmond Doss to keep up this regular program of prayer and Bible study amid the difficulties of war. It was not easy to remain true to the principles of God's Word when those around him mocked. But he had determined to put God first in his life, regardless of the consequences. Because he honored God, God honored him.

ZEPPELIN EXPLOSION

Set a watch, O Lord, before my mouth; keep the door of my lips. Psalm 141:3.

Have you ever seen a zeppelin? Probably not. However, fifty years ago these huge, cigar-shaped airships were familiar sights in the skies. A lighter-than-air gas was used to raise them in the same way that a balloon is lifted. Hydrogen, the lightest gas available, was used in most of them.

Seven million cubic feet of hydrogen filled the sixteen bags of the 803-foot *Hindenberg,* the largest zeppelin in the world. Its four diesel engines propelled the craft through the air at eighty knots an hour, making the trip from Germany to the United States in three days.

On its thirty-sixth flight, the *Hindenberg* exploded just minutes before landing at Lakehurst, New Jersey. Within seconds the whole airship was ablaze. Thirty-six of the ninety-seven people on board died in the explosion. The date of the tragedy was May 6, 1937.

No one knows what caused the explosion. Some thought an electrical charge from storm clouds ignited the hydrogen. A small match could have done it, or even a tiny frictional spark.

It is that way, too, with your tongue. James says it is like a small fire. Just as great power for destruction is in a small spark, so great power for evil is in the tongue.

A hasty word can destroy a friendship. An ill-chosen phrase can set a town on fire. An angry comment can set a nation aflame. Wars have been fought over careless words.

Ellen White once wrote: "The tongue is a little member, but the words it frames, made vocal by the voice, have a great power. . . . Words have kindled fires that have been hard to quench."—Letter 34, 1899.

In the *Youth Instructor* of March 5, 1903, she wrote: "Too often, fretful, impatient words are spoken, words which stir the worst passions of the human heart. Such ones need the abiding presence of Christ in the soul. Only in His strength can they keep guard over the words and actions."

Realizing the tremendous potential for destruction that lies in your tongue, will you not ask God today to set a watch before your mouth and keep the door of your lips?

SECRET CARGO

Cleanse thou me from secret faults. Psalm 19:12.

Shortly after two o'clock on the afternoon of May 7, 1915, the *Lusitania,* the largest and finest ship afloat, was torpedoed and sunk off the southern coast of Ireland. Nearly twelve hundred people lost their lives.

The tragedy happened so quickly that escape was all but impossible. An enemy submarine fired a shot that hit the starboard side of the ship just behind the bridge. This was followed by a second explosion from somewhere within the ship. Within eighteen minutes the vessel was under water.

For many years there was mystery surrounding the sinking of the *Lusitania.* What caused the second explosion? Was there a secret cargo on board?

Yes, as a matter of fact, there was. The ship's manifest produced at the time of judicial inquiry stated only that there were sundries and lard on board. Not until many years later, when a carbon copy of the original manifest was discovered, did the world hear what was really on that ship.

The secret cargo consisted of more than sixty tons of ammunition. It was not the torpedo that sank the *Lusitania.* That simply ignited the explosives, causing the second explosion.

Do you have a secret cargo on board your ship? Are you doing things you know are wrong? Have you kept certain acts secret from your family and friends? Someday your life's story will be open before the universe. All will then be able to see your "cargo," be it good or bad.

In writing about that day of judgment, Ellen White says, "In the solemn assembly of the last day, in the hearing of the universe, will be read the reason of the condemnation of the sinner. For the first time parents will learn what has been the secret life of their children. Children will see how many wrongs they have committed against their parents. There will be a general revealing of the secrets and motives of the heart, for that which is hid will be made manifest,"—*Child Guidance,* p. 560.

How much better to come to God now and ask Him to cleanse you of all sin, open or secret. Only as you let Him remove the secret cargo from your life will you be sure of reaching heaven.

RUNAWAYS

There is no peace, saith the Lord, unto the wicked. Isaiah 48:22.

After five years, eight months, and seven days the European part of World War II came to an end. May 8, 1945, was celebrated throughout the Western world as V-E (Victory in Europe) Day.

Many leaders of the defeated Nazis committed suicide. Others surrendered. Some, like Adolf Eichmann, disappeared.

Mr. Eichmann expected to be tried for the murder of 6 million Jews, should he be caught. To avoid this he changed his name to Ricardo Klement and went to Argentina.

There he got a factory job. None of his neighbors suspected his real identity. Not until fifteen years later did Israeli agents locate him and bring him to justice.

Before his trial Adolf Eichmann wrote out a confession in which he said, "I realize that there is no point in continuing to evade justice. . . . I want at last to achieve inner peace."

Adolf Eichmann learned that there is no peace for the transgressor. For fifteen years he escaped punishment, but he could not escape his own conscience. He ran thousands of miles from the scenes of his murders, but he could not run away from himself. A false passport did not change who he really was. With such a burden of guilt, inner peace was not possible.

Many today are like Adolf Eichmann, trying to run away from who they really are. Some try to escape through alcohol and drugs. A few run away from home to join cults and communes. Some change their names and others their schools. For some, reading forms a means of escape. Still others turn their stereo sets on full volume to try to drown the voice of conscience. Whatever the method, it does not work.

Are you trying to run away from yourself or something that you have done? Are you trying to escape punishment that you deserve? Wherever you run, guilt will meet you there. Until you face up to the reality of your life and do something about it, you will have no rest. Until you confess your sins and repent, inner peace is not possible.

Come to Jesus today. Whatever you have done, He loves you. He will accept you. He will give you pardon and peace.

LIVING BY DYING

I am crucified with Christ: nevertheless I live; yet not I, but Christ liveth in me: and the life which I now live in the flesh I live by the faith of the Son of God, who loved me, and gave himself for me. Galatians 2:20.

"Died November 10, 1848.

Fell asleep on May 9, 1882."

This unusual inscription is on the tombstone of George Cobb in Brunswick, Maine. It seems strange at first to imagine a man walking around for thirty-four years after his death, and yet this is exactly what happened.

Mr. Cobb was well known for his drinking and swearing. No one wanted to be around when he had a fit of temper. Then one day something happened to the old George Cobb everyone knew. He responded to a call for surrender made by Elder James White at a revival meeting that was held in a schoolhouse. Right then, the old George Cobb died and a new George Cobb was born.

"What?" people asked. "George Cobb is not smoking and drinking anymore? What caused the change?"

George Mueller, of Bristol, was often asked a similar question. He had lived a life of sin for many years and then suddenly he began having an outstanding Christian experience. "What is the secret?" his friends wanted to know.

He opened his Bible and read Galatians 2:20. "There came a day when George Mueller died," he said.

There came a day in Paul's life, too, when he died. He accepted Christ's death and resurrection. The old Saul who wanted to kill the Christians died; a new Paul who wanted to preach Christ was born.

Do you find it hard to give up certain habits in your life? Do you have a struggle with impure thoughts or an evil temper? Would you rather read a novel than your Bible? Would you rather watch television than pray? Do you find church boring?

Why is it so hard to live the Christian life? Ellen White gives the answer on page 127 of *Messages to Young People:* "Because professed Christians are not dead to the world. It is easy living after we are dead."

The secret of living a successful Christian life, then, is in dying. Daily we must come to Jesus, be crucified with Him, and rise to walk in newness of life.

DIAMOND ANNIVERSARY

Behold thy mother! John 19:27.

Today is the diamond anniversary of Mother's Day. Seventy-five years ago today the first Mother's Day was celebrated in the Andrews Methodist church in Grafton, West Virginia. Pastor H. C. Howard used today's verse as his sermon text.

Let us for a moment behold *your* mother. We will look at her, as it were, through a diamond, using the letters of that word to tell something about her character and beauty.

D is for the dreams she has for your life. She wants you to be happy and successful, but most of all she wants you to love God. When she rocked you to sleep long ago she pictured you grown up—somehow, somewhere working for the Lord.

I is for illnesses—all those times she sat by your bed and held your hand. Her tender loving care did more than any medicine to make you well and strong again.

A is for appreciation. When you have done your best, Mother is always there to smile her approval. A hug from Mother is worth more than all the trophies you might win. It is better than an "A" on your report card or a blue ribbon at the fair.

M is for the melodies you learned at your mother's knee. It is for memory verses she taught for Sabbath school. Bits of those songs and verses will come back to you just when you need them most.

O is for obedience, learned the hard way through Mother's discipline. Sometimes you had to be punished, but now you love and obey God because she taught you how.

N is for nature—all the beautiful things of God's creation that she helped you to see. You are reminded of trips to the zoo, Sabbath afternoon walks, bird watching, star gazing, gathering flowers, and planting gardens.

D is for dresses and denims—all the time she spends washing, ironing, mending, and sewing so that you can look your best.

Put them all together, they spell DIAMOND, the most precious of jewels. And that is exactly what Mother is to us today and every day.

No doubt you did something for Mother already last Sunday. However, why not give her another surprise on this special day?

HEAVENLY CENSUS

For man looketh on the outward appearance, but the Lord looketh on the heart. 1 Samuel 16:7.

Caesar Augustus was Emperor of Rome when Jesus was born. It was he who called for a census of all the people of his kingdom, causing Joseph and Mary to travel to Bethlehem where Jesus was born.

Three times during his rule Augustus called for a numbering of the people. The final census was completed on May 11, A.D. 14. On that day a special ceremony was held in Rome. Large crowds gathered to watch Augustus offer a sacrifice to the pagan gods, imploring them to withhold calamity from the people in the new age that was starting.

Almost every country today takes a census. The word has come to mean a regular check on the number and condition of the people in a certain area.

Such questions are asked as: What is your name? Age? Birthplace? Citizenship? Occupation? Are you married? How many children do you have? How many rooms are in your house? Do you own or rent your home? What is your religion?

After all the information is collected, books are published with a list of the various localities and their population. Government leaders can then see where more jobs are needed and where houses must be built.

As useful as a census is, there are limits to what it can tell. No census can show how many criminals there are, for such people will not tell the truth. It may register what work a person does, but not whether he is honest on the job. A census might reveal how many people call themselves Christian, but it cannot show how many have a real experience with the Lord Jesus Christ. Only a heavenly census will reveal that.

A striking statement is found in *Messages to Young People:* "From what has been shown me, there are not more than half of the young who profess religion and the truth, who have been truly converted."—Page 131.

Having our names on the clerk's books as baptized members of the church means nothing if we are not genuine Christians. Many of us are holding back from a full surrender to Jesus Christ. Are you one of these? Won't you give your all to Him today? You cannot deceive the heavenly census taker.

THE LITTLE NURSE

I was not disobedient unto the heavenly vision. Acts 26:19.

"Why, Florence," said Mother, "what are you doing home so soon? I thought you had gone with the others on a picnic."

"I can't go," answered the little girl as she held up her puppy for Mother to see. "Frisky is hurt and I must help him."

Mother looked at the deep gash on the front leg of the dog and sent for a veterinarian.

"May I help you?" asked Florence when the doctor came.

"Of course you may, little nurse," he said, smiling.

Florence often acted out the part of "little nurse." She would rather help the sick than go to parties. She cared for the sick farmers on her wealthy father's estate. When everyone was in good health, she pretended her dolls were ill and nursed them.

When Florence grew too old for games, she knew that she must be a nurse for real. Her parents were shocked. In England in those days, nurses were often drunken women who were not fit to care for the sick. Hospitals were dirty places. No wealthy girl had ever done such a thing.

Florence insisted, "I believe that God wants me to be a nurse."

Like Paul, Florence Nightingale, who was born on this day in 1820, was determined not to be "disobedient unto the heavenly vision." Neither the pleading of friends, the demands of parents, nor the glitter of wealth could take her eyes from her goal.

When the Crimean War broke out Florence Nightingale was ready. She transformed the British military hospitals from houses of death into halls of hope. She became known as the lady of the lamp as she walked up and down the hospital corridors bringing comfort and hope to the wounded and dying.

Though you are young, God can speak to you, giving you a vision of what He wants you to do for Him. Florence Nightingale was just a child when she received the challenge to be a nurse. Samuel was but a boy when he heard God's voice in the Temple. David was still young when God anointed him to be king. Ellen Harmon was a teen-ager when God called her to be His messenger.

You are not too young for God to direct your life. When He shows the way, do not be disobedient to *your* heavenly vision.

BLOOD, SWEAT, AND TEARS

Fight the good fight of faith. 1 Timothy 6:12.

In 1940, Great Britain stood alone in her fight against the advancing army of Hitler. The British military had just suffered several defeats when Winston Churchill was asked to become the prime minister.

On May 13 Churchill stood before the Parliament and said, "I have nothing to offer but blood, toil, tears, and sweat." His worried countrymen accepted the offer. They were willing to sacrifice anything if victory might be theirs.

Wherever Winston Churchill went he held up two fingers in a V for victory salute. This became an inspiring symbol to people of many nations. It gave them hope that though they might lose some battles, they could still win the war.

The Christian life, too, is a battle. In Ephesians 6, Paul urges us to be prepared as soldiers to fight against the enemy. We are not fighting against men equal in strength to ourselves. We are fighting a much stronger foe, a supernatural enemy, one trained for six thousand years in methods to bring about our defeat.

If we are earnest about gaining the victory in this fight, then it may take "blood, toil, tears, and sweat" before it is achieved.

"[Only] those who would rather die than perform a wrong act . . . will be found faithful," we are told in *Messages to Young People*, page 74. It is possible we might have to shed our blood before this victory is gained.

Of toil and tears there will be plenty. We have to work hard in order to maintain our position near to Jesus. It takes effort to dress with the breastplate of righteousness, the girdle of truth, the helmet of salvation, and the sword of the Spirit, but without these we will surely lose the battle.

No one said it would be easy, but we do have the assurance that if we remain with Jesus and His truth, we will be victorious.

On the cross of Calvary the arms of Jesus were outstretched in a glorious sign of victory for you and me. Millions look to that sign and have hope. It says to us, "Though you may lose some battles, do not be discouraged. We will win the war."

VACCINATION OF THE UNIVERSE

Affliction shall not rise up the second time. Nahum 1:9.

Do you like injections? Of course not. Who does? If you had lived two hundred years ago you could have escaped trips to the doctor for "shots." But then, you might also have gotten bubonic plague, yellow fever, typhoid, rabies, diphtheria, or smallpox.

Dr. Edward Jenner, a physician in rural England in the late 1700s became interested in preventing smallpox. As he traveled around he noticed a relationship between that disease and cowpox. Dairymen and milkmaids often caught the milder sickness, from the cows. Dr. Jenner noticed, however, that such people never contracted the more serious smallpox.

To prove his theory, Dr. Jenner got permission from the parents of 8-year-old James Phipps to inoculate their healthy son. On May 14, 1796, the doctor made a small cut on the boy's skin and put pus from a cowpox sore into the wound. In a few days James developed one small sore and had a slight fever.

Six weeks later Dr. Jenner made another cut on James and gave him some pus from a smallpox patient. Nothing happened. James did not get smallpox. Dr. Jenner had been successful with the first vaccination. Today, because of widespread vaccination, smallpox is a very rare disease. Soon it may be completely gone.

God has done something like that with the sin problem in the universe. Long before this world was created, sin began with Lucifer in heaven. One third of the angels caught the "virus" of sin from Satan. From there it spread to Adam and Eve and since to all the inhabitants of Planet Earth.

Unfallen beings on other worlds have been watching the sin disease take its course in the lives of men and angels. One day soon, Satan and all who follow him will be destroyed. The disease of sin will never again mar the universe that God has made. The experience of the last six thousand years, including the sacrifice of Christ on the cross, will act as a giant vaccination for God's creation.

Praise God! The day is coming when no one will ever sin again. Evil will disappear never to return. Suffering and death will come to an end. Temptation and trouble will be no more. The world will once again be the happy, loving place God intended it to be.

MILESTONES

For none of us liveth to himself, and no man dieth to himself.
Romans 14:7.

The sun was not yet up the morning of May 15, 1764, when Thomas Wharton and Jacob Lewis met at Front and Market streets in Philadelphia. They inspected the wagonload of stones and checked their tools while they waited for the surveyor general of the province to show up.

The Philadelphia insurance company had decided to pay for putting milestones on the road from Philadelphia to Trenton. Mr. Lewis and Mr. Wharton would dig the necessary holes and plant the stones. The surveyor general would measure off the 5,280 feet between each stone. By the end of the day thirty-one stones had been planted marking off the distance between the two Colonial cities. The first milestones in the new world had been set out.

Although large reflecting signs have replaced milestones along the super highways of America and Europe, some countries still use stones to mark off the miles. Such stones are important, for they name your destination and give the distance you will have to travel to get there. Careful observance of the milestones will help you to reach your goal.

Have you ever thought of yourself as a milestone along the highway of life? The books you read, the places you go, and the things you eat will influence others. The music you play, the television programs you watch, and the jokes you tell will affect those around you. When people look at you, what do they see?

Your life is leading people closer to Christ or farther away from Him. A thoughtless word or action may start someone on the downward trail. A victory gained may inspire someone else to do the same. A life lived for Jesus will point others to the way of happiness.

Remember, there are only two ways for travelers in the journey of life. There is the broad way that leads to eternal destruction and the narrow way that leads to everlasting life. You are pointing in one direction or the other.

To which destination does your life point? Is it leading others to heaven or hell? If your friends and acquaintances were to follow your example would they be saved or lost? What kind of milestone are you?

THE LOST PEARLS

The kingdom of heaven is like unto a merchant man, seeking goodly pearls. Matthew 13:45.

When Mary, Queen of Scots, fled to England on May 16, 1568, she took with her a valuable string of black pearls given her by a cherished friend.

When Mary was beheaded a few years later, Elizabeth I, Queen of England, asked her private agents to find this necklace. Officials of the British Museum, Scotland Yard, and hundreds of private investigators tried in vain to locate it. For 350 years the whereabouts of those pearls remained a mystery.

Then one day two young American women, Lavinia and Lucy, of New Haven, Connecticut, were touring England. In the English town of Newhaven, they wandered into the dusty secondhand shop of Martin Lazenby.

"Do you have something small and cheap that we could take back to America as a gift for a friend?" Lavinia asked.

Looking around the cluttered room, Lazenby noticed a dirty string of beads hanging from a nail in the wall. Taking it down he offered it to them. "This isn't much, but it is small, and I can let you have it for a shilling."

Lucy bought the beads, thinking they might have possibilities if they were restrung and cleaned up a bit. The next day she took them to a jeweler in London, who promised to have them ready by the next morning.

When the girls returned, they were invited into the manager's office. There an official of the British Museum told them the story of the lost necklace. He said, "We have found the missing pearls. We will give you 25,000 dollars for them."

You can just imagine how Martin Lazenby, of the cluttered junk shop, felt when this news reached him! For years those beads had hung on his wall. He didn't know the value of the treasure he possessed.

How many of us today are making the same mistake? The Bible, a treasure of inestimable worth, is gathering dust in many of our homes. The promises of Scripture are like precious pearls to be gathered and worn near one's heart. Do you know the value of the treasure you possess? Take a second look at your pearls.

LET THEM LAUGH

Woe unto you that laugh now! for ye shall mourn and weep.
Luke 6:25.

Today is the birthday of Edward Jenner, the doctor who discovered that smallpox could be prevented by vaccination.

Dr. Jenner realized that millions of lives could be saved if others knew about his discovery, so he wrote a scientific report of his experiments and presented it to the president of the Royal Society of London.

"We are doing you a favor by *not* publishing your paper," the president wrote back. "You will only expose yourself to ridicule if you print such a paper."

"They can ridicule me if they like," Dr. Jenner said. "I know that what I have written is true. I will print the paper myself."

Although he was at first scorned in his own country, scientists in other countries did not laugh. Physicians in France began to vaccinate immediately. Catherine the Great of Russia instructed her doctors to vaccinate everyone. Napoleon ordered all of his soldiers to be inoculated. In the United States, President Thomas Jefferson had his whole family vaccinated.

Dr. Jenner possessed the quality of character that Christian youth need today, that ability to hold on to what you know is right regardless of what others say. You may be ridiculed for keeping God's Sabbath day holy and for believing the Word of God in this modern scientific age. You may be scorned because you do not take part in worldly amusements. You may be laughed at because you believe that God answers prayer.

Let them laugh, for one day the tables will be turned. The time is coming when those who mock you now will wish that they had followed you. They will cry for the rocks and the mountains to hide them from the face of Jesus whom they will see coming in the clouds of heaven.

Among those who will weep in that day will be many who laughed at Jesus. They found it amusing that He had done so much for others and yet would not save Himself. Jesus let them laugh because He was determined to die that we might live. Surely we can endure a little ridicule for His sake now.

GOD'S SECRET

But of that day and hour knoweth no man, no, not the angels of heaven, but my Father only. Matthew 24:36.

In 1986, Halley's comet will return after an absence of about seventy-six years. It is a sight seen usually only once in a lifetime. This spectacular display was last seen in 1910, when your great-grandparents were young.

On May 18 of that year Halley's comet was observed passing over the sun, frightening hundreds of thousands of people who believed it signaled the end of the world. Thousands sought the safety of churches. Others camped in cyclone cellars, hoping to escape the destruction.

The New York *World* reported: "New York is keyed up to a high pitch of expectancy at the prospect of being sprinkled with star dust and the possibility of being smothered with noxious gases or bombarded with meteorites."

When the day was over people came out of hiding and went about their normal duties. Like so many other predictions of the end of the world, it was a false alarm.

In the year A.D. 1000 multitudes in Europe expected Christ to come and hundreds of pilgrims went to the Holy Land to await His return. In 1524, a German preacher, Mr. Stoeffler, predicted that the Lord would send a flood to end the world that year. His followers built rafts and arks and waited for the end that did not come.

In 1844, followers of William Miller preached that Christ would come on October 22, but again people were disappointed. Since then many other dates have been set. In the 1960s some were proclaiming that Christ would come before 1975. Now there are those who declare the end is coming in the year 2000. The day is to be May 5 of that year.

Do not be deceived by such predictions. Christ is coming soon, there is no doubt about that. The signs all tell us the world cannot last much longer. However, we do not know *when* He will come. The Bible tells us that nobody—neither the astronomers, the preachers, nor the world leaders—knows when the world will come to an end. That is a secret known only to God. He has kept such information from even the angels in heaven.

The important thing for you and me is to be ready today and every day.

THE DARK DAY

Immediately after the tribulation of those days shall the sun be darkened, and the moon shall not give her light. Matthew 24:29.

The disciples had heard Jesus preach about the end of the world, but He had not told them when it would be. They wanted to find out, and went in search of Him. They found Jesus on the Mount of Olives and, gathering around Him they asked, "How will we know when the time has come?"

Carefully Jesus explained about the troubles that His followers would face. Then he said, "Immediately after the tribulation of those days shall the sun be darkened, and the moon shall not give her light."

It happened just as Jesus predicted. For several hundred years Christians were persecuted. Many who stood true to God's Word were thrown into prison. Some were burned at the stake. Others had to hide in the mountains and caves of the earth.

Just as this period of great trouble was coming to an end, the signs that God had promised began to appear. On May 19, 1780, the sun was darkened and the moon did not give its light.

A Boston newspaper reported that "cocks crowed in answer to one another as they commonly do in the night: Woodcocks, which are night birds, whistled as they do *only* in the dark: Frogs peeped—In short, there was the appearance of midnight at noonday."

"A sheet of white paper, held within a few inches of the eyes, was equally invisible with the blackest velvet," wrote Samuel Tenney.

A report by Samuel Stearns said that "Cows left their pastures and plodded homeward to be milked. Birds and barnyard fowls sought their perches and dropped their heads in sleep. Dogs whined and put tails between their legs. People spoke in hushed voices. They lighted candles in the houses, and as the blackness grew deeper toward noon great numbers of them fell upon their knees at home or in churches and sent up fervent prayers."

From that day to this no satisfactory explanation has been found for that dark day. Jesus had promised that it would happen and it did. The dark day of May 19, 1780, is one of the signs that Jesus is coming soon.

A PROBLEM OF WEIGHT

Let us lay aside every weight, and the sin which doth so easily beset us, and let us run with patience the race that is set before us. Hebrews 12:1.

At 7:40 A.M. on May 20, 1927, a tall, lean young man walked across muddy Roosevelt Field outside of New York and climbed into a tiny monoplane called the *Spirit of St. Louis*. Charles A. Lindbergh was planning to fly alone nonstop across the Atlantic Ocean and win the coveted $25,000 prize.

Four men had already died in the attempt. Two others were missing. The problem was one of weight. How could they carry enough fuel? The *Spirit of St. Louis* held 451 gallons of gasoline and twenty gallons of oil. In order to make room for so much fuel, every unnecessary gadget was stripped from the plane. Even the gas gauges were removed.

Charles Lindbergh ripped out spare pages from his notebook and discarded the sections of charts he would not need. He had special flight boots that were several ounces lighter than normal. He did not take a radio, because without it he could carry ninety pounds more gasoline. The parachute was left behind because it was twenty pounds he could not afford.

A stamp collector offered him 1,000 dollars if he would carry one pound of letters to Paris. Lindbergh refused, because that pound might be the difference between life and death.

Thirty-three and one-half hours after takeoff, the *Spirit of St. Louis* touched down on Le Bourget Field near Paris, where huge crowds greeted Lindbergh's arrival. Where others failed, Charles A. Lindbergh succeeded because he solved the problem of weight.

You and I also have a flight to make and a goal to reach. We are in a race and whether we win or lose will depend on whether we have gotten rid of the unnecessary weight in our lives.

Some of us need to get rid of friends who are leading us in the wrong direction. There are bad habits we need to discard and words we must stop using. Might it be books or a radio that we need to dump? Perhaps certain records should be left behind. Old grudges will have to go, as will gossip and lies. There will be no room for pride and selfishness.

Whatever is weighing you down, get rid of it so that you might go on with confidence to win the prize of eternal life.

CHAIN REACTION

And sin, when it is finished, bringeth forth death. James 1:15.

Ordinary uranium is quite harmless. Once it has gone through certain processes it becomes what is known as enriched uranium. Assemble enough of this and a chain reaction will automatically take place, resulting in an explosion.

Forty years ago scientists did not know much about this process so it was necessary to experiment. Louis Slotin was in charge of the testing.

Louis set up a table with a rack. On the rack he placed two half spheres of uranium. In itself, neither had enough mass to cause a chain reaction. Then very slowly, using a screwdriver, he would push the two pieces of material together and watch the reaction build up. Just before the mass was ready to explode, he would push the two pieces apart. Louis felt sure he could control the experiment. He did it at least fifty times without incident.

Then on the afternoon of May 21, 1946, something went wrong. His hand slipped, and the two pieces of uranium were pushed dangerously close together. Hurling himself forward, Louis tore the two half spheres apart with his bare hands before the explosion could occur. He was then rushed to the hospital, where he died nine days later from radiation.

Sin is like uranium. It often appears quite harmless, and unsuspecting youth do not realize the powerful potential for death locked up inside. Somewhat like scientists in a laboratory, they play around with sin.

A young person may say, "I'll go to the movies, but only good ones. I'll drink, but only a little with friends. I'll take a few drugs just for fun. I can manage. I am in control."

Then comes the realization that he or she has lost control. Too late comes the understanding that a chain reaction has been set up that will end in eternal death.

Is there no hope for such a one? Is there not some way to stop the process? Yes, but the person himself cannot do it. Jesus Christ is the only one who can break the deadly power of sin. He died on Calvary's cross for this purpose. Will you claim Him as your Saviour today?

TSUNAMI

And the world passeth away, and the lust thereof: but he that doeth the will of God abideth for ever. 1 John 2:17.

Have you ever heard of a tsunami? These are big tidal waves caused by explosions under water. From the center of the blast waves move out in ever-widening circles. At least one of these has occurred every year since 1800. Approximately every 10 years a severe tsunami causes great damage.

The year 1960 was one of those years. On May 22 an earthquake was recorded off the western coast of South America, causing huge tidal waves to begin moving out across the Pacific, reaching as far as New Zealand and Japan. Traveling at a speed of forty-five miles per hour, thirty-foot waves exerted forty-nine tons of pressure on every square yard of beach they hit.

In Hilo, Hawaii, $20 million worth of damage was done when the tsunami broke over the sea wall and hit the town. Two hundred and thirty buildings collapsed under the power of the waves. Sixty-one people were killed. Only solid rock remained unharmed.

Perhaps Ellen White had such a picture in mind when she wrote: "Worldly influences, like the waves of the sea, beat against the followers of Christ to sweep them away from the true principles of the meekness and grace of Christ; but they are to stand as firm as a rock to principle. It will require moral courage to do this, and those whose souls are not riveted to the eternal Rock will be swept away by the worldly current."—*Fundamentals of Christian Education,* pp. 288, 289.

Newspapers, magazines, books, television, radio, and billboards pour out a continual flood of propaganda upholding the fashions and practices of the world. It seems that everybody is doing the things we cannot. If we are not careful the tidal waves of worldly influence will bear down upon us with tsunami force, destroying our determination to follow Christ and taking us out into the main stream of worldly life and pleasure.

It is not easy to stand up under such strong pressures, but we must if we would not be destroyed with the world. Make sure today that your life is hid with Christ in God so that you can remain true to principle, like the mighty rocks that remain unchanged by the waves beating against them.

BORN BLIND

Jesus answered, Neither hath this man sinned, nor his parents: but that the works of God should be made manifest in him. John 9:3.

May 23, 1945, was a black day for the Krents family. That Wednesday Mrs. Krents wrote in 8-month-old Harold's baby book: "We have just returned from the eye specialist in Boston. My baby is blind."

In spite of his handicap Harold learned to type, play football, and ride a bicycle. He played second violin in the high school orchestra and was president of the student council. He was accepted in Harvard Law school and did well. Then one month before graduation a day came when everything seemed to go wrong.

Discouraged, Harold went to the chapel to pray. "Why me?" he cried in his anguish. "Why did this have to happen to me?"

The organ began to play softly and Harold sobbed as he thought about his sightless future.

"Suddenly," Harold said, "I was aware that God was holding my hand and a sense of peace warmed me."

From that moment on he knew that God was not punishing him for anything he or anyone else had done. He realized that God had a purpose for his life. He knew that the One who had been with him all of his dark days would continue to guide and help him.

Of course, God can do anything. He could heal the blind man who sat by the wayside in the Bible story, and He did. He could also heal Harold Krents, but He did not. With Harold, as with the apostle Paul, God chose rather to make His works manifest by giving him courage to rise above his handicap.

Harold went on to graduate from Harvard. He passed the bar examination and was employed by a Washington law firm. He became happily married to the girl who was his reader during law school days. His example has done much to encourage others who have to live with handicaps. For Harold, life definitely does have meaning and purpose.

Do you have a handicap or problem in your life? Perhaps God is going to use that very thing to make His works manifest before the world. Ask Him to use you and your handicap for His glory today.

BLESSED ASSURANCE

And hereby we know that we are of the truth, and shall assure our hearts before him. 1 John 3:19.

John had been brought up in a Christian home, but he did not have assurance in his heart that he was a child of God. He was a preacher's son, but he did not know that his sins were forgiven. He tried hard to be good, but failed so many times. He envied the quiet assurance of his Moravian friends who believed the promises and knew that they were accepted by God.

On the morning of May 24, 1738, John Wesley prayed earnestly for faith to believe that God had accepted him. Then he opened his Bible and read: "Whereby are given unto us exceeding great and precious promises: that by these ye might be partakers of the divine nature" (2 Peter 1:4). Somehow he must believe that those promises were for him. Turning to the Bible again, he opened it to the text: "Thou art not far from the kingdom of God" (Mark 12:34).

All that day God continued to speak to John. In the afternoon a choir anthem touched his heart with words from Psalm 130: "Let Israel hope in the Lord: for with the Lord there is mercy, and with him is plenteous redemption" (verse 7).

That evening John attended a meeting where someone read an article by Martin Luther about righteousness by faith. It told how we are saved, not by what we do, but by what Christ has done for us.

"About a quarter before nine, while he was describing the change which God works in the heart through faith in Christ, I felt my heart strangely warmed," wrote John Wesley about that night. "I felt I did trust in Christ, Christ alone, for salvation; and an assurance was given me, that He had taken away *my* sins, even *mine,* and saved *me* from the law of sin and death."

It was as if a great load had been lifted from his shoulders. What a joy to know for sure that he was a child of God!

Do you have that assurance today? Can you sing with joy, "Blessed assurance, Jesus is mine"? Do you know for sure that God loves you and has forgiven your sins?

If not, go to Jesus now and ask Him for that peace. He does love you! He died for you. He will surely accept you, for He has promised: "Him that cometh to me I will in no wise cast out" (John 6:37).

THE STRANGEST NAVY

And the Lord said unto him, What is that in thine hand?
Exodus 4:2.

By May 25, 1940, the British Army fighting in France had retreated to the beaches of Dunkirk. Slowly the enemy was closing in. With their backs to the sea, the English could retreat no further. Thousands of soldiers thought their end had come.

Then the miracle of the little boats began. The word was spread in England that small boats were needed to evacuate soldiers.

Within hours the strangest navy in history was formed. Pleasure boats, fishing craft, yachts, tugs, and barges poured out of the rivers and harbors of England. Shrimp catchers, ferries, rowboats, and motorboats all headed for Dunkirk. Some one thousand small craft of all descriptions went to the rescue, manned by bankers, dentists, fishermen, young and old.

Thankful soldiers waded into the English Channel to meet them the next day. Those small boats were able to rescue more than 350,000 men.

What if some of the people had said, "My boat is very small. I will stay at home." Or what if others had thought, Of what use is my old rowboat. It goes so slow. Fortunately for the stranded soldiers, the people of England decided to use whatever they had to accomplish the task.

God often uses small things to accomplish His purposes, too. When, at the burning bush, Moses expressed his fear of failure, the Lord said to him, "What is that in thine hand?" It was only a small rod, just a stick of wood, but the Lord promised to use it to His glory.

Because Moses was willing, God used that small stick to work miracles. It became a serpent and swallowed the rods of the Egyptian magicians. Waved over the land of Egypt it brought the ten plagues. When the rod was lifted above the Red Sea, the waters parted. Hit against the rock, it was used by God to bring forth water.

What do you have in your hand? A cup of cold water, a guitar, or a bicycle can be used of God. It may be only a pencil, but God can use it. Whatever you have, however small it may be, God can use it today to help rescue men and women besieged by the enemy of souls.

THE MYSTERY MAN OF EUROPE

That being justified by his grace, we should be made heirs according to the hope of eternal life. Titus 3:7.

On this day in 1828, a 17-year-old boy stumbled into Nuremburg, Germany. As if in a daze he wandered along the streets until he was spotted by a shoemaker, George Weichman.

"Can I help you?" the shoemaker asked. "Where are you going?"

The boy did not know where he was going, nor where he had come from. He could not speak German. All he knew was his name, Kasper Hausman. A note he carried said he had been abandoned as a baby and now he wanted to be a soldier. He knew nothing of such common things as fire, time, and money.

Under the care of a teacher, Kasper learned to speak. Then he told what he remembered of his life. From the earliest time he could remember, he had been kept in a room six feet long, four feet wide, and five feet high. It had a dirt floor and two closed windows. He had slept on a pile of straw and he had been fed only a meager diet.

Kasper became known as the Mystery Man of Europe. Many tried to trace his relatives. Some believed that he was of royal birth and began gathering facts to prove it. However, before his identity could be established, Kasper was killed while walking in the park. Evidently someone knew who he was and did not want his identity known.

Was Kasper a prince? Was he heir to a fortune or throne? I don't know, but I do know that you are. Yes, you are a prince or a princess, an heir to a palace, a robe, and a crown. Jesus died on Calvary's cross that you might be called a child of the heavenly King. He is now in heaven getting things ready for you to enjoy.

However, Satan will do his best to keep you ignorant of who you really are. He does not want you to claim your inheritance. He wants to keep you locked up in the prison house of sin so that you might never know the honor and happiness that should be yours as a son or daughter of God. He will stop at nothing to hide your true identity. He would rather see you dead, than see you claim your eternal inheritance.

Only Jesus can set you free. Call on Him today. The inheritance of eternal life can be yours.

154

THE STOLEN SUITCASES

Whither shall I go from thy spirit? or whither shall I flee from thy presence? Psalm 139:7.

Where can we go that God cannot reach us? The answer, of course, is nowhere; for God is everywhere present.

We may try, like Jonah, to run away; but, remember, God found him even in the belly of a big fish. For fear of Jezebel, Elijah hid in a cave; but God found him there. Read all of Psalm 139 and you will discover that God can reach us anywhere, under the most unusual circumstances.

Take for instance the story of Jim Lacey. God reached him during a robbery. One Saturday night Jim left home with a chisel, intent on stealing the contents of some car. On Fifty-seventh Street he found an auto with the ventilator window ajar. In a matter of minutes he had opened the door and removed two suitcases.

Once inside his dingy basement room, Jim opened the luggage and found clothes and stacks of music. He immediately pawned the clothes for $140. Back in his room he began stuffing the music into bags for disposal.

Then it was that Jim saw the sheet music for a song he remembered singing in church school. In his mind he could hear again the choir and the organ background. Memories flooded back: church, Bible stories, prayer. It was all so foreign to the life he was now living.

Laying aside that piece of music he picked up another and read the words: "Everyone must have a friend to tell his troubles to; And I found mine, O dearest Lord, My truest friend is You."

That night Jim Lacey lay awake, remembering. The conviction came that God was even now calling him to a better life. Jim never stole again. He got a job and began attending church. He wrote a letter to Alfonso D'Artega, the conductor whose suitcases he had stolen, asking his forgiveness. He began saving money to repay what he had taken.

On May 27, 1954, Jim Lacey sat in Carnegie Hall watching Mr. D'Artega conduct the orchestra. For the first time he saw the man whose suitcases had led him back to God. Jim's heart was filled with gratitude that God had found him, even in the midst of a robbery.

SELF-CONFIDENCE

We should not trust in ourselves, but in God. 2 Corinthians 1:9.

Peter's experience of walking on the water is an example of what can happen when someone has too much confidence in his own ability. Self-confidence caused Peter to look to himself rather than to Jesus, and he nearly drowned.

Self-confidence leads us to think we know everything and no one should tell us what to do. Tragedies often occur because someone trusted his own wisdom rather than seeking help from a more experienced person.

A case in point is what happened the night of May 28/29, 1914, on the St. Lawrence River. The *Empress of Ireland* was headed downstream with 1,477 people on board. Coming up the river was the Norwegian collier *Storstad*. The two ships exchanged whistle signals just before a dense fog settled between them.

When the fog cleared a few minutes later, horrified passengers on the *Empress* saw the steel-clad bow of the Norwegian ship coming straight for their starboard. A warning was sounded, but it was too late. Within fifteen minutes the *Empress* sank, taking with it 1,014 lives.

The fault was with the Norwegian ship. Her first officer, Alfred Toftenes, was inexperienced. He should have called the ship's captain to the bridge at the first sign of fog. He needed advice from one who had been through such problems before. Instead, trusting his own judgment, he changed course and pushed full steam into the other ship.

Many youth today are like that ship's officer. They want to be their own captain. They want to do their own thing, to be in control. Advice of parents and teachers is not sought.

As Ellen White wrote, "Many of our youth suffer shipwreck in the dangerous voyage of life, because they are self-confident and presumptuous."

Not only should we seek the advice of our elders, we also need heavenly wisdom to guide us through the dangerous waters of life. The fog is there and we cannot trust ourselves. We need the Captain. Will you not ask Jesus to come to the bridge of your ship today? He will see you safely through.

CLIMB THE HIGHEST MOUNTAIN

With God all things are possible. Matthew 19:26.

At 11:30 in the morning of May 29, 1953, Edmund Hillary, of New Zealand, and Tenzing Norgay, a Nepalese tribesman, stood on the top of the world. For the first time man had reached the summit of 29,028-foot Mount Everest, the world's highest mountain.

After pausing a few moments to enjoy the beauty of the white-capped peaks spread out beneath him, Mr. Hillary took a camera from inside his shirt and photographed the scene. He also snapped a picture of Tenzing waving his ice ax, on which were strung the flags of the United Nations, Great Britain, Nepal, and India. Fifteen minutes later the two men started down.

Two months of struggle and hardship preceded that moment of triumph. Several men had died attempting to scale Everest, where avalanches, crevasses, strong winds, soft snow, fierce cold, and high altitude combine to make the climb almost impossible.

No, it was not an easy thing they had done. The endurance of Hillary and Norgay was tested to the limit. Many times they became so exhausted that they questioned whether to give up or continue their push to the top.

Life is a lot like a mountain. Great men and women are those who struggle on in spite of difficulties and reach the top. Step by step they overcome each problem. Inch by inch they move ahead. They are willing to attempt the impossible.

What difficulties are you facing in your upward climb of life?

Some of the dangers you may encounter are crevasses of sin and avalanches of temptation. These can be avoided by the careful climber. There are icy winds of ridicule and persecution. It takes courage to press on in spite of the cruel things people say about us.

Physical handicaps, loneliness, difficult family situations, poverty, and past failures all may be obstacles on our way to the top. Praise God, each of these can be overcome with His help. Step by step we can reach our goal.

With God all things are possible. With His help you can climb the highest mountain.

FAITHFUL UNTO DEATH

Be thou faithful unto death, and I will give thee a crown of life. Revelation 2:10.

Six hundred years ago Bibles were written in Latin and chained to monastery walls. Ordinary people were forbidden to read the Scriptures, and to study and proclaim the sacred teachings often brought imprisonment and death.

In Bohemia, Huss and Jerome boldly taught the Bible. They would not accept what the pope said about religious matters unless it agreed with God's Word. For this, Huss was put to death by burning at the stake and Jerome was put in prison.

Once when Jerome was weak and sick he lost courage and said that the church was right in condemning Huss. Afterward, alone in his cell, he was unhappy with what he had done. He knew that he had denied his Lord and determined that if given another chance he would stand up for the truth.

After a year in prison Jerome was again brought to trial. "I was wrong in condemning Huss," he said.

"Take that back," his friends urged, "or you will surely be put to death."

"Prove to me from the Bible that I am wrong," he said.

"Heretic!" the people cried. "To the flames! To the flames!"

On May 30, 1416, Jerome was taken to the very spot in Constance where Huss had been killed. He was tied to an upright stake around which wood and kindling were arranged.

When the executioner went behind him to light the fire, Jerome said, "Come forward boldly; apply the fire before my face. Had I been afraid, I should not be here."

As the flames licked at his feet he sang a hymn. His last words before the smoke choked him were a prayer, "Lord, Almighty Father, have pity on me, and pardon my sins; for Thou knowest that I have always loved Thy truth."

The crowd stood amazed at the martyr's courage. What was it in the Bible that inspired men to die in its defense? Many who watched Jerome burn that day went home to search the Scriptures. Some were later converted to the truth for which he laid down his life.

Whether you are called upon to die for your faith or to live for it, be faithful, and you, too, will receive a crown of life.

OUR TASK

And this gospel of the kingdom shall be preached in all the world for a witness unto all nations; and then shall the end come. Matthew 24:14.

Nearly two hundred years ago a meeting of ministers was about to end in an English village. The leader said, "We have covered our agenda. Is there anything else to discuss?"

William Carey, a shoemaker-turned-preacher, stood up.

"Yes, Brother Carey?" the leader questioned.

"Sir, Jesus said, 'Go ye into all the world and preach the gospel to every creature.' Let's talk about these words of His. Don't you believe that He was telling His disciples and us as well, to preach the gospel in every country on earth? We must send missionaries to the countries that do not have the Bible."

"Sit down, young man," the leader interrupted. "If God wants to convert the heathen, He will do it without our help. This meeting is adjourned."

William Carey was disappointed but not discouraged. He wrote a tract expressing his concern for the thousands who had never heard about Jesus.

On May 31, 1792, Carey was asked to be the speaker at another ministerial meeting. This was held in the back parlor of a cottage in Kettering, England. He concluded with the words, "Christ said, 'Ye are my witnesses!' He has commissioned us to carry His message of salvation to every creature under heaven. There are thousands, yea millions who live and die in far-off countries without Christ . . . without hope. God is faithful. He will help us to do this work for Him. We must expect great things from God. We must attempt great things for God."

The men were about ready to leave when Andrew Fuller arose and said: "I believe that God expects us to respond to the message we have heard today. God has impressed me that now is the time to act. Please, brethren, let us consider what we can do to help the lost."

That day the first missionary society was organized and later, William Carey was sent to India as its first missionary.

Our task today is the same as it was then. There are yet millions who have never heard about Jesus. Who will tell them? Will you?

DON'T GIVE UP THE SHIP

Behold, I come quickly: hold that fast which thou hast, that no man take thy crown. Revelation 3:11.

Capt. James Lawrence lay dying on the deck of the American frigate *Chesapeake*. Moments before, on June 1, 1813, the captain had been hit by a bullet fired from the British ship *Shannon*. Battle-weary sailors made him as comfortable as they could on the rough wooden floor. Summoning his remaining strength, Captain Lawrence looked into their faces and said, "Don't give up the ship!"

Those words electrified the men and gave them courage to fight on. That brief sentence became the watchword of the United States Navy, bringing courage to faint hearts in many battles. When men might have run from enemy fire, they have been held to their post of duty by those words, "Don't give up the ship!"

During World War II, a group of soldiers became separated from the main body of troops. Surrounded by the enemy, without food or water, some felt they must surrender. It was then that a plane flew over dropping packages of food and canteens of water. On one of the packages was scribbled a portion of that message from Captain Lawrence: "Don't give up!" The soldiers held on and were rescued in a few days.

Victory is often just around the corner from defeat. Success is the other side of failure. It is when the battle is roughest that we must hold on. Victory will come.

"What's the use of trying?" Satan whispers. "Defeat is certain. Can't you see I'm going to win? See how small your church is. You cannot hope for victory. Abandon your ship. Join my side. This is where the action is."

Mrs. White once had a dream about a man who faced a similar temptation. It seemed to her that he was on a boat that was being battered by the enemy and tossed by the waves. He said, "I shall get off; this vessel is going down." But the captain said to him, "No, this vessel sails into the harbor. She will never go down."

In today's verse Jesus is telling us: "Don't give up the ship! Stay in the church. Keep your faith. I am coming. Hold on! Fight on! Victory will be yours!"

160

ALMOST . . . BUT LOST!

Then Agrippa said unto Paul, Almost thou persuadest me to be a Christian. Acts 26:28.

Amelia Earhart, woman aviator, was nearly home. Already she had flown 22,000 miles on her globe-circling trip, making thirty stops in nineteen countries. Now she was in New Guinea and as soon as the weather cleared she would head home to the United States, with a short stop at Howland Island. Soon she would be greeted by cheering crowds honoring her as the first woman to fly around the world.

In the very early morning hours of June 2, 1937, Amelia took off from New Guinea. At two-forty-five a.m. she made contact with a United States coast guard ship. At six-fifteen she asked for help in getting her bearings. At seven-forty-two she said: "We cannot see you. Gas is running low. Unable to reach you by radio. We are flying at altitude 1,000 feet."

The weather became worse. Visibility was zero. At eight-forty-five Amelia gave her last message: "We are running north and south."

Amelia Earhart was almost home; however, almost was not enough to save her life. She was almost home, but lost.

When Jesus comes and the books of record are opened we will be able to read the story of many lives about whom it can be said, "Almost, . . . but lost."

King Agrippa: Almost persuaded to be a Christian, . . . but lost.

Bud: Almost gave his heart to the Lord during a Week of Prayer, . . . but lost.

Judy: Surrendered almost everything, . . . but lost.

Speaking of those who do not make an entire surrender of their lives to Jesus Christ, Ellen White says, "Almost Christians, yet not fully Christians, they seem near the kingdom of heaven, but they cannot enter there. Almost but not wholly saved, means to be not almost but wholly lost."—*Christ's Object Lessons,* p. 118.

"'Almost' cannot avail, 'Almost' is but to fail!
Sad, sad the bitter wail, 'Almost—but lost!'"

These words are part of a hymn written by P. P. Bliss. It is number 228 in *The Church Hymnal.* Why not take a few minutes to sing the entire song?

STAYING THROUGH

I have finished the work which thou gavest me to do. John 17:4.

Nineteen-forty. The retreat from Dunkirk was nearly finished. For more than a week little boats of every description had been coming to the beaches to pick up British soldiers.

Planes droned overhead. Machine guns sputtered nearby and shells exploded all around. Men waded into the pounding surf, trying to reach the evacuation boats.

In the midst of all this two British army nurses went about their duties unmindful of the danger, they worked over the wounded soldiers brought to them, giving medicine, applying bandages, and speaking words of hope.

"Into a boat, you two," an officer commanded.

To disobey a commanding officer was a serious offense, but how could these dedicated nurses leave so many men yet unattended? Without a look at the boat that had come to rescue them, the two young women shook their heads and continued to work.

"We are staying through," one of them said. Those two brave nurses did not leave the battlefield until every soldier in their care was either dead or on a boat to England.

It is very easy to begin a task, but not so easy to finish it, particularly if the going is rough. Look around your house and see how many half-finished jobs you can locate. Perhaps in a bottom drawer there is a dress someone cut out weeks ago but never finished. Maybe there is a half-completed airplane model on some shelf or a partly done painting gathering dust. Uncompleted class projects, unfinished poems, and half-mowed yards all reveal a weakness common to many of us.

Ask God to give you the ability to endure to the end of a task. Ask Him to help you persevere until your jobs are done. Ask Him to help you finish whatever you start.

If you learn perseverance in the small tasks you have to do each day, when you tackle the big jobs of life, you will be able to see them through just as those nurses did on the beach at Dunkirk.

Strive to be like Jesus, who was able to say at the end of His life on earth, "I have finished the work."

ALONE ON THE ATLANTIC

What is man, that thou art mindful of him? and the son of man, that thou visitest him? Psalm 8:4.

The weather was fair and the sea calm on the late afternoon of June 4, 1966, as a twenty-foot-long dory pulled away from Cape Cod. The two occupants, John Ridgeway and Chay Blyth, were setting out to row their boat to England.

Some of the dangers they expected to encounter were whales, sharks, and freighters. It would be necessary for one of them to be awake at all times. While one slept the other rowed. Before long their muscles were sore and their hands were blistered. They weathered two hurricanes, during which it seemd as if the sea was one giant roller coaster.

Alone on the vast expanse of the Atlantic Ocean with an immense sky above them, the men had time to reflect on the message of the plaque nailed to the wall of their boat: "Oh, God, Thy sea is so great and my boat is so small."

Chay wrote in his log book: "I pray quite a lot now."

At first John refused to pray. He had not bothered with God when things were going well, and now that they were having to struggle for their lives, he was too proud to pray. Eventually, John admitted that without help they would not reach England, for storms had delayed their progress and taken them off course. Supplies were nearly exhausted. In the face of all this, he, too, began to pray.

A British trawler stopped and offered supplies. "It is almost as if some divine hand had provided the conditions to test us and then to guide us home," John wrote.

Some of us are like John and Chay. We think we can make a go of things on our own. You may be young and strong and don't feel the need of God. If such is the case, it may be good to be put into a position where you cannot cope. Sometimes we need to realize how small and insignificant we really are.

How small is man in the great universe of God! Isn't it amazing that God cares about us? He is delighted when we realize our need of Him. He wants us to come to Him with our problems large and small.

God will hear our sincere cries for help, just as He did those of Chay and John. The wonder is that we go to Him so little, that we struggle so much alone.

163

VISION FOR FITNESS

Know ye not that ye are the temple of God, and that the Spirit of God dwelleth in you? 1 Corinthians 3:16.

As the sun set on Friday, June 5, 1863, a dozen or so people gathered for worship in the home of A. Hilliard in Otsego, Michigan. Someone read a text from Scripture and Ellen White was asked to pray.

Ellen prayed particularly for her husband, who was very depressed because of ill health. She moved closer to him and placed her hands on his shoulders. As she did so, she was taken off in vision. God's glory seemed to surround the company and Elder White's depression vanished. The vision continued for forty-five minutes.

What Ellen had seen was a plan for fitness. It was all so new, so different from the way the people were living, that she could not tell them that day. Little by little she wrote the message out.

The vision began with a scene from the Garden of Eden where Ellen saw Adam and Eve in their perfection. Then she viewed the decline of the human race to the place where everyone seemed to be sick, and most people didn't expect to live beyond 40 years of age. This, she learned, was partly a result of the addition of meat to the human diet.

Ellen spoke of the harmful effects of alcohol, tobacco, tea, coffee, spices, rich desserts, and drugs. She spoke against the evils of overeating and overworking. She said that it is unwise to eat between meals and just before going to bed.

Besides encouraging people to overcome bad habits, she spoke of forming good ones such as drinking lots of water, exercising in the fresh air, allowing sunlight into the home, and taking a daily bath.

Today we have abundant scientific proof that what God showed Mrs. White is true, but one hundred years ago Adventists simply took it by faith and began to put the principles into practice.

As the believers did so, their health greatly improved. When they felt well they could better understand the truths of the Bible and could work harder in preaching God's message. Adventists began to understand that their bodies were indeed temples in which the Holy Spirit wanted to dwell.

RAINBOWS IN THE RAIN

Nor height, nor depth, nor any other creature, shall be able to separate us from the love of God, which is in Christ Jesus our Lord. Romans 8:39.

Although George Matheson was blind, with the help of his devoted sisters and friends, he became a successful preacher. He had hoped to marry and have a family, but the girl he loved turned him down because of his blindness. Broken-hearted, he never tried to win anyone else.

Perhaps it was the thought of what he was missing in not having a wife that was bothering George Matheson on his sister's wedding day, June 6, 1882. She begged him to attend, but he would not go.

At the time of the service, George sat alone in his house near the sea in western Scotland and thought about his life. He remembered the shock of losing his sight at the age of 18. He must have thought of the struggles to finish his education and the terrible pain of losing the girl he loved. He knew she had loved him; why then had she let go of that love and turned her back on him?

Suddenly, as if sent as a gift from God, the words of a poem came into his mind. Within five minutes he had written them down just as you will find them in Number 145 of *The Church Hymnal.*

In the poem, George calls Christ the Love that would not let him go, the Light that followed him, and the Joy that brought relief from pain. He speaks of opening up his heart to Christ and being able to trace "the rainbow through the rain." If you don't know "O Love That Wilt Not Let Me Go" you should learn it today. Perhaps someday it will be a comfort to you as it has been to many people during the past one hundred years.

You never know when a friend will turn his back or when someone dear and precious may die. Many things can happen to take love away from your life.

When that happens you will feel as if the bottom has dropped out of everything. The pain is so great that you wonder how you can possibly go on living.

At such a time you can find in Jesus the love, light, and joy that you will need to survive. He will never let you go. He will help you find the rainbows in the rain.

GOD'S FLAG

Moreover also I gave them my sabbaths, to be a sign between me and them, that they might know that I am the Lord that sanctify them. Ezekiel 20:12.

What is a flag? A piece of colored cloth? Yes, but it is more than that.

Take some red, white, and blue pieces of material and stitch them together into the Stars and Stripes and Americans everywhere feel a special thrill when they see the familiar colors waving in the breeze. Make those same pieces into the Union Jack and Britishers will respond with cheers. Sew them into three vertical bars and you have the Tricolor for which Frenchmen will give their lives.

In past wars flags were important. The flag was a sign of loyalty to a particular government.

During the American Civil War a certain captain was sent to New Orleans to raise up the United States flag in a prominent place. As soon as the soldiers were gone, William Bruce Mumford, a Southern sympathizer, tore the flag from its post.

A few days later when the general came with two thousand troops to take over St. Charles Hotel, William Mumford was among the crowd that gathered there.

Loudly Mumford boasted of his exploit in tearing down the United States flag. He called it "the old rag of the United States." Because of his actions, he was called to trial on June 7, 1862, and publicly hanged for treason.

The way you treat your flag is important. It shows whether or not you are loyal to your country.

God, too, has a flag. It is the Sabbath. Keeping the Sabbath holy is the sign that we are loyal to Him and that He is protecting and helping us.

The false Sabbath is Satan's flag. Before Jesus comes, all the world will line up under one of these flags, Sabbath or Sunday. It will make a big difference which flag you fly. It will show where your loyalty lies.

Where you will stand in that last great conflict depends a lot on how you treat God's flag now. Do you treasure the Sabbath, or do you dishonor it by your actions? Do you fly your flag proudly? By so doing, you show your loyalty to God every week.

THE BIBLE IN THE PILLOW

Thy words were found, and I did eat them; and thy word was unto me the joy and rejoicing of mine heart. Jeremiah 15:16.

The Judsons were sitting down to supper the evening of June 8, 1824, when Burmese soldiers walked into their home and arrested them. Adoniram Judson persuaded them to release his wife, Ann, but he was bound with rope and dragged through the streets of Ava to the filthy prison.

Meanwhile, Ann ran about the house destroying letters and papers that might be used against her husband. The Judsons' most precious possession was the translation of the Bible into Burmese that Adoniram had been working on for more than ten years. Somehow she must save it. Wrapping it carefully, she buried it in the corner of the garden.

Soon afterward the soldiers came back to search the house, but they did not find the translation of the Bible. As soon as possible Ann dug it up and sewed it into a hard pillow. This she took to the prison.

"It's your Burmese Bible!" she whispered.

"Bless you, Ann!" Adoniram whispered back. Every night he slept with the manuscript under his head. No one bothered to steal such a dingy-looking hard pillow.

Nearly a year later the prisoners were moved to a different jail. This time they were not allowed to take any possessions. The old pillow was left behind.

Meanwhile, one of the Judson's Burmese converts went to the old cell to see if there was anything he could take as a souvenir of his friend. He saw the dirty pillow and took it home. Inside he discovered the precious manuscript. As he read, the words spoke peace to his heart and he knew that he must keep the Bible safe so that someday all Burmese could know its wonderful message.

After almost two years of imprisonment, Adoniram Judson was released. Imagine his surprise to find the manuscript of the Bible still safe in the home of his friend! He immediately resumed work on the translation. Fifteen years later the Bible was ready to print. Because of it, thousands of Burmese Christians today know the happiness that only God's Word can bring.

You, too, can discover this joy by reading God's Word.

167

BE STILL AND KNOW

Be still, and know that I am God. Psalm 46:10.

On May 27, 1974, 24-year-old Debbie Dortzback was making her nursing rounds in an Ethiopian mission hospital when she was confronted by a masked man with a gun. She was kidnapped by the Eritrean Liberation Front and kept for twenty-six days in a remote village hideout.

"The hardest part of the ordeal was not eating from a tin can or finding my home in a shelter of logs or staring at the machine guns the men held," Debbie wrote later. "Instead it was sitting still, resting in the fact that God was yet in control."

On June 9, God did something to show Debbie that He was still in charge. On that day she was given the use of a radio by one of her captors. Toying with the knobs, she found only static and a babble of strange languages. Then, suddenly, she heard someone speaking English. She turned up the volume, pressed her ear close to the speaker, and heard a minister in a far-off land say:

"What do we do when problems come our way, when we are faced with separation from someone we love, when we come to the utter end of our own resources?"

That's me, all right, Debbie thought as she strained to catch the speaker's next words:

"Everything about us may change, but there is one thing that is changeless. God's Word stands unmoved. God Himself cannot change. It is in Him we must put our confidence and find Him completely able to bring a solution, and peace."

The voice faded and a Swahili program came on. Leaving the radio, Debbie went outside. Now, it seemed that everything about her spoke of God's love. Insects moving through the grass, a raven flapping overhead, a butterfly poised on a rock, and the excited cry of a child herding sheep, all reminded her that God was near. She was learning to sit still and learn of God.

Have you learned how to "Be still?" Find a few moments today. Go to a quiet spot where you can be alone and think of God. For a little while, get away from your family and friends, from the television, radio, and cassette player. Just be still and let God speak to you.

LOST IN THE WOODS

And we know that all things work together for good to them that love God, to them who are the called according to his purpose. Romans 8:28.

"I am so happy to meet you again!" a woman said to Ellen White at the Michigan camp meeting in 1875.

"Do you remember calling at a log house in the woods near Vergennes twenty-two years ago?"

Mrs. White said she rememberd the occasion well.

Ellen and her husband had been traveling from Bedord to Vergennes when somehow their guide lost his way. When they could find no water, Ellen had fainted. With a borrowed ax the group had cut their way through the forest until they came to a clearing in which sat a log cabin. There they had been given bread and milk and a place to sleep. The Whites prayed and sang with the family and left them a little book to read.

"You talked to me of Jesus and the beauties of heaven. You spoke with such fervor that I was charmed," the woman continued. "I read the book and lent it to my neighbors. Since then the Lord has sent ministers to preach the truth and now a group of Sabbathkeepers meets there each week. In all, twenty people have been converted because you called at our house."

Elder and Mrs. White could not understand why they were lost in the woods on June 10, 1853. They were only fifteen miles from their destination. Their driver had passed over that road repeatedly, and was well acquainted with it. But that day he traveled twenty-five miles out of his way through woods, over logs and fallen trees where there was hardly a trace of a road. They had thought the experience annoying at the time, but God had brought good out of it.

Not everything that happens to us in life is good. There are unpleasant incidents. Many things happen that we wish had not taken place. Sometimes we may seem to be lost in the woods, wasting our time. However, God can bring good out of every experience of life.

We may not understand why our plans are sometimes upset and troubles come. Instead of fretting and worrying because things are not as we would like them, let us trust in our wise and loving heavenly Father to work everything out for our good. In all that happens to us, God is at work.

SUNSHINE BAND

Ye are my witnesses, saith the Lord, and my servant whom I have chosen. Isaiah 43:10.

Fourteen-year-old Luther Warren wanted to witness for Jesus. He thought how great it would be if all of his friends could work together to spread the message of Christ's soon return.

One day he shared these ideas with his 17-year-old friend, Harry Fenner. They were walking along a country road in Michigan, and Luther suggested, "Harry, let's go over the fence and pray about it."

Together, the boys climbed the rail fence and found a secluded spot behind some bushes where they could pray. They consecrated themselves to the task of taking the gospel to the world and asked God to help them recruit young people in the project.

"Come join our youth society," Luther and Harry urged their friends. Soon nine teen-age boys were meeting each week to pray and witness. They went on errands for the sick, gave out tracts, and wrote missionary letters.

Luther Warren grew up to become a Seventh-day Adventist minister. As such, he still felt a burden that the youth should have a part in God's work. In this he was encouraged by Ellen White who wrote in 1892:

"Young men and young women, cannot you form companies, and, as soldiers of Christ, enlist in the work, putting all your tact and skill and talent into the Master's service, that you may save souls from ruin? Let there be companies organized in every church to do this work."—*Christian Service,* p. 34.

Luther Warren was one of the first to organize such companies of young people. On June 11, 1894, a youth society was organized in Alexandria, North Dakota. They called themselves the Sunshine Band. Their purpose was to help others and to take the gospel into all the world.

Today the Adventist Church has a worldwide network of youth societies where children and young people can be trained for witnessing activities such as Voice of Youth efforts, jail bands, literature distribution, and inner-city projects. There are many things that you can do for Christ. What witnessing projects does your youth society have? What are you doing?

THE BROKEN TYPEWRITER

If any of you lack wisdom, let him ask of God, that giveth to all men liberally, and upbraideth not; and it shall be given him. James 1:5.

It was June 12, 1977. I sat at my typewriter trying to complete one part of the manuscript for this book. The space bar kept sticking, making a mess of the page. It would have to go to the repair shop.

The repairman, however, was out of town. "He'll be back tomorrow," his helper said.

I knew from experience that "tomorrow" meant any time in the next week. I couldn't wait until then, nor even until the next day to get the typewriter fixed. I had to type the manuscript. We were leaving on furlough in a few days. Company was expected. There was no time to wait. I must get it repaired now.

"I'll fix it myself," I said, and went home.

Now, I know nothing about the inner workings of a typewriter. For two hours I banged, poked, and oiled, but the machine still did not work any better.

Frustrated, I folded my hands over the typewriter and prayed, "Dear Lord, please help me. I need this typewriter now. I cannot waste any more time. You have promised that if we lack wisdom we should ask You and You will give it to us. Please, show me what to do to fix this typewriter."

Within minutes the machine was working beautifully, and I wondered why I had waited so long to ask for help.

How often I have done the same thing with my life. I have struggled on for hours and days on my own, trying desperately to make things work. I have gone doggedly on in face of failure, still trying to find out where things went wrong. Finally, when thoroughly exhausted, I have done what I should have done in the beginning, gone to Jesus for wisdom. How quickly things then fell into place!

Are there things for which you need wisdom? It may be for a difficult subject in school, a problem situation at home, or a decision about your future. Whatever it is, go to God with your perplexity. He has promised to give you wisdom. Put your trust in an all-wise and loving God. He will show you what to do. He will not fail you.

171

THE CONQUEROR

In all these things we are more than conquerors through him that loved us. Romans 8:37.

Alexander the Great lived about three hundred years before Christ. He conquered the ancient world from Greece to India. His fame as a general spread far and wide. People worshiped him as a god.

He was 32 years old and had great plans for the future. However, his ideas were never realized, for in the year 323 B.C. Alexander threw a big party. No one ate or drank more than he. He drank all one night and all the next day. While lying in his room in a drunken stupor he caught a cold, which developed into malaria.

On the tenth day of June he fell into a coma and his men knew he was dying. A long parade of soldiers filed by his bed. He roused just enough for someone to ask him to whom his kingdom should go. He murmured faintly, "To the strongest." On June 13 he died.

Alexander the Great had conquered almost the whole world, but he had not been able to conquer himself. He had controlled millions, but he did not control his own appetites and passions. He had been victorious in a hundred campaigns, but he lost the most important battle of all.

The warfare against self is the greatest battle that we have to fight.

Have you seen this battle take place in the classroom? Johnny feels angry because of what someone has said. He tries to get even. Perhaps there is a fight. He may even win, but he has lost the battle with self.

Have you seen this battle in the home? Betty doesn't get something she wants. She feels that everyone is picking on her. Grumbling and complaining, she makes life unpleasant for the entire family. She pouts and whines until she gets her way. Betty gets what she wants, but she loses the battle with self.

Have you seen this battle at the table? Bill eats anything he wants. He never knows when to stop. He stuffs himself until he is sick. He has lost the battle with self.

"Everyone who enters the pearly gates of the city of God will enter there as a conqueror, and his greatest conquest will have been the conquest of self."—*Testimonies,* vol. 9, p. 183.

KEEPING ON COURSE

Thou shalt guide me with thy counsel, and afterward receive me to glory. Psalm 73:24.

Charles Lindbergh was not the first to fly nonstop across the Atlantic Ocean. Arthur Brown and John Alcock, two Britishers, did it eight years earlier.

On June 14, 1919, the two men started out from Newfoundland in a converted bomber named the *Vimy*. Sixteen hours and twelve minutes later they landed in a pasture in Ireland.

So many things went wrong that it is a wonder Brown and Alcock made it. Within six hours of take off the wind-powered generator tore loose from the wing. Their radio stopped working. Then they saw part of the exhaust pipe fall into the sea.

A few hours later they rode into a treacherous North Atlantic storm, with hail, rain, lightning, and gusting winds. They were tossed around like a fragile kite. Alcock lost control of the plane and it spiraled into a dive toward the ocean, five thousand feet below. Just sixty feet above the white-capped waves he was able to right the plane.

In a few minutes Brown pointed to the compass and Alcock had a good laugh. The storm had turned their craft around and they were going full speed back toward Newfoundland!

Fortunately, the compass was working. Once they saw their error it was easy to turn around and head in the right direction. In the storm there was no other way to get their bearings. Without the compass they might have wandered in circles over the ocean until they ran out of fuel. Without the compass it is unlikely that they would have reached their goal.

You and I have a goal to reach, our heavenly home. We, too, need a compass to guide us through the stormy weather of life. We need a sure and true guide if we are going to keep on course and reach our destination.

The Bible is the only safe guide. Every day we need to check with it to see if we are going in the right direction. We can trust our heavenly compass. It will always point the way home. Have you checked your position lately? Are you traveling in the right direction? If not, do what John Alcock did in the storm; turn around and head the right way.

LOMA LINDA MIRACLE

Whatsoever he saith unto you, do it. John 2:5.

One spring day in 1905, Elder John A. Burden opened a letter from Ellen White who was then in Washington, D.C., attending the General Conference. He read: "Secure the property by all means."

The property in question was seventy-six acres near Redlands, California, at a place called Loma Linda. It seemed to be an ideal spot for a medical and educational institution. The owners had first asked $110,000, but had now reduced the price to $40,000.

"Move forward in faith, and money will come from unexpected sources," the letter said.

Elder Burden decided to trust the word of the Lord as given through Mrs. White. He personally took out a $1,000 loan and made the first payment. The next installment of $4,000 was due on June 15. Where was he to find so much money?

Elder Burden heard of an Adventist brother who had recently asked the conference if they needed money. Perhaps he would give for Loma Linda. So Elder Burden took the electric train from Los Angeles to within one and a half miles of the ranch where the man lived.

When he finally located the cabin, no one was there. Disappointed, Burden returned to the track to await the next train. Lost in thought, he forgot to signal, and the cars passed without stopping. It would be two hours until the next one.

"Return to the cabin," a voice seemed to say. So back to the cabin he walked, and he found the family eating supper. Elder Burden quickly explained about Loma Linda.

"Praise the Lord!" the man exclaimed. "I have just sold some property and I am sure the Lord wants the money for Loma Linda." He gave 2,400 dollars and someone else loaned the rest.

The next payment was to be made in July, and on the day it was due a letter came in the morning's mail with a draft for 5,000 dollars from a lady in New Jersey. It was the exact amount needed. All other payments were also met in a miraculous way.

When God speaks to us, we need to be willing, like Elder Burden, to go forward in obedience. As we obey we can expect to see the miracle-working power of God.

KLONDIKE GOLD

It cannot be gotten for gold, neither shall silver be weighed for the price thereof. Job 28:15.

On Wednesday, June 16, 1897, a ship from Alaska steamed into San Francisco harbor. As soon as the boat docked, a motley group of bearded men got off, staggering under their loads of gold. The precious metal was in their pockets and in their suitcases. It was stuffed in old coffee pots and glass jars. Some carried homemade moosehide bags full of it. Altogether, $750,000 worth of gold came off that one ship.

This was the first the outside world knew of the richest gold strike in history. On hearing the news, one hundred thousand people walked off their jobs and away from their homes, heading for Alaska and the Klondike River.

Most were unprepared for the rigors of northern trails that must be followed across treacherous mountain passes, through wild blizzards, and over raging rapids. It took an average of sixteen weeks on the trail to reach Dawson City. Only one in four made it.

Fevered by the desire for riches, men seemed willing to endure any hardship in the hopes of finding a fortune. In their frantic search many lost that which is far more valuable than gold. Some lost their lives and others their health. In the rough mining-town life many lost their religious experience and their good name. They gave up their principles to fight for gold.

We need to get our priorities straight today. It is important to know what things are of lasting value. We should be pursuing these goals with all the earnestness of the Klondike miners.

Character is the Christian's gold. All the riches in the world cannot buy a pure heart, a clear conscience, or a good name. Love for God, faith in His promises, and salvation are more precious than gold.

David said, "Therefore I love thy commandments above gold" (Ps. 119:127). Job declared about wisdom, "The gold and the crystal cannot equal it" (Job 28:17). Solomon said, "A good name is rather to be chosen than great riches, and loving favour rather than silver and gold" (Prov. 22:1).

Should we not, like the Klondike miners, be willing to sacrifice anything, undergo any hardships, that we might have that which is more valuable than gold—an upright character?

175

BATTLE OF BUNKER HILL

Submit yourselves therefore to God. Resist the devil, and he will flee from you. James 4:7.

There are two generals in the battle of life: God and the devil. James urges us to join Christ's side and fight against Satan. If we do, victory is assured. If we keep fighting, the devil will retreat.

The Battle of Bunker Hill illustrates this. It was the first real battle of the American Revolution. Bunker Hill was one of two hills on a peninsula just north of Boston, separated by a causeway from the mainland.

General Thomas Gage, British commander, planned to fortify those hills as soon as reinforcements came from England. When the Americans learned of this plan, they decided to take the hills first.

On the morning of June 17, 1775, General Gage saw that the Americans were in control. He immediately sent 2,500 soldiers to capture the hill.

He ordered his men to advance up the steep and difficult incline to the top. It appeared at first that there would be no resistance. The British marched forward in ordered procession, but just as they reached the top, the Americans began to fire. So strong was their resistance that the British were forced to retreat.

General Gage ordered his men to advance a second time. Again they were beaten back by the strong fire of the Americans.

On their third attempt, the British succeeded in gaining the top of the hill and capturing some guns. The Americans fled; they were out of ammunition and could no longer resist.

In a similar way the devil launches attacks against us daily. As long as we have ammunition and keep resisting, Satan will have no choice but to retreat. He has, however, the same quality of perseverance as those British troops. He keeps attacking, hoping sooner or later to find us without defense.

What is our ammunition? The Word of God. Remember that when Satan assaulted Jesus in the wilderness our Lord sent the devil flying with an "It is written." Paul says we must fight Satan with "the sword of the Spirit, which is the word of God."

How is your ammunition supply?

VICTORY AT CALVARY

Thanks be to God, which giveth us the victory through our Lord Jesus Christ. 1 Corinthians 15:57.

On this day in 1815, Napoleon Bonaparte led the armies of France against the Duke of Wellington and was defeated at Waterloo. So complete was his rout that to this day we say that someone who has suffered a crushing blow in life has "met his Waterloo."

The news of the British victory was taken by sailing ship to the southern coast of England. London was notified by an apparatus known as a semaphore that used two flags held in various positions to spell out the words.

Londoners anxiously waited as the semaphore on top of St. Paul's Cathedral slowly spelled out the words: "W-E-L-L-I-N-G-T-O-N D-E-F-E-A-T-E-D . . ."

Just then a dense fog settled over the city, cutting off the remainder of the message. Stunned, people began to plan the defense of their homes against the French invasion they now expected.

Suddenly the fog lifted and the signals continued: "W-E-L-L-I-N-G-T-O-N D-E-F-E-A-T-E-D N-A-P-O-L-E-O-N A-T W-A-T-E-R-L-O-O.

A whoop of joy went up from the waiting crowd. People laughed and shouted to one another. Victory was theirs!

Today we are in a similar situation to that of the Londoners on the day when the fog came down. We look at the trouble and chaos in the world and it appears that evil has triumphed. Tales of murder and brutality fill the newspapers. Innocent people suffer while enemy countries settle their arguments with missiles and bombs. Everything seems to spell out the sorrowful message: "C-H-R-I-S-T D-E-F-E-A-T-E-D."

But one day soon the fog will be rolled away. The sky will be filled with the glory and brilliance of Christ's return. As if in letters of fire, the whole world will read: "C-H-R-I-S-T D-E-F-E-A-T-E-D S-A-T-A-N A-T C-A-L-V-A-R-Y."

What a day of rejoicing that will be! The trumpet will sound. The dead in Christ shall be raised and we shall all be changed and rise to meet the Lord in the air. Victory over sin and death will be ours! Let us praise Him today for the assurance of that victory.

IN HIS HANDS

Thou art my God. My times are in thy hand. Psalm 31:14, 15.

Today is the birthday of José Rizal, who has been called the George Washington of the Philippines. He never commanded an army or held a public office. Rather, he was a medical doctor who wrote books exposing the oppression of his people.

José's name is on many roads, schools, colleges, and business firms in the Philippines. His statue is in dozens of Philippine towns. Children are named for him and a day of parades and speeches is held in his honor every year.

Because of his writings, the Spanish rulers banished José Rizal to Dapitan on northwest Mindanao for four years. Although he took no part in the Revolution of 1896, he was arrested and shot by a firing squad.

A military doctor present at José's execution was amazed at the calmness with which he faced death. Stepping up to the prisoner, the doctor asked, "Comrade, may I feel your pulse?" He found it strong and normal.

When all was in readiness, the soldiers raised their rifles. The signal was given and José Rizal, the hero of the Philippines, fell dead. His death encouraged those fighting for freedom, and fifty years later the goal was realized.

What kept José Rizal calm during that trial and execution? The answer can be found in a letter he wrote to his parents: "I believe that wherever I might go I shall always be in the hands of God, who has control over the destinies of all men."

You and I need such faith if we are going to stand in the trying days that are coming. The time is approaching when youth who insist on obeying the Word of God may be treated as was José Rizal. They will be considered participants in a revolution. Speaking of this time, Mrs. White wrote: "Children will be disinherited and driven from home. . . . As the defenders of truth refuse to honor the Sunday-sabbath, some of them will be thrust into prison, some will be exiled, some will be treated as slaves."—*The Great Controversy,* p. 608.

Regardless of what your future may hold, this much we do know, you will be in God's hands.

DAVID'S BIBLE

Peace I leave with you, my peace I give unto you. . . . Let not your heart be troubled, neither let it be afraid. John 14:27.

Sam Tannyhill did not know what peace was. From boyhood he had been on the run, trying to avoid being caught for stealing. He was born on June 20, 1929, and died twenty-seven years later in the electric chair at Ohio State Penitentiary for killing a waitress.

Two Seventh-day Adventist men from Fremont, Ohio, felt a special burden for this young man. They visited him in his cell and talked to him about the love of God. Keith Collins promised to give Sam a Bible, but when he got home he couldn't find the spare one he thought was there. His 9-year-old son, David, had just been given a new Bible for his birthday.

"Daddy, you can give my Bible to Sam," the boy said.

Sam accepted David's Bible and promised to read it. When he ran out of other books he finally picked it up to pass the time. About this experience he wrote:

"I found a place where a guy named Jesus sent some of His gang to bring Him a mule. For this I thought Him a horse thief. Then I ran across a place where He made wine. For this, I called Him a bootlegger. Then I found a place where He raised the dead, healed all manner of sickness, and cast out evil. Now I wondered, What manner of Man is this? So I started at Matthew and read all the part called the New Testament. By that time I found Him, not a horse thief or a bootlegger, but the Son of God."

Sam wanted the peace he read about in John 14:27. Would God give it to him, a murderer? From Tuesday to Saturday he cried and prayed. He asked God to forgive him every sin. He put his whole life and future in God's hands and received the peace he had been seeking. For the first time in his life Sam was able to sleep at night. His burden of guilt was gone. He had the peace that only Jesus Christ can give.

In a letter to Keith Collins, Sam said, "Now I know that Jesus is real. He lives in my heart. . . . Thank David Paul for the Bible."

Peace such as this is available for all people. Come to Jesus today with all your guilt. Hand over your life and future to Him. He will bring you peace and everlasting happiness.

DEVIL IN DISGUISE

For there shall arise false Christs, and false prophets, and shall shew great signs and wonders; insomuch that, if it were possible, they shall deceive the very elect. Matthew 24:24.

Satan's impersonation of Christ will be his masterpiece of deception. The devil will appear in different parts of the earth as a majestic being of dazzling brightness, resembling the description of the Lord as given in Revelation. So great will be his glory and so marvelous his works that people will be convinced he is Jesus. Many will go to him to be blessed and will believe him when he says that he has now changed the Sabbath to Sunday. Most people will be willing to obey his command that all should worship on that day.

Millions will be deceived, but you need not be misled. You can know that this being is Satan. How is that possible? A story from the French Revolution will help us to understand.

It happened on June 21, 1791. The people of Paris had turned against King Louis XVI and Queen Marie Antoinette because they lived in luxury while the common people starved. So angry were the people that an armed guard had to be posted about the palace to protect the king and queen. Realizing the seriousness of their situation, the royal couple attempted to escape.

Early in the morning of June 21, the king ordered a carriage brought to the back door of the palace. Disguised as commoners, he and the queen and their children set out for the eastern border of France. On the way the carriage was stopped for a short rest period, and a peasant recognized the king from his picture, which was on the paper money then in circulation. He reported to the police, and the royal couple soon were returned to Paris under guard.

That uneducated man easily recognized the king from his picture. So you and I will be able to recognize Satan in his disguise. We will know the devil by his false teachings and by the counterfeit manner of his appearing, because we will have in our minds a clear picture of how Jesus will come.

Only those who have studied the Bible carefully will not be deceived by Satan's clever disguise. Read pages 624 and 625 of *The Great Controversy* for a description of what Satan will try to do. Study Matthew 24:24-31 and Revelation 1:7 for a clear picture of how Christ is going to come. Do not be deceived!

WAKE UP!

Now it is high time to awake out of sleep: for now is our salvation nearer than when we believed. Romans 13:11.

"Wake up, Christians!" Paul is saying to us. "Don't you know what time it is? Jesus is coming soon."

Now as never before it is important for us to be awake so that we can understand the signs around us. We need to be alert to the warnings so that we might be prepared for Christ's coming.

The story of what happened on June 22, 1918, is an example of the disaster that can come when those who should be awake are sleeping.

A twenty-five-car circus train left Michigan City, Indiana, that night for Hammond, Indiana. Besides fourteen flat cars carrying tents and equipment, there were seven animal cars and four sleeping cars for the circus personnel.

At Ivanhoe the engineer had to stop to check on an overheated brake box. No other train was due for an hour, but as a precaution, the flagman set up flares behind the train. Automatic signals farther down the track were also set in operation.

Back in Michigan City, an empty troop train left the station early and headed west behind the circus cars. It rumbled through a number of yellow caution signals and finally a flashing red light. The flagman frantically waved his lantern at the approaching engine, but it was no use. The troop train barreled ahead, ramming into the back of the circus train, killing sixty-eight people and many animals.

The engineer of the troop train had taken a pain pill before leaving Michigan City. It had put him to sleep, and he hadn't seen the warning signals.

Satan is trying to put us all to sleep so that we will not see the red light and the yellow warning lights. Wars, famines, earthquakes, storms, and diseases of every description should tell us something if we are awake. The increasing number of crimes, strikes, and mini-wars announce Jesus' soon return. If they do not, we must be asleep. It is time to wake up! Jesus is coming soon!

181

MAKING CHOICES

No man can serve two masters: for either he will hate the one, and love the other; or else he will hold to the one, and despise the other. Matthew 6:24.

You cannot have your cake and eat it too. You cannot be in London and Paris at the same time. You cannot serve two masters. Somewhere along the line you must make a choice.

Edward Albert Christian George Andrew Patrick David, better known as the Duke of Windsor, knew that such choices are not easy. He once had a very difficult one to make.

Born on this day in 1894, Edward was destined to be the King of England. When his father, King George V, died, Edward inherited the throne of the British Empire.

Before the year was out he was faced with a most difficult decision. Either he could be King of England or he could marry Wallis Simpson. He could not do both. The laws and customs of his country would not allow a king to marry a divorced woman. He asked for special legislation to allow it. When it was refused, he had to make a choice.

"I am going to marry Mrs. Simpson and I am prepared to go," the king decided. On December 11, 1936, he gave up his throne, saying, "I have found it impossible . . . to discharge my duties as king as I would wish to do without the help and support of the woman I love."

Whether Edward was right or wrong in his decision is a matter of opinion. He had a choice to make. In making it he revealed what was most important to him.

Every day you and I have choices to make. Some are of little significance, simply revealing our likes and dislikes. Others are very important, revealing which master we serve.

Christopher had to decide between a new car and going away to a Christian academy. He chose the Christian education. Do you think he was wise?

Karen played violin in the community orchestra. The conductor said they must practice on Friday nights for the big concert that was coming. He told Karen that she must attend or she could not play in the concert. She chose not to play in the concert. Did she choose correctly?

Consider well the choices you make today!

GOD'S HEROES

Even a child is known by his doings, whether his work be pure, and whether it be right. Proverbs 20:11.

"I have tried so hard to do right!"

These words were spoken by Grover Cleveland, a former President of the United States, just before he died on June 24, 1908. Those who knew him said that those last words pretty well summed up his life. In his long career as a public office holder, Cleveland had tried to make his decisions on whether or not something was right, not whether it was the popular thing to do.

As mayor of Buffalo he vetoed so many dishonest contracts that he was known as the "veto mayor." When he became President he had the courage to say No when he felt something would not be good for the country, even if it cost him votes.

Mrs. White must have had such men in mind when she wrote: "We should choose the right because it is right, and leave consequences with God. To men of principle, faith, and daring, the world is indebted for its great reforms."—*The Great Controversy*, p. 460.

Daniel is an example of a man who stood for the right under severe trial. Praying was not the popular thing to do. But it was right, and he did it.

It certainly was not the popular stand that Shadrach, Meshach, and Abednego took on the plain of Dura, but it was the right one.

Moses could have been a popular ruler of Egypt; but he remembered his mother's teaching and chose the right, rather than the popular course.

When faced with a course of action, we should, like these great men, ask ourselves, "Is it the right thing to do?"

"Be steadfast, my boy, when you're tempted,
    To do what you know to be right.
Stand firm by the colors of manhood,
    And you will o'ercome in the fight.
'The right,' be your battle cry ever
    In waging the warfare of life,
And God, who knows who are the heroes,
    Will give you the strength for the strife."
—Phoebe Cary

CUSTER'S LAST STAND

Be strong in the Lord, and in the power of his might.
Ephesians 6:10.

The truth about all that happened on June 25, 1876, during the Battle of the Little Bighorn will never be known. We do know that George A. Custer was asked to lead a regiment of 650 soldiers into the valley of the Little Bighorn River and capture an Indian village.

When the general spotted the settlement, it appeared to be a small one. He decided there couldn't be more than a thousand people there. It would be easy for his men to surround the camp. He saw no need to wait for reinforcements. Dividing his soldiers into three groups, Custer sent one column to the right, one to the left, and led the other straight forward.

To the surprise of all, between 2,500 and 5,000 hostile Indians were gathered in that village. General Custer and all of his men were killed. Not one was left to tell the story of Custer's Last Stand.

One thing seems certain: General Custer made a wrong guess as to how many Indians were in the village. He underestimated the strength of the enemy. He should have waited for reinforcements.

Let us not make the same mistake today in our battle of life. We are not fighting an ordinary enemy. We are struggling against one who has had six thousand years of experience. He has plenty of demons to help him. One third of the angels of heaven were cast out with him into the earth.

To our inexperienced minds things may not look all that bad. We go forth alone to meet temptation, and we are defeated. We are no match for the devil and his demons. We dare not stand alone. We need heavenly reinforcements.

Christ does not intend that we stand alone against the devil. It is His strength, not ours that can defeat the enemy. It is "in the power of his might" that we have hope.

All power in heaven and earth belongs to God. Satan's host of demons are outnumbered two to one by loyal angels. We are told that God would send every angel in heaven to our rescue, rather than see us overcome by the evil one. There is no need for defeat in our lives today. All we have to do is ask for the help to come.

THE PIED PIPER

Thou shalt not follow a multitude to do evil. Exodus 23:2.

According to an old German legend, this is the day the Pied Piper stole away the children of Hamelin.

In the year 1284, so the story goes, there was a plague of rats in the town of Hamelin. Mousetraps and poison proved useless. In order to get rid of the vermin the town imported eleven hundred cats from Bremen, but still the rats got thicker.

Then one Friday a strange-looking man dressed in a red jacket, pointed hat, wide breeches, and gray stockings came to the town fathers and offered to clear the town of rats for a hundred ducats.

After the bargain was made, the man took out a pipe and began to play a tune. Soon rats and mice by the thousands came from every garret, hole, tile, and rafter. They flocked around the piper as he played his weird music. He led them all into the Weser River, where they drowned.

But when he went to collect his one hundred ducats, the town fathers paid him only ten. He did not protest, but he returned the next Friday and played again upon his pipe. This time all the children in town came flocking to him as if hypnotized. He led them out of the city to a hill called Koppenburg and into a cavern. The music became fainter and fainter until at last it was gone. Never again did the people of Hamelin see their children. One hundred and thirty children disappeared.

There may not have really been a Pied Piper of Hamelin seven hundred years ago, but there most certainly is one today. We might call him the Pied Piper of Everytown. You can hear him playing in the movie theater and at amusement parks. His tunes can be heard over radio and television.

"A love for music leads the unwary to unite with world lovers in pleasure gatherings where God has forbidden His children to go. Thus that which is a great blessing when rightly used, becomes one of the most successful agencies by which Satan lures the mind from duty and from the contemplation of eternal things."—*Patriarchs and Prophets,* p. 594.

Don't be fooled by this modern Pied Piper.

HIS NAME IS GOD

Worship him that made heaven, and earth, and the sea, and the fountains of waters. Revelation 14:7.

White-capped waves dashing against a rocky coast. An eagle soaring high above the valley floor. A doe with her fawn drinking from a still, blue lake. These tell us of God's care. An arctic tern flying 11,000 miles to its nesting site, a chipmunk scampering along a fallen tree, and a line of ants taking food to their underground home—all show us something of our Creator.

What would it be like if you had no eyes to see the blues, golds, and crimsons of an autumn day? What if you could not hear the thundering of a waterfall or the beat of rain upon your roof? What if you could not see the early morning sun turning dew drops into diamonds? What if you could not hear the soft purr of your kitten? What if you were blind and deaf?

Helen Keller, whose birthday is today, was such a person. When she was 19 months old her world suddenly became dark, silent, and frightening. It remained that way until her teacher, Anne Sullivan, taught her about the world through the sense of touch.

When Helen was 10 years old, her parents decided it was time to teach her about God. They asked a pastor friend to come to their home and talk to her about the Creator. With Miss Sullivan as interpreter, he spoke to Helen about the mountains, sky, sea, birds, flowers, and animals. He told her that the Maker of the beautiful world in which she lived was called God.

Helen's face lit up with joy and understanding. Quickly she spelled out with her fingers, "I have known Him all the time, but I never knew His name."

God has given you eyes that you might see His power in a sprouting bean. He has given you ears that you might hear His voice in the pounding surf. He has given you a nose that you might sense His love in the fragrance of honeysuckle. He has given you fingers that you might feel the softness of a baby's hand and know He cares for you. He has given you a tongue to taste the sweetness of a strawberry, and by so doing know Him better.

God wants you to know who He is. He wants you to worship Him as your Creator today.

BE PREPARED

Be thou prepared. Ezekiel 38:7.

It was June 28, 1778, two years after the beginning of the Revolutionary War. At daybreak on that summer morning the British army began to move through New Jersey.

General George Washington, commander of the American troops, ordered Charles Lee to attack the marching British soldiers from the rear and sides and destroy all they could.

It did not work out that way. Charles Lee was late in getting his soldiers moving. By the time the Americans were ready for battle, it seemed hopeless. When General Washington saw his men retreating, he rode to the front and took command. He found the British just six hundred feet away.

He must station his men for a fight, but he had no information about the surrounding land. There was no time to draw up maps. He needed information now. Was there anyone who could help?

"David Rhea says he knows the area well, sir."

"Send for David Rhea!" Washington ordered.

Within a few minutes General Washington had the information he needed. "There's a ravine here and a bridge there. That hill is the highest one around and has a trail leading up this side. Over there is an orchard with a hedge that could be used for protection."

Immediately General Washington stationed his men in the correct places. Three times the British charged the troops behind the hedge, but they could not break through. All afternoon the battle raged. The Americans held their positions and by the next morning the British had slipped away. The outcome of the battle might have been very different had it not been for the man who was ready with the answers when his general needed them.

We must be like David Rhea, ever ready to help our General. We never know when the Lord may need us. We never know just what we might be called to do.

If God calls you to do a task for Him, will you be ready? Are you studying faithfully so that you will be prepared when the time comes? When there is a need, will you be able to say, "Yes, I can help."

NEEDLESS PAIN

Cast thy burden upon the Lord, and he shall sustain thee. Psalm 55:22.

One hundred and fifty years ago there wasn't much that could be done to stop pain. By 1850 ether and chloroform had been discovered and a few doctors were using them for pulling teeth and minor surgeries.

Although these anesthetics worked, few were willing to use them. Some said that God meant us to be in pain, and that to stop it was to cooperate with the devil. Those who used these pain killers were said to be "caught in the snares of Satan."

On June 29, 1850, the famous English statesman, Sir Robert Peel, was thrown from his horse while riding on Constitution Hill. His left collar bone and several ribs were broken. He was bleeding heavily and in severe pain.

Although Peel was attended by the queen's personal physician and the most famous surgeon was called to his side, they could do nothing to help him. He was in such great pain that the doctors couldn't even bandage him. He was left to suffer the severest agony for three days until he died. Help was available at the nearest chemist shop, but it wasn't used. Peel's doctors did not want to be among those who "cooperated with the devil."

How wrong these physicians were to think that pain is part of God's plan for His children. Pain is the result of sin. God does not want us to suffer. Even when pain is caused by our own transgression of the laws of health, Jesus looks down with pity on us. He wants to do everything possible to help us bear our suffering. He, too, suffered pain on the cross and He can sympathize with us.

Jesus wants us to come to Him with all our burdens, physical or mental. He understands. He cares. He is the great Physician who has medicine for every hurt. He can ease any pain and soothe any heartache.

You must have sung these words by John Scriven many times:

> "O what peace we often forfeit,
> O what needless pain we bear,
> All because we do not carry
> Everything to God in prayer."

NIAGARA DAREDEVIL

Believe on the Lord Jesus Christ, and thou shalt be saved.
Acts 16:31.

Thousands of people gathered on the cliffs of the Niagara River on this day in 1859 to see Charles Blondin walk the quarter mile of tightrope stretched 200 feet above the water near the roaring falls.

Wearing bright pink tights and a spangled tunic of yellow silk, Blondin left from the American side of the river carrying a fifty-pound balancing pole. In the center of the rope he sat down, got up, and went on. Then he lay down and balanced the pole on his chest. He turned a backward somersault and walked the rest of the way. He started back across the rope carrying a chair. Midway across he balanced it on the rope and sat down.

Blondin walked the tightrope above Niagara River many times during the next two years. Each time he had new stunts to perform: standing on his head, dancing a jig, walking across blindfolded, crossing backwards, and walking on stilts.

Mr. Blondin advertised that a large sum of money would be given to anyone who would ride on his back across the rope. Impetuously, several volunteered.

"Do you believe I can make it to the other side?" he asked each one.

"Oh, yes," each agreed. "I believe you can do it."

"Are you ready to come across with me?"

But the candidates looked at the narrow rope swaying in the breeze above the rushing water, and it was too much. Not one had enough faith in Blondin to get on his back. Each said that he believed in the stunt man, but none was willing to trust his life to him.

Finally, Blondin persuaded his assistant to climb on his back. Three hundred thousand people watched as he walked across the rope with the man on his shoulders. A cheer went up from the crowd when they reached the other side.

In the Christian life, believing in Jesus Christ is more than saying, "Yes, I believe." It is being willing to rest your whole life in Him, trusting Him to see you safely across the tightrope of life.

UNCLAIMED RANSOM

For there is one God, and one mediator between God and men, the man Christ Jesus; who gave himself a ransom for all. 1 Timothy 2:5, 6.

The whole world has been taken captive by Satan. You and I are prisoners of the devil. He claims us as his own. And our release required a redemption price. Jesus Christ, the Son of God, paid the redemption for you and me. He gave His life on Calvary's cross so that we might be free to our heavenly Father.

The story of Charley Ross might help us understand this better. On this day in 1774, 4-year-old Charley was playing with his 6-year-old brother, Walter, in the yard of his home in Philadelphia. Two strange men drove up in a wagon. Grabbing the two small boys, they put them in the wagon and drove away. For some reason Walter was put out of the wagon five miles from home, but Charley was never seen again.

Three days later Charley's frantic parents received a scribbled, misspelled note that said:

"Be not uneasy. Your son, Charley Bruster be al writ. We is got him and no power on earth can deliver him out of our hand. You will have to pay us before you git him from us, an pay us a big cent."

Charley's father was willing to pay. Notices were posted that $20,000 would be paid as the price for the return of Charley Ross; but no one claimed the money.

Mr. Ross spent the next twenty-three years of his life looking for his lost boy, but he died a heartbroken man. No one knows why the ransom was never claimed.

Until he died Mr. Ross never gave up searching. He put ads in many papers, and traveled widely following clues that might lead to his son. He spent his life and fortune looking for his loved one.

God is something like that father. He loves us all so much that He paid the supreme price in giving His Son, Jesus Christ, as the ransom for our souls.

Still there are lost boys and girls who have not been found. Their redemption price has been paid, but as yet they are captives still. Are you one? Don't make Him wait any longer. You are free. Come home to your Father.

GUARDIAN ANGEL

Are they not all ministering spirits, sent forth to minister for them who shall be heirs of salvation? Hebrews 1:14.

Dan Smith, of Orillia, Ontario, Canada, has a good reason to remember July 2, 1975. On that day he was driving a tractor-trailer loaded with thirty tons of gravel along Highway 400 toward Barrie. Without warning, his right rear wheel eased off the road onto the soft gravel at the edge of a thirty-foot embankment.

For about 200 yards Dan fought to gain control, but he saw that it was hopeless.

"Dear God," he prayed, "please take over now. I have done everything I can!"

Dan clung desperately to the steering wheel as the rig turned upside down and then righted itself. When the truck came to a stop, Dan scrambled out unhurt except for three broken ribs and some minor scratches and bruises.

How do you account for such a miraculous deliverance? Dan and his family believe that his guardian angel took control of the truck in answer to his prayer.

Did you know that your guardian angel was appointed to you the moment you were born? Throughout your life he keeps you from many dangers of which you know nothing.

When you are tempted to do wrong, it is he who is beside you prompting you to take a better course. If you ask, he will help you choose the correct words to speak each day.

On the day when Jesus comes, your guardian angel will be there to welcome you. If you should die before that time, he will mark your resting place, and will be the first person to greet you on the resurrection morning.

There are some things that can cause your guardian angel to leave you. He will not follow you into places of worldly amusement where Christians should not go. He will not follow you into meetings where error is being taught. Unfaithfulness in keeping the Sabbath and a thoughtless, careless attitude drive him away. He leaves your home when harsh, angry words are spoken.

This morning, thank God for your guardian angel, and pray that he might be with you every moment of this day.

THE TURNING POINT

To day if ye will hear his voice, harden not your heart. Psalm 95:7, 8.

On July 3, 1863, the Union forces were holding forth on Cemetery Ridge at Gettysburg, Pennsylvania. General George Pickett led his Confederate troops on a charge up the hill under heavy enemy fire. His men broke through the Union lines, and soldiers fought a hand to hand battle. Before the sun had set that day, two thirds of Pickett's men had been killed or captured, and the rest retreated.

History books say that this battle was one of the great events of American history. It was the turning point of the Civil War. From that time on, the North began to have the upper hand. The South never regained the power it had before that day.

In all wars, whether fought on a nation's battlefield or in a person's heart, there comes a turning point for good or ill.

For Joseph the turning point may have been the day he was sold as a slave. We are told that in one day he was changed "from a petted child to a man, thoughtful, courageous, and self-possessed" *(Patriarchs and Prophets,* p. 214).

As Joseph saw the hills of home receding in the distance he cried his heart out. Would he ever see his father again? What would the future hold?

He finally stopped crying and tried to remember the stories his father had told him about God. He remembered how angels had come to Jacob when he was in a strange land. This made Joseph feel better. He was sure that his father's God would care for him, too.

On the road to Egypt, Joseph gave himself fully to the Lord and prayed for His presence to go with him to the strange land ahead. On that road he determined to be true to God regardless of the circumstances. That day was the turning point of Joseph's life.

God is speaking to you today. As you respond to Him, something very real can happen. You can give yourself and your future into His hands as Joseph did. Today can be the turning point of your life.

TO BE FREE

Stand fast therefore in the liberty wherewith Christ hath made us free. Galatians 5:1.

Two hundred and seven years ago today America's Declaration of Independence was signed in Philadelphia. This document stated the reasons why the United States wished to be free.

It is time that some Christian young people agreed to a similar document declaring their independence from the kingdom of Satan. It might read such as this:

When in the course of human events it becomes necessary for people to dissolve the bands that have connected them to the world and to assume the free station to which they are entitled, decency demands that they should declare the causes that impel them to the separation.

We hold these truths from God's Word, that all men were created in the image of God and that they were given certain rights and privileges, that among these are eternal life, liberty, and happiness.

That from the time Lucifer began his reign these rights have been denied mankind. To prove this, let these facts be submitted:

That he has brought mankind a knowledge of evil that has taken away their happiness.

That those who follow him are not free. Instead, they are bound by the chains of sin and evil habit to do his will.

That he has deceived one third of the angels of heaven and now uses them to bring mankind to destruction.

That wherever he rules, quarrelling, fighting, wars, and violence never cease.

And whereas we have come to know that Jesus Christ, God's Son, came into this world and died on Calvary's cross to set us free from the power of this tyrant,

And whereas every person who accepts Jesus Christ as his Saviour will be restored to his rightful place as a son or daughter of God, inheriting eternal life, liberty, and happiness,

I do, therefore, accept Jesus Christ as the Lord and Master of my life and do declare that I am henceforth free from Satan's power. He shall no more rule my life. From this day on I am free through Jesus Christ my Lord.

NO GUNS

Thou shalt not kill. Exodus 20:13.

Is there a time when it is right to kill? What about in time of war? Should not Christians support their government by joining the army and helping to wipe out the enemy?

No. The Ten Commandments clearly tell us not to kill. We must somehow honor our country without dishonoring God.

Seventh-day Adventist young people who are drafted into the armed forces are encouraged to declare their noncombatancy status. This means they will serve their country in any way possible during time of war, but without guns.

Conscientious objector is another name for a person who, because of religious conviction, will not take up a gun against another human being.

Private Stanley W. Crook was a conscientious objector. He twice won the Silver Star Medal for bravery on the battlefield in Korea.

Once he was sent with a night patrol to seek out the enemy position. On the way the soldiers walked into a mine field and several were badly wounded. In full view of the enemy, Stanley gallantly did his job of caring for the wounded and the dying.

On July 5, 1953, he was in the thick of the battle. Under heavy fire, he helped many wounded to safety, then stayed behind to give plasma to an injured man. There he was hit by enemy guns and killed.

The United States Army proclaimed Stanley a hero. But in his own words, written home after being notified of his first honor, he said, "I'm not a hero. I was just doing my job the way God wanted me to."

That is what being a noncombatant is all about: not fighting, not carrying a gun, not killing, but serving your country in the way God wants you to—saving life rather than taking it.

Knowing this, should Christian boys and girls be playing with toy guns and setting up mock battles?

Is Jesus pleased when He hears someone on the playground angrily shout, "I'll kill you!"?

If God wants us to be noncombatants in war, not taking life, but saving it, don't you think He holds the same standards for our play?

MIDNIGHT EXPRESS

Therefore hear the word at my mouth, and give them warning from me. Ezekiel 3:17.

At eleven o'clock on the night of July 6, 1881, 15-year-old Kate Shelley stood on the porch of her small home on the east bank of Honey Creek, Iowa, and watched the worst storm she had ever seen.

Wind howled, lightning flashed, thunder boomed, and rain came down in gale-whipped sheets. The usually-placid creek was now a raging torrent beating against the railroad trestle. Then Kate saw the dim light of a freight engine round the curve beyond the west side of the bridge. She watched as it rolled onto the wooden trestle. There was a splintering crash, and the engine plunged into the swollen creek.

Kate ran inside to tell her mother. "I've got to cross the creek to the station and stop the midnight express, or lots of people will die," she said. "There isn't much time. I must hurry."

"Don't go!" pleaded her mother. "You might die yourself!"

"I have to try," Kate insisted. "It is my duty. I can't simply stand here and watch the train fall into the water and listen to the screams of the dying people. I must go."

"Go then, but be careful," her mother said. "I'll be praying for you."

Kate ran out the door into the blinding storm. Slowly she crawled across the narrow catwalk that was still intact. Gale force winds threatened to blow her off the shaky ledge.

It seemed an eternity before she reached the other side. Once there, she raced to the station. Throwing open the door she shouted, "The bridge is out! Stop the express! Quick! The freight engine has gone into the creek!"

The stationmaster dashed outside and flagged the express train to a stop. Another minute and it would have been too late!

It is now minutes to midnight in this world's history. People are rushing down the track of life toward eternal death. They don't know the bridge is out. Someone must warn them before it is too late. God has given that message to you and me. It is our duty. If we do not do it, lives will surely be lost.

BROKEN WALLS

For he is our peace, who hath made both one, and hath broken down the middle wall of partition between us. Ephesians 2:14.

People have been building walls for a long time. Sometimes walls are good and necessary. They can safeguard your property and protect your privacy.

There are other walls, invisible ones, that we build to keep people out of our lives.

We build such walls of color, nationality, language, religion, and financial status. Such barrier-building leads us to think that we, and those like us, are the only ones that matter in this world. *We* are God's chosen people. *We* are the favored ones. *We* are the ones that count.

Sometimes these walls are simply a nuisance, keeping people apart who should be together. At other times such divisions result in tragedy. Like the time seventy-eight people drowned in Alwar, India.

On July 7, 1973, a flash flood washed away the road and swept a bus load of passengers into a swollen river one hundred miles southeast of New Delhi. Only eight people survived. All might have lived had it not been for an invisible wall called *caste.*

The passengers belonged to two high-caste communities that normally would have no relationship with each other. They would not eat together. Their children would not marry. They would not worship together.

On the day of the flood, there was only one rope by which the people could be rescued. They must work together and use the same rope. They refused. Each group wanted exclusive right to that rope. While they squabbled, seventy-eight persons drowned.

This world is doomed. There is only one way of salvation for you and me. That one way is through Jesus Christ, who died on Golgotha's Hill so long ago. He is the way, the truth, the life, the door—and, yes, the rope by which we may all be saved.

We must all share in the provision God has made for our rescue. There will be no ghettos in heaven. The multitude that gathers on the sea of glass will not be divided by walls. If we plan to be in that happy land we ought now to tear down the barriers that separate us from one another.

SHAWNEE TOM

And that they may recover themselves out of the snare of the devil, who are taken captive by him at his will. 2 Timothy 2:26.

Tom Ingles was captured by Shawnee Indians on July 8, 1755, when he was 4 years old.

Tom grew up knowing nothing of the English language nor the ways of his people. He liked his teepee home with its bearskin rug and cozy fire. He dressed as did the Indian boys, ate the same food, and played the same games. Still, he knew that he was different.

"Why are my skin and hair lighter than yours?" he asked his Indian mother. "I look more like the French trader than I do you and father."

"You were not born an Indian," the squaw explained. "Your family was captured by Shawnee warriors. You were brought back to our village, and I don't know what happened to the rest of your family."

Actually, Tom's real mother and father had escaped to Virginia and were constantly searching for their lost son. Years went by and the parents heard that he was in a Shawnee village near the Scioto River. They sent a messenger with $100 in ransom money to bring him back. Tom didn't want to leave his Indian home. He pretended to be happy to go, but that night he slipped away and returned to the Shawnees.

Later, Mr. Ingles himself returned with the messenger to try to persuade his son to come home. When Tom Ingles saw the man who claimed to be his father, he knew that what he said was true.

"We do look alike," he said through an interpreter. "I believe what you say. I will go with you wherever you want to take me."

If you are like Tom Ingles, a long way from home and lost from your heavenly Father, why not return to Him today? You need not remain a captive of Satan. Jesus Christ paid the ransom for you with His own blood on Calvary's cross. Take a good look at Him today. You are His child, made in His image. He wants you back home where you belong. Will you accept His offer? Will you return with Him today?

SOWING TIME

He that goeth forth and weepeth, bearing precious seed, shall doubtless come again with rejoicing, bringing his sheaves with him. Psalm 126:6.

One hundred years ago the land in Australia, where Avondale College now stands was wild, uncultivated, and far from the cities where Adventists lived. Mrs. White and a few others moved to the place and tried to get something started, but it was very discouraging.

During this time Mrs. White had a beautiful dream that encouraged the workers. On the night of July 9, 1896 she dreamed that she and her husband were going for a walk on their farm near Cooranbong, and as they walked they talked about the needs of the school. (Elder White had been dead for some time, but in the dream they were together again.)

Mrs. White said, "'I know not where means are coming from. . . . We have to break the soil at a venture, plow in hope, in faith. . . . So we must sow this missionary soil with the seeds of truth.'" Elder White said, "'It must be carried on in simplicity and faith and hope, and eternal results will be the reward of your labors.'"

Elder and Mrs. White walked the full length of the garden and started back. On the way they noticed that the vines were covered with berries, which they immediately began to pick. As they worked, Mrs. White spoke: "'I thought these plants were inferior, and hardly worth the trouble of putting into the ground. I never looked for such an abundant yield.'"

Her husband reminded her of cities in America where they had preached. At first there seemed to be few results, but afterward there was a wonderful harvest. "'You are to sow in hope and faith, and you will not be disappointed,'" he said.

Shortly after this dream, funds came from Africa and the school was built. Today abundant fruit of their sowing can be seen in the hundreds of preachers, teachers, secretaries, accountants, and missionaries who have come from that school.

When you give out a gospel tract or do a kind deed for a neighbor you are sowing seeds of truth. Do not be discouraged if you don't see many people join the church now because of what you do. God will bless the seeds you sow and someday you will see the harvest.

HOW HOT IS HELL?

And the elements shall melt with fervent heat, the earth also and the works that are therein shall be burned up. 2 Peter 3:10.

On July 10, 1913, the thermometers in Death Valley, California, registered 134 degrees Fahrenheit.

My mother's treatment for the colds and fevers of my childhood was a hot tub bath. She would begin the bath at about 100 degrees and gradually raise it to around 120 degrees. How I cried and begged her to stop! She would smile, put a cold cloth on my head and tell me it would make me better. I was sure that such temperatures were a foretaste of the fires that will cleanse the earth.

Perhaps you have experienced 212 degrees Fahrenheit, the boiling point of water, and got a painful blister as a result. Cookies and cakes bake at around 350 degrees Fahrenheit, and you know how hot that oven is when you open the door.

Gas furnaces can produce temperatures of 2,800 degrees Fahrenheit, and electric furnaces go as high as 5,000 degrees. A solar furnace can reach a temperature as high as 8,000 degrees.

How hot will hell be? Hot enough to melt all the elements! Tungsten, the metal used as a filament in incandescent lamps, melts at 6,160 degrees Fahrenheit. Graphite is often used to make pots for melting other metals because it can withstand temperatures up to 6,390 degrees. In the fires of hell, tungsten and graphite are going to melt!

Some people believe that the fires of hell will burn for eternity and that the wicked will be alive and suffering, crying out for help through the ceaseless ages of time. But the Bible teaches a hotter hell than that! Sin and sinners are going to be burned up completely, destroyed.

Malachi says, "For, behold, the day cometh, that shall burn as an oven; and all the proud, yea, and all that do wickedly, shall be stubble: and the day that cometh shall burn them up, saith the Lord of hosts, that it shall leave them neither root nor branch" (chap. 4:1).

What a day that will be when sin is finally destroyed! If any of us are consumed in the fires of hell, it will be because we have rejected Jesus Christ and have held on to our sins.

Won't you accept His salvation today, before it is too late? Do not neglect Him any longer.

199

THE GOLDEN RULE

"Therefore all things whatsoever ye would that men should do to you, do ye even so to them. Matthew 7:12.

These words are often called the golden rule. Do they make sense in today's world, where there is stiff competition in sports, school, and business? Some people seem to think they must put the other fellow down in order to win, trying to reach the top regardless of what happens to anyone else.

John Wanamaker, who was born on this day in 1838, was one who thought the principles of the Bible are still good. Something happened when he was young that helped him make up his mind to live by the golden rule.

With only a few dollars in his pocket, John went into a store to buy his mother a Christmas present. Wanting to buy the best possible gift with the little money he had, he carefully examined the various items in the showcase. The clerk became impatient. Finally, John said, "I'll take that one."

As the clerk was wrapping it, John saw something he liked better. "Please, sir," he said, "I have changed my mind. Would you give me this one instead?"

"It's too late to change, young man," said the clerk. "You have bought this one and you will have to keep it."

When John grew up he determined to have a store where people could get what they wanted. It would be a store where the clerks were always courteous. He would give better quality at lower prices. The price would be the same for everyone, with no bargaining to try to get as much as possible out of the customer. He would put the customer first, treating them as he would like to be treated. If someone wasn't satisfied with his purchase, he could bring it back and have his money refunded.

People in Philadelphia were amazed. Merchants predicted Wanamaker would go broke; but they were wrong. Customers flocked to his store and he soon opened a larger one. Before long he had many stores which made up the largest retail clothing business in America. Following the golden rule brought him both wealth and happiness.

The world would certainly be a better place if we all followed Jesus' rule of life. Whatever happens today, try putting yourself in the other person's shoes and ask yourself, If I were that person, how would I like to be treated?

THE UNCONQUERABLE GOD

He will swallow up death in victory; and the Lord God will wipe away tears from off all faces. Isaiah 25:8.

Today is the birthday of Julius Caesar, Emperor of Rome. Wherever he led his army into battle, they won. Caesar conquered all of Europe west of the Rhine River. He won outstanding victories in North Africa and the Middle East. Reporting on one of these battles, he told the senate, "I came, I saw, I conquered."

Unfortunately, the glory seemed to go to Caesar's head. He was not content with the title of Emperor for one year at a time. He demanded that it be given him for life.

When the new calendar was brought out, he had the name of the month *Quintilus* changed to July in honor of himself.

Still not satisfied, Caesar had a statue made of himself and placed it in a temple alongside the other gods the people worshiped. On it was written: "To the Unconquerable God."

Shortly after setting up this statue, Caesar was stabbed to death as he entered the senate meeting. He had conquered many enemies, but he could not conquer death.

Jesus Christ is the only unconquerable God. He is the only one who has conquered death.

Forty years after Caesar died, Jesus left the glories of heaven and came to this earth to be born as a baby in a cattle shed in Bethlehem. At the age of 33 He was led from His place of prayer by Roman soldiers and sentenced to death by a Roman governor. A crown of thorns was placed upon His head, and a purple robe was thrown about His shoulders. The King of the universe stood silently while men mocked Him. He was beaten, spat upon, and nailed to a wooden cross. There He suffered and died for your sins and mine.

On the third day an angel from the throne of God came with a blinding flash of light and rolled away the stone of His tomb. Jesus Christ walked forth from that grave as the conqueror of death.

One day soon He will come again and call forth those who are now sleeping in their graves. Because He lives, they too shall live. He will take us all to a land where no one will ever die again.

BLACKOUT

Yet a little while is the light with you. Walk while ye have the light, lest darkness come upon you. John 12:35.

The blackout of July 13, 1977, is an illustration of what happens when the lights go out. On that night a summer storm knocked out a high-voltage power line near New York City and nine million people were without light for twenty-five hours. Subways stopped and elevators stalled. Water pumps, toilets, refrigerators, and televisions ceased to function. Shops had to close.

Into the darkened streets poured men, women, and children intent on evil. They broke into shops and carried off clothes, appliances, furniture, groceries, and cars. Nearly fourteen hundred stores were robbed and still the rampage of violence, and crime continued through the night.

A thousand buildings were set on fire. The fire fighters couldn't keep up with the calls. One hundred policemen were injured by bottles, bricks, baseball bats, and broom handles. The mayor of New York called it a "night of terror." Not until the sun came up the next morning and illuminated the streets and alleys of that great city did the looting and violence stop.

Just before Jesus comes there will be a worldwide spiritual blackout. The light of God will be withdrawn from the earth and mankind will be left under Satan's power. Under the influence of evil angels terrible destruction and violence will take place. Cruelty, hatred, and evil passions will have full sway. There will be a great time of trouble such as we have never dreamed of. A world that has rejected Jesus will be left in darkness.

God's work of judgment in heaven will be finished. All cases will have been decided. There will no longer be a need for the Holy Spirit to plead with human beings to repent and come to God. He will no longer be here urging people to be kind, helpful, and decent. He will no longer be present to restrain the powers of darkness.

When that night of terror comes it will be too late to repent and come to Jesus, for the Holy Spirit, who brings us to repentance, will have left the earth. Today is the day of salvation. Accept Jesus now before the light goes out.

BASTILLE DAY

Whatsoever things are true, . . . if there be any virtue, and if there be any praise, think on these things. Philippians 4:8.

Today is Bastille Day in France. It is a national holiday marking their independence.

The Bastille, a prison in Paris, somehow became the symbol of oppression by the king and the nobles. On July 14, 1789, a large, angry mob of merchants, farmers, and working men gathered outside its walls to protest against the government. They could do little more than shout slogans, for they had no weapons. Nor did they have any way of reaching the prison itself, since it was protected by a moat.

It might have remained only a noisy disturbance, except for the fact that the governor of the prison lowered the drawbridge to allow some artillery of the royal guard to enter.

The angry crowd rushed in, killed all the soldiers and set the prisoners free. The next day the mob began to tear down the hated prison and today only a monument marks the place where the castle fortress once stood.

In some ways your mind is like the Bastille. No enemy can enter except as he comes through a gateway. Therefore, we need to guard well the gateways to our minds. We dare not let down the drawbridge lest Satan find an entrance for evil thoughts.

Mrs. White has written this warning to us: "Those who would not fall prey to Satan's devices must guard well the avenues of the soul; they must avoid reading, seeing, or hearing that which will suggest impure thoughts. . . . The heart must be faithfully sentineled, or evils without will awaken evils within, and the soul will wander in darkness."—*The Acts of the Apostles,* p. 518.

Are you guarding the gateways to your mind? Have you placed a sentinel to watch your eyes, ears, and mouth?

Are you careful about the books you read and the pictures at which you look? Do you choose wisely the programs you watch on television? What kind of music do you listen to, and what is its effect on your mind?

Today guard diligently the castle of your mind. Be careful what thoughts enter there.

MIDGET CHRISTIANS

*Desire the sincere milk of the word, that ye may grow thereby.
1 Peter 2:2.*

At birth, Charles Stratton was a normal, healthy baby weighing nine pounds. He developed as other babies do until he was 6 months old, and then he stopped growing. At that time he was twenty-five inches long and fifteen pounds in weight. When he was 6 years old he was still the same size.

"He is the smallest child I have ever seen who could walk alone," Mr. P. T. Barnam said. "I will ask him to join my circus."

At the age of 6, Charles Stratton did join the circus, where he was known as Tom Thumb. He dressed in a variety of costumes and entertained the audience. He would appear as a cupid with his bow and quiver full of arrows or perhaps a Revolutionary War soldier with a ten-inch sword. Or he would come onto the stage playing the part of Napoleon Bonaparte or of David fighting Goliath.

Tom Thumb became very popular, even traveling to Europe and entertaining kings and queens. He spent his entire life amusing people. By the time he died on July 15, 1883, 20 million people had paid to see this little man.

Although Tom Thumb was rich and famous, none of those who came to watch him wanted to be like him. Every boy and girl wants to grow up to be like other people. They don't want to spend their lives dangling legs from too-high chairs and straining to reach the doorknob.

Isn't it strange that boys and girls who will eat good food so that they can grow up to their full physical height are sometimes content to remain midgets in their spiritual lives? Instead of growing up into mature Christians they stay at the kindergarten stage. They do not continue to grow in their knowledge of God. They neglect their spiritual food and become dwarfed.

Christians who stand tall for Christ are those who spend time every day reading the Bible, learning its promises, and thinking about their meaning. They exercise their faith through prayer and grow every day to be more like Jesus.

Are you a midget Christian? You don't have to stay that way.

FAMOUS LAST WORDS

For I know whom I have believed, and am persuaded that he is able to keep that which I have committed unto him against that day. 2 Timothy 1:12.

The last words Ellen White spoke before she died on July 16, 1915, were to her son, William. She said, "I know in whom I have believed."

Many times she had used these same words to comfort those who were mourning the loss of a loved one. In 1893 she used them to bring comfort to parents who had lost children at sea. She wrote, "Whatever may be your circumstances, however dark and mysterious may be the ways of Providence, though the path may be through the deep waters, and trials and bereavements may afflict again and again, the assurance still comes, 'All things work together for good to them that love God' (Rom. 8:28). 'I know whom I have believed, and am persuaded that he is able to keep that which I have committed unto him against that day' (2 Tim. 1:12)."—*Selected Messages,* book 2, p. 261.

To Mary, her daughter-in-law who had tuberculosis and would die at the age of 33, Mrs. White wrote, "Thank God, Mary, the light afflictions which are but for a moment, work for you a far more exceeding and eternal weight of glory. You know in whom you have believed and are persuaded that He is able to keep that which you have committed unto Him against that day. The trials may be severe, but look to Jesus every moment—not to struggle, but to rest in His love."—*Ibid.,* p. 249.

During a period of time when Mrs. White was ill, helpless, and in great pain, she could only sleep about two hours a night. At such times she would talk to Jesus. About this experience she said, "Jesus was sacredly near, and I found the grace given sufficient, for my soul was stayed upon God, and I was full of grateful praise to Him who loved me and gave Himself for me. I could say from a full heart, 'I know whom I have believed.'"—*Ibid.,* pp. 241, 242.

You, too, can have the beautiful assurance that Jesus is your friend and helper. You need never doubt. Like Paul and Ellen White you can rejoice in whatever life brings, because you know God.

GIANT CHRISTIANS

But grow in grace, and in the knowledge of our Lord and Saviour Jesus Christ. 2 Peter 3:18.

One morning while 10-year-old Isaac Watts was kneeling with his parents for worship, he began to giggle. As soon as the prayer was finished his father asked, "Isaac, why did you laugh during prayers? You know it is not allowed!"

Isaac pointed to the bell rope that hung by the fireplace and said: "I saw a little mouse run up the rope and these lines came into my head: 'There was a mouse for want of stairs, ran up a rope to say his prayers.'"

Father decided Isaac must have a lesson administered to the seat of his pants. The boy began to cry, and said, "Oh, Father, Father, pity take, and I no more will verses make."

Despairing of getting his son to stop making verses, Father Watts suggested that he use this ability to create better songs for the worship services. Isaac accepted the challenge. Altogether he wrote 761 hymns, 31 of which appear in *The Church Hymnal*.

Isaac Watts, who was born on this day in 1674, was not a large man. Although hardly a midget, he was smaller than most other people.

One day as he was standing near a restaurant with some friends, he overheard a man say, "Who is that odd-looking little man?"

"It is Isaac Watts," someone answered.

"Really? Is *that* the great Dr. Watts?" the man questioned, surprised, unable to believe that such a small man could have written so many beautiful hymns.

This was too much for Isaac Watts. Soon after he wrote,

"Were I so tall to reach the pole,
Or grasp the ocean with my span,
I must be measured by my soul:
The mind's the standard of the man."

Although Isaac's physical body did not grow very tall, he became a giant of the mind and spirit. He could not increase his height, but there was nothing to stop him from growing tall in his love for Jesus and in his ability to share that love with others. In this he became a giant, and so can you.

LITTLE LOST BOY

For the Son of man is come to seek and to save that which was lost. Luke 19:10.

Nine-year-old Kevin was lost. He hadn't meant to get lost, of course. He just wanted to explore the wonderful world of mountain and forest near the place where his family had been picnicking. He had grown tired of swings, slides, and table tennis. With a ping-pong paddle in hand he walked off down the Crimson Dawn Trail on Casper Mountain, Wyoming.

Kevin had a good time singing, whistling, and talking to the birds. He slapped the paddle against the trees as he walked through the woods. The trail led him into Elkhorn Canyon, a forbidding area of huge cliffs, deep chasms, bears, and rattlesnakes.

As evening shadows closed in, Kevin tried to find his way back, but the paths all looked the same. The stars came out, and he knew that he was lost. It was cold, and he wished that he were home in his warm bed. However, he had to settle for a pile of pine needles in the dark woods. Maybe in the morning he would find the way home.

The next day Kevin walked deeper into the canyon. After five days and nights in the forest he was too weak to go on. He lay down to die beside a sparkling brook that ran through a mountain meadow.

That is where the rescue team found him after five days of search that had begun Sunday evening, July 18, 1971.

Mike Murphy was the first to see Kevin's crumpled form lying on a sunny patch of grass near the mountain stream. He took a deep breath and held it as he ran to the boy. Then he exhaled and smiled. Kevin was alive! In that wonderful moment both Mike and Kevin knew how precious life is.

Jesus was even more aware of the value of life. That is why He left the splendors of heaven and came to this dark world to search for lost boys and lost girls. You are one for whom He came. The Bible says that "All we like sheep have gone astray; we have turned every one to his own way" (Isa. 53:6).

Jesus, the Great Rescuer, never gives up His search. He loves you. He is looking for you. Will you let Him lead you home?

RESCUE BY ROPE

I drew them with cords of a man, with bands of love. Hosea 11:4.

On the afternoon of July 19, 1960, Philip Reeves was working in the headhouse atop a 100-foot-high concrete grain elevator when he was knocked down by two tremendous explosions that shattered the elevator and rocked the area like an earthquake.

Soon the headhouse became a roaring chimney, its windows belching fire and smoke. Philip Reeves made his way to a top-floor window. Leaning out as far as he could, he called down to the gathering crowd, "Help me! Please, help me!"

Someone grabbed the electronic bull horn from the fire truck and called back, "Hang on! God will show us how to save you. Don't lose hope! We will help you!"

Meanwhile a frantic effort to save Philip was in progress. A small airplane flew over and dropped a rope, but it simply floated on the hot air rising from the fire. Next an Air Force helicopter made an attempt to reach him but broke one of its rotor blades. Another helicopter was called. But for young Reeves there wasn't much time. He collapsed over the window sill, with his head pointing toward the horrified spectators below.

A man was lowered in a sling from the second helicopter. He reached the now-unconscious boy and pulled his blistered body to safety. The hoist operator wound up the cable and Philip was on his way to the hospital.

Every man from Adam to the present time has been, like Philip Reeves, trapped and doomed to die. We have all sinned, and "the wages of sin is death" (Rom. 6:23). We had no hope. It seemed that all mankind must perish, that there was no way of escape for a lost world.

Then from the sky a rope of salvation was let down to us. It was a rope of love and caring. Jesus Christ left the security of His place in heaven to come down to this perishing planet. He risked all that we might be saved.

Today the rope is there. It is within your reach. Don't wait any longer. Time is short. Grasp that rope today and be saved. There is hope for all who call upon the name of Jesus.

SPACE ADVENTURE

Ye are my friends, if ye do whatsoever I command you. John 15:14.

On July 20, 1969, millions watched as the Apollo 11 lunar module touched down on the rocky plain called the Sea of Tranquility. They saw Neil Armstrong climb out of the spacecraft and step onto the moon's surface. It seemed impossible that all of this was happening more than 238,000 miles away.

Today a trip to the moon doesn't sound all that interesting. Men have their hearts set on further goals such as, Mars, Jupiter, Saturn, and beyond. Earth beings, including myself, want to find a way to get beyond their solar system.

I am planning on a space trip that will take me thousands of light years away to the most beautiful land imaginable. I have read that it is a land of rolling hills covered with velvety green grass, graceful trees, and never-fading flowers.

In that far distant spot in space there is a city glorious to behold. It is built in the shape of a square, measuring 360 miles on each side. The walls appear to be made of gold and the foundations sparkle with the colors of precious jewels. Each wall has three gates and each gate, I am told, is one huge pearl.

Inside the city, the streets are of gold, and the brightness is beyond description. In the center of that city is the throne of God and from the throne flows the river of life. A most unusual tree grows by that river. It looks like two trees, but is really one, with a trunk on one side of the river and a trunk on the other side with the branches joined above. The fruit is most delicious, and those who eat of it will never die.

There is a lovely home and mansion in that far-off land for anyone who wants one. There everyone will live as princes and princesses. Best of all Jesus will be there and He will walk and talk with the redeemed. The music is magnificent and there is so much to see and do.

Do you want to join me in taking that space flight? The requirements are simple. God's astronauts need only to be His friends, those who love Him and by His grace, keep His commandments. Reservations are being made today. Make sure you get yours.

MONKEY TRIAL

God created man in his own image, in the image of God created he him. Genesis 1:27.

The biggest news story of 1925 concerned a high school teacher in Dayton, Tennessee, who taught the theory of evolution to his students. According to Tennessee law at that time, only the story of Creation as recorded in the Bible could be taught. For disobeying this law, John T. Scopes was brought to trial.

Two famous lawyers, Clarence Darrow and William Jennings Bryan, argued the issue in court for eleven days, from July 10 to July 21. All over the world people followed the debates and had their own backyard quarrels about man's origin. If the monkeys had also taken up the argument, it might have gone something like this:

"Have you heard what they are saying about us these days?"

"No, what is that?"

"People claim that they descended from us!"

"How can that be? We don't act like them. Did you ever hear of a monkey taking drugs and blowing his mind?"

"No, nor have I heard of a monkey getting drunk and beating his wife and children."

"Neither do we drop bombs on each other and send missiles to destroy our neighbors."

"There really must be some mistake. Man descended from someone, but he did not descend from us!"

Of course, the truth is that we descended from Adam and Eve, who were formed by the hands of Jesus Christ, in His own image. What a beautiful thought! We were made to be His sons and daughters. We were made to reflect His character.

Sin, of course, has come into the world and almost wiped out the image of God in man. One of the reasons that Seventh-day Adventists operate so many schools is to help the young people understand their true origin. They have been established to help bring men and women, boys and girls, back to God, so that His image can again be reflected in them. They have been built so that young people can learn to know the One who created them.

God made the world. He made you. He wants you to reflect His image today.

JOHN'S DISCOVERY

Let no man despise thy youth; but be thou an example of the believers, in word, in conversation, in charity, in spirit, in faith, in purity. 1 Timothy 4:12.

J. N. Andrews, who was born on this day in 1829, became the first Seventh-day Adventist foreign missionary. Did you know that he could read the Bible in seven languages? Did you know that he memorized the entire New Testament?

As a teen-ager John Andrews was very much interested in Bible study. It was actually he who led his whole family to keep the Sabbath. It happened like this:

A family by the name of Stowell sold their farm because they were so sure Jesus would come on October 22, 1844. When He did not come, they were stranded. Mr. Andrews invited the Stowells to share the Andrews' large home.

While there, 15-year-old Marian Stowell read a tract explaining that Saturday is the Sabbath. She shared it with her brother, Oswald, and together they kept their first Sabbath.

The next Monday Marian gave the tract to 17-year-old John Andrews. He was immediately convinced that Christians should worship on Saturday.

"Have your father and mother read this?" John asked.

"No," Marian replied, "but I have, and I know now that we are not keeping the right Sabbath."

"I also believe that this is the truth," said John. "Will you keep the true Sabbath with me, Marian?"

"Of course," she answered. "Oswald and I have already kept one Sabbath. This week you can join us. Why don't you give the tract to your folks to read?"

"All right," said John. "I will." Mr. and Mrs. Andrews immediately accepted the Sabbath truth and passed the little paper on to Mr. and Mrs. Stowell. The next Sabbath the two families were united in obeying God's command.

Although we should respect those who are older, they do not always know the full truth from God's Word. In such cases God expects young people to do what they know is right and thus be an example to their elders, as were John, Marian, and Oswald.

Your example and faithfulness may be the means of winning an older person to Jesus and His truth.

JOURNEY TO JERUSALEM

Some trust in chariots, and some in horses: but we will remember the name of the Lord our God. Psalm 20:7.

It was a sad day as well as a happy one for the five thousand campers by the River Ahava. It was no doubt hard for the people to say goodbye to the land that had been their home for so long. They had sold or given away most of their possessions. What was left was packed, and they were ready to go. Last minute purchases for the journey had been made, and the animals were readied for the trip to Jerusalem.

"What's the holdup, Ezra?" someone must have asked as the leader of the expedition made his rounds of the tents.

"We cannot go without a priest," Ezra replied. "I have sent messengers to find one to go with us."

Eventually a priest was found, but the departure was further delayed. "We will have a prayer meeting before starting," Ezra announced. "We must ask God to show us the way to Jerusalem and to protect us on our journey."

"But aren't any of the king's soldiers coming along? After all, he is the one who has made the decree for us to return to rebuild the Temple. He is also sending gifts to help us. Surely he will spare a few soldiers if you ask him."

"I can't do that," Ezra said. "I am ashamed to require of the king a band of soldiers and horses to help us against the enemy in the way, 'because we had spoken unto the king, saying, the hand of our God is upon all them for good that seek him; but his power and his wrath is against all them that forsake him' (Ezra 8:22)."

So the five thousand people had a day of fasting and prayer there by the riverside. On or about April 7, 457 B.C., they took down their tents, loaded the camels, and started out. Throughout the journey God blessed them, so that they arrived safely in Jerusalem on or about July 23. After a three-day rest they held a special thanksgiving service to praise God for His guidance and protection along the way.

The returning Jews had put their trust in the Lord, and He had not failed them. It is good for us to remember, too, that with God on our side we are safer than with a police escort or an army's protection.

PASSING INSPECTION

And there shall in no wise enter into it any thing that defileth, neither whatsoever worketh abomination, or maketh a lie: but they which are written in the Lamb's book of life. Revelation 21:27.

At 12:50 P.M. on July 24, 1969, the journey of Apollo 11 ended in a splashdown in the Pacific Ocean. The three astronauts— Neil Armstrong, Michael Collins, and Edwin Aldrin—were immediately scrubbed with disinfectant to kill possible moon germs. Then they were put into a seventeen-day quarantine aboard the U.S.S. *Hornet* to see whether they had brought back any harmful bacteria from their moon journey.

Before you and I can enter the kingdom of heaven we must undergo a similar inspection of our character. Nothing unclean will be allowed through the gates of the New Jerusalem.

Can you imagine a fistfight under the tree of life? Can you picture someone telling a dirty joke in the presence of the angels? Would it seem right to hear unkind words along the banks of the River of Life?

In Psalm 24 David asked the following question: "Who shall ascend into the hill of the Lord? or who shall stand in his holy place?" The answer: "He that hath clean hands, and a pure heart" (verses 3, 4).

If you and I are going to be allowed to take the greatest space trip of all time, then we must, with Jesus' help, get rid of the things in our lives that would bar our entrance to that holy land.

In *The Youth's Instructor* of January 17, 1901, Ellen White wrote: "One defect, cultivated instead of being overcome, makes the man imperfect, and closes against him the gate of the Holy City. He who enters heaven must have a character that is without spot or wrinkle or any such thing. Naught that defileth can ever enter there. In all the redeemed host not one defect will be seen."

Today has been given us so that we might come to Jesus with all our filthiness and be cleansed and made righteous through His blood.

Not only will He forgive the sins of our past, but He will keep us from falling again and will present us faultless before the throne of God. By His grace and power we can pass inspection and be eligible for entrance into the city of God.

OVERHEATED ENGINES

Blessed are the peacemakers: for they shall be called the children of God. Matthew 5:9.

Seventy-five years ago Blériot's airplane engines were unreliable and overheated rapidly. Usually the motor did well for about twenty minutes and then began to miss so badly that the pilot was forced to land.

Using his own engine, Louis Blériot won a prize on July 25, 1909, for making the first flight across the English Channel. The airplane he used looked something like a bicycle pulling a man-sized box kite. To make the crossing he had to depend on one of his unreliable engines. If it overheated too soon Blériot might fall into the choppy waters below. However, that day there was a light rain that cooled his engine and kept it running smoothly for the thirty-seven minutes it took him to fly from France to England.

Do you know some people who are like those old airplane engines in that they become angry very quickly when things don't go their way?

Then there is another type of person who is like the cooling summer rain. Instead of fighting with the angry person and thus making him hotter, this peacemaker is like water putting out the fire. Not long ago I overheard a conversation that illustrates these two types of individuals.

"You tripped me on purpose!"

"I did not. You didn't watch where you were going."

"You did so! You're just jealous because we're winning."

"Don't call me a liar! If you want to fight, I'll . . ."

These two "engines" were really getting hot! You could almost smell the smoke! Then along came the "cooling rain."

"Come on, let's play!" he said. "We won't count the last point. Having fun is more important than winning. Let's get on with the game and have a good time."

Like magic, the overheated "engines" cooled down and the game had a happy ending.

Jesus said that those who are like "cooling rain" to "overheated engines" will be called the children of God. Will you be a peacemaker today? It's really quite easy. Why not give it a try?

UNCONDITIONAL SURRENDER

So likewise, whosoever he be of you that forsaketh not all that he hath, he cannot be my disciple. Luke 14:33.

On July 26, 1945, the leaders of Britain, the United States, and Russia met at Potsdam, Germany, and issued an ultimatum calling for Japan to make an unconditional surrender or suffer "prompt and utter destruction."

Two days later a reply came from Japan that they wanted peace, but certain conditions must be met. The Allies refused to allow any conditions. A few days later the first atomic bombs were dropped on Hiroshima and Nagasaki.

Surrender followed swiftly. It was unconditional. Nothing was held back. And with that surrender peace came once more to the world.

Unconditional is the only kind of surrender that Jesus Christ will accept from us. He will be your Lord of all or He will not be your Lord at all. He will have all of your heart or He will have none of it.

We need to be like the old Indian chief. After hearing the story of Jesus' death on the cross, he was overcome with gratitude. He must give something to the One who had given so much for him. He brought a lovely pair of beaded moccasins to the pastor, saying, "I will give these to Jesus."

"No, chief, that is not what Jesus wants," the pastor said.

Next he brought a pair of finely woven snowshoes.

"No," the pastor said again, "that is not what Jesus wants."

Finally, the old chief went into his tepee and brought out his most treasured possession, an automatic rifle.

"No, that is not what Jesus wants," the pastor said for the third time.

Suddenly the light dawned on the old chief's mind, and he said, "I will give Jesus this poor Indian."

"Yes," said the pastor, "that is what Jesus wants."

That is what Jesus wanted from the rich young ruler, too. He wanted him to surrender himself completely and unreservedly, holding back nothing. The young man refused to make that surrender and went away sorrowful.

Jesus is calling you today. Will you make an unconditional surrender of all you have and are? It is the only way to peace.

OBEDIENT GRASSHOPPERS

And I will rebuke the devourer for your sakes, and he shall not destroy the fruits of your ground. Malachi 3:11.

On July 27, 1931, a swarm of grasshoppers descended on the States of Iowa, Nebraska, and South Dakota, destroying thousands of acres of crops. A similar plague was reported in several other parts of the world.

When the insects swarmed over the African country now known as Kenya, every green thing was consumed, and the government had to step in to save the people from starvation.

In that country, one Christian man decided to claim God's promise of Malachi 3:11. "Dear Lord," he prayed, "I have been faithful to You in giving my tithes and offerings. Now I ask that You will keep Your promise and rebuke the devourer for my sake. Please protect my crops from the grasshoppers."

"Nothing can stop those insects from coming here," his neighbors taunted. "Your God is no better than ours!"

When the grasshoppers arrived, the sky was dark with their bodies. They settled down over the countryside, eating every blade of grass and every stalk of corn. There was not even a leaf left on the trees.

But not one touched the garden of the Christian man who had claimed God's promise. His field stood out like a green oasis in the midst of a dry desert.

People came from miles around to see the garden that the grasshoppers wouldn't eat. To each, the man told the story of how God had kept the promise of His Word.

"We don't understand it," the people said. "Are you sure you didn't put out some kind of poison?"

"I did not," he answered. "I simply prayed to God. He spoke to the grasshoppers, and they obeyed and stayed off my property."

If you were faced with a similar situation, would you be able to pray to God and expect an answer? Do you always pay a faithful tithe of all the money that comes to you? You may not earn much on your summer job, but you will owe God one tenth of all you earn. To keep that one tenth for yourself would be robbing God of what belongs to Him.

Only as we are faithful to God will we have the confidence that will enable us to pray as that man did about the grasshoppers.

THE SUBSTITUTE

But God commendeth his love toward us, in that, while we were yet sinners, Christ died for us. Romans 5:8.

In July, 1794, the dungeons of Paris were crowded with men and women who were destined for the guillotine.

One night an old man roamed the prison where he had been brought that day. As he looked at the sleeping forms, he was suddenly startled by the face of one he saw there. He stopped and gazed at the form on the floor. Could it be? Yes, he was sure it was his own son.

The father sank down beside the boy and tried to think of some way to deliver him from the awful fate that would be his.

"Aha! I know what I can do," the old man spoke to himself as a smile played upon his wrinkled face. "We both have the same name. I can answer for him and go to the guillotine in his place."

All night the father sat beside his sleeping son, hoping he would not wake up. Early the next morning three soldiers came into the dungeon and one called out: "Jean Simon de Loiserolle."

"Here I am!" the father said as he jumped to his feet.

On the way to the execution they passed the office where the records were kept. His name was again called out. "Jean Simon de Loiserolle, age 37."

"The name is correct," answered the old man, "but my age is 73."

"Stupid mistake!" the soldier muttered and made the correction, then checked off the name.

Later, the son awoke, expecting to be called at any moment to his death. One of his comrades finally spoke: "An old man sat beside you all night. When the guard came this morning and called your name he answered for you and went to his death."

Three days later on July 28, 1794, Robespierre, a leader of the French Revolution, was himself taken to the guillotine and the Reign of Terror came to an end. When the prison doors were opened, Jean Simon de Loiserolle, Jr., walked out a free man.

Jesus did the same for you. He answered when your name was called. He died that you might go free.

THE IMPOSTOR

For there is nothing covered, that shall not be revealed; and hid, that shall not be known. Matthew 10:26.

When Albania became independent on July 29, 1913, the country had neither president nor king. Therefore, the people asked Halim Eddine, a Turkish prince, to come and lead their nation.

Prince Eddine wasn't sure he wanted to be the King of Albania, so for some time he neglected to send a message, and the people became anxious. Then one day a telegram arrived stating that the prince was on his way to Durazzo, the capital city.

A few days later the new leader arrived in a golden coach. He wore a striking uniform decorated with medals. At his side he carried a shining sword. He was tall and looked very much as a king should look. When he spoke everyone listened. For five days he was honored at banquets and by parades throughout the city.

Then another telegram arrived from the Sultan of Turkey, stating that the man in Durazzo was an impostor. Prince Eddine was still in Turkey.

The people couldn't believe it. Quickly they went to their "king" to get an explanation, but he had gone. He knew that his disguise was no longer possible. Actually, he was Otto Witte, a circus performer, who looked a great deal like the prince.

Judas Iscariot was another impostor. He pretended to love Jesus, but betrayed Him with a kiss.

Ananias and Sapphira were impostors. They pretended to be generous supporters of the church by giving all of their property, while in reality they kept part for themselves.

Are you acting as an impostor? Do you dress like a Christian, talk like a Christian, and go through all the motions of being a good Christian, when down deep you are something different? You may fool your friends, but you cannot fool God. The time is coming when all the hidden things of your heart will be revealed. In that day the whole universe will know you for what you really are.

So what is the use of pretending now? Let Jesus come into your heart and take away your sham and pretense. Let Him make you a genuine Christian from the inside out.

ASSEMBLY LINE CHRISTIANS

Which is Christ in you, the hope of glory. Colossians 1:27.

Henry Ford, whose birthday is today, was a pioneer in building affordable cars. To accomplish this he decided to make only one model and that by the assembly line method. Soon the price of his model T dropped to less than $300.

By installing a moving assembly line, Ford decreased the time it took to make a car from twelve and one-half to one and one-half hours. The frame of the car moved through the plant on a conveyor belt, and workmen on each side added a part as it passed by.

There is one thing that modern cars have in common with the old model T. They are of very little use until someone climbs into the driver's seat and operates the mechanism to make them go.

A car might be air-conditioned and gold plated, but still it needs a driver behind the wheel if it is going to be driven outside of the factory. With a driver, a car can take people to work, school, or the lake. It can win a race or rush people to the hospital.

Your life is something like an automobile. From the time you were born you have been moving along the conveyor belt of learning. Your parents, brothers, sisters, aunts, uncles, and grandparents may have all done their share in building the chassis of your life. You have moved past a long line of Sabbath school teachers, counselors, ministers, and schoolteachers. They have all added something to your character.

It may seem that you have moved along from one stage of life to another with very little effort. However, before long you will have come to the end of the assembly line. No one will be there anymore to push you in the right direction.

From that point you must have a driver for your life. There comes the time when you must choose who that will be. Will you choose the Lord Jesus Christ?

Only as Christ takes over the controls will you have the assurance of reaching your destination safely. Give Him the keys of your life today. Put Him in the driver's seat and all will be well. He is sure to get you to the place you want to go.

SLAVES OF JESUS

Know ye not, that to whom ye yield yourselves servants to obey, his servants ye are to whom ye obey? Romans 6:16.

The word *servant* in this verse actually means "a slave." What is it like to be a slave?

One hundred and fifty years ago it meant that cruel men invaded your village, burned huts, killed the old and sick, and took you who were strong in chains to the coast, where you were loaded on a boat—like cattle—and shipped to a marketplace in the New World.

There you were purchased as so much property and put to work on plantations of cotton, sugar, or bananas. From the moment you were bought you had no choice but to obey your master and do his bidding. You belonged to him, and he could do with you as he wanted. You went nowhere and made no decisions without his permission.

No wonder there was such wild rejoicing on the night of July 31, 1834, when at the stroke of midnight 800,000 slaves held under the British flag were set free.

Slaves of all ages crowded the churches in the British West Indies on that night and waited for the bells to ring out their freedom. With the first peal the newly-freed people leaped to their feet with a shout of joy that seemed to lift the roofs. How glorious to be free!

This is what happened to the human family. For many years we were slaves of sinful desires and evil habits. When the devil snapped his fingers we obeyed. Then one glorious day Jesus set us free. The bells rang and angels sang. The whole world lay before us, and now we were free men and women, boys and girls, in Christ Jesus.

Now we want to obey a new master. We love Him so much for setting us free that we have vowed to serve Him the rest of our lives. Willingly, gladly, we will do His every bidding and obey His every command. Where He sends us, we will go. What He tells us, we will do. Now, by choice, we are "slaves" of Jesus Christ, for we have yielded ourselves to Him.

Whom do you obey? Who directs your life? To whom do you belong? Are you a slave of Christ or Satan? The choice is yours.

BORN AGAIN

Verily, verily, I say unto thee, Except a man be born again, he cannot see the kingdom of God. John 3:3.

William Wilberforce was born into a wealthy home in England more than two hundred years ago. He was brilliant, and by the age of 21 had graduated from Cambridge University and was elected to Parliament. He was an excellent public speaker. Everyone expected him to have an outstanding future.

Then, when William was 25, something happened that changed the course of his life. He was traveling with Pastor Isaac Milner by carriage through Europe on a holiday. The two men talked constantly about God and His purposes for mankind. They read the Bible together and prayed.

Somewhere along the way William Wilberforce gave his life to the Lord Jesus Christ. He was born again, became a new person. From that time on, he lost all interest in worldly ambition and could think only of living for Christ.

As William prayed about what God wanted him to do, he felt impressed that he should dedicate his life to putting an end to the slave trade. For nearly fifty years Mr. Wilberforce worked to get a bill passed in the British Parliament that would stop the buying and selling of slaves.

Because of William Wilberforce and the change that came into his life when he was born again, the 800,000 slaves in the British territories were set free on August 1, 1833.

When we are born the first time, we are born as sinners. As such we are selfish creatures who cannot please God.

To be born the second time is to have an experience such as that of William Wilberforce. We come to Jesus just as we are and ask Him to create a new heart and life within us. With that new heart come new thoughts, new desires, new hopes, new ambitions, new friends, and new actions. We no longer live for ourselves but for Him who died that we might live.

You cannot make this change yourself. You cannot accomplish it by determination. Wishing to be a better person will not bring it about.

To be born again means to be made a new creature in Christ Jesus. It is something He does for you when you accept Him as Lord and Master of your life. Have you made that choice?

AWARDS DAY

And, behold, I come quickly; and my reward is with me, to give every man according as his work shall be. Revelation 22:12.

On the night of August 2, 1943, Lt. John F. Kennedy was in command of Pt-109 when it was rammed by a Japanese destroyer. The boat was cut in two and sank almost immediately. Two men died. Lieutenant Kennedy was thrown against the wall of the cockpit, injuring his back; but he was able to hold on to wreckage until daybreak.

He then commanded the ten survivors to swim with him to a nearby island. One of the men was badly injured so Kennedy took the man's life preserver and swam with him to shore. Eventually the group was able to find some Christian natives of the Solomon Islands who helped them to safety.

For these deeds of bravery John F. Kennedy was awarded the Navy and Marine Corps Medal and the Purple Heart.

Look up Decorations and Medals in the encyclopedia and you will find a colorful display of bronze and silver medallions offered by various countries.

Those who do great service for Japan are given the Supreme Order of the Chrysanthemum. Sweden offers the Royal Order of the Seraphim. France awards membership in the Legion of Honor, and Britain gives the Victoria Cross.

Very few people receive these awards. However, it will not be that way when God gives out His medals. Everyone who is saved will receive an award on that day.

In vision Ellen White saw what it would be like. She saw all of God's children gathered before Him on the sea of glass. With His own right hand He placed a golden crown upon the heads of the redeemed of earth. He gave them harps of gold and placed palms of victory in their hands. She saw that not all the rewards would be equal. Some had crowns that appeared heavy with stars while other crowns were not so bright. But all were satisfied with their crowns. It all depended on what work the redeemed one had done.

Do you feel sometimes that no one takes notice of what you do? Are you passed by when the trophies are given out? Jesus sees all that you have done for Him. He will give you a reward. So cheer up. Awards Day is just around the corner.

THE BEST TRANQUILIZER

Behold, he that keepeth Israel shall neither slumber nor sleep.
Psalm 121:4.

Early on the morning of August 3, 1923, Calvin Coolidge was awakened and told that President Warren Harding had died. Coolidge dressed and knelt in prayer before going downstairs to take the oath of office, thereby becoming the thirtieth President of the United States.

President Coolidge then went back upstairs, undressed, and went back to bed. Wonder of wonders, in spite of the sudden responsibility thrust upon him, he slept. People wondered how he could possibly rest when suddenly all the problems of the world had been thrown into his lap.

His experience was similar to that of an old woman during the bombing of London during World War II. Every night the bombers came dropping their deadly weapons. The air-raid sirens, the drone of the approaching engines, the deafening explosions, and the cries of the injured kept most people awake and in a constant state of nerves. People noticed, however, that this grandmother seemed to be relaxed by day and slept well at night.

"How do you keep so calm?" a neighbor asked. "Don't you know what is happening? Aren't you afraid?"

"Yes," she replied. "Every night I says my prayers, and I worries about what Hitler is going to do tonight. Then I remembers how the parson said God was always watchin', so I goes to sleep. After all, there's no use for two of us to lie awake."

Trust in God is better than a tranquilizer. Prayer is better than a pill. The next time you have trouble sleeping, get out of bed and kneel down to pray. Tell God all about the things that worry you. Tell Him you are going to leave everything in His hands for the night.

How comforting to know that there is Someone all powerful who is in charge of the circumstances of our lives. We can trust Him. We can rest all our cares and worries on His shoulders. We can go to sleep knowing that while we rest He is working things out for our best good.

We can be like David who said, "I will both lay me down in peace, and sleep: for thou, Lord, only makest me dwell in safety" (Ps. 4:8).

ONLY ONE DOOR

Neither is there salvation in any other: for there is none other name under heaven given among men, whereby we must be saved. Acts 4:12.

It was not safe to be a Jew in Amsterdam in 1942. Since the invasion of Holland by Hitler's army two years before, the Jews had been brutally persecuted and many were deported to extermination camps in Germany and Poland.

Otto Frank realized that the only hope for his family was to find a safe hiding place. Behind his office was a small house known as the annex. The two were connected by a narrow passageway. Mr. Frank began laying in provisions and preparing the back house as a hideaway for his family.

There was only one way to reach the rooms in the back house and that was through a door in a room on the second floor. A special bookcase was built to fit over this door so that no one would suspect that it existed. Behind that door eight people hid successfully for two years.

Then on August 4, 1944, Nazi police searched the house and discovered the hidden door. The eight people were captured.

Just as there was only one way to enter the Frank family's secret hiding place, there is only one way by which we may enter heaven. Some people think that you can enter heaven through any "door" you choose, be it Hinduism, Islam, Buddhism, or any other religion. Such people say, "It doesn't really matter how you reach heaven as long as you get there. All religions are good. They all lead to the same place."

This is not true. The Bible declares that there is only one way, only one "door," and only one name whereby we can be saved. The name of Buddha will not save you. Neither will the name of Mohammed, Krishna, or any other man.

Noah's ark is often used to illustrate God's kingdom. In that ark there was only one door. All the animals and the eight people who were saved from the Flood entered in through the same door. So it is with the kingdom of heaven. There is only one "door," and that "door" is Jesus Christ.

When this world comes to an end there will be only one place of safety. There is only one door to that secret hiding place in the shadow of God's wings, and that "door" is Jesus Christ. Today that "door" stands open for you and me.

SAVED FROM DROWNING

I will heal their backsliding, I will love them freely: for mine anger is turned away from him. Hosea 14:4.

August 5, 1972, was a beautiful, sunny Sabbath. The Kortenbachs should have been in church; but were instead on the banks of the Cowlitz River, blowing up rafts and planning a lazy day floating downstream.

Over the months Sabbath had ceased to have the special significance it once had had for the Kortenbachs. Little by little they had grown careless, until the family stopped going to church altogether.

On this Sabbath the family of five had not gone far when their rafts were caught in the swift rapids, thrown against dense overhanging branches, and upended. In a twinkling the rafts disappeared, and so did Father and Susan. Mother, Heidi, and Bill were left clinging to branches, fighting for their lives against the current.

I have said my last No to God, Mother thought in those brief moments. We are all going to drown. We have deliberately ignored God's Sabbath and now we have no hope. We cannot even pray, for He will not hear us.

Though not called upon, God was still there, looking after His wandering children.

Heidi and Bill were able to scramble to safety along the branches. Mother found herself securely stuck against some big roots in the water and was able to climb out.

Neither Father nor Susan could swim, but Father was able to hold on to a loop of the raft and keep afloat.

Susan was struggling to keep her head above water when a most unusual thing happened. One minute she was in the water and the next she seemed to fly through the air. She doesn't know how she got into the raft but suddenly there she was. After a little while the water became shallow, and she and her father climbed out and found their way to the others.

It was a very sober family that drove home in their soggy clothes that afternoon. The following Sabbath morning all five of them were in Sabbath school.

You see, God loves us very much, whether we are good or bad. When we slip away from Him, He feels sorry and goes out to search for us. If we do not resist, He will heal our backsliding.

SAVED BY A ROCK

The Lord is my rock, and my fortress, and my deliverer.
2 Samuel 22:2.

On August 6, 1916, a tugboat was pulling a barge in the Niagara River when something happened to the connecting cable. The barge broke away and was carried by the swift current straight toward the falls. The two men aboard were sure it was their last boat ride.

"The barge is loose!" shouted a dozen voices.

"Stop it!"

"Save the men!"

"Somebody do something!"

But there was nothing anyone could do but watch the barge rush to its doom. Bystanders were powerless to help. The tug did not dare pursue. All hope seemed gone, when suddenly, with a mighty lift of the current, the barge was deposited on top of a huge rock hidden beneath the surface. There it stopped, just seconds away from the falls. Now there was something people could do.

"Phone the police!"

"Call the boat company."

"Bring a rope."

Lifesavers threw a rope to the barge, and the men were rescued. How thankful they were for the rock that saved their lives.

We, too, are saved by a Rock. That Rock is the Lord Jesus Christ, the mighty Rock of Ages. Without Him we have no hope. Just as surely as the Niagara River flows over the falls, so surely is the sinner headed for destruction. Just as that barge was helpless in the current, so are we powerless to save ourselves. The swift-flowing river of sin will take us to certain death.

But, praise the Lord, in the middle of that river there is a Rock. Those who reach Him will be saved. As long as you cling to Him nothing can harm you. Let temptations come. Let the waters beat around you. Let the current pull as hard as it likes. In Him you are perfectly safe and secure. Unbelief, impure thoughts, and bad habits can flow all around you, but they cannot move you as long as you hold to Him.

The Lord is our Rock and our Deliverer. Won't you cling to Him today?

226

CALLED TO PREACH

Therefore be ye also ready: for in such an hour as ye think not the Son of man cometh. Matthew 24:44.

Fifty-year-old William Miller sat at his desk in Low Hampton, New York, one Saturday morning in August, 1831. Before him was an open Bible. As he read again the verses that told of Christ's soon return he was overwhelmed with the conviction that God was calling him to tell this message to others.

Could you have looked in on him that summer morning you would have seen that he was troubled. William Miller was not a preacher, but a farmer. Was God really calling him? Would anyone listen to him?

"Dear Lord, is this really a call from You? If it is, then please send someone to ask me to preach. If You do that, I will go."

A few moments later there was a knock on his door. It was his nephew, Irving Guilford, from the nearby town of Dresden. "Father sent me to ask you to come and preach at our place tomorrow morning. We want you to tell us about what you have studied on the second coming of Christ."

William Miller was stunned. He had not really expected an invitation to preach. After spending some time praying in the maple grove beside his house, he surrendered to God's call. That afternoon he made the sixteen-mile journey to Dresden.

The following morning, probably August 7, William Miller stood up to preach before a congregation gathered in the kitchen of the Guilford home. When he was finished the people urged him to stay and tell them more. He remained for one week, carefully explaining how he had arrived at the year 1843 as the time when Jesus would come.

He read them Daniel's prophecy about 2,300 days and explained that in prophecy one day equals one year. This prophecy began in 457 B.C. with the decree to rebuild Jerusalem. Subtracting this number from 2,300, he got the year 1843.

People were electrified. Only twelve more years! Whole families gave their hearts to the Lord that week.

William Miller was wrong in giving a date for the Lord's return, but we do know it will be soon. Are you ready?

A MATTER OF PRIDE

Pride goeth before destruction, and an haughty spirit before a fall. Proverbs 16:18.

Spain was proud of her navy. It was the strongest in the world, and her merchant ships brought back untold wealth from lands afar. Three hundred years ago the Spanish Empire included the Philippines, most of South America, and parts of North America and Africa. Spain had reason to be proud, for she was the most powerful country in the world.

When English pirate ships began attacking Spanish boats and stealing their gold, Spain was not greatly worried. After all, they had the strongest navy.

The King of Spain decided to invade England and bring it into his empire. One hundred and thirty ships were prepared. Seven thousand sailors and more than 17,000 soldiers boarded the ships. There was great enthusiasm as Spanish success was taken for granted. The fleet of ships was called The Invincible Armada and was sent off with great fanfare. Defeat was not possible.

However, the Spanish had not counted on the bad weather. This delayed their progress and gave the English time to organize a navy. They were not prepared for the eight fire ships that the English floated into their carefully planned formation, scattering the Spanish ships, driving them out to sea. Neither had the invaders counted on the swiftness with which the small British ships could maneuver.

The Invincible Armada was defeated by the English on August 8, 1588. Half of the ships remained and slunk home in shame.

Pride is still around today.

If you think you're the most popular person in school and expect everything to come your way, be careful; you may be headed for a fall.

If you think you're the best ballplayer on your team and thus victory will always be yours, watch out; you may be beaten.

If you think you're so smart that you will automatically be at the top of the class without half trying, beware; someone will prove you wrong.

If you consider yourself a good Christian in no danger of falling into sin, watch your step; a fall is certain.

WHY JESUS CRIED

The Lord is not slack concerning his promise, as some men count slackness; but is longsuffering to us-ward, not willing that any should perish, but that all should come to repentance. 2 Peter 3:9.

One Sunday afternoon nineteen and one-half centuries ago, Jesus sat on a donkey on the Mount of Olives and cried. He looked at the beauty of Jerusalem glistening in the setting sun, and His body shook with agonizing sobs. The happy throng that accompanied Him grew silent, and some cried with Him out of sympathy.

Jesus saw the city compassed round about with Roman soldiers. He saw the terrible starvation and death that would come to those people. He saw children and parents grabbing food from one another and mothers eating the dead bodies of their own children. He saw the soldiers setting fire to the Temple and the beautiful city lying in ruins with not one stone left upon the other.

Even though Jesus knew that Jerusalem would be destroyed, He wanted to save all whom He could. He didn't want any to die, so He gave some information to His disciples a few days later. If this were heeded, the lives of His followers would be saved.

Jesus said, "When ye shall see Jerusalem compassed with armies, then know that the desolation thereof is nigh. Then let them which are in Judea flee to the mountains; and let them which are in the midst of it depart out" (Luke 21:21).

For forty years after Christ's crucifixion God gave those within the city time to repent. The disciples pleaded with the people to accept Christ. And many did so.

In A.D. 66, when the Roman army under Cestius Gallus surrounded the city, the Christians knew that the time had come to flee. Just at the moment when attack seemed certain, Cestius Gallus drew back and the Jews followed to do battle. In the brief time that the gates were open the Christians escaped. None of them perished when the city was destroyed on August 9, A.D. 70.

God loves you just as much as He loved those people inside Jerusalem. He doesn't want you to die. He will save you if you will let Him. If you reject Him, how sad He will be!

CORRECTION BY FIRE

Thou shalt also consider in thine heart, that, as a man chasteneth his son, so the Lord thy God chasteneth thee. Deuteronomy 8:5.

In 1902 there was a concentration of Adventists in Battle Creek, Michigan. There were located the General Conference headquarters, a world-famous sanitarium and hospital, a medical school, the Review and Herald Publishing House, and a large tabernacle seating 3,500 people.

Then on February 18 the main building of the sanitarium burned to the ground. On December 30, the Review and Herald was completely destroyed by fire.

"God is trying to teach us something," A. G. Daniells said. "God has always disciplined His people like a Father; and when He permits calamities to come upon them, . . . there is meaning in them. And that meaning we must discover and heed."

When Mrs. White heard about the fire in the publishing house, she wrote: "Everyone connected with the office should ask himself, 'Wherein do I deserve this lesson? Wherein have I walked contrary to a "Thus saith the Lord," that He should send this lesson to me?'"

For thirty years the testimonies of Mrs. White had warned Adventists that they were concentrating too much of their work in Battle Creek. No one had seemed to be listening. Now they were ready to pay attention. It was decided to relocate.

After much prayer and investigation, the committee decided on Washington, D.C. Mrs. White gave her approval and on August 10, 1903, the General Conference headquarters and the Review and Herald Publishing Association moved to Washington.

The Adventist leaders of 1903 set us a good example. When troubles come we should spend some time asking ourselves the questions they asked: "Have I been following the Lord whole-heartedly? Have I heeded the warnings and reproofs that God has sent? Have I been following my own way?"

An honest look at our lives will often show us why God permits certain things to happen.

Just as earthly parents punish their children to make them understand that they are doing wrong, so our heavenly Father corrects us by allowing troubles and calamities to come our way.

POWER TO GET WEALTH

But thou shalt remember the Lord thy God: for it is he that giveth thee power to get wealth. Deuteronomy 8:18.

Andrew Carnegie entered the United States as a poor boy, but by the time he retired in 1901 he was worth at least 400 million dollars. He spent the next nineteen years giving that money away, for he believed it was a sin to die rich.

It is difficult to comprehend 400 million dollars. Let's just say that you could spend one dollar for every single minute of your life. At that rate, in one hour you could spend 60 dollars or 1,440 dollars per day. If you could go on spending that much every day it would take you almost two years to spend your first million dollars and a fantastic 760 years to spend as much as Andrew Carnegie had.

Mr. Carnegie felt that once the needs of his family had been cared for, the remainder of his riches should be used to benefit mankind. He gave much of it to schools and universities. He built 2,509 free libraries. He set up a special fund to help heroes who risked their lives to save others. He gave much to his former employees and also to a number of churches. Before he died on August 11, 1919, he had spent 350 million dollars.

What I have read about Andrew Carnegie leads me to believe that he would have agreed with Mrs. White when she said, "God has not given us riches to use just as we shall fancy, to indulge impulse, to bestow or withhold as we shall please. We are not to use riches in a selfish way, devoting them simply to our own enjoyment. This course would not be doing right toward God or toward our fellow men, and would bring at last only perplexity and trouble."—*Review and Herald,* March 31, 1896.

It is not a sin to be rich. In fact, the Bible says it is God who gives us the ability to get wealth. The talent of making money is a valuable gift, and when used wisely can be of great benefit to the world.

What do you do with the money you get? Do you waste it? Do you spend it all on yourself? Do you hoard it? Do you put any aside for God? Do you think about the millions who go to bed hungry every night?

Remember who gives you the power to get money. He is waiting to see what you will do with it today.

ERASING THE TAPE

If we confess our sins, he is faithful and just to forgive us our sins, and to cleanse us from all unrighteousness. 1 John 1:9.

On August 12, 1877, Thomas A. Edison stood in front of a small metal cylinder wrapped in tinfoil and mounted on an axle that could be turned. Next to this cylinder was a small mouthpiece. Edison began to rotate the cylinder as he spoke: "Mary had a little lamb, Its fleece was white as snow, And everywhere that Mary went, The lamb was sure to go."

As he spoke, the diaphragm of the mouthpiece vibrated, causing a needle to vibrate. As this happened, the needle made small dents in the tinfoil. Then another needle was attached to the diaphragm and the cylinder turned again. This time back came Edison's voice: "Mary had a little lamb . . ." For the first time a human voice had been recorded and played back.

Today's stereo is a far cry from the first phonograph. Now we have tape recorders, cassette recorders, mini-cassette recorders, dictating machines, and videotape recorders. With the press of a button anybody can record anything, from his own voice to a symphony.

If you have a tape recorder available, try this experiment. Push the record button and say, "This is the record of Peter's life. He disobeyed his mother last week. He stole money from her purse and then lied to her when she asked whether he had done it. He cheated on yesterday's math quiz. He is a bad boy and cannot go to heaven."

Listen to the recording you have made. Would you like to have a record like that kept in heaven of your sins?

Now, just suppose that Peter is sorry for his sins. Going to his room he kneels down and asks Jesus to forgive him for each bad thing he has done. In that very moment Jesus wipes away all Peter's sins and gives him a clean new tape.

Rewind the tape you made of Peter's life, to the beginning. Push the record button and say: "This is the record of Peter's life. Peter never did anything wrong. He was always honest and obedient and faithful. He has always been just like Jesus. There is a place in heaven for him."

Listen now to the new recording. Wouldn't you like to have that kind of record of your past life? You can have it the moment you confess your sins to Jesus.

THE HAND THAT TURNS THE DIAL

Discretion shall preserve thee, understanding shall keep thee.
Proverbs 2:11.

What is wrong with television? Is your set really an "idiot box," as some people say? Is it an "invention of the devil"? Should Christians have one in their home?

If there is a problem with television, I maintain that the fault does not lie with the set, but with the hand that turns the dial.

Television can make us aware of what life is like in other parts of the world. We can see the launching of a satellite or the effects of war on a Cambodian refugee. Through it famous men and women can come into our homes. A twist of the dial might bring us a symphony concert or a glimpse of a cattle roundup.

Television can help catch shoplifters, teach isolated children the three R's, and bring a message of salvation to a man in jail.

At the same time it can keep mothers from their housework, and children from getting enough outdoor exercise. It can dominate a household to the point where normal conversation is almost impossible, and family members become strangers for lack of communication.

Surveys indicate a connection between the large amount of time some children spend watching television and their inability to concentrate in school.

Do the scores of murders, gun battles, and fistfights that are enacted each week on television have anything to do with the rising amount of violence in the streets?

Do the sentimental love stories portrayed every afternoon on the "soap operas," in which divorce is the accepted thing, have anything to do with the large number of homes that are splitting up these days?

These are probably not questions John Logie Baird, the Scottish inventor whose birthday is today, asked himself when he gave the first public demonstration of this modern-day wonder. However, they are questions that Christian young people need to consider carefully when they reach for the television dial.

CHARACTER CONSERVATION

Thou shalt not go up and down as a talebearer among thy people. Leviticus 19:16.

At 1:00 P.M. on August 14, 1933, the man in the lookout tower high on Saddle Mountain, Oregon, noticed what appeared to be a small forest fire over in Gales Creek Canyon. This was an area where lumbermen were working, and everyone expected them to put out the fire, but they couldn't.

By the time regular firefighters reached the camp the fire was raging out of control. Volunteers joined the crew, making an army of three thousand men fighting the blaze. Still they were powerless to stop it. Sparks and smoke rose 8,500 feet into the air. The heat was so intense that no one could go within a quarter mile of the blaze.

It was the worst forest fire in history. A total of 270,000 acres of timber were destroyed, an amount equal to all the lumber used at that time in the United States in one year. The loss was estimated at more than $200 million.

Gossip is something like a forest fire. It begins with just a small spark of information. At that point it would be so easy to put out. Instead, talebearers fan the spark into a flame, adding fuel to the fire as they pass it on. Before long it has spread out of control.

In a certain school gossiping and tattling became so bad that the teacher had to think of a way to stop it. So one morning she brought to class a cardboard box on which were pasted pictures of birds. In the lid there was a small slot. The teacher suggested that if the pupils had any gossip, they tell it to the birds. They were to write any bad things they heard about someone on a piece of paper and put it into the box. The first day the box was full. After a few days it was empty. The children had learned that it was no fun to tell it to the birds, because the birds didn't tell. They also discovered that everyone in class was much happier.

If you hear any gossip today, keep it to yourself. Let the fire stop with you.

A good sign for Smokey the Bear would be: "Help Prevent Gossip Fires." The conservation of character is every bit as important as the conservation of resources.

ARC DE TRIOMPHE

For he hath made him to be sin for us, who knew no sin; that we might be made the righteousness of God in him. 2 Corinthians 5:21.

Today is the birthday of Napoleon Bonaparte, who was Emperor of France just after the French Revolution. In 1806, on his thirty-seventh birthday, the foundation stone was laid for what was to be the largest triumphal arch ever constructed, the Arc de Triomphe.

Built to honor the revolutionary armies, the Arc de Triomphe stands 15 stories (160 feet) tall. It is 146 feet wide and has a central arch that is 48 feet across.

Many victorious armies have passed through that archway and more than one flag has flown from its top. Perhaps the most dramatic parade occurred on the day the armistice of World War I was celebrated. Reports say that twenty thousand Frenchmen marched through the Arc de Triomphe that day.

On a platform raised above the arch sat a choir which sang out the question: "By what right do you come to the arch of victory?"

"We come by the blood-red banner of Verdun!" was the reply. They had fought the enemy and had come home victorious.

Before long you and I may take part in another glorious victory celebration. We may stand on the sea of glass before the walls of the New Jerusalem. The pearly gates will swing open wide and, led by Jesus Himself, the saved ones will march through that great archway.

Should the angel choir sing out the question: "By what right do you enter this Holy City?" the reply may be shouted back: "By the blood-red banner of Calvary!"

Because of what happened at the middle cross on Calvary's Hill nearly two thousand years ago, you and I can claim the right to enter the heavenly city. Jesus, the perfect Son of God, suffered for your sins and mine.

The blood that flowed from His hands and feet that day was for you. It can cover all the ugliness of your past life and allow you to stand as a perfect, spotless individual who is worthy to enter the presence of God. It is that blood which provided your victory. That blood can make you a conqueror. Thank God for Calvary!

235

TAKE A REST

And he said unto them, Come ye yourselves apart into a desert place, and rest a while. Mark 6:31.

If James White had followed this counsel of Jesus perhaps he would not have been stricken with paralysis on the morning of August 16, 1865.

Elder White had been working very hard preparing pamphlets on health and temperance. He also needed to deal with many problems concerning Adventist men who had been drafted into the army. He was in constant demand as a speaker and there was simply no time for him to rest. He worked night and day.

On June 5 of that year God had sent James a special message through his wife, Ellen. He must stop working so hard and let others bear some of the responsibilities while he took time out for exercise and rest. However, the work seemed so urgent that he kept on, giving no heed to the demands of his body and mind for relaxation.

On August 16, while Elder and Mrs. White were taking a brief walk before breakfast, he suddenly became paralyzed. As he was trying to open an ear of corn, Mrs. White heard a strange noise. She looked up and saw her husband's face flushed and his arm hanging limp at his side. He could not speak, and his wife had to help him into the house. For fifteen months he was unable to work.

That experience shows that we cannot go against the laws of health without suffering the consequences. We must have periods of rest and relaxation. Indoor work must be balanced by exercise in the open air. Times of mental strain must be followed by periods of vacation.

What about you? Are you following the counsel the Lord has given regarding study?

"Students should not be permitted to take so many studies that they will have no time for physical training. The health cannot be preserved unless some portion of each day is given to muscular exertion in the open air."—*Fundamentals of Christian Education,* p. 146.

If you take time for outdoor exercise, you will find your mind fresher and more able to understand your lessons. Your body will also become stronger and you will not so easily get sick.

FULTON'S FOLLY

For we have not an high priest which cannot be touched with the feeling of our infirmities; but was in all points tempted like as we are, yet without sin. Hebrews 4:15.

"Fulton's Folly" is what someone called it. The thing was described by one writer as "an ungainly craft looking precisely like a backwoods sawmill mounted on a scow and set on fire." The *Clermont* was actually a steamboat, one of the first in the United States.

August 17, 1807, was the date scheduled for the ship's public trial. A large crowd gathered on the banks of the Hudson River to see if it would work.

"I'll bet you anything it won't go!" said one.

"What a lot of noise it makes!" said another.

"To say nothing of all that fire and steam and smoke."

"She'll never make it!"

Robert Fulton ignored their comments and made ready to prove that the ship would work.

Slowly the boat began to move away from the wharf. It headed toward the center of the river where it made a clean-cut turn upstream and was on its way. A shout went up from the spectators.

"There she goes!"

"It works!"

"Look at her pass the other boats!"

At the amazing speed of about five miles an hour the *Clermont* steamed up the river to Albany and back in thirty-two hours. The news that the ship really worked spread all over New York, and soon there were plenty of passengers and freight to keep it busy.

The attitude of those spectators on August 17, 1807, is still around in 1983. People look at Christianity and say, "It will never work. It is not possible to live by the ideals of the Bible."

Jesus Christ came into this world to prove that it does work. He came to demonstrate the reality of the things He taught.

Jesus was once a child. He became a teen-ager and faced the same problems you face. By His life He proved that it is possible for a young person to grow up in a wicked world and yet not sin. He had no resources you do not have. He demonstrated what you can become through His grace and power.

DISQUALIFIED

For whosoever shall keep the whole law, and yet offend in one point, he is guilty of all. James 2:10.

In 1926 Gertrude Ederle became the first woman to swim the English Channel. She might have claimed that honor one year sooner had she not inadvertently broken one little rule.

On August 18, 1925, 18-year-old Trudy dived into the English Channel from a rock on the French shore. Nine hours later she had covered seventeen miles in spite of heavy seas.

"Only six more miles!" her trainer yelled from the tugboat beside her. "You can make it! Keep going!"

Just then a huge wave broke over Trudy and she disappeared. When she came up she was not swimming. She had stopped to spit out some salt water and catch her breath. However, her trainer thought she had collapsed. Frightened, he called out to the man who was swimming beside her, "Get Trudy! She's in trouble."

Immediately he was at her side with his arm around her.

"Oh, Jim, why did you do it?" Trudy sobbed. "I was all right. I could easily have gone on. I wasn't in trouble."

Very much disappointed, Trudy climbed into the boat. There was no use going on. It didn't matter that she had kept all of the other rules. She had broken one and she was disqualified.

The following year she broke no rules and became the first woman to swim the English Channel.

God says that is how it is with us, too. Breaking even one of His commandments disqualifies us for entrance into heaven. One small lie will keep us out just as surely as will a hundred bigger sins.

Does it seem unfair to you that God demands obedience to every one of His commandments? Your teachers are not that strict, are they? Whoever heard of a teacher failing a student because he missed one point out of a ten-point quiz? Yet this is God's way. You score either perfect or zero.

It really isn't unfair, for God has provided a way by which we may all have a perfect score. Whether our sins are big or small they must be confessed and forsaken. When we come to Jesus, He forgives our sins and wipes out the record. He then gives us a perfect score on the books of heaven. Through Jesus Christ we can be qualified to enter the Holy City.

CHOOSING A CAREER

Lord, what wilt thou have me to do? Acts 9:6.

When you were a small child everything was decided for you. Life then was quite simple.

When you become a teen-ager life gets more complicated. You are expected to begin making your own decisions. Your parents are not always around. You have to learn to stand on your own two feet and take the consequences of the choices you make. Sometimes this is frightening!

One of the big decisions that faces a young person is What career shall I follow? Will it be teaching? Nursing? Farming? Engineering? Construction? How can you know for sure what is best?

Bernard Baruch, a statesman whose birthday is today, faced the same problem. He just couldn't make up his mind, so his mother took him to a phrenologist. The man ran his fingers over Bernard's skull for a few minutes and asked, "What would you like this boy to be?"

"We thought to send him for medicine," Mrs. Baruch replied.

"A doctor? Never! Put him instead into business. He will do big things."

It was decided. Because of the bumps on Bernard's head, he was going to be a businessman. Is there no better way for Christian youth to come to a decision? Must you go to fortunetellers or look up your horoscope to find the answer?

God, who brought you into existence, knows all about your abilities. He has a plan for your life. You are qualified to do one task better than any other.

Ellen White once wrote: "God has given to every man his work, and no one else can do that work for him."—*Testimonies,* vol. 4, p. 615.

The important thing, then, is to find out what it is that God wants you to do. Since He has the master plan, wouldn't it make sense to go to Him for guidance about your career?

You don't have to have somebody feel your head in order to find your answer. Neither is it necessary to be worried and perplexed about your future.

Just whisper the words, "Lord, what wilt Thou have me to do?" When the time comes, you will know. Meanwhile, be assured that God is leading you in the right direction.

PLAYING WITH SNAKES

And the great dragon was cast out, that old serpent, called the Devil, and Satan, which deceiveth the whole world. Revelation 12:9.

You can't trust a snake. One day it may seem to like you, the next day it may try to kill you.

I know from experience, for I kept a pet python for two years. It was so well trained that I could, without fear, let it wrap itself around my arm. When I flicked its tail it always unwound. Then the day came when it tightened its grip instead. I panicked, and it squeezed tighter still. My hand became numb, and I screamed for help. My husband came to my rescue and unwound the snake. That was the last time I played with it. I was glad I lived to make the choice.

Jean-Guy Leclair, of Montreal, was not so fortunate. On August 20, 1978, he was strangled by his pet boa constrictor while performing in a nightclub.

Mr. Leclair laid down on the floor and let the eight-foot snake coil around his body as he had done countless times before.

"If I'm not on my feet in twenty minutes you can put me in a coffin," Mr. Leclair told the audience. Then he seemed to lose control of the snake and it twined around his neck. The manager called the police. Four of the officers struggled to free Mr. Leclair, but it was too late; he was dead.

Satan works in the same way. His temptations appear to be harmless as long as we keep control. A little of this or that, as long as it is just a little for excitement, can't do any harm. Such reasoning shows that we are falling for Satan's lies.

That is what happened in the Garden of Eden. As Eve listened to the serpent talk, she thought he was trying to be her friend. He promised her an exciting world of knowledge if she would taste a little of the fruit.

"Just take one small bite," the serpent said. "Nothing will happen. I have eaten it and I am still alive. See how wise I am. Why don't you also eat and become wise?"

Eve took a bite and shared the fruit with her husband. Oh, the terrible results of that one small sin!

Playing with snakes is not a safe hobby. Neither is playing with sin.

CHARTER OAK

Whosoever therefore will be a friend of the world is the enemy of God. James 4:4.

Friendship with the world is one of the greatest dangers we face. Little by little Satan persuades Christians to listen to popular music, read best-seller books, watch award-winning movies, and wear the latest fashions. Slowly, worldliness creeps into their daily habits until there is little difference between the followers of Christ and the world.

The Charter Oak, which once stood in Hartford, Connecticut, illustrates this process. When James II was King of England, he sent Sir Edmund Andros to America to take back the charter from the legislative assembly in Connecticut. The day he asked for the document there was a debate that lasted until after dark. Candles were lighted, but suddenly they flickered out. When they were relighted, the charter was gone. The story is that Joseph Wadsworth took the document during those moments of darkness and hid it in the hollow of the oak.

That tree became famous, and people from far and near came to see the oak that had saved the Connecticut charter. Each wanted a piece of the wood as a souvenir. After 169 years of chipping away at the old tree, the original hole had enlarged enough to hold twenty-five men. As a result, on August 21, 1856, the giant tree fell during a gale.

A storm is coming upon this old world of ours. Some who have appeared as mighty oak trees in the church will fall. Why?

About this time, Mrs. White wrote: "The time is not far distant when the test will come to every soul. The observance of the false Sabbath will be urged upon us. The contest will be between the commandments of God and the commandments of men. Those who have yielded step by step to worldly demands, and conformed to worldly customs will then yield to the powers that be, rather than subject themselves to derision, insult, threatened imprisonment, and death."—*Prophets and Kings,* p. 188.

Today, while there is still time, we ought to think seriously about the habits of our lives. Is something chipping away our faith? What about our spare time activities? Is there anything that indicates our friendship with the world? Are we another Charter Oak?

SOWING TIME

For whatsoever a man soweth, that shall he also reap.
Galatians 6:7.

James White sowed wrong health habits and he reaped poor health. When he grew up in the early 1800s people knew very little about how to keep from getting sick. Like most people, James ate the wrong things at the wrong times. He overtaxed his mind by close study at school. While still a teen-ager he began preaching with such zeal that he took no thought for proper food, rest, and exercise.

James White was often sick with fever, stomach trouble, and colds. Three times he was paralyzed. Once he was so ill that he could do no work for fifteen months. Many times special prayer was held for him that he might recover enough strength to continue leading the Adventist Church. One of these special seasons of prayer took place on August 22, 1877. The Lord raised James White from his bed of sickness as He had done before.

It is wonderful that God can and does heal in answer to prayer. Did you ever consider that it is just as wonderful that He has given us information as to how we can live without getting sick?

Why do you think God gave such detailed instruction to us through the Spirit of Prophecy? Might it not be so that you and I can maintain good health? Perhaps it is because He doesn't want us to suffer as our pioneers did.

There are many health habits that God has given us. Here are a few:

1. Eat meals at a regular time every day.
2. Do not eat anything between meals.
3. Do not snack before bedtime.
4. Eat plain, simple food rather than rich, spicy food.
5. Exercise every day in the fresh air.

It would make an interesting research project for you, your family, or your class to go through Mrs. White's writings to see how long a list of health habits you can make. Divide them into categories such as diet, eating habits, rest, exercise, use of water, clothing, et cetera. Perhaps you will find ways to improve your health. Remember that ten, twenty, or thirty years from now you will reap what you sow today.

REBELS

If ye be willing and obedient, ye shall eat the good of the land: but if ye refuse and rebel, ye shall be devoured with the sword: for the mouth of the Lord hath spoken it. Isaiah 1:19, 20.

Two hundred and eight years ago the British were having trouble with the American Colonies. Many people were not loyal to the king, whom they felt was a tyrant. They did not want to obey the governors and soldiers he had sent to rule over them. They refused to pay what they considered to be unjust taxes. They organized volunteer armies.

Fighting broke out between these colonial soldiers and the king's men. They fought at Lexington and Concord in April and at Bunker Hill in June. By August 23, 1775, King George III and his ministers had to admit that they had a revolution on their hands. On that day the king made a public statement in which he labeled the colonists as "rebels."

The dictionary says that a rebel is one who resists authority. In some cases we might also use the words *disobedient, uncontrollable, ungovernable, unmanageable,* and *insubordinate* to describe such a person.

These words could also be used to designate an unconverted person. Such a one does not want to yield to the authority of Jesus Christ. He doesn't want to obey God's laws or do God's will. He wants, rather, to run his own life, make his own rules

During the American Revolutionary War those who were willing to obey the king, even though he was a tyrant, were called "loyalists." Wouldn't this be a good name for young people today who are faithful, true, and loyal to King Jesus, who is always fair and just?

In the Revolutionary War the so-called rebels won. In the final war on this earth the loyalists will be the victors.

Those who are willing and obedient subjects of King Jesus will inherit a new heaven and a new earth. Beautiful things are in store for those who are faithful and true.

However, Satan and his host of rebels will all be destroyed. Not one rebel will be left in the whole wide universe that God has created.

Today we must line up on one side or the other. Are you a "loyalist" or a "rebel"? If you are a rebel, it is not too late to switch sides. Do it now.

POMPEII'S LAST DAY

The day of the Lord so cometh as a thief in the night. For when they shall say, Peace and safety; then sudden destruction cometh upon them. 1 Thessalonians 5:2, 3.

August 24, A.D. 79, began like any other day in the Italian city of Pompeii. Housewives prepared breakfast for their families and went to market. Men made their way to work. Children played in the streets. No one noticed anything strange about the 4,000-foot mountain that rose from the plain behind the town.

At one o'clock in the afternoon there was a mighty explosion that shook the city. People rushed into the streets. Terrified, they stared at a black cloud that rose high into the sky then seemed to fall back into the crater of the volcano. Soon there was a second explosion, greater than the first. This time the cloud darkened the whole sky and from it hot ashes and stones began to fall.

Within twenty-four hours the city and thirty thousand of its citizens were buried under fifty feet of ash and stone. The few who lived to tell the story were those who ran from Pompeii toward the sea at the sound of the first explosion.

The sudden destruction that came to Pompeii gives us a picture of what it will be like at the end of the world. People will be carrying on life as usual. No doubt the theaters, liquor shops, and gambling casinos will be busy. In many homes the radio and television sets will be tuned in to the usual shows.

Perhaps the programs will be interrupted for an emergency announcement: "A strange object from outer space seems to be headed directly for Planet Earth. Coming from the direction of the constellation Orion, it now appears about half the size of a man's hand in the eastern sky."

Frightened people will rush out into the streets. They will see the cloud grow until it fills the whole sky. They will see Jesus Christ, whom they have rejected, sitting on the throne, surrounded by all the angels of heaven. They will seek shelter, but they will find none. Those who have not been friends of Jesus will be destroyed by the brightness of His return.

In that hour there will be no opportunity to repent. Today, while there is still time, run to Jesus. In Him you will be safe when disaster strikes.

FISHERS OF MEN

Follow me, and I will make you fishers of men. Matthew 4:19.

On August 25, 1950, John Napoli was fishing for salmon thirty miles beyond San Francisco's Golden Gate bridge. By early afternoon his boat was full, and he headed for home.

Two miles from the bay, John was shocked to see hundreds of heads bobbing about on the waves. In the shallow water he could see the ship that had just sunk. As he looked at the people struggling for life, his eyes filled with tears. "I must save as many as possible," he said, and set to work.

His was the only boat in sight. From all sides people begged for help, and John worked as fast as he could. He threw his $3,000 catch of fish overboard to make room for more people. After six hours of work he had fifty-four crowded on board. Still there were cries for help, and John threw a rope into the water and towed sixteen more people into the harbor.

When asked why he had worked so hard to save the seventy people, John said, "I knew the tide was changing and would soon run out into the Pacific Ocean, sweeping all those people into the open sea. If I did not rescue them, who would? I had to do it then, before it was too late."

Millions in this world are in a position similar to those drowning people. The tide is changing. Time is running out. Fishermen with the courage of John Napoli are needed to help save those who are lost.

How can you rescue people from the destruction that is soon to come upon this world? How can you become a fisher of men?

There are many ways that you can do your part. Inviting your friends to Sabbath school, church socials, and Pathfinder Club meetings is one way you can work. You can share church papers with people in your neighborhood. You might hold a Junior Voice of Youth meeting. You can learn to give Bible studies. Teen-agers in many countries are doing this with great success. You can conduct a branch Sabbath school or a Story Hour for the children in your community. You can sing and pray with the shut-ins.

If you really do want to fish for men, God will help you to find a way to do it.

SWALLOWED BY A WHALE

Then Jonah prayed unto the Lord his God out of the fish's belly. Jonah 2:1.

On August 25, 1891, James Bartley was on board the ship *Star of the East* near the Falkland Islands when the crew spotted an eighty-foot sperm whale. James was one of the crewmen who went in rowboats to harpoon it. The whale was wounded and lashed out, almost overturning the boats. When the men returned to the ship with the dead whale they noticed that James Bartley was missing.

On August 26, when the men were removing blubber from the whale they were startled by a movement in the stomach. Cutting it open they discovered Bartley. He was unconscious, but after a bath of cold sea water he recovered and told his strange story.

He had been tossed from the rowboat by a flip of the whale's tail and had landed in its open mouth. The inside was soft and spongy, and James felt himself slipping along a smooth passage. Sudenly he found himself in what was like a tremendous sack, much larger than his body. All was completely dark. He felt around with his hand and came in contact with several fish that squirmed away at his touch.

For a short time James struggled and tried to call out, but breathing became difficult, and the heat was unbearable. His head began to ache terribly, and he felt he had only a few more moments to live. Then he lost consciousness until cold water was poured over him, and he found himself on the deck of the ship.

It must have been something like that for the prophet Jonah. There in the darkness, heat, and slime of the fish's stomach he knew that he would die unless God worked a miracle for him. He called out to God for deliverance, and the fish became sick and vomited him up on the beach in answer to that prayer.

Sometimes you may feel that your life is in a real mess, but you cannot be in a worse situation than Jonah. If God could hear him from the stomach of a fish at the bottom of the sea, He will surely hear your prayer, wherever you are, and whatever your circumstances. Reach out to God in faith and He will deliver you.

THE BLANKET METHOD

The kingdom of heaven is like unto treasure hid in a field; the which when a man hath found, he hideth, and for joy thereof goeth and selleth all that he hath, and buyeth that field. Matthew 13:44.

Back in the mid-1800s, when George Bissell used his savings to purchase an old oil field near Titusville, Pennsylvania, he didn't have in mind a treasure of gold, silver, and precious stones. He was after a sticky, black substance that was oozing out of the soil. Rock oil, as it was then called, was sold as a medicine.

Five years passed by without much success in gathering the oil. Mr. Bissell got a few barrels by making trenches and allowing the oil to slowly fill in.

Edwin L. Drake was hired to find a way to get to the underground treasure. He rigged up a walking beam that caused a drill bit on a rope to rise and fall and bury itself in the soil. The steam engine used to operate the drill filled the forest with its groans. People in the area laughed at the contraption and called it Drake's Folly.

At thirty-six feet the drill hit solid rock. Then, late on the afternoon of August 27, 1859, at a depth of sixty-nine feet, the drill dropped through the rock into an opening. The drilling crew drew up the iron bit and stopped work for the day.

By the next morning the well was filled with oil. Before long twenty-five barrels a day were being pumped out of that hole. The news spread like wildfire, and thousands of people rushed to Pennsylvania to drill for oil. A few of the wells yielded thousands of barrels a day, and some who risked everything to buy a small patch of field became rich overnight.

It's a lot like that with God's Word. The treasures of the Bible, too, are found deep under the surface. Only those who take the trouble to drill deep will be rewarded.

Too many Christians use the "blanket method" of Bible study. They hope to soak up their religion from contact with their parents, teachers, and friends. There is, of course, some benefit to be gained by this method, but how small compared to the abundant riches available!

The treasure you can find in God's Word is worth everything it costs you to get it. The field is before you. Begin drilling today.

RIGHTS

Let this mind be in you, which was also in Christ Jesus. Philippians 2:5.

On August 28, 1963, two hundred thousand people marched for civil rights in Washington, D.C. Posters and speeches demanded that the government of the United States give to the Negroes the rights they had been denied.

Speaking from the steps of the Lincoln Memorial, Martin Luther King, Jr., proclaimed, "There will be neither rest nor tranquillity in America until the Negro is granted his citizenship rights."

Since that day twenty years ago we have heard a lot about rights: civil rights, women's rights, teachers' rights, students' rights, human rights, workers' rights, and children's rights. Everywhere people are standing up and demanding that they be treated as they deserve. Through riots, marches, sit-ins, hunger strikes, and rallies, people have been trying to make sure their rights are granted.

Do you consider these approaches correct ones for a Christian? Should we take part in a riot for a good cause? Ought we to participate in a strike? Will a Christian make angry speeches demanding that his rights be honored? Can you picture Jesus Christ carrying a placard and shouting slogans?

"Jesus did not contend for His rights. Often His work was made unnecessarily severe because He was willing and uncomplaining. Yet He did not fail nor become discouraged. He lived above these difficulties, as if in the light of God's countenance. He did not retaliate when roughly used, but bore insult patiently."—*The Desire of Ages,* p. 89.

When Jesus was taken prisoner He had the right to a fair trial, but He did not demand it. He had the right to live, but He did not hold on to that right. He had the right to be treated with honor as the King of heaven, but He died in disgrace for you and me.

As Christians we must be like Christ, having His mind and possessing His character. In the Sermon on the Mount we are instructed not to resist those who mistreat us. Instead, when someone hits us on one cheek, we are to allow them to hit us on the other cheek also.

HELP FROM ABOVE

Save me, O God; for the waters are come in unto my soul.
Psalm 69:1.

It was nine-twenty-two on the morning of August 29, 1973. Roger Mallinson and Roger Chapman were trapped in a submarine at the bottom of the Atlantic Ocean 150 miles southwest of Cork, Ireland.

Minutes before, they had been on the surface, being hauled in to the support ship. During the operation the towline got caught around the hatch lock of the sub's rear buoyancy sphere. The hatch came off, and more than a ton of water poured into the sphere. The sub sank rapidly to the ocean floor.

With their sphere full of water there was no way that Chapman and Mallinson could raise the sub. They had a 90-minute supply of oxygen left. Help must come soon or they would surely die. Any efforts made to save themselves would be worse than useless, for they would use up the oxygen supply more quickly. There was only one thing they could do: relax and wait for help from above.

No man had ever been saved from such depths, but would-be rescuers were willing to try. Two more submarines were rushed to the spot. With their help, strong cables were hooked around the stranded sub, and she was winched up to the surface. Mallinson and Chapman came out of the sub alive.

You and I are in a position similar to that of those two men. Like the water in the sub's buoyancy chamber, sin has filled our hearts and lives, holding us down. There is nothing whatever that we can do to save ourselves. All efforts to lift ourselves will be in vain. We can strive until we are exhausted, but we will be lost unless help comes from above.

Only in Jesus is there any hope of our salvation. We must put all our trust in Him. He will save us, for He has promised. He will reach down with His arms of love and help us to overcome our sins and live a life of joy in the sunshine.

It doesn't matter how far down sin has taken you. You may have sunk to the very bottom of the sea, but God can reach you there. Wherever you go, His love can rescue you. He is able to lift you from the very depths. Won't you let Him save you today?

DR. PATON'S WELL

For without me ye can do nothing. John 15:5.

Dr. John Paton and his wife arrived in the New Hebrides on this day in 1858. They soon discovered that there was a shortage of fresh drinking water.

"I am going to sink a deep well down into the earth to see if our God will send us fresh water up from below," Paton announced.

Namakei, the old chief, feared that the doctor was going to look foolish, so he tried his best to prevent it. "O Missi," the chief said, "your head is going wrong; you are losing something, or you would not talk wild like that! Don't let our people hear you talking about going down into the earth for rain, or they will never listen to your word or believe you again."

Dr. Paton paid no attention to the chief. He went ahead with his plans for digging. He was able to convince some of the native people to assist him, but when the well was twelve feet deep one of the sides caved in. From then on Paton had to do the digging while the helpers stood above and pulled up the buckets of sand.

One day, at about thirty feet, the doctor was delighted to note that the dirt was moist. He said, "I think that Jehovah God will give us water tomorrow from that hole!"

"Never!" the helpers laughed. "Rain comes from the sky, not from the ground."

However, the next morning there was water in the well. The old chief felt it, looked at it, and finally tasted it. "Rain! Yes, it is rain! Missi, wonderful is the work of your Jehovah God!"

Soon everyone wanted to dig wells. Six or seven were sunk by the islanders, but the water was salty in every one. The islanders said, "We have learned to dig, but not how to pray, therefore Jehovah will not give us rain from below."

Many people in the world are like these islanders. They dig away at their wells, keeping busy doing many good and commendable things. There is only one thing missing. They have not learned how to pray, not realizing that it is the vital, living connection with Christ that puts life-giving water in their wells.

HOUSE BUILDING

Every man's work shall be made manifest: for the day shall declare it, . . . and the fire shall try every man's work of what sort it is. 1 Corinthians 3:13.

Silently, almost unnoticed, you are building a spiritual house. Day by day you are adding bricks to this character building. Is it one that will stand firm through storm, fire, and earthquake?

Or will it be like the mud huts in the village of Dasht-i-Bayoz in northeast Iran? Those houses looked good. Their owners had whitewashed them and decorated them with bright colors. Then came the test.

On August 31, 1968, an earthquake shook the northeast corner of Iran. Sixty thousand houses were destroyed and some 18,000 to 22,000 people were killed. Scores of villages were flattened.

Investigation revealed that the main cause of the many deaths was the way in which the houses were constructed. They were made of mud bricks topped with a domed brick roof. Those roofs looked pretty, but they were not able to withstand the violent shaking of the earth. The domes caved in, burying the occupants of the houses under the rubble.

Jesus told a similar story about two houses. One was built on sand and the other on rock. One was a fair-weather house that collapsed with the first big storm. The other was a house for all seasons, and it stood firm when the rains came.

If you want your house to be like that of the wise man, how will you build?

Paul tells us that your house of character must have Jesus Christ as its foundation. Upon that base you can add the bricks of obedience to Christ's commandments. Love, understanding, kindness, and courtesy are also good building materials. You should use some patience, temperance, and tolerance. Honesty and truthfulness should be built in somewhere. Your house should contain peace, joy, and reverence.

Under no circumstances should the mortar of sin be used to hold any of the bricks together, for it will weaken the entire structure.

Take a good look at the house you are building. Is it strong? Is it sure? Will it stand the time of test?

251

WHEN THE FIRE COMES

Behold, God is my salvation; I will trust, and not be afraid.
Isaiah 12:2.

On the morning of September 1, 1894, a pall of blue-gray smoke hung over the town of Hinckley, Minnesota, blotting out the sun. For weeks thousands of pine stumps had been smoldering in the cleared lands around the village.

At one o'clock in the afternoon a brisk wind came out of the southwest and fanned the smoldering stumps into flame. The wind carried sparks and fire into the town where the wooden buildings and sawdust-covered streets were soon ablaze.

"Run for your lives!" parents called to their children. "Run to the river! Run to the gravel pit! Run to the lake!"

More than one hundred persons sought safety in the gravel pit along with horses, cows, cats, and dogs. The pit's two acres of shallow stagnant water protected them from the holocaust that raged around them.

About three hundred people made it to nearby Skunk Lake where they held wet clothing over their heads as protection against flying sparks. When the heat became too intense, they immersed themselves for a few seconds. All in the lake survived.

One family was running from the blaze when they encountered a driverless team of horses pulling a wagon. Climbing aboard they discovered four barrels of water. Crouching in these they were able to live through the fire.

All who sought refuge in water that terrible day survived. Four hundred and eighteen people who couldn't make it to water perished.

One day soon this earth will burn up. In a mighty sea of fire everything and everybody will be consumed. Only those who have hid themselves in Christ, from whom flows the water of life, will survive that day. His righteousness, like cooling water, is our only hope.

Jesus Christ is the only way of escape. Run to Him today. Find your refuge in the water of life. Immerse yourself in His love and grace, and you will be saved.

If you accept the salvation that Jesus offers now, then you will have nothing to fear when the fire comes. You will be safe because you trust in Him.

THE SILVER LINING

In every thing give thanks. 1 Thessalonians 5:18.

For the Christian, every cloud has a silver lining and every tragedy masks a blessing.

Take for instance the great London fire that began in the early morning hours of Sunday, September 2, 1666. Within four days two thirds of the city lay devastated. Two hundred thousand people were left homeless and eighty-nine churches were destroyed. Could there be anything to thank God for in such a tragedy? Is it possible that there was a blessing in circumstances so terrible?

Yes, even that tragedy held a blessing. The fire wiped out Old London with its open sewers, ramshackle wooden houses, smelly slums, and dirty streets. The city was rebuilt with better buildings and a much improved sewer system.

The fire seemed to have a purifying effect on the air. It killed thousands of rats and apparently destroyed the last germs of the bubonic plague that had taken thousands of lives the previous year. What seemed a tragedy at the time actually was a blessing in disguise, saving thousands of lives and making London a better place in which to live.

Another example of blessing out of tragedy is found in what happened to Corrie ten Boom and her sister Betsie, who were put in a concentration camp during World War II. One day the sisters were transferred to Barracks 28 and found their beds full of fleas. They didn't see how they could live in such a filthy place, much less thank the Lord for it.

Then Betsie read today's verse. "Don't you see," she said, "we must thank God for everything about this place."

"Must we thank the Lord for the fleas?" asked Corrie.

"Yes, even for the fleas," Betsie answered.

Several days later they learned that because of the fleas the guards refused to enter the room. This gave the sisters the freedom to read their Bibles and witness that they would not have otherwise had.

When something really bad happens to you, try praising God. When you feel discouraged and blue, try praising God. When everything seems to go wrong, try praising God. Thank Him for everything, good and bad. Ask Him to help you find the silver lining behind your dark cloud.

THE BLESSINGS OF WORK

And that ye study to be quiet, and to do your own business, and to work with your own hands, as we commanded you. 1 Thessalonians 4:11.

Do you know how to work with your hands? Have you learned to enjoy it? Do you know the pleasure that comes from having done a job well? Have you been taught the true dignity of labor? If you can answer Yes to these questions you are a fortunate person.

Many people do not want to work. They look upon manual labor as degrading. Some strive to get an education, thinking they won't have to work so hard. Others would rather accept a handout than do an honest day's work. They seem to feel the world owes them a living.

"These need to learn that no man or woman is degraded by honest toil. That which degrades is idleness and selfish dependence. Idleness fosters self-indulgence, and the result is a life empty and barren—a field inviting the growth of every evil."—*Education,* pp. 215, 216.

When God created Adam and Eve He gave them work to do in caring for their garden home. That work was meant to be a blessing. When Jesus came into this world to live He worked in a carpenter shop that He might be an example to us.

What are some of the advantages that come from labor with our hands? Look up "work" in the *Index to the Writings of Ellen G. White,* and you will find a long list of benefits. Today, which is the anniversary of the first Labor Day, celebrated throughout the United States in 1894, would be a good time to make such a study. When school begins, perhaps your teacher would be willing to use your findings to make an attractive bulletin board display on the benefits of labor.

Here is a sample of what you will find:

"Useful occupation was appointed them as a blessing, to strengthen the body, to expand the mind, and to develop the character."—*Education,* p. 21.

"Practical work encourages close observation and independent thought. Rightly performed, it tends to develop that practical wisdom that we call common sense. It develops ability to plan and execute, strengthens courage and perseverance, and calls for the exercise of tact and skill."—*Ibid.,* p. 220.

CAFETERIA CHRISTIANS

We then that are strong ought to bear the infirmities of the weak, and not to please ourselves. . . . For even Christ pleased not himself. Romans 15:1-3.

Even as a child, Jesus lived to bless others. We are told that He sometimes gave up His own meal so that someone else could eat. He was constantly looking for ways to brighten the lives of those around Him. Even the animals of the forest benefited from His selfless service.

How different His life was from the way most of us live. Self rules in the hearts of old and young alike. We want to please ourselves rather than make someone else happy.

Perhaps we could call selfish people cafeteria Christians, for in a cafeteria everyone serves himself.

The first self-service restaurant was opened on this day in 1885 on New Street in New York City. Called the Exchange Buffet, it immediately became popular. Since then all sorts of self-service enterprises have come into being: car washes, gasoline stations, photo booths, supermarkets, and even department stores.

Self-service is the way of the world, but it is not the way of heaven. A true follower of Jesus Christ will not live to please self, but rather to make others happy.

Perhaps you have heard about the man who dreamed that he went to hell. There he was surprised to see a long table laden with beautiful fruit, nuts, and a wide variety of foods. It was a feast fit for a king, yet the people were starving and in terrible misery. They all had arms that would not bend at the elbow and thus they could not feed themselves.

Then it seems that man was transported to heaven, where he saw the same scene of food spread on a long table. Everyone was happy and well-fed. However, he noticed that they, too, had arms that would not bend, but each person was feeding someone else.

Heaven will be for those who are like Jesus, those who are selfless, kind, helpful, and thoughtful of others. It will be for those who live to serve others rather than themselves. There won't be any cafeteria Christians at the marriage supper of the Lamb.

255

WORTH THE SACRIFICE

He shall see of the travail of his soul, and shall be satisfied.
Isaiah 53:11.

On the afternoon of September 5, 1970, two young Austrians reached the top of the more than 17,000-foot Mount Kenya and started down again. Roped together, Gerd Judmaier and Oswald Oelz descended the sheer face of the mountain to a patch of level ground. There Oswald searched for a solid rock around which to fasten the rope. Gerd leaned out over a large boulder to check the route down.

Suddenly, the rock broke loose. With a cry for help Gerd disappeared. Oswald braced himself and held on to the rope. It burned his flesh as it ripped through his palms. Before the rope played out he was able to wind it around his arm and stop Gerd's fall. Then he fastened the rope and climbed down to the ledge where his friend had fallen.

Gerd's leg was badly fractured and was bleeding profusely. Oswald did what he could to make Gerd comfortable. After tying him securely to the ledge, he left to find help.

On the fourth day a helicopter, flown by Jim Hastings, was on its way to take Gerd to a hospital. No one knows how it happened, but the helicopter crashed, killing the pilot.

That night Gerd was feverish, frostbitten, and sick at his stomach. In spite of his hopeless condition, he stubbornly refused to give up to discouragement. "If I die now, that pilot's life was wasted," he said. "I must live for his sake."

Eventually another team of rescuers got the injured man down the mountain and into a hospital, where he recovered. Over and over Gerd expressed his thankfulness for those who had risked their lives to save his.

"The name of Jim Hastings will never be forgotten in our household," Gerd said.

Some 1,950 years ago on another mountain in another land a young man gave His life in a rescue attempt. On Mount Calvary, Jesus died that you might have eternal life.

If you feel discouraged sometimes, just remember that Jesus died on the mountain for you. If you are lost, then His sacrifice was in vain. For His sake, because He loved you so much, you must be true! When He sees you saved eternally, He will be satisfied that it was worth the sacrifice.

PART OF THE BODY

And whether one member suffer, all the members suffer with it. 1 Corinthians 12:26.

Today's verse is taken from a letter Paul wrote to the church at Corinth, Greece. Evidently the members there were not working together as they should. Because of certain talents they possessed, some felt they were better than others. Those not so gifted felt they were not needed.

"No," Paul said, "this is not true. God has given you different abilities and all are important to the church. Look at your own bodies. What good would you be if you had only an eye or an ear? Each part is necessary and all are needed to make up your body."

Some boys and girls feel that they are not very important because they are not able to do what adults can do. They feel that it doesn't really matter whether they attend meetings or not. Maybe some adults make them feel that way, but this is wrong.

Look at your fingers for a moment. They are very small in comparison with your arms, but what a struggle you would have without those fingers! Even very young children are important parts of the church, and each has a special work to do for Jesus.

It matters whether or not you attend meetings. It matters if you neglect prayer and Bible study. It matters whether or not you take part in questionable activities. If you are not in good spiritual health, the whole church will suffer.

You know that if you have one bad tooth, you can feel miserable all over. An infected appendix can give you much pain and put your whole body in the hospital. Little things are important!

Take, for instance, what happened on Monday, September 6, 1943. The *Congressional Limited,* full of holiday crowds, was traveling between Washington, D.C., and New York. As the train sped through the Philadelphia suburbs a wheel bearing froze on the seventh car, causing the train to halt suddenly. As it stopped, the disabled car jumped the track, rolled down an embankment, and hit a signal tower. The other cars followed, piling into one another. Seventy-nine people died, and one hundred others were injured—all because of the failure of a small wheel bearing.

DAM BUILDING

But I keep under my body, and bring it into subjection. 1 Corinthians 9:27.

On this day in 1936, Hoover Dam was completed. Its 726-foot height makes it one of the tallest dams in the world. It is 660 feet wide at the base. There is enough concrete in this dam to pave a sixteen-foot-wide highway for three thousand miles.

All that cement is there to control the Colorado River, which at certain times of the year used to flood the countryside. At other times the water level was so low that it could not be used for irrigation.

Rivers, you see, have no self-control. If snow melts in the mountains, the river swells and rushes madly to the sea. It cannot say, "No. It would be better if I slowed down. I will save some of myself for the dry season."

Have you seen people who are like a river, unable to control their thoughts, feelings, and actions? If they are annoyed such people may let loose with a torrent of angry words. They may overeat to the point of making themselves sick. When the crowd flows along toward some forbidden place of amusement, they are washed along with it.

It is possible for teachers and parents to act as dam builders, putting up rules and regulations to keep children under control. That is fine when the adults are around, but what happens when they are absent?

"While under authority, the children appear like well-drilled soldiers; but when the control ceases, the character will be found to lack strength and steadfastness. Having never learned to govern himself, the youth recognizes no restraint except the requirement of parents and teachers."—*Education,* p. 288.

Self-control is difficult because of our sinful natures. Centuries of disobedience have made us all like water. Only as we give our wills to Jesus Christ do we have the power of self-control.

The will is that part of us that is used in making decisions, that governs our actions, and helps us choose the right. When we choose to use this part of ourselves with Jesus' help, we are linking our weakness to His strength, and we may thus build our own "dams" to control our lives.

258

IN TIME OF STORM

And every one that heareth these sayings of mine, and doeth
them not, shall be likened unto a foolish man, which built his
house upon the sand. Matthew 7:26.

A modern version of Christ's story about the two houses took
place on Saturday, September 8, 1900, in the island city of
Galveston, Texas. On that day a hurricane struck, destroying
$17 million worth of property and killing many people.

Writing about it in the Galveston *Tribune,* Editor Richard
Spillane said, "To go out on the streets was to court death.
Cisterns, portions of buildings, telegraph poles, and walls were
falling. The noise of the wind and the crashing of buildings was
terrifying."

That night a large tidal wave put most of the city under
water. Ocean steamers were deposited into the downtown
business section. Houses crumbled like cardboard playthings.
The strongest homes were washed away. Waves tore open
graves, and coffins floated alongside cars, houses, and furniture.

Just a few miles away the same storm left houses standing.
Why? Part of the answer lies in the location of Galveston. This
city had been built on a narrow sand bar twenty-five miles long
and two miles wide. No part of the island was more than five feet
above sea level. Houses there were built on sand and in the time
of storm they collapsed. Two miles away on the mainland the
houses were built on solid ground and remained firm.

Some Seventh-day Adventist young people today are like so
many houses on sand. They have heard the gospel story since
they were in cradle roll. They know what they ought to do and
how they ought to live. They know what the Bible teaches but
they do not follow it in their lives. There is a distinct separation
between what they hear in church on Sabbath and how they live
during the week. To live at such a low spiritual level is to court
disaster.

A storm is coming upon this old world. Before Jesus comes
there will be a "time of trouble, such as never was since there
was a nation." Only those who have a close connection with the
Lord Jesus Christ will be saved out of this time of trouble. Only
those who are doers of the word, as well as hearers, will find
their spiritual house secure in that day.

Where have you built your house?

259

NO POLICEMEN NEEDED

And the gates of it shall not be shut at all by day: for there shall be no night there. Revelation 21:25.

Long ago cities in Europe and Asia were surrounded by high stone walls. Huge gates were closed at night or in time of danger. Guards stood at the gates and watchmen were posted on the walls.

In 1983 there are few cities protected by walls, gates, guards, and watchmen. Instead, policemen patrol the streets in cars or on motorcycles.

Can you imagine New York, Tokyo, London, or Mexico City without policemen? What would a modern city be like without some means of holding crime in check?

On this day in 1919, the city of Boston had such an experience when its 1,117 policemen went on strike. For three days there were no officers patroling the streets. No criminals were booked and no investigations were made. Thieves and hoodlums had a heyday, and honest citizens feared to leave their homes at night.

In this world of sin and trouble no one wants a city without a police force. Law-abiding people want protection from murderers and thieves. Because of sin, walls, gates, and policemen are necessary.

When Jesus comes the third time sin will come to an end. Satan and all his evil angels will be consumed by fire. All evil men will perish. The only people left alive will be those who are kind, honest, truthful, loving, and helpful. For such people there will be no need of policemen.

The New Jerusalem will thus be a city without a police force. The gates will remain open, for there will be no enemies to keep out. There will be no heavenly FBI with its fingerprint file of the saints. There will be no jails or prison camps.

There will be no sadness in that city. Nothing ugly or cruel or mean will be there. There will be no bruised, battered, and neglected children. There will be no alcohol, drugs, or vice. There will be no fear, disappointment, or death. Everything you own will be safe. No one will steal your golden crown.

Now is the time to prepare to live in that city. Let Jesus come into your heart and give you love, joy, peace, long-suffering, goodness, and gentleness. Only such people will be there.

OF MOSS AND TREES

Casting all your care upon him; for he careth for you. 1 Peter 5:7.

You may not have heard of the African explorer whose birthday is today. If you want to read a true story of thrilling adventure, read about the journeys of Mungo Park. In 1905 he explored the Niger River for more than one thousand miles, traveling where no civilized man had ever been.

On one occasion Park was lost and desperately ill. He felt that even God had forgotten him. Lying on the ground in the jungle, he had almost talked himself into dying when his eyes rested on a piece of fresh, green moss. The beauty of it somehow brought life and hope to the sick and discouraged man.

Mungo Park said to himself, No human eye but mine can see that little piece of moss, and yet God keeps it green and beautiful. Even if I had never seen it, God would still love it and care for it. If God is so gracious and kind as to look after that moss, I am sure He cares for me, so here goes to make another try.

Still sick, Mungo got up from his jungle bed and stumbled on. Soon he found food and made his way to friends. He completed his task and returned home triumphant. Many honors were heaped upon him, none of which he would have received had it not been for that piece of moss and the certainty it gave him that God did care.

Teen-age Jennifer had a similar experience. For some reason she was terribly discouraged and wondered how she could go on living. Home was far away, and she could think of no one to talk to about her troubles.

Closing her books, Jennifer left the dormitory and walked across the campus to a stretch of woods that bordered a bubbling brook. She sat down under an oak tree and looked up toward its top, so high above her. Something in the greenness of the woods and the strength of the trees spoke hope and peace to her. Her thoughts were turned to God, and she told Him about all her problems.

Jennifer returned to her room that day smiling, for she had left her cares with the One who had made the trees and the bubbling brook.

MYSTERIES

It is given unto you to know the mysteries of the kingdom of heaven. Matthew 13:11.

On September 11, 1937, Kuda Bux, of Pakistan, gave a hair-raising performance in Liverpool, England. Fully blindfolded, he walked along a narrow ledge atop a two-hundred-foot building. A slight misstep would have sent him to his death.

Another time this amazing man went to a hospital and requested a doctor to blindfold him. The physician began with dough plasters over which he placed thick pads of cotton wool. Next he used three rolls of bandages, completely covering the man's head.

"I'll guarantee that you cannot see," the doctor said.

"Thank you very much, Doctor," Kuda Bux said. He then turned and left the room. Reporters watched as he boldly strode down the hospital hallway. Outside he mounted a bicycle and rode in and out of the rush-hour traffic without accident. He steered as though he could see perfectly.

How did he do it? Nobody knows. It is a mystery.

The Bible is full of mysteries, too. Some of these we can understand with the guidance of the Holy Spirit. As you study and pray, many things that are mysteries to the person who does not love Jesus will become clear.

There are other mysteries that will take longer for us to understand. We will be studying these throughout eternity.

Scientific experiments cannot explain how salvation takes place. There is no way of describing how long eternity is. The fact that God has no beginning and no end is a mystery.

We cannot understand how the infinite God could come from heaven and be born as a tiny human being in this world. We cannot comprehend how someone who has been dead for thousands of years can come to life again.

It is impossible to explain the process by which the love of God can change a drunken man into a kind and loving father. We do not know how prayer travels to the throne of God.

We cannot understand how God can know the future as well as the past. We are puzzled when trying to figure out what life really is and how it begins.

These are all mysteries that we will study throughout the ceaseless ages of eternity.

CAUGHT OFF GUARD

Watch and pray, that ye enter not into temptation. Matthew 26:41.

You and I are in the army of Jesus Christ. We are expected to be ready at all times to resist the devil. If we fail to watch and pray we may be taken off guard as were the French in the Battle of Quebec.

Under the leadership of the Marquis de Montcalm, France had five thousand soldiers stationed at Quebec. This was an ideal place for a fort because the city stood on heights overlooking the Saint Lawrence River.

The English, under the leadership of General James Wolfe, were repelled when they tried to attack east of Quebec. Montcalm expected that they would next attack at Cap Rouge, west of the city, so he sent his soldiers there.

However, Wolfe decided to land at the foot of the cliffs directly below the Plains of Abraham. On the calm, cloudy night of September 12, 1759, five thousand British soldiers scaled the cliffs and readied themselves for battle.

At dawn on September 13 the surprised French general quickly summoned his troops, but they were not prepared and fired too quickly. The British advanced in unbroken ranks, saving their fire until within close range. After only fifteen minutes of fighting the French retreated. What a different outcome there might have been had Montcalm been watching all possible approaches! Had French soldiers been guarding the cliffs that night, they could have picked off the British as they climbed.

Satan is a clever general. He searches for our weakest side and waits until we forget to watch and pray. Like the British attacking Quebec, he comes unexpectedly, and we are overcome before we can marshall our spiritual resources.

Betty's weakness was pride in her grades. She had always been first in her class until Carole moved to town. Suddenly, Betty had to work a lot harder to stay on top. She began skipping her morning worship time to study. One day Satan saw his chance. Betty couldn't think of an answer on a test. By a slight turn of her head she could see what Carole had written. Betty was not on guard that day. She saw the answer and wrote it.

Be sure you stay on guard today!

SIN CARRIERS

For as he thinketh in his heart, so is he. Proverbs 23:7.

If Satan is to succeed in persuading a person to sin, he must somehow reach his mind and cause him to think sinful thoughts. Satan's problem is how to get into the mind and change thought patterns. He cannot just open the door, as it were, and walk in. The way in which yellow fever is spread gives us a clue as to how Satan can spread sin.

You can live right next to a person sick with yellow fever and you will be quite safe unless a certain kind of mosquito bites the sick person and then bites you. The mosquito gets the disease virus from the blood of the sick person and puts it into your blood. There the virus can grow and may even eventually kill you. The mosquito is called the *carrier* of the disease.

Walter Reed, whose birthday is today, discovered how yellow fever is spread. In 1900 he was sent by the United States Army to Cuba to combat this terrible disease that threatened to destroy the whole army. Once Reed identified mosquitoes as the carriers of the sickness, he was able to eradicate it from Cuba by destroying the insects.

If we are to protect ourselves against the virus of sin, then we must find out what carriers Satan uses to give us sinful thoughts.

Some of the most common sin carriers are bad books, magazines, and newspapers. As we read about the evil deeds of other people, those actions are impressed onto the cells of our brains. The memories are then recalled in our leisure time. As we think about the sinful deeds of others we are more and more tempted to commit the same actions ourselves.

Movies and television programs can also be used as carriers to infect us with Satan's thoughts. He can also use the conversations of our friends.

If we want pure lives we must think pure thoughts. If we want pure thoughts we must be careful what goes into our minds.

For this reason God has counseled us: "Those who would not fall a prey to Satan's devices must guard well the avenues of the soul; they must avoid reading, seeing, or hearing that which will suggest impure thoughts."—*Happiness Homemade,* p. 152.

THE BLOOD-SPRINKLED BANNER

Thou hast given a banner to them that fear thee. Psalm 60:4.

William Beanes was captured by the British and kept prisoner aboard a warship in Chesapeake Bay. On September 13, 1814, two of his friends received permission to board the warship and speak to the British on his behalf.

The English agreed to release Mr. Beanes, but not until they had finished bombarding Fort McHenry. The three men were put on a prisoner exchange boat at the rear of the British fleet so that they could not get any message to the Americans on shore.

All night Beanes and his friends paced the deck of the ship. As morning came, the smoke and haze were so thick that they could not tell whether the flag was still there. They feared that the British had won.

Suddenly, at seven o'clock on the morning of September 14, the sun broke through the mist and shone upon the star-spangled banner that was waving in the breeze. One of the men, Francis Scott Key, was so moved by the sight of his country's flag gleaming bright red, white, and blue that he wrote a poem to express his feelings. Taking an envelope from his pocket, he quickly scribbled down the words that are now part of the national anthem of the United States.

> "Oh, say can you see
> by the dawn's early light
> What so proudly we hailed
> at the twilight's last gleaming?"

Sometimes we may feel as William Beanes and his friends felt that misty morning after the bombardment of Fort McHenry. It seems that there is so much evil and injustice in the world that surely Satan must be in control. Wrong appears so strong, and it is hard to believe that God is still the Ruler.

But if we will look through the mists, we can see the banner of King Jesus bright in the morning sun.

Satan bombarded the Son of God with all his might almost two thousand years ago on the cross. It appeared that Friday afternoon that God had lost. However, on Sunday morning it became clear that it was Satan who had lost. God's banner of love was still flying!

Thank God, that bloodstained banner still flies!

OUR INHERITANCE

Wherefore, as by one man sin entered into the world, and death by sin; and so death passed upon all men, for that all have sinned. Romans 5:12.

One of the most infamous crimes of this century was committed by Bruno Richard Hauptmann. In the spring of 1932 he kidnapped the baby son of Charles and Anne Morrow Lindbergh. He collected 70,000 dollars in ransom money, although he killed the baby.

For nearly three years Mr. Hauptmann eluded the police. Then one Saturday morning, September 15, 1934, he drove into a gas station and paid for his gas with a $10 bill. An alert attendant wrote the car license number on the back of the bill. Through this the police were able to trace the criminal.

A few days later when Mr. Hauptmann drove away from his house the police surrounded him and stopped his car. They pulled him out and snapped handcuffs on him. Ransom money was in his wallet, and the balance of the cash was found behind a false wall in his garage.

After a six-week trial Mr. Hauptmann was found guilty and was sentenced to death in the electric chair.

But what about you and me? We have not done anything as bad as that. We are really quite good by comparison. We have not murdered anyone. The lies we have told have been small ones, after all. If we have stolen, it was only little things such as pencils, food, or a few cents. Surely *we* don't deserve to die!

Oh, yes, but we do! Even if we had never done anything wrong, we would still be sinners, for we were born that way. Sin is more than acts that we do. It is a condition inherited from our forebearers.

Sin can be traced all the way back to Adam. When we compare his sin with all the terrible crimes committed today, it seems a small thing. All that he did was eat a piece of fruit because he loved his wife. Yet, in eating the fruit he disobeyed God, and that was sin. Since that day every human being born into this world has been born with sinful tendencies, without a way of escape, and thus must die eternally.

However, God has opened such a way for us. Jesus died in our place. Through Him we can have eternal life.

266

PILGRIMS

But now they desire a better country, that is, an heavenly: wherefore God is not ashamed to be called their God: for he hath prepared for them a city. Hebrews 11:16.

On September 16, 1620, the *Mayflower* sailed from Plymouth, England, with 102 passengers on board, most of them Puritans who had separated from the Church of England.

To find freedom to worship God according to their conscience a group of Puritans had emigrated to Holland. After a few years as strangers in that land they decided to go to America, where they felt things would be better. So they returned to England and then, with a few others, sailed for a new country.

After weathering stormy seas for sixty-five days, the ship arrived at Cape Cod. For almost a month the Pilgrims, as they were called, explored the countryside until they found what they considered the ideal spot for their colony near Plymouth Harbor. There was a stream of pure water, some cleared land, and a hill that could be fortified.

That first winter was a hard one. Half of the Pilgrims died before they had a chance to enjoy their new home. The land was hostile, and the remaining Pilgrims might not have made it had not friendly Indians come to show them how to farm, hunt, and fish.

The term *pilgrim* was a good name for those 102 people who sailed on the *Mayflower,* for the word means "wanderer," or "wayfarer." These people had been strangers in a strange land, wandering from place to place in search of religious freedom.

They were like Abel, Enoch, Noah, Abraham, Isaac, and Jacob—"strangers and pilgrims on the earth." These men and their families were also seeking a better country.

Are not you and I pilgrims and strangers in this world? This is not our permanent home. We are going someday to a better land, where there will be no more sorrow or crying.

A favorite song of the early Adventist believers was "I'm a Pilgrim," No. 666 in *The Church Hymnal.* If you cannot sing it, at least read the words and you will understand a little better what it means to be a spiritual pilgrim, wandering, ever looking for the city where "the glory is ever shining" and "the fountains are ever flowing." Soon Jesus will come to take us, if we're faithful, to heaven, where we will be pilgrims no more

267

CITIZENSHIP DAY

Let every soul be subject unto the higher powers. For there is no power but of God: the powers that be are ordained of God. Romans 13:1.

Today is the day on which the Constitution of the United States was signed in 1787. Since 1952 it has been celebrated as Citizenship Day. What does good citizenship mean? Can a Christian be a good citizen?

C—A good citizen is CONCERNED. He does all he can to uphold right and make his country a better place in which to live.

I—He keeps INFORMED about the political issues around him and does what he can to support good causes.

T—A good citizen is TOLERANT of people of other religions, races, creeds, and cultures.

I—He is also INDEPENDENT. A good citizen will not expect the government to supply the needs of his family. He obeys the command of God, "Six days shalt thou labour." He is not a burden to the community.

Z—A good citizen will be "ZEALOUS of good works" as Paul admonished in his letter to Titus. He will participate in community projects.

E—He will be an EXAMPLE of all that is good, true, honest, and clean.

N—A good citizen is NEIGHBORLY. He is friendly and goes out of his way to show kindness to someone in need.

S—A good citizen will be "SUBJECT unto the higher powers." He will not resist that government, but will obey the laws and pay his taxes.

H—He will be known as a HELPFUL person. If his neighbor is in trouble, he will do what he can to be of service. He gives clothes to the naked, food to the hungry, and support to the widow and orphan.

I—A good citizen is INDIGNANT when he sees evil. He speaks out against crime of every type.

P—A good citizen will be PEACEFUL. He will not quarrel with his neighbor but will look for ways to be friends. He will not participate in violence. He will not disturb the peace of others.

Yes, a Christian can be, indeed he must be, a good citizen. Are you one?

THE MYSTERIOUS PRISONER

For God shall bring every work into judgment, with every secret thing, whether it be good, or whether it be evil. Ecclesiastes 12:14.

At exactly three o'clock on the afternoon of Thursday, September 18, 1698, the massive oak doors of the Bastille swung open as the carriage of the governor of the prison rolled into the courtyard. Behind it stopped a heavily curtained litter carried by four servants.

The governor jumped out of his carriage and hurried to the litter and drew aside the curtains. He watched as two soldiers helped a tall, white-haired man alight then marched with him to one of the prison towers. The tower gate slammed shut behind the man, and he was never seen again.

Who was the prisoner? None knew for sure. His face was never seen since it was covered at all times by a black velvet cloth. The man spent thirty-four years in prison, but his name was never mentioned in any correspondence. When he died he was buried under a false name.

In some ways, many people are like that mysterious prisoner. They do not show their true selves. They are what we call hypocrites. Such a person may be a baptized member of the church and perhaps even hold an office. He or she may attend Sabbath school, church, prayer meetings, camp meetings, being in the right place at the right time going through the right motions.

Before Jesus comes some of these people will leave the church. About such Mrs. White wrote: "Many a star that we have admired for its brilliance will then go out in darkness."—*Prophets and Kings,* p. 188.

The day is coming when we will appear before the judgment seat of Christ. In that day all masks will be ripped off, and the universe will see who we really are. Our thoughts, motives, and secret actions will be revealed.

God has given us today that we might with His help bring our lives into harmony with our words. We must do more than *say* we are Christians. We must learn of Jesus so we can *be* Christians, through and through.

IT COULDN'T HAPPEN

But they refused to hearken, and pulled away the shoulder, and stopped their ears, that they should not hear. Zechariah 7:11.

Seven children and nine adults clung to the roof of the Greens' house and prayed for their lives. They were soaked to the skin from the rain, and hurricane winds tore at their clothes and hair. Giant waves rocked the house beneath them.

When the storm struck, the group had been downstairs in the living room having a party. As the house began to flood, they all fled to the attic. But the water rose higher, and even there they didn't feel safe, so the men cut a hole in the roof, and they all climbed out to cling to the slanting surface.

Suddenly a large section of the house broke away, and the frightened people were set afloat at the mercy of the waves. Miraculously, the wind drove them toward a raised portion of beach and deposited them there. All sixteen were rescued.

Not everyone was so fortunate. This worst hurricane ever to hit the northeastern seaboard of the United States killed 600 people and left 60,000 homeless.

Most of the lives could have been saved had people not stopped their ears to the warning that was given on September 19, 1938. On that day the hurricane passed by the Florida coast giving all a scare, but not touching the mainland. Grady Norton, of the Jacksonville Weather Bureau, predicted that the New England States would be hit.

There was a small article about the approaching storm on page 27 of the *New York Times* the next day. No one really believed that a hurricane would come to the northeastern United States. Hurricanes happened only in the tropics. Apparently even the weather forecasters ignored the strange atmospheric conditions that confirmed the fact that the storm was indeed headed for New England. It couldn't happen here, they thought; but it did. Stopping their ears did not stop the storm!

We need to be careful that we do not ignore the warning like the people of New England did in 1938. We should keep our ears open to the warnings God gives us through the Bible and the Spirit of Prophecy. Even if we don't like what God says at times, we must not be so foolish as to think that closing our ears will prevent His words from coming to pass.

HE THAT ENDURETH

And ye shall be hated of all men for my name's sake: but he that endureth to the end shall be saved. Matthew 10:22.

Juan Sebastián del Cano was the first man to sail around the world. On September 20, 1519, he was one of 240 men who set sail with Ferdinand Magellan in search of a westward route to the Spice Islands.

Of the five ships that began the journey, only the *Trinidad* and the *Victoria* reached their destination, where each took on a load of cloves.

The commander of the *Trinidad* tried to sail back across the Pacific and was never seen again. Del Cano took the *Victoria* west around the tip of Africa and reached home after almost three years.

Del Cano and his men endured tremendous hardships on their journey. During the trip they sailed for ninety-eight days without seeing any land except two uninhabited islands. Food ran out and water was rationed. They lived on sawdust and rats, and many died of starvation and sickness. Others were murdered by hostile natives in the islands where they stopped. Of the original 240 men who began the voyage, only 18 received a reward, for they alone had endured.

A time of great trouble is coming to this earth before Jesus comes. Daniel said it would be worse than anything that has happened in the world before. There will be terrible famines, earthquakes, and strange new diseases.

"The people of God will not be free from suffering; but while persecuted and distressed, while they endure privation and suffer for want of food they will not be left to perish."—*The Great Controversy*, p. 629.

It is evident that God's people will not have an easy time in those days. They will be hated. Their lives will be in danger. They will not be allowed to buy or sell. They may have to flee their homes and live in remote areas where there are no modern conveniences.

Not wanting to endure suffering and hardships, many will be tempted to give up when such troubles come. Those who stay close to Jesus will not give up. With His help they will endure unto the end.

Will you be among that group? If so, you will be saved.

DOES GOD LIE?

God is not a man, that he should lie; neither the son of man, that he should repent: hath he said, and shall he not do it? Numbers 23:19.

A man whom we will call Mr. Smith lived on Long Island near the sea. He had thought for some time that it would be interesting to have a barometer so that he could know what kind of weather to expect. He found just what he wanted in a New York City store and asked that it be delivered to his home.

On the morning of September 21, 1938, the barometer arrived by post. Eagerly Mr. Smith opened the box and inspected it. He was annoyed to see that the needle pointed below 29, where the dial read "Hurricanes and Tornadoes."

"Something must be wrong with this barometer," Mr. Smith said. "The weather outside is fine. It doesn't look like a hurricane at all." So saying, he packed up the offending instrument and drove to the post office to mail it back to the store.

At two-thirty that afternoon, while he was still in town, the hurricane struck. One-hundred-mile-an-hour winds tore across the island. A forty-foot wave swept several miles inland. Mansions as well as humble cottages were washed away. A radio tower disappeared. Trains and boats were broken apart by the force of the waves. Mr. Smith's house disappeared. The barometer had told him the truth, but he would not accept it.

God's Word is like that barometer. As we look at it, we can receive a warning of the approaching storm. The prophecies are all clear. Even though the weather seems fine right now, things will change for the worse very quickly.

Getting rid of the barometer will make no difference to what happens, but that seems to be what many people are doing.

"The world is no worse than it has ever been," such folks say. "I can't believe that the Bible really means what it says."

In spite of what people may think about the barometer, the storm is going to come. Christ will return to take His people home. This earth will be destroyed. All will happen just as the Bible says, for God does not lie. His prophecies are always true.

When Jesus comes in the clouds of heaven, how sad it will be if we are not ready because we refused to heed the barometer.

272

WITCHES AND DEVILS

Be sober, be vigilant; because your adversary the devil, as a roaring lion, walketh about, seeking whom he may devour. 1 Peter 5:8.

On this day in 1692, the last person was hanged for practicing witchcraft in the American Colonies. By this date, 250 women had been arrested and twenty had been executed.

After this, interest in witches declined and they came to be thought of as make-believe characters. They appeared in fairy tales and in decorations around Halloween.

Today all is changed. After 291 years, witches are back in business. There are thousands of real witches in the world today, an estimated 500 in Manhattan alone. They dress in ordinary clothes, but they claim to have extraordinary powers to cast spells and work black magic. Most acknowledge that their power comes from Satan.

Visit a bookstore and you will see a large section devoted to witchcraft, Satan worship, sorcery, devil possession, astrology, and the occult. Many colleges offer courses in witchcraft and spiritism. Some of the most popular movies of the past few years have been about witchcraft and Satan worship.

As we get nearer to the end of time the devil is working harder than ever to bring as many people as possible under his banner. God has warned us to have nothing to do with the devil's program.

"There shall not be found among you any one that maketh his son or his daughter to pass through the fire, or that useth divination, or an observer of times, or an enchanter, or a witch, or a charmer, or a consultor with familiar spirits, or a wizard, or a necromancer. For all that do these things are an abomination unto the Lord" (Deut. 18:10-12).

In spite of this plain instruction, King Saul consulted the witch at Endor. Because God was no longer with Saul, he turned to the devil for counsel. That is what is happening today. People do not know Jesus Christ, so they turn to devils and witches.

If you would be safe, stay away from anything that belongs to the occult. Do not play with the devil, for when you do you are walking on forbidden ground.

Put your faith in the living God. His knowledge and power far exceed that of Satan.

BOLD AS A LION

The wicked flee when no man pursueth: but the righteous are bold as a lion. Proverbs 28:1.

The two ships were unevenly matched. The British warship *Serapis* carried 44 guns, throwing 315 pounds of metal in a single shot. The American ship *Bonhomme Richard* had 42 guns, throwing only 258 pounds of metal with each shot.

The battle began on Thursday, September 23, 1779, at seven-fifteen in the evening. The sky was clear and the moon full as the two ships drew close together. Soon most of the guns on the American ship were smashed and more than half of its 140 men killed or wounded.

Within a matter of minutes the *Bonhomme Richard* would sink. Something must be done quickly! Commander John Paul Jones ordered: "Let us close with the enemy. We must get hold of him!"

The *Bonhomme Richard* sailed in close to the *Serapis*. The remaining crew of the American ship put out grappling hooks.

"Are you ready to surrender?" asked Captain Pearson.

"No! I have just begun to fight!" replied John Paul Jones. And fight he did in a hand-to-hand battle. Finally, a grenade thrown into a hatch of the *Serapis* caused a terrific explosion and killed fifty men. The captain, with no more heart for resistance, handed over his sword and took down his flag.

John Paul Jones won that battle because he had the courage to fight on in spite of apparent failure.

David was another man who was bold in battle. He was not afraid to walk out to fight the giant with only a slingshot and five smooth stones. Saul's soldiers compared Goliath's size to their own and felt pretty small. David compared the giant's size to God and saw no problem at all.

John Paul Jones and David had several things in common. They were both small in comparison with their opponent. In both cases strength was apparently with the enemy. To win against such odds seemed impossible to both, but they nevertheless kept up the fight. Instead of fleeing in despair, they walked boldly up to face the foe.

You and I need that kind of boldness in our fight against the devil. We should never let the size of the opposition scare us into surrender. One with God is a majority.

IMAGE WORSHIP

Thou shalt not make unto thee any graven image. . .: thou shalt not bow down thyself to them, nor serve them. Exodus 20:4, 5.

The second commandment clearly says that we are not to worship images. Yet there are millions of Christians who have these in their homes. When they go to church they bow down before statues of the virgin Mary, Saint Peter, Saint Paul, and hundreds of others. Why do they do this when the Bible clearly says that they should not?

In the beginning of the Christian church there were no images. Peter, Paul, and John did not teach people to break the second commandment. For about three hundred years after Christ, images were not permitted. Then little by little people began to copy their heathen neighbors who worshiped idols. They made statues of Jesus, Mary, and the disciples.

When Leo IV became emperor of the Eastern Roman Empire in A.D. 775, he made a law that no one could worship images. This made a lot of people unhappy.

In those days most people could not read. Even if they could, Bibles were too expensive for the common people to have. Therefore, they did whatever the priests taught them to do. These leaders thought it was easier for the illiterate people to pray to God if they had an image in front of them. Also, the use of pictures and images made the churches more attractive to the heathen people who were used to idol worship.

After Leo died, Empress Irene called a church council to be held at Nicaea in what is now Turkey. The purpose of the council was to settle the question of image worship. The Second Nicaean Council, which began on this day in 787, decided it was all right for Christians to bow down to images. Soon the churches were again full of images.

But just because the Second Council of Nicaea voted that it was OK to use idols in worship does not make it right in God's sight. Man's law did not change God's law. His commandments are everlasting.

We must be careful every day to test the laws that men make by the Word of God. If we must make a choice between obeying men's laws and God's laws, I will choose to obey God's law. What about you?

MORE BEYOND

If in this life only we have hope in Christ, we are of all men most miserable. 1 Corinthians 15:19.

Spanish explorers who first reached the South American continent were elated. They could not imagine anything more beyond. Joyously they sent word back to Spain: "We have reached the limits of the world!"

Spanish government officials were so excited that they made coins on which were stamped the words, "Ne Plus Ultra," meaning "No More Beyond."

How wrong they were! As explorers began to push inland through the dense tropical jungles, they discovered that the world went on and on.

On September 25, 1513, Vasco Nuñez de Balboa stood on top of a mountain and gazed out over the vast expanse of the Pacific Ocean. There was still more beyond.

New Spanish coins were made without the *Ne*. They said "Plus Ultra," meaning, of course, "More Beyond."

Many people are like those first Spanish explorers. They believe that this life is all they have in which to love, laugh, grow, build, study, explore, experiment, travel, and do all the exciting things that they now enjoy. Heaven, as they view it, is a sort of non-existence where spirits float around on clouds. No wonder they are not eager to go there!

There are many good things to enjoy in this world, and there is "more beyond" in heaven for you. Christ died that you might not only enjoy life now but that you might enjoy it forever.

"There every power will be developed, every capability increased. The grandest enterprises will be carried forward, the loftiest aspirations will be reached, the highest ambitions realized. And still there will arise new heights to surmount, new wonders to admire, new truths to comprehend, fresh objects to call forth the powers of body and mind and soul.

"All the treasures of the universe will be open to the study of God's children. With utterable delight we shall enter into the joy and the wisdom of unfallen beings. We shall share the treasures gained through ages upon ages spent in contemplation of God's handiwork. And the years of eternity, as they roll, will continue to bring more glorious revelations."—*Education,* p. 307.

APPLES GROW ON APPLE TREES

Ye shall know them by their fruits. Matthew 7:16.

Today is the birthday of John Chapman, better known as Johnny Appleseed. When John was 18 years old he went to southwestern Pennsylvania, where he built a four-room log-and-stone house and began to grow apples. His orchard was the wonder of the wilderness.

Pioneers on their way west were always welcome at Johnny's home. When they were ready to continue their journey by flatboat down the Ohio River, he gave them deerskin bags full of apple seeds to plant at their new homes.

One day John decided to travel down the river himself. He made the journey in two canoes that he lashed together. Each contained a load of apple seeds. Wherever he found a good spot he stopped to plant seeds.

For forty years Johnny Appleseed wandered up and down the Ohio Valley assisting settlers. With his knowledge of herbal remedies he helped care for the sick. He aided settlers in clearing land and planting crops. And, of course, everywhere he gave away apple seeds and helped start orchards.

In his lifetime Johnny gave away thousands of apple seeds and young apple trees. Although you and I have never watched any of his apple seeds grow, we can be certain of one thing. They grew into trees that produced apples. We can be certain that none of his apple trees bore cherries, pears, or peaches. It is one of the laws of life that apples grow on apple trees, and cherries grow on cherry trees.

Jesus said that the same principle holds for people. Just because someone says he is a Christian does not make him one. Just as we know an apple tree by its fruit, so we can know a Christian by the fruit he bears.

Our words and actions are our fruit. You will not find unkind words, selfish acts, or dishonest behavior in the life of a real Christian. These are the fruit of a different kind of tree.

Those who are Christians will produce the fruit of the Spirit: love, joy, peace, long-suffering, gentleness, goodness, faith, meekness, and temperance.

LIAR, THIEF, GAMBLER, DRUNK

*For God so loved the world, that he gave his only begotten Son,
that whosoever believeth in him should not perish, but have
everlasting life. John 3:16.*

George Mueller was born at Kroppenstaedt, Prussia, on
September 27, 1805. He was born again one Saturday in
November of 1825. In the twenty years between those two
birthdays George Mueller was a very bad boy.

Before he was 10 years old, George was a practiced thief and
liar. When Mr. Mueller missed money from government funds
entrusted to him, he suspected his son, but could prove nothing.
To catch the thief, he laid a trap by placing money where he was
sure George would find it. A little while later George took the
money, hiding it in his shoe. Before he could spend it, his father
called him.

"George, I laid some money down here and now it is gone. Do
you know what happened to it?"

"No, Father. I don't know anything about it. I didn't see any
money."

"We'll see if you are telling the truth," his father said, as he
began to search George from head to foot. Of course, the money
was discovered. The boy took his punishment, but was no better
for it.

George went from bad to worse. He began to play cards,
gamble, and carouse. The night his mother died George
staggered through the streets of the city, drunk. He was only 14
years old at the time.

George went to church twice each year, but this slight
exposure to religion seemed to have no influence on his life. He
didn't own a Bible. He never prayed.

Then one day George attended a prayer meeting with a
friend. The Prussian habit was to pray standing up and here, for
the first time, he saw someone praying on his knees. The
earnestness of those believers in prayer and the message of
God's love for him turned George Mueller around. His old habits
disappeared and in their place came habits of prayer, Bible
study, and witnessing. He was happier than he had ever been in
his life.

You, too, can find the happiness and victory that George
Mueller found in Jesus. God's love can change your life.

278

HEADSTRONG HAROLD

Where no counsel is, the people fall: but in the multitude of counsellors there is safety. Proverbs 11:14.

In 1066 King Edward of England lay dying in his palace. Although he had promised the throne to William of Normandy, he changed his mind and gave it to Harold instead.

Immediately, William gathered his soldiers to invade England and secure the British throne by force. While he was marshaling his army and preparing the fourteen hundred ships that would take them across the channel, the King of Norway invaded England in the north. While King Harold hurried north to defend that part of his realm, William landed on the undefended southern coast. The date was September 28, 1066.

Harold and his men defeated the northern invaders, but at a great loss of soldiers. In spite of this, the king planned to march immediately south and fight William.

"Don't do it," his counselors urged. "Your army is too small and weak from fighting the Norwegians. Wait until you can gather more men and face William with confidence."

"How can I wait?" the king said. "William is burning farms and plundering villages in my kingdom. I must defend the people. I will go."

"If you go now, you will surely lose," his advisors said. "Wait and you will have some chance of winning."

But Harold would not listen to his counselors. He did not want to follow their advice. He marched southward and met William at the Battle of Hastings. Just as his counselors had warned, his army was defeated and he was killed in battle. The victorious leader, who became known as William the Conqueror, became the King of England. The outcome might have been quite different had Harold listened to those older and wiser than himself.

What would you have done if you had been Harold? Would you have listened to the advice of your counselors? Or would you have closed your ears and rushed on to your destruction at Hastings?

How do you react to advice in your everyday life? Are you willing to seek counsel from your parents, teachers, and pastor? Do you recognize that it is safer to follow the counsel of those who have had more experience in life?

CHAIN REACTIONS

Freely ye have received, freely give. Matthew 10:8.

On September 29, 1901, a baby boy was born in Rome who, as a man, would help develop the atomic bomb. He grew up to become a teacher of physics in Italy and later in the United States. In 1942 Enrico Fermi made the first atomic piles and produced the first nuclear chain reaction.

This particular experiment was important because it showed a way to create nuclear power from the splitting of atoms. The splitting of just one atom produced only a small amount of energy. But that energy was used to split other atoms which produced more energy which was used to split still more atoms. This process kept on growing, producing more and more energy all the time.

The energy created in a nuclear chain reaction can be used for destruction, as in the case of the atomic bomb. Or it can be used for such useful purposes as generating electricity, heating houses, running cars, and operating submarines. It can be used in medical research and space exploration.

There is also great power produced in chain reactions among people. A destructive type of chain reaction was started in the Garden of Eden. Satan tempted Eve to eat the forbidden fruit. She in turn offered it to Adam. Through Adam the knowledge of evil was passed on to his sons and through them to their sons and through all the succeeding generations to you and me.

Chain reactions can also work for the good and happiness of mankind. Jesus came into the world to demonstrate love, healing, and blessing. We are reaping the result of that chain reaction in all the good things we enjoy as Christians in 1983.

Would you like to begin a chain reaction today? Find ways to share the love and kindness of Jesus with others. For instance, try to smile at everyone you pass today. Speak some happy words to all you can. Look for ways to be helpful and courteous to those around you.

The people whose lives you touch will be a little bit happier because they met you. Perhaps they will then smile and say something nice to the people *they* meet. Think what a lot of happiness you could set in motion today! Why not get started right away?

THE OPEN SPACE IN ORION

If there be a prophet among you, I the Lord will make myself known unto him in a vision, and will speak unto him in a dream. Numbers 12:6.

"I am not convinced that Sister White is a prophet of God," Joseph Bates said after hearing her speak for the first time.

A few months later Bates witnessed Ellen White in vision. He was most interested when she began to talk about the stars. Since his days as a sea captain he had been interested in astronomy and had read many books on the subject.

Joseph Bates was thrilled with her description of the great open space in the constellation Orion. He had often seen the nebula of Orion that appears in the center of the three stars of the hunter's belt. He had read Lord William Rosse's description of a "gap in the sky" and a Dutch astronomer's statement about an opening "through which one had a free view into another region which was more enlightened." He had read other reports of this corridor of light which was so broad that ninety thousand earth orbits could stand side by side in it.

During Mrs. White's vision Elder Bates jumped to his feet and exclaimed, "That is the best description I have ever heard of the open space in Orion. I wish Lord William Rosse were here tonight."

"Who is Lord William Rosse?" James White asked.

"He is the great English astronomer who has written so much about the nebula in Orion."

As soon as Mrs. White came out of vision, Joseph Bates questioned her. "Where did you study astronomy?"

"I have never studied astronomy," Ellen replied. "As far as I know I have never even looked inside a book on astronomy."

Mrs. White had never read any of Lord Rosse's books, nor had she looked through a telescope. She could not have seen any pictures of the open space in Orion, because the first photograph of this nebula was not taken until September 30, 1880, thirty-four years after her first vision on this subject.

"Now I am convinced that God is speaking to us through Mrs. White," Joseph Bates testified.

Today we have much more evidence than Elder Joseph Bates had that the writings of Ellen G. White are sent from God. If we study them carefully, we, too, will believe.

SUPERNATURAL STRENGTH

The Lord will give strength unto his people. Psalm 29:11.

On October 1, 1965, Mrs. Gene Perryman, of Jasper County, South Carolina proved that God does give strength to those who need it.

On that bright fall morning this 25-year-old mother was standing on the back porch holding her baby. Her 8-year-old son and an older daughter had just gone around to the front of the house to wait for the school bus. Suddenly there was the screech of car brakes and the sound of screaming.

Mrs. Perryman laid the baby in a crib on the porch and ran around the house to the highway. A car was stopped some distance from the house. Wedged underneath between a rear wheel and the gasoline tank was her son.

"I was afraid that the gas tank would catch fire," Mrs. Perryman said later. "I knew I had to get my boy out."

Although she was a small woman and not particularly strong, that desperate mother lifted the rear of the car off her son and sent the car into the ditch. The automobile weighed nineteen hundred pounds. Mrs. Perryman weighed less than one hundred.

In the Bible we also have stories of unusual strength. David killed a lion and a bear single-handedly. Samson carried the huge gates of a city on his back.

How did these people manage such feats? They did not have that much strength of themselves. At their moment of great need God gave them what they needed.

On January 21 you read the story of Pastor Jesson trapped in a burning railroad car. From somewhere he received the strength to free a fellow passenger. "Someone lifted with me," Pastor Jesson said.

There will be emergencies in your life, too, when you will need more strength than you possess. The need may not always be for physical strength. At times you may require supernatural strength of will to overcome temptation. In your life there may be times of great sadness that will call for emotional strength.

Whatever your challenge, God can give you the power to meet it.

GRASSHOPPER FEAST

With men it is impossible, but not with God: for with God all things are possible. Mark 10:27.

Jed and Mary stood at the edge of their potato field looking over the neat rows they had planted together. They had counted on a good crop to see them through the winter and had hoped for enough to sell so that they could finish building the house and barn. But now, suddenly, it seemed their hopes were to be shattered.

Swarms of grasshoppers had invaded their valley in north-central Utah. Without a Please or a Thank you the insects were helping themselves to potato plants.

At first Jed and Mary had tried to kill the grasshoppers but for every one they destroyed hundreds more came. Theirs was not the only farm affected; a neighbor had brought news that it was the same throughout the valley. There was no hope. All the farmers would be ruined.

"What will we do, Jed?" asked Mary as she slipped her small hand into his large one for comfort. "What *can* we do?"

"It will take a miracle to save our crops now," said Jed, shaking his head as if to clear his mind of the awful sight.

"Perhaps God will send the grasshoppers away," said Mary. She wanted so much to find words to make them both feel better. "God can do anything. Surely He will hear our prayers. Nothing is impossible with Him."

Then they saw it—a long-winged white bird, about the size of a pigeon, swooping down out of the sky. It landed in the middle of their potato field and began to gobble down grasshoppers. The first bird was followed by another and another until hundreds had come for the grasshopper feast.

"Praise the Lord!" said Jed. "He has heard our prayers. Our crop is saved."

All up and down the valleys of north-central Utah that day in 1848 the story was the same. Flocks of gulls from Great Salt Lake destroyed the grasshoppers, and the crops were saved.

On this day, some years later, a monument to the seagulls was unveiled in Salt Lake City. Passing by the glistening statue of those two birds, we are reminded that nothing is impossible with God.

PRAYER IN A COTTON FIELD

They that seek the Lord shall not want any good thing. Psalm 34:10.

Mary Jane McCleod was born into a black family in South Carolina twelve years after Abraham Lincoln had freed the slaves. Although theoretically Mary was as free as any white girl, she soon learned there were some things white girls did that she couldn't do. The thing that bothered her most was that she couldn't read.

One hot Saturday afternoon when Mary was 10 years old she went with her mother to the home of some white neighbors. The two girls invited Mary Jane into their playhouse. She pretended that she was the nursemaid and rocked a beautiful doll while her two hostesses pretended to be grown-up ladies. While Mary was rocking the doll, she noticed a book lying on a small table. She reached over and picked it up.

"Put that down!" screamed one of the girls.

"I won't hurt it," said Mary Jane. "I just want to feel it."

"No!" shouted the other sister. "Books are for people who can read. You can't read."

Mary put the book down and placed the doll on the chair. Then she ran out of the playhouse and down the pathway where she met her mother and sobbed out the story.

"I *will* learn to read," Mary Jane said.

Her mother smiled and said nothing, for she knew that her daughter could not go to school. She had to work in the cotton fields.

Mary Jane picked cotton, but as she did she chanted a little prayer, "I want to read! I want to read! Please, dear God, let me go to school."

Before long a teacher came to the area and started a school. Mary Jane attended. Later she went away to college, and became a teacher. On October 3, 1904, Mary Jane McCleod Bethune opened her own school in Daytona, Florida. This school grew so large that it became a college, and Mary Jane was its first president. Later she met many important people, but wherever she went, Mary Jane told how God had heard her prayer in the cotton field.

You can pray anywhere. God will hear your prayer, just as He did Mary Jane's.

SPACE TRAVEL

And God shall wipe away all tears from their eyes; and there shall be no more death, neither sorrow, nor crying. Revelation 21:4.

The Space Age didn't really begin on October 4, 1957. True, that was the day on which the first artificial satellite was launched by Russia. But that was not the beginning of man's desire to escape the troubles of Planet Earth.

Long before the birth of Christ, David sang: "Oh that I had wings like a dove! for then would I fly away, and be at rest" (Ps. 55:6).

Other men had the same wish and some of them tried it. An ancient Greek myth tells about a father and son who made wings out of feathers and wax. The son, Icarus, was so delighted with his ability to fly that he soared higher and higher until the sun melted the wax, and he fell into the sea and drowned.

About two hundred years after Daniel spent a night in the den of lions, someone in Greece made a wooden pigeon that could fly. The Chinese invented kites about the same time.

Then two thousand years passed by with no progress in achieving man's dream of traveling to the moon and stars.

Today we take space travel for granted. Man has been to the moon and photographed the planets. There is talk of interplanctary "bus" service and space vacations.

Man now has, as it were, the wings of a dove. He can fly away from earth and its atmosphere and wing his way to the moon and planets. But even out there he cannot find rest.

Astronauts have learned that your troubles don't vanish when you escape earth's gravity. Worries about sick loved ones, money problems, and misunderstandings travel right along into space. Selfishness does not disappear when men enter a spacecraft. A spacesuit cannot cover up a sinful nature.

Until sin is destroyed there can be no lasting peace and happiness, regardless of where man may be able to go for a vacation in space.

There will still be tears, heartaches, sickness, and death until the day when Jesus comes in the clouds of heaven and takes us on the greatest of all space journeys to the throne of God.

I hope that day will be soon, don't you?

ANGEL MESSAGES

And the Lord God of the holy prophets sent his angel to shew unto his servants the things which must shortly be done. Revelation 22:6.

Does God still give messages to His people through angels? Avondale College stands as a testimony to the fact that He does. It happened almost one hundred years ago when Mrs. White was working in Australia.

One night she had a vision in which she seemed to be looking over a property that was being considered for the new college. She seemed to be walking through a deep woods with some friends. Suddenly they came into a small clearing where they saw a neatly cut furrow about six feet long and nine inches wide. Two men approached and began to examine the soil. "It is not good," the men said. "It will not grow crops."

While they were speaking Ellen White looked up and saw an angel standing on the furrow. He said, "False witness has been borne against the land. This is good soil. Fruits and vegetables will grow here. The Lord is able to set a table in the wilderness."

A few days later Mrs. White was called to look at some property that was for sale about seventy miles from Sydney. While traveling on the train she related her dream to her companions.

When they arrived at the property, it was exactly as she had seen in her vision. The group passed through a dark wood and came to a clearing where there was a fresh furrow. No plow was in sight. The grass around it had not been trampled down. There were no signs that any human being had been there, except for the furrow that measured six feet long and nine inches wide. Two men who had not heard her tell about the dream came from opposite directions. They both knelt down to examine the soil.

"It will not raise a thing," they agreed.

Then Mrs. White told the men of her vision and the message of the angel. They were amazed, but they accepted the message and purchased the property.

On October 5, 1896, about thirty-five people gathered near where the furrow had been to witness Mrs. White lay the cornerstones for the first building of the college.

The angel's message proved true. The farm produced abundant fruits and vegetables in the years to come.

BIBLE BONFIRES

The grass withereth, and the flower thereof falleth away: but the word of the Lord endureth for ever. 1 Peter 1:24, 25.

On this day in 1536 William Tyndale was strangled and then burned at the stake near Vilvorde Castle in Belgium. His crime? He had translated the New Testament into English.

As a young man just out of college William read the Greek Bible and through its pages found the Lord Jesus Christ. After that experience he was determined that all English-speaking people should be able to read the words of Scripture. He said, "If God spares my life, I will, before many years have passed, cause the boy that driveth the plow to know more of the Scriptures than the priests do."

William kept his word, but he had to flee England to do it. In Germany he completed his translation and got it printed. With the help of traders he smuggled it into England.

People sold their most precious possessions in order to buy a copy of the Bible. The books were hidden and brought out at night to be read by candlelight. Many were punished for owning a copy.

Ten years after Tyndale's death, the English parliament made a decree that all English New Testaments should be brought on a certain day and given up to be openly burned. Hundreds were destroyed in the bonfires.

Other European nations made similar laws. Fires were kindled across Europe with Bibles as fuel.

The story is told of a prince who held one of these burnings in his courtyard. A huge pile of Bibles were gathered, and he sat down with friends to watch them burn.

Page by page the precious volumes were destroyed. As the flames leaped upward, the wind caught one of the burned pages and dropped it, with edges blackened and scorched, into the prince's lap. As he looked down he read of today's verse: "The grass withereth, and the flower thereof falleth away: but the word of the Lord endureth for ever."

The prince took this as a message sent from Heaven condemning his actions. Stunned, he rose from his chair and left the scene of the bonfire to think upon the message of the verse.

God's Word still endures in spite of Satan's efforts through the centuries to get rid of it. Do you treasure that Word?

WHAT A KING!

And being found in fashion as a man, he humbled himself, and became obedient unto death, even the death of the cross. Philippians 2:8.

The year was 1942. The place was Denmark. World War II was in progress. Since 1940 the country had been occupied by enemy soldiers, though the government was allowed to continue as long as the leaders obeyed Hitler's commands. One day the order came that all Jews should be marked for death by wearing the Star of David.

In response, King Christian attended a service in a Copenhagen synagogue on October 7. To show his sympathy for his subjects he said, "If the Jews are to wear the Star of David then we shall all wear it. You are all Danes. You are my people."

Many Danish Jews wept to think their king loved them enough to identify himself with them. What a king!

Go back now nearly six thousand years. The place is the Garden of Eden. The world was occupied by the enemy. God looked down and saw the terrible results of yielding to the demands of Satan. He felt so sorry for His people.

So in due time He left His throne in glory and came down to this dark, miserable planet called Earth. He became a baby in a poor home. He grew up in poverty and hardship. He knew what it meant to be hungry, tired, and cold. He suffered as all mankind must suffer.

It was just as if He were saying: "So you have sinned. You must bear the mark of death. You must suffer and die. Since that is the way it is, I have left My throne in heaven to come and share your lot with you. I, too, will wear the mark of death. You are all My people."

King Christian did a beautiful thing by identifying himself with his subjects. But Jesus did something much more beautiful. He not only lived with us and suffered with us; He died in our place.

Because He left all, we may inherit all. Because He suffered, we have hope. Because He shared our life of sorrow and trouble, we may share His life of glory and peace. Because He died for us, we may live forever with Him. Because He was raised from the dead, we do not need to fear death. Because He loved us so much, we also love Him. What a king!

CHICAGO FIRE

Behold, now is the accepted time; behold, now is the day of salvation. 2 Corinthians 6:2.

On Sunday night, October 8, 1871, Dwight L. Moody preached to a large crowd in Chicago. In vivid detail he described the trial of Christ before the rulers. His conclusion emphasized the words spoken by Pilate: "What shall I do then with Jesus which is called Christ?" (Matt. 27:22).

"I wish you would take this text home with you and turn it over in your minds," said Pastor Moody to the congregation. "Then next week we will come to Calvary and the cross and we will decide what to do with Jesus."

But next week never came for many people in Chicago. While Dwight Moody was preaching, a fire started in the barn of Patrick O'Leary at 137 De Koven Street. Peg-legged Daniel Sullivan was even then frantically trying to loosen the tethered cows. By the time Moody had finished his sermon a whole city block was ablaze. The closing song was never finished, for the sound of fire engines broke up the meeting.

Within minutes, much of Chicago was on fire. The 185 firemen were helpless to stop the racing flames. Seventeen horse-drawn engines, twenty-three hose carts, and four hook-and-ladder wagons were no match for the blaze. By twelve-thirty fires had broken out in all three of Chicago's districts.

By Tuesday morning 17,500 buildings had been destroyed, with damages of some $400 million. Three hundred people had died and 100,000 more had been left homeless.

As Moody watched the city burn he wondered how many of the large crowd he had addressed on Sunday night had died. How many of those had perished eternally because he had not urged them to give their hearts to Jesus that very night?

Later Mr. Moody declared, "I would rather have my right hand cut off than give an audience now a week to decide!"

Today you and I must answer the question, "What shall I do then with Jesus which is called Christ?"

Now is the only time you have. Will you accept Him as your Saviour today? Next week or next year may never come for you. Now is the only time you can claim with any certainty. Now is the accepted time. Now is when you must decide.

NO WINEGLASSES

Look not thou upon the wine when it is red, when it giveth his colour in the cup, when it moveth itself aright. At the last it biteth like a serpent, and stingeth like an adder. Proverbs 23:31, 32.

Edward Bok, who was born on this day in 1863, worked for the *Brooklyn Eagle* newspaper as a reporter. One day he was assigned to report the speeches of General Ulysses Grant and President Rutherford B. Hayes, who were speaking in the city.

In those days it was the custom to serve wine to reporters. It was Bok's first assignment and he knew he would have to make a decision. Calling one of the waiters, he said, "Please remove my wineglasses. I do not wish to drink."

Young Bok thought no more about it and proceeded to take down the speech of General Grant. It was easy, for the general spoke slowly. However, President Hayes talked rapidly and none of the reporters could keep up with him.

After the meeting Edward Bok went to the President and told him his difficulty. Mr. Hayes looked at him curiously and said, "Wait a few minutes; I'll be back."

About fifteen minutes later the President came to Edward Bok and said, "Tell me, my boy, why did you have the wineglasses removed from your place?"

Edward was surprised that anyone had noticed, but he decided to be honest. "I did it, Mr. President, because I wanted a clear head. Long ago I made up my mind to be a total abstainer and I saw no reason to make tonight an exception."

The President then asked Edward for his name and address. He took the young man in his own carriage and on the way handed him a copy of his speech. Edward Bok's newspaper was the only one to publish the President's speech.

The next day Edward received a note from the President that said, "I have been telling Mrs. Hayes what you told me at the dinner last evening. She was very much interested. She joins me in asking you to call on us at eight-thirty this evening."

Many years later, after Edward Bok became a famous editor, he said that his decision that night was one of the most important of his life.

What would you do in a similar situation? Would you, like Edward Bok, have the courage to stand up for your convictions? God will give you strength to do so when the time comes.

THE TOWER

The name of the Lord is a strong tower: the righteous runneth into it, and is safe. Proverbs 18:10.

On October 10, 1813, a baby boy was born in a small village in northern Italy. He later became a famous musician, and if you are taking music lessons, look in your books for something composed by Guiseppe Verdi. The world almost missed hearing his beautiful music because of the tragedy that came to Guiseppe's village while he was still a baby.

Napoleon, Emperor of France, was defeated in the Battle of Leipzig by the combined armies of Austria, Prussia, Russia, and Sweden. The victorious soldiers then invaded northern Italy, driving out the French and killing many Italians as well.

A farmer rushed to the inn owned by Guiseppe's father to warn him of the danger. "The Cossacks have come!" he shouted. "Hide!"

Mr. Verdi ran up the stairs calling to his wife, "Luiga, the soldiers have come. Take the baby to the church!"

Mrs. Verdi wrapped Guiseppe in a blanket and dashed out, while her husband stayed behind to hide his valuables under the floor. But the church was already crowded with old people, women, and children, all huddled around the altar.

Looking around for a safer hiding place, Mrs. Verdi noticed the stairs to the bell tower. Clutching Guiseppe tightly to her bosom, she quickly mounted the stairs and pressed herself against the wall of the small platform under the bell. Above the loud beating of her heart she could hear the galloping hoofbeats of the Cossack horses.

The horses stopped in front of the church, and the cruel soldiers battered down the door and killed everyone there. However, they never thought to check the tower, and Guiseppe and his mother were saved.

The wise man says that the name of Jesus is like that tower. To Him we may flee for refuge and strength. In Him we are able to hide from those who seek our destruction. When temptation presses about us we can call our Lord's name in prayer. The moment we do, it is as if we are lifted high above the world into a strong tower where we are safe.

UGLY DUCKLING

The king's daughter is all glorious within. Psalm 45:13.

Thirteen-year-old Eleanor was not pretty. Her mouth was too big and her teeth too prominent. Her chin was small and receding. Her blond hair was uncontrollable, and freckles spotted her nose. Her few dresses were plain and out of style.

The girl had been shy from babyhood, sensing somehow that she was a disappointment to her beautiful mother, who had wanted a boy. The child overheard remarks that impressed upon her that she was plain to the point of ugliness.

"She's so old-fashioned," her mother would explain to visitors, and Eleanor felt that she wanted to sink through the floor in shame because she did not live up to the maternal expectations. She didn't like parties because her plainness and awkwardness always made her feel ill at ease.

Before Eleanor was 10 years old both her mother and father died and she went to live with her grandmother, who had many other responsibilities that took her attention. From then on, the girl felt even more isolated and alone in the world. How she longed to belong to someone who really loved her in spite of her looks!

The sadness of Eleanor's life made her more sensitive to the hurts of others. On one occasion while visiting with friends away from home, she carefully wrote a letter to her brother every day.

One morning her hostess said, "Come, let's go out and do something."

"Let me finish this letter first," said Eleanor.

"But you wrote to your brother yesterday!"

"I write to him every day," said Eleanor. "I want him to feel he belongs to somebody."

Eleanor Roosevelt, the shy, plain, little orphan girl whose birthday is today, became the First Lady of the United States. People all over the world loved her because of her inward beauty revealed in thoughtfulness of others.

Millions came to think of Eleanor, not as an ugly duckling but as a beautiful swan because of the lovely character she developed. She had learned that the girl on the inside was more important than the girl on the outside.

LAND HO!

And when these things begin to come to pass, then look up, and lift up your heads; for your redemption draweth nigh. Luke 21:28.

At two o'clock in the morning of Friday, October 12, 1492, Roderigo de Triana, a sailor on the *Pinta,* sighted the New World. He, along with eighty-seven other adventurers from Spain aboard three ships, had been eagerly looking for land.

On September 18 they had seen birds and low-lying clouds that made them think land was near. On the twenty-fifth someone raised the cry of "Land ho!" but it proved a false alarm. On October 7 another false alarm was sounded.

Four days later crewmen on the *Pinta* fished up a cane, a pole, a rod that seemed to be made of iron, and a board. Someone on the *Niña* spotted a branch with berries on it. The men breathed a sigh of relief. Surely this time they were near land. That night their leader, Christopher Columbus, saw a light on the horizon and knew that before morning they would be ashore.

He was right. In the early morning moonlight a sailor sighted a distant limestone cliff. By dawn they put down anchor, and the men stepped onto the shore of Watling Island. There they knelt to kiss the ground and give thanks to God for a safe journey, their tears of joy mingling with the sand. The men thought they had reached India, but instead they had come upon a new world.

You and I have also set sail for a new world. It won't be long now before we will walk the streets of its golden city and feast on its life-giving fruit. No, it can't be far away. The heavenly land is just over the horizon. All the signs tell us that it is so.

There are wars and rumors of wars. Land is just ahead!

There are famines and earthquakes. These are sure signs of our journey's end.

There is violence in our streets, and men seem to live by hatred. It can't be long now!

The churches are full of people who do not have the power of Christ in their lives. We must be almost there!

The gospel is rapidly being carried to the farthest corners of the globe. The new world is just ahead!

There are false prophets and false Christs! Land ho!

Look up! Be happy! We will soon be there!

293

NO GREATER LOVE

Greater love hath no man than this, that a man lay down his life for his friends. John 15:13.

On this day in 1881, a large, well-equipped steamship, the *Crypian,* sailed from Liverpool, England, in the midst of bad weather. Within a few hours she was caught in a fierce gale.

The ship might have survived the storm if other problems had not arisen. First the steering mechanism broke. Then one of the boilers burst. Large waves swept overboard and extinguished the fires in the ship. There was nothing left to do but drift at the mercy of the storm.

Soon the ship was foundering dangerously near the rocky coast of Wales. The captain summoned the passengers and told them it was every man for himself.

The frightened people grabbed what they could to use as buoys and began to swim for shore. Finally there were only two people left on board—the captain and a stowaway, a young street urchin.

As the captain was putting on his life belt he noticed the terror-stricken boy huddled in a corner. Without hesitation the man removed his life jacket and strapped it onto the child.

Both the captain and the boy jumped into the waters just as the ship went under. The boy made it to shore, but the captain was drowned.

The boy told those who had gathered on the shore the story of his rescue by the captain, ending by saying over and over, "He gave himself for me! He gave himself for me!"

The boy was not a passenger. He was a lawbreaker. He deserved to drown. He had no business on that ship. In spite of this, the captain gave his own life that the young boy might be saved.

Because the stowaway accepted the gift of the life jacket that the captain offered, he was saved. Had he refused it, he would surely have drowned.

It is that way with our eternal salvation. We must accept the "life jacket" that Christ offers us. What He did on Calvary makes it possible for us to be saved.

Christ loves us so much. He gave Himself for you. He gave Himself for me. Oh, wonderful, wonderful love! He died that we might live! Surely there is no greater love!

DAVID'S BAD LEG

And the prayer of faith shall save the sick. James 5:15.

"We may have to amputate David's leg," the doctor said. "It looks bad."

Little David lay on his bed in Abilene, Kansas, and listened to the conversation. He was feverish and semidelirious as a result of raging infection caused by a cut from a jagged tin can. He was horrified at the thought of losing his leg.

How could he run through the Smoke Hill River with only one leg? He couldn't hang from the rafters in the old barn by his toes like the other boys. He wouldn't be able to walk tightrope along the rooftree of the barn. With one leg gone, he wouldn't be able to play baseball or do a hundred other things that boys like to do.

Calling his older brother, Edgar, to his side, David said, "Promise me that you won't let anyone cut off my leg. I'd rather die than be a cripple."

For the next three nights Edgar slept on the doorsill of David's room. He was going to make sure no one cut off his brother's leg!

Meanwhile, of course, the whole family was praying for David's recovery.

We can imagine Father and Mother with their five other sons gathered in the living room for family devotions. Father reads a bit from the Bible, and they all bow in prayer as he pleads for the life of his third son. "Dear Lord, please help our David's leg to get better. We don't want to have it amputated. Please heal the infection and take away the fever. Make him well again, if it is Your will."

God gave an answer of Yes to their prayers and Dwight David Eisenhower was soon running and playing with the other boys again. This boy, whose birthday is today, grew up to become a great U.S. Army general, and later, President of the United States.

Many people's lives have been saved by prayer after the doctors have given up hope. Jesus is the Great Physician. We should never hesitate to go to Him in prayer. He will always hear and will do what He knows is best.

BRIDGE COLLAPSE

In God have I put my trust. Psalm 56:11.

Morale was low among the workmen on the 2,590 meter West Gate Bridge in Melbourne, Australia. Word got around that a similar bridge had collapsed in Great Britain.

"This bridge isn't safe," the men grumbled.

Jack Hindshaw, the engineer in charge of construction, called the men together to explain why the bridge in Great Britain had collapsed. "That will not happen here," he promised them. "If I didn't think it was safe I wouldn't be working here."

Not long after, on the morning of October 15, 1970, Jack Hindshaw received an urgent message: "There is trouble. Come to the bridge at once."

Hindshaw arrived within half an hour to find that the bridge had buckled in one section. The men were doing their best to find a way to correct it.

Suddenly there was a terrible wrenching of metal and a whole section of the bridge crumbled and fell to the river below. Thirty-five of the sixty-eight workers were killed. Among them was Engineer Jack Hindshaw.

Mr. Hindshaw believed in his project. He had faith in the work of his company. He was sure the span would remain secure. But his faith was wrongly placed, and he fell with the bridge to his death.

It is possible for us to do the same in the spiritual realm. Some people put their trust in money and others in their own abilities. Too many place their faith in a particular person. They honor him so much that should he fall they will fall with him. Others put their trust in a church. They feel as long as their names are recorded they will be safe. They think that because the church has been around for centuries it will not let them down. Someday they might be surprised.

It is not wise to put our faith in a person or in a system of beliefs. The Bible says that if we do we will be disappointed. There is only one sure support on which we can rely and that is the Lord Jesus Christ. He is the same yesterday, today, and forever. He will not fail us. We can count on Him. In Him we will be safe.

VICTORY OVER PAIN

Neither shall there be any more pain: for the former things are passed away. Revelation 21:4.

The time is ten-fifteen on Friday morning, October 16, 1846. The place is the operating theater of the Massachusetts General Hospital in Boston. The seats above the surgical pit are full of interested students and staff members. The patient, Gilbert Abbot, is strapped to the red-plush operating chair. The large tumor on his jaw can be seen by everyone. The instruments are ready. The surgeon, John Collins Warren, and his assistants stand ready to operate.

At that moment Dr. William T. G. Morton strides into the theater carrying a glass globe. He nods to those present and proceeds to a small room behind the amphitheater seats. There he saturates a sponge with ether and places it in the glass globe which he then corks. Carrying the globe with the sponge he again enters the operating theater.

Crossing to the patient he says, "Are you afraid?"

"No," Mr. Abbot replies. "I am not afraid."

Dr. Morton puts a tube from the glass globe to Mr. Abbot's lips and tells him to breathe through his mouth. After three or four minutes the doctor removes the tube from the patient's mouth and says to the surgeon, "Your patient is ready."

Dr. Warren holds the large tumor in one hand and a knife in the other. Steeling himself for the customary screams of agony, he makes the first incision.

There is no cry or movement from the patient. The operation proceeds as quietly as though the doctor were working on a corpse. He closes the wound and washes the patient's face. For the first time surgery has been performed without pain.

Today we take it for granted that operations will be painless. We expect teeth to be pulled without hurting. A wide variety of injections and pills are available to put a temporary end to discomfort. Yet, in spite of man's scientific advances there is still pain in the world.

Pain will be here as long as sin exists. Only when sin has been destroyed will there be complete victory over suffering. Let us pray that Jesus will come soon.

UNRECOGNIZED GLORY

The glory of this latter house shall be greater than of the former, . . . and in this place will I give peace. Haggai 2:9.

In 586 B.C. King Nebuchadnezzar marched into Jerusalem and destroyed Solomon's Temple. When his soldiers returned to Babylon, they took with them golden vessels from the Temple and many captives.

Years later, another king of Babylon held a feast for one thousand of his government officials. The king poured wine into those vessels and passed them around for all to drink. There was much laughter as they drank the wine and praised their heathen gods.

While the feast was in progress, the army of Cyrus diverted the waters of the Euphrates River, which ran through the city. Using the dry riverbed the troops marched unopposed into Babylon.

King Cyrus permitted the Jews to return to their homeland in order to rebuild the Temple. However, there was a general feeling that the new building would not be as beautiful as Solomon's Temple.

On October 17, 520 B.C. God spoke to the prophet Haggai and said that the Temple was going to be more glorious than Solomon's Temple, for the Lord Himself, the long awaited Messiah, would come and fill it with His glory.

Five hundred years later Jesus left the glories of heaven and was born in Bethlehem. When He grew up He visited the Temple. Sick were healed, sinners saw in Him their hope of salvation, and those who were troubled found peace.

The glory of the Lord was in the Temple at Jerusalem because Jesus was there. However, many did not recognize His glory. They did not find His peace.

Through the Holy Spirit, Jesus comes to church each Sabbath to fill the sanctuary with His glory. Did you find His glory and peace last week, or were you busy writing notes, reading *Guide,* or whispering to your neighbor?

This week why not try something different? Enter the church on tiptoe. As soon as you sit down, bow your head and ask God to show you His glory and peace. Wait, watch, and listen. You will not be disappointed.

BURIED TREASURE

Where your treasure is, there will your heart be also. Luke 12:34.

About twenty miles north of Burlington, Vermont, near Lake Champlain, is the small town of St. Albans. Somewhere between the town and the Canadian border lies a buried treasure of $114,522 in gold. There is a reward of $10,000 for the person who discovers it, but so far no one has claimed the reward. That treasure has been hidden away since the evening of October 18, 1864.

For several days before that date, strangers began to appear in St. Albans. Then on Tuesday afternoon the twenty-two newcomers gathered on the village green. When the clock struck three they divided into groups and headed for the three banks that faced the village square. Some of the men held the townspeople at bay with their guns. Others entered the banks and took the money. With the loot, they mounted their horses and galloped out of town.

The twenty-two men were Confederate soldiers who planned to use the funds to help them rob other New England towns. However, fourteen of them were caught in Canada, and no other towns were robbed. The captured men refused to tell where they had hidden the money.

After the war one of the soldiers came back to St. Albans to search for the gold. A local farmer followed him from a distance, and noticed that he wandered up and down the Vermont side of the Canadian border as though looking for something. But either the landmarks were not the same, or the former robber had forgotten some important details. He left without the gold.

During times of war some people bury their family treasures in the back yard or in the cellar before they flee. Wherever possible those people return to find their treasure.

Where is your treasure hidden? Is it in heaven? Have you been using your money for missions and evangelism? Have you been helping the poor and suffering?

Of course, Satan is also trying to get you to lay up treasure in his territory. He knows that where your treasure is there your heart will be also. That's what he wants, your heart, your allegiance, and your devotion.

Where is your heart? Where have you put your treasure?

IT IS FINISHED

When Jesus therefore had received the vinegar, he said, It is finished. John 19:30.

On this day in 1781, Lord Cornwallis surrendered at Yorktown, thus insuring the American triumph in the Revolutionary War.

In the Yale University Art Gallery hangs a painting of the ceremony of surrender done by Artist John Trumbull. It shows George Washington and his officers lined up to receive the British. Marching down the center is the British general that was sent by Cornwallis riding on a white horse followed by a long line of red-coated British soldiers. The defeated men look so sad. The British general, slouched on his horse, looks glumly at the ground. Even the horse appears unhappy.

In contrast, Washington and his men are sitting proud and straight. They have won the battle and the look of triumph is on their faces. The winning officers seem to be holding back their spirited horses, which have one hoof raised as if ready to charge.

When the surrender was completed and all the arms were turned over to the victors, the British soldiers broke into a mournful rendition of an old English song: "The World Turned Upside Down."

For the winners, of course, it was a joyous occasion. They had fought hard and won. Their country would be free. George Washington echoed their thoughts when he said, "The work is done and well done."

These words remind us of those spoken by another General nearly two thousand years ago. Hanging there on the cross Jesus said, "It is finished."

What did He mean? What was finished? Was His life finished and done? No, for He rose again on Sunday morning. Was it the work of telling everyone about His Father's love? No, that work is still going on.

It was the work of redemption that was finished on the cross. At that moment when Jesus Christ gave His life as a sacrifice for your sins and mine, the price was paid and the atonement was made. From that time on the triumph over Satan was an accomplished fact. That moment on the cross assured the final victory and freedom of this world from sin and death.

CAPTAIN BLIGH'S BIBLE

For the word of God is quick, and powerful, and sharper than any twoedged sword, piercing even to the dividing asunder of soul and spirit. Hebrews 4:12.

An example of the power of God's Word is seen in the story of Capt. William Bligh's Bible, which was packed away in the captain's sea chest when he went sailing for Tahiti on the ship *Bounty*. On the way back the crew mutinied. They put Captain Bligh and eighteen of his supporters into a small boat and set them adrift on the Pacific Ocean.

The mutineers took six men and twelve women from Tahiti and headed for Pitcairn Island, where they hoped to hide from the British Government.

It was not much of a paradise, however, for one of the men knew how to brew liquor, and soon they were spending most of their time getting drunk. In this condition they fought over the women and killed one another off. Within ten years only one man, John Adams, was left alive.

John became very sober as he realized the responsibility he had for so many women and children. He wanted to organize a school, but he had no textbooks. Then he remembered the sea chest. He opened it and discovered Captain Bligh's Bible. He read it earnestly and gathered the women and children around him each day to teach them from its pages.

The still, where liquor had been made, remained idle. The children grew up to be clean, well-behaved, peaceful, and orderly. They learned to read and write. A church was built. In the place of curses, words of laughter and praise were heard throughout the island. The news of this tremendous change spread around the world.

James White sent a box of Adventist literature to the island and later John I. Tay, a ship's carpenter, spent five weeks telling them about the Sabbath and the soon return of Jesus. Mr. Tay promised to tell the General Conference about the desire of the island people to be baptized.

As a result, on October 20, 1890, with a missionary crew on board, the schooner *Pitcairn* set sail from San Francisco harbor. The people of Pitcairn Island were baptized, and a church school was established. Now there is Adventist work on many South Sea islands. It all began with Captain Bligh's Bible.

301

UNITY IN BATTLE

That they all may be one; as thou, Father, art in me, and I in thee, that they also may be one in us. John 17:21.

"253 269 863 261 471 958 220 370 4-27-19-24."

Signal officers on twenty-six ships of the British Royal Navy spelled out the coded message from Admiral Nelson's flag ship, the *Victory.* Their hearts beat a little faster as they deciphered its message: "England expects that every man will do his duty."

The day was Monday, October 21, 1805, and one of the most famous sea battles of history was about to be fought. The place was near Cape Trafalgar just off the southern coast of Spain, near the Strait of Gibraltar. The combined French and Spanish ships were 33 to the British 27.

Although the English sailors were outnumbered, they determined to do their duty. Every man was alert. Nelson ordered his fleet to be split into two columns. One squadron, led by Admiral Collingwood, headed for the center of the enemy fleet, cutting the line of ships in half and breaking their orderly formation. Admiral Nelson then headed for the lead ship, and within four hours of fighting the victory was gained. Eighteen enemy ships were sunk and the rest captured.

Two things helped the British to win that battle. One was the unity of the ships and their sailors. Every man did his duty as it was outlined, working together to carry out the Admiral's plan.

A second reason for their success was their ability to divide the enemy. They struck at the middle of the line of thirty-three ships, cutting off sixteen that could not then come to the aid of their lead ship. The unity of the enemy was broken.

If the British ships had each acted independently in the battle, they could not have won. It is the same with God's church on this earth. Everyone must do his duty, working together to follow the plans of the Leader. This is why Christ prayed for His disciples, and for us, that we might all be united. He knows that this is the only way to win our battle with the enemy.

Is it possible that something you or I might do could destroy unity and cause defeat? Let us resolve to do our duty today for God and our church.

THE GREAT DISAPPOINTMENT

But of that day and that hour knoweth no man, no, not the angels which are in heaven, neither the Son, but the Father. Mark 13:32.

Suppose for a moment what it might have been like for a young person of your age to be looking for Jesus to come on October 22, 1844.

Imagine the excitement there would have been in your church on the previous Sunday.

"I can hardly wait for Tuesday to come," says one of your friends.

"Me, too!" agrees another. "Just think how exciting it's going to be to look up into the sky and see thousands of angels and the glory of Jesus, brighter than the sun!"

"Won't it be fun to feel ourselves going up and up and up into the air to meet Jesus?" you suggest.

"Yes," replies a friend. "And I'm going to see Grandma and Grandpa, who died last year."

"And I can talk to Aunt Elizabeth again," you respond.

"Father says we are going to have a wonderful feast when we get to heaven," someone adds. "It will surely be better than beans and potatoes."

"Our neighbors who are not ready are going to feel so sad," says another friend. "We have tried to tell them the truth, but they wouldn't listen."

Monday comes and goes with much the same thoughts of expectation. No one wants to go to sleep on Monday night. Mother insists that you go to bed about ten o'clock, but you do not sleep. You lie there listening to the adult voices and looking out the window.

Midnight comes and some people go outside to watch the sky for the first sign of light from heaven. You go, too. The frosty fall air chills your toes.

No one feels like breakfast, for all are anticipating a heavenly feast. At noon you eat a little and continue to wait.

By evening the neighbors come to see whether you are still here. "He'll come tonight. Just wait and see," you say. But you go to sleep late that night sad and disappointed. You don't want to wake up again. How will you face the neighbors? Why didn't He come?

OPERA HOUSE FIRE

Christ died for our sins. 1 Corinthians 15:3.

It took four days for news of the surrender of General Cornwallis to reach the village of Collinsville, Pennsylvania. The day the news came, October 23, 1781, was a day of great rejoicing.

It was planned that a Thanksgiving service would be held in the church. However, as the hour for the meeting approached, it was evident that the little church could not hold everyone. At the last moment the meeting place was switched to the town opera house, which was on the second floor above several stores.

People from miles around came to the meeting, packing even the larger quarters. Pastor Coons had not yet returned from the war, so one of the church elders took charge of the meeting. Mrs. Coons sat on the front row.

Suddenly there was a scream of "Fire! Fire!" A large tongue of flame leaped up the wall behind the speaker. Smoke quickly filled the room.

People jumped to their feet and headed for the narrow door that led to safety. In the panic of that moment it seemed that surely many lives would be lost in the stampede.

Then above the shouting of the struggling mass of people a song was heard. People turned to look and saw Mrs. Coons standing on the platform before the backdrop of flame. Her eyes were turned toward heaven. Her arms were outstretched. Her sweet voice was raised in a simple hymn that everyone knew. One by one the people joined in singing. The traffic jam at the door seemed to melt away. Order was restored and the people left the building in a quiet and orderly fashion.

All, that is, except Mrs. Coons. She was coming down the steps from the stage when the roof fell in. Her voice was stilled forever.

No wonder that the people of Collinsville put up a statue to commemorate her brave deed. No wonder they placed a bronze plaque in her honor on the little frame cottage where she was born. They wanted the world to know that they appreciated what the pastor's wife had done for them.

Once, long ago, Jesus died for you and me. What are we doing to tell the world that we appreciate that love?

PITCAIRN SIGN

And hallow my sabbaths; and they shall be a sign between me and you, that ye may know that I am the Lord your God. Ezekiel 20:20.

Four years before the missionary ship *Pitcairn* set sail from San Francisco, John Tay made up his mind to go on his own missionary trip to the little Pacific Island for which the boat would be named.

John found work on a ship going to Tahiti and from there he caught another ship bound for Pitcairn. The islanders welcomed him, and soon he was conducting Bible studies every evening. Soon the meetings had to be moved to a larger building.

On Sunday, October 24, 1886, after only six days on the island, Tay was asked to preach the Sunday sermon. He spoke for half an hour about the true Sabbath.

"The seventh day is the Sabbath of the Lord," John Tay announced. "God made the world in six days and rested on the seventh. He sanctified that day and He expects us to worship Him on Saturday not on Sunday."

"We never heard of such a thing!" someone said after the meeting. "Why haven't we seen this before?"

"Why does everyone keep Sunday?" others questioned. "Didn't Jesus change the day from Saturday to Sunday?"

"You must speak to us again on Tuesday," another suggested.

So it was that John Tay again preached about the Sabbath on Tuesday night at the prayer meeting. By the time he had finished speaking someone said, "I will keep the Sabbath."

"I see it, too," joined in another voice. "I also will keep the Sabbath."

One by one the people of Pitcairn Island made up their minds to keep the very next Sabbath. John Tay got permission to have the meeting on Saturday. When the bell rang for the first Sabbath meeting on Pitcairn, every person on the island came.

All day long on that first Sabbath they discussed the new light they had received. The next day every person on the island went to work. From that day to this only the seventh-day Sabbath has been observed on Pitcairn. Each week as the people meet for Sabbath school, they are reminded that the Sabbath is a sign God has given them of His love and power.

A MOTHER'S LOVE

Can a woman forget her sucking child, that she should not have compassion on the son of her womb? yea, they may forget, yet will I not forget thee. Isaiah 49:15.

On October 25, 1966, Mary Carson was sewing a dress for her 6-year-old daughter, Ginny, when 10-year-old John ran into the house shouting, "Ginny's been hit by a truck!"

Mrs. Carson rushed out to find her daughter lying in a pool of blood beside the road. Within minutes an ambulance was speeding the child and her mother to the hospital emergency room.

Eventually the doctor came out to explain to Mr. and Mrs. Carson that without an operation Ginny could not live. Her head was badly fractured and even with surgery there was only a slight chance that she would pull through, and if she did, she might be helpless the rest of her life.

Ginny lived through the operation but she did not wake up for nearly a month. During those weeks most of Mrs. Carson's time was spent beside her bed. She talked to Ginny and read her stories by the hour, even though there was no response from the child. Mrs. Carson helped massage her body and exercise her legs and arms.

After a month Ginny woke up, but she couldn't speak or walk. Mrs. Carson faithfully continued her visits until, after 143 days, the little girl was able to leave the hospital. During all that time every available moment was devoted to Ginny.

Why did Mrs. Carson spend so much time in the hospital with her daughter? Because she loved her, of course. Perhaps more than anything else, it was that love that pulled the child through. Today Ginny is a capable, happy young woman who thanks God for life and a wonderful mother.

"The Miracle of Ginny" is what the *Reader's Digest* called this story. Perhaps a better title would have been "The Miracle of a Mother's Love."

As great as a mother's love can be, God says that His love for us is even greater. It is possible that sometime a mother might forget her child, but God will never forget His children.

Through all of our trials and difficulties, He is there. In times of darkest discouragement He is by our side. His love is always sure. His love will see us through.

THREE LONELY CHILDREN

The Lord is nigh unto them that are of a broken heart. Psalm 34:18.

Johnny, 7, Edith, 4, and Edward, 2, huddled together in the small cave and listened to the shouts of Indians as they came closer, beating the brush in the woods. The children crouched motionless, scarcely breathing, until the search party was gone.

After a long time Johnny pushed aside the brush that hid the entrance to the cave and cautiously crept out to survey the situation. He found his home burned to the ground, his parents killed.

Returning to the cave he took his brother and sister by the hand and started out for the nearest neighbor two miles away. When the little trio reached the clearing they found that the warriors had been there, too. Nothing remained.

By evening the children had arrived at a third clearing, but no one was there. The house had been looted, and they were afraid to stay for fear the Indians would return.

They moved deep into the woods and took shelter under a bush, where they huddled together for warmth. The hooting of an owl, the howl of a coyote, and the scream of a bobcat frightened them. Soon all three were sobbing uncontrollably. They were cold, hungry, alone, and so frightened. Oh, how they wanted their mother!

When the sun came up, the children began walking again. They came to a clearing and saw an Indian approaching. Too exhausted to run or hide they could only wait to see what would happen. How happy they were to discover it was their old friend, Tom, who had worked for their father. He took them by canoe to Seattle, where friends gave them a home and love.

Surely Jesus was very near to those three heartbroken children on that long-ago October 26. It was He who comforted them as they cried together in the bushes. It was He who watched over them in their little cave. It was He who sent Tom to find them in the forest. It was He who provided them with a new home and someone to love them.

God was very near to those three lonely children and He'll be near to you, too, whenever you need His love and protection.

SALAMANACA VISION

Let your light so shine before men, that they may see your good works, and glorify your Father which is in heaven. Matthew 5:16.

On Monday afternoon, October 27, 1880, Ellen White had just knelt to pray in Salamanaca, New York, when it seemed that the room was filled with a soft silvery light. Then God gave her a vision in which she seemed to be in Battle Creek. An angel said, "Follow me," and took her to a room where a group of men were discussing the *American Sentinel* magazine.

She saw one of the men hold a copy of the magazine high over his head, and say, "Unless these articles on the Sabbath and the Second Advent come out of this paper, we can no longer use it as the organ of the Religious Liberty Association."

The next morning Mrs. White began to tell the curious vision but she got only as far as the part about the angel leading her and could not remember the rest of what she had seen.

Several times during the next few months she tried to tell that vision but each time she could get no further than the angel's leading her.

Then at three o'clock one morning in March during the time of the General Conference session, Mrs. White was awakened and instructed by the Lord to go to the early morning meeting and tell the vision. She did this and spoke for an hour counseling the workers to let their light shine regarding the message of the Sabbath and the Second Coming.

When she sat down a man in the back of the room stood up and said, "At three o'clock this morning I was in that long-lasting meeting. I am the man who made the remarks about the articles in the paper, holding it high over my head. I . . . was on the wrong side. . . . I take this opportunity to place myself on the right side."

Mrs. White was surprised. She thought the meeting had taken place five months before when she had seen it in vision.

One after another the men who had been in the meeting stood and confessed their mistake and promised to follow the counsel the Lord had given.

Sometimes you and I are like those men, are we not? Sometimes we feel ashamed to let our light shine. We should never be ashamed. God will bless us if we follow His counsel and let everyone know what we believe.

LIBERTY

Come unto me, all ye that labour and are heavy laden, and I will give you rest. Matthew 11:28.

L—is for *Lady Liberty*. This 151-foot-1-inch copper woman holds in her left hand a tablet bearing the date of the American Declaration of Independence. Her right hand is extended high in the air, holding a glowing torch. At her feet is a broken shackle.

I—is for *Isére*, the name of the French ship on which Lady Liberty traveled from France where she was made, to New York where she stands as a symbol of hope to refugees and immigrants of many lands. It took 214 packing cases to hold the 450,000 pound statue.

B—is for *Bartholdi*, the French sculptor who designed the Statue of Liberty and raised the money to make the dream a reality. The people of France gave $250,000 for the statue, and the people of the United States gave about $280,000 for the pedestal on which Lady Liberty would stand.

E—is for *Eiffel*, Alexandre G. Eiffel, the man who built the supporting iron framework of the statue. Spiraling inside of this framework is a stairway with 168 steps.

R—is for *Representatives* of France and America who were present on October 28, 1886, when the statue was unveiled. President Grover Cleveland dedicated the statue as a symbol of liberty for all oppressed and homeless people of the world.

T—is for *Tyranny,* the opposite of liberty. Newspapers are full of stories of riots, revolutions, coups, and rebellions. Hundreds of thousands of people are still risking their lives in search of freedom. Refugees from tyranny are still roaming the world in search of liberty.

Y—is for the *Yearning* that every human being has to be free. Lady Liberty symbolizes this natural longing of the human heart. She says, "Give me your tired, your poor, Your huddled masses yearning to breathe free." However, the "huddled masses" need more than beautiful words to make them really free.

The shackles of sin must be broken if man is to have true liberty. Man needs to escape the tyranny of Satan. This is possible only by heeding the words of the Author of Liberty, "Come unto me, all ye that labour and are heavy laden, and I will give you rest."

309

FIFTEEN YEARS OF LOVE

And he shall turn the heart of the fathers to the children, and the heart of the children to their fathers, lest I come and smite the earth with a curse. Malachi 4:6.

Carefully, slowly, Mrs. William Gille copied out today's verse and thought of her own dear son, Billy, whom she loved very much. He had attended an Adventist school. She and Dad had hoped he would be a worker for the Lord, but Billy had strayed away from the faith of his parents. He didn't go to church any more, and they felt so sad.

Fifteen years of work was now completed, work done in love for her wandering boy. She had begun the project in 1936 with Matthew 1:1 and finished it on October 29, 1951, with Malachi 4:6. During all of those years she had kept the Bible open on the kitchen table and whenever she had a few minutes she sat and wrote and prayed for her son.

One thousand eight hundred twenty-eight sheets of paper, eighteen bottles of ink, and no one knows how many prayers went into this handwritten copy of the Bible.

That Christmas Mr. and Mrs. Gille gave a most unusual gift to their son, a Bible hand-written by his mother. The book was four-and-one-half inches thick and weighed nine pounds.

Placing the Bible in her son's hands, Mother Gille said, "Billy, darling, remember that every word was written with love, but I can't begin to love you as the Lord does." Tears were in her eyes, and she had to swallow hard as she watched her son take the precious book in his hands and leaf through its pages. Would he read it? Would its message reach his heart and make a change in his life?

Only eternity will tell the results of that one mother's love for her son. What a joy it would be for Mother Gille to meet Billy in heaven and know that her labor of love was not in vain.

Most Christian parents are somewhat like Mrs. Gille. They are trying in one way or another to give their sons and daughters the very best gift they can imagine, a love for Jesus, the Bible, and the church.

It is this desire that makes fathers and mothers work long hours so that their children can attend a Christian school. This is why they urge their children to attend church and spend time every day reading the Bible.

310

INVASION FROM MARS

And for this cause God shall send them strong delusion, that they should believe a lie. 2 Thessalonians 2:11.

"RADIO LISTENERS IN PANIC
Taking War Drama as Fact"

This was the headline of the *New York Times* on Monday, October 31, 1938. The article told of the mass hysteria that had taken hold of thousands of radio listeners in Eastern United States between eight-fifteen and nine-thirty on the evening of October 30.

At that time there was a broadcast dramatizing H. G. Well's science fiction, "War of the Worlds." This program was so well done that people were led to believe there actually had been an invasion from Mars.

Thousands of people in New York and New Jersey ran from their homes to escape the "gas raid from Mars." Many had to be treated for shock. Some walked around with wet towels covering their faces. Others began moving furniture out of their homes. City parks were crowded with frightened people. Telephone lines were jammed by callers who wanted to know how to protect themselves against the Martians.

This all goes to show that most human beings are easy to deceive. Most people believe what their eyes see and their ears hear. If they read something in the newspaper they accept it as true. If they see something on television news they take it as a fact.

In 2 Thessalonians Paul tells how Satan will work among people in the last days with lying wonders in order to trick them. He says that because people do not know and love the truth of God they will be deceived into believing lies.

If you and I are not going to be among that group of people then we need to study our Bibles carefully so that we can clearly understand what is truth and what is a lie.

One of these days the big news story is going to be the so-called return of Jesus. There will no doubt be pictures of him taken by newsmen who have gone to some far off place to hear him speak and to watch him perform miracles. People who know their Bibles will not be among the thousands who throng to see him. They will not be deceived. They will know that it cannot be Jesus, for His coming will be in the clouds and every eye shall see Him.

311

LUTHER'S 95 REASONS

The just shall live by faith. Romans 1:17.

In 1517 you could get to heaven by paying money. At least that is what many people in Saxony believed.

A priest by the name of Tetzel sold certificates that assured people that their sins were forgiven, and they could go straight to heaven when they died.

It was possible to buy certificates for those who were already dead and who were supposed to be suffering for their sins in a place called purgatory. Tetzel said, "Once the money in the box rings, the soul from fiery purgatory wings."

It was even possible to buy certificates that stated that the sins a person planned to commit in the *future* would be forgiven. One could thus go out and purchase pardon before committing a crime.

Tetzel was not the only one who sold these certificates. Frederick of Saxony also handled them. He had 17,413 so-called holy objects that he kept in his house. There were such things as a piece of wood supposedly from the cross, a thorn said to be from the crown of Jesus, or a tooth purported to have belonged to one of the apostles. People could pay money to see these objects and thereby get 128,000 years of release from purgatory.

There was in Saxony at least one man who did not believe what Tetzel and Frederick were saying. Martin Luther had studied the Bible carefully and had learned that you cannot buy salvation. It is a free gift of God. Jesus paid the price of sins on Calvary's cross. He took our punishment. We can receive forgiveness by simply having faith in Him.

So late on the night of October 31, 1517, Martin Luther walked up to the doors of the church in Wittenberg. He unrolled the large piece of paper on which he had written his objections to the sale of the certificates. He had listed ninety-five reasons why people should not buy them. He nailed that paper to the church door.

To all who read that document it proclaimed: "The just shall live by faith." And that, we are told, was the beginning of the Protestant Reformation.

THE LISBON EARTHQUAKE

And there shall be famines, and pestilences, and earthquakes,
in divers places. Matthew 24:7.

The most famous of all earthquakes is the one that destroyed Lisbon, Portugal, on November 1, 1755.

There were actually three earthquakes on the same day. The first one was the worst and happened at nine-forty in the morning. The shock lasted about six minutes, and thirty thousand people were killed by the falling buildings. Hundreds of people died in churches where they had gone to attend All Saint's Day mass.

Every large public building was destroyed, as well as twelve thousand private homes. The shock of the quake was felt at least seven hundred miles away. The earthquakes caused the formation of new lakes as far away as Norway and Sweden.

Those people who were not killed by the falling buildings ran out into the streets, gathering in parks and along the riverside. Then large tidal waves, twenty feet high, swept over the city and drowned many more. Following that, a fire broke out that lasted for six days and destroyed what was left of the city. Some sources estimate that altogether sixty thousand people died that day.

Sailors on ships in the harbor had as it were ringside seats to this performance of destruction and death. They saw the buildings fall, and the people throng the riverside. They watched the tidal wave rush in to flood the city and witnessed fires raging through the rubble. They saw terrified people struggling to find shelter and safety. Some of the sailors put down the small boats from the ships and went out to rescue those who survived.

People thought the world was coming to an end, but the Lisbon disaster was just the beginning of many terrible earthquakes that would follow. Sixty thousand people perished in an earthquake in Italy in 1783, and more than seventy-five thousand died in that country in 1908. A quake in China in 1915 claimed the lives of 180,000 and five years later 143,000 died in the Tokyo area of Japan. Other severe earthquakes have since occurred in Peru, Iran, Chile, Ecuador, and many other places.

Each new earthquake partially fulfills the prophecy of Matthew 24 speaking God's message: "Jesus is coming soon!"

313

MAKE-BELIEVE INDIAN

Marvel not that I said unto thee, Ye must be born again. John 3:7.

Daniel Boone was born on November 2, 1734, when most of America was still a wilderness. When he grew up he helped to build a settlement called Boonesboro in Kentucky.

Once, in 1778, Daniel was taken captive by the Shawnee Indians, who took him north of the Ohio River to show him off. Chief Blackfish admired him for his ability as a hunter and decided to adopt him into the tribe.

With much ceremony the Indians went about the task of making Daniel Boone one of them. They plucked out all the hair from his head except for one small tuft on the top which was called a scalp lock. They ceremonially "washed away" his white blood and used the juice of certain plants to stain his skin brown. It was then proclaimed that he was the son of Blackfish and a Shawnee Indian. Daniel pretended to love Indian life. He went on hunting trips with the braves and took part in their feasts and councils.

Then one day Daniel learned that a large war party planned to attack his settlement of Boonesboro. He ran away from the Indian camp and traveled four days to warn his relatives and friends. When the war party of four hundred Indians, led by Chief Blackfish, attacked the fort, Boone and his men were ready for them. The attack was not successful.

There are some people who are Christians in the same way that Daniel Boone was an Indian. They dress like Christians. They talk like Christians. They sing the songs that Christians sing. They might even attend church on Sabbath, but that does not make them Christians.

When the testing time comes, make-believe Christians will reveal that they belong to their father, the devil.

To be a real Christian, then, you must be born into the family of Christ. Accepting Jesus as your personal Saviour, you give yourself completely to Him. Through His Holy Spirit you are given a new heart and a new mind. You are changed into a completely new person, one who not only acts like a Christian but who is one inside out.

Are you a Christian? Have you been born again?

HIGHWAY BUILDERS

Prepare ye the way of the Lord, make straight in the desert a highway for our God. Isaiah 40:3.

Have you ever watched engineers at work building a new highway? First they survey the area to see where the road should go. Then caterpillars and bulldozers do their work.

In some places the land is very low and piles of rock must be hauled in to build up the roadbed. In other areas whole sides of hills are removed by dynamite to make a level road.

Bridges are built across rivers and deep chasms. Where necessary, tunnels are built through mountains. Hundreds of thousands of tons of gravel and asphalt are used to make a highway as smooth as possible.

On this day in 1942, the Alaska Highway was completed. This 1,523-mile road runs between Dawson Creek, British Columbia, and Fairbanks, Alaska. It is the only highway linking Alaska with the road systems of the United States and Canada.

The highway was built during World War II at a cost of $140 million. The United States did not hesitate to spend that huge sum of money because they knew it was important that they be able to get military supplies and equipment into Alaska in case of an invasion from Japan.

The Japanese did invade the Aleutian Islands in June of 1942. But by November the highway was completed, and the United States was able to move in troops and military equipment. Within a short time the enemy was driven out.

You and I are called upon by God to be highway builders. The road we are to construct is not for military use. It is for the coming of the King of the universe, our Lord and our God.

This highway is built within our hearts and is completed as we prepare for the coming of Jesus. We have to straighten out the crooked places in our hearts. Sin must be blasted out of our lives. The low places in our characters must be filled with the graces of the Holy Spirit.

Just as a modern highway cannot be built without powerful equipment, so we are not left to build our highway unaided. Just as the big machines level the roadbeds and make them smooth, so we must allow the Holy Spirit to work in our lives, making them smooth and ready for the coming of the Lord.

GOLDEN TREASURE

Whosoever believeth in him should not perish, but have eternal life. John 3:15.

Tutankhamen was about 12 years old when he became Pharaoh of Egypt. When he died at the age of 18, a wonderful funeral ceremony was held in his honor. His burial mask was made of pure gold inlaid with precious stones. The young king was buried in a golden casket and surrounded with golden furniture. Then the door was sealed, and the passageway was filled with rocks, and yet another door was sealed and covered.

Centuries came and went without anyone looking upon the glories of King Tut.

Howard Carter, an American archeologist, searched for this tomb for thirty years. He explored many places where he thought it might be, but each time he was disappointed. In November, 1922, he began work on a new site. For three days the men dug away tons of stone without finding anything. Then at six o'clock on the morning of November 4, Howard Carter came to the diggings and found his men talking excitedly.

"Look what we've found!" one of the workers exclaimed. "It is a step cut into the ground."

Within the next few days twelve more steps were excavated. These led to a door behind which, Carter felt sure, lay the treasure of King Tut. He sent a telegram to his backer, Lord Carnarvon, to come at once.

When Lord Carnarvon arrived, the two men watched anxiously as the door was opened. Behind it they found only a stone-filled tunnel that led to another mighty door.

There was great excitement as Carter chiseled a hole in the second door. When it was large enough they looked through it into a room filled with golden treasures magnificent beyond description: beautiful boxes and beds, vases and chairs, statues and musical instruments, a golden throne and glittering jewels.

As wonderful as King Tut's treasure is, a still more wonderful treasure awaits your discovery. All who search the Bible will find the tomb. But unlike King Tut's tomb, this one is empty. King Jesus—the buried Monarch—stepped forth, the Conqueror of death. The treasure He wants to give you is eternal life. Will you accept it today?

GUY FAWKES' DAY

A soft answer turneth away wrath: but grievous words stir up anger. Proverbs 15:1.

Today is Guy Fawkes' Day in England. Tonight, in that country, there will be fireworks and bonfires to celebrate the day in 1405 when Parliament was not destroyed.

Underneath the Houses of Parliament there were many cellars, which at that time were rented out to local merchants to store their goods. A group of terrorists rented one of these cellars, and with the help of Guy Fawkes, filled it with thirty-six barrels of gunpowder. The barrels were then covered with bundles of firewood.

A slow fuse was prepared and Guy Fawkes was chosen to light it. The explosion was to take place on November 5 when Parliament would be meeting. However, the explosion never happened, because the plot was discovered.

One of the plotters had a friend in Parliament whom he did not want to be killed in the explosion. He warned him with a note that said: "Have care for your life. I advise you, if you love your life to make some excuse so that you need not go to Parliament. God and men are agreed to punish the wickedness of this time. Go to the country where you will be safe."

So the cellars were searched and the gunpowder was discovered. Guy Fawkes, along with other plotters, was arrested and executed.

There are times when we are like Parliament, sitting as it were on barrels of gunpowder. A problem comes up, there is some misunderstanding, and we are faced with an angry person who is about to explode. All he needs is for someone to light the fuse and the damage will be done.

This is a plot of Satan to destroy friendship. It is one of his methods of putting an end to peace in homes and communities.

If we are wise we will search our relationships to see where barrels of gunpowder are hidden. Then we will make sure the fuse is never lit.

One of the best ways to put a stop to explosions of temper is to speak kind words, soft words, tender words, to the person who feels he has some reason to be angry.

Are there any "gunpowder plots" in your life? "A soft answer turneth away wrath" and prevents explosions.

THE MUSICAL RUNAWAY

Teach me thy way, O Lord, and lead me in a plain path. Psalm 27:11.

Thirteen-year-old John Philip planned to run away from home. When the circus left town on a certain night, he would be with them. He had gotten himself a job in the circus band at $12.00 a week, and he was excited at the prospects of being on his own and doing grown-up things.

"Don't tell your parents," the band leader said.

"I won't," John Philip promised. However, the secret was just too good to keep, and he had to tell someone. He told his friend Ed Accardi.

"Don't tell your parents," John Philip warned.

"I won't," Ed promised. But the thought of the excitement John Philip was soon to have was too much for him. Ed didn't want to run away, but he thought he might persuade his mother to let him join the circus. Mrs. Accardi guessed what was happening and told John Philip's mother.

The next morning John Philip's father got up early and paid a visit to the commandant of the Marine Corps and explained the problem. Then the father went back home and woke up John Philip. "Put on your best clothes and come with me," he said.

Father took John Philip to the home of the commandant, who greeted him with, "Welcome to the Marine Band, John Philip!" So instead of joining the circus band, the young musician joined the Marine Band in which his father played trombone.

John Philip Sousa, who was born on this day in 1854, later became a famous conductor of the United States Marine Band and wrote many marches.

John Philip Sousa had a father who loved him and understood the desire of teen-age boys to be independent. He saved his son from doing something foolish, and at the same time helped him to be happy.

You and I have a heavenly Father who is like that. Often He interrupts our plans for life so that He can give us something better. He knows your longings and desires to do something important with your life. He will lead you if you will let Him. He knows what will make you happy.

DEADLY RAYS

Wash me throughly from mine iniquity, and cleanse me from my sin. Psalm 51:2.

Marie Curie, who was born on this day in 1867, discovered radium, a rare, silver-white metal. There is only a very limited quantity of it in the whole world.

Radium is often mixed with other substances and looks like table salt. However, I would not advise you to eat it with your potatoes! This element gives off intense radiation that can produce severe, hard-to-heal burns.

The effects of radium do not appear immediately after exposure. Several days may pass before the skin becomes red and sore. The deadly rays can also destroy red corpuscles.

Marie Curie twice received the Nobel Prize for her work with radium. She worked tirelessly over kettles of boiling pitchblend in order to extract just a few milligrams of this metal. The constant exposure burned her skin many times and left her scarred. She did not realize that the rays were silently destroying her red blood cells. Her body could not manufacture new corpuscles fast enough, and she died as a result of her experiments.

In some ways sin is like radium. Its harmless appearance is a deception. We may not see the results immediately, but eventually it will bring death.

Sometimes the effects of radium can be seen in the scars it leaves. Sin also leaves visible scars. We see these marks in the lives of the drunkard, the dope addict, and the habitual thief. We can see the scars of sin in diseases of the mind and the body and in the faces of unhappy, selfish men and women.

However, just as much of radium's damage is inside the body where it destroys the blood cells, so sin also works inside, quietly, unnoticed, secretly destroying life.

Even though we may not show the evidences of sin in our lives immediately, if we continue to be exposed we will eventually die because of its devastating radiation just as Marie Curie died as a result of her exposure to the rays of radium.

Our only hope is to pray the prayer of David, "Wash me throughly from mine iniquity, and cleanse me from my sin."

GOD'S FOOTPRINTS

The heavens declare the glory of God; and the firmament sheweth his handiwork. Psalm 19:1.

Early one morning two Arabs sat in their tent discussing God. "How do you know that He exists?" one man asked.

"How do I know a camel passed by my tent in the night?" inquired the other.

"You know by the footprints," was the reply. Looking out the door they could plainly see the marks of the camel's feet in the sand.

"That is how I know there is a God," said the other Arab. "I can see His footprints."

Have you seen God's footprints lately? Look out your window. Can you see that God has been near your house in the night? What do you see that makes you think of God?

After lunch today perhaps your family can go for a walk in the country or through a park. Climb a mountain or walk around a lake. Look for God's footprints. Don't forget to look up into the sky, for His footprints are there, too.

In about three years you will be able to see a very rare footprint of God in the sky. At that time Halley's comet will return. Sir Edmund Halley, a British astronomer whose birthday is today, was the one who discovered that this comet comes back to adorn our skies only once every seventy-six years or so. There is a record of it as far back as 240 B.C. It was last seen between August, 1909, and July, 1911. So it is about time for Halley's comet to come again.

This is a footprint of God that you will probably see only once in your lifetime. And what a glorious footprint it will be! Its head will be as bright as the most brilliant stars. Its long, luminous tail will stretch across one third of the visible distance of the sky.

The fact that this comet is coming soon, on a schedule and a path that God set for it ages ago when He put it into space, tells us something about the Creator whom we serve. It tells us of His mighty power. He is able to keep suns, planets, moons, and comets all traveling through space at tremendous speeds without traffic jams or collisions. What a marvelous and mighty God we worship!

A HIDING PLACE

Thou art my hiding place; thou shalt preserve me from trouble; thou shalt compass me about with songs of deliverance. Psalm 32:7.

If you have been caught in a bad storm, you know how important it is to have a hiding place from the wind and rain. In time of flood it is even more important to find a place where you are safe from the raging torrents.

In the Bangladesh cyclone of 1970 at least one million people perished because they could not find a hiding place. Along with them died a million head of livestock. When the flood waters receded they left behind everywhere decaying bodies.

It all started about nine o'clock on the morning of November 9 when a low pressure area formed in the Bay of Bengal southeast of Madras. By the next day it had developed into a storm, with winds of fifty-five miles per hour. By the following morning the storm was only 650 miles southeast of Chittagong. Warnings of the approaching storm were broadcast, and those who could do so found a safe place for their families, but for most there was no place to go.

Winds were traveling at a speed of more than one hundred miles per hour when the storm reached the mouth of the Ganges River. Huge waves flooded islands and coastal areas. On thirteen of the islands not one person was left alive. All the houses were gone, the crops destroyed. Nothing remained but mud and debris. Hundreds of ships were washed onto the shores.

As the storm approached, people rushed to the highest point of land they could find. Some climbed trees and others watched the storm from rooftops. Many people had their "hiding place" washed from beneath them.

The terrible destruction of that cyclone is an illustration of the destructive power of evil. There are times when trouble and calamity come upon us like a storm. Sometimes Satan brings in temptation like a mighty flood.

In such times we need a safe retreat, or we will be washed away. The only place we can flee for safety is to Jesus Christ, the mighty Rock of Ages. The storms of life can blow with gale force, but we are secure in that hiding place.

Are you safe in the Rock? If not, surrender to Jesus today. When the storm comes you will be ready.

HIDE AND SEEK

But without faith it is impossible to please him: for he that cometh to God must believe that he is, and that he is a rewarder of them that diligently seek him. Hebrews 11:6.

Of course you have played hide and seek. Remember what it was like to be "It"? You closed your eyes and counted to one hundred while your friends ran away and hid.

At last you shouted, "Coming! Ready or not you shall be caught!" Then you looked cautiously around and began to search for your friends. You could not see them, but you knew they were there somewhere, and you were determined to keep on looking until you found them.

Sometimes there are real-life situations that are like hide and seek, only they are not a game. They are for real. One of these searches came to an end on November 10, 1871.

The person who was hidden was Dr. David Livingstone, the famous explorer and missionary. He had been on an expedition into the heart of Africa for many months. No one in the outside world had heard from him and many thought that he was dead. However, Gordon Bennett, of the *New York Herald,* believed that Dr. Livingstone was alive. He sent a newspaper reporter, Henry Morton Stanley, to find him.

Mr. Stanley searched for Dr. Livingstone for seven and one-half months in the wild jungles of Africa before finding him. When possible he traveled by boat. Other times he walked. He suffered illness and hardships of all kinds. But he did not give up. He believed that Dr. Livingstone was there somewhere, and he kept on until he found him at Ujiji, near Lake Tanganyika.

In your games of hide and seek with your friends, you know that they are out there somewhere and you believe that if you keep looking, you will find them. So you do keep looking, and sure enough, you do find them.

That's how it is in the game of hide and seek we have with God too. We are "It," and God is the One who is in hiding. He is not in hiding on purpose. It is sin that has "hidden" Him from us.

If we will believe that He is there, then go looking for Him, we will surely find Him.

You are "It." Let your search begin now!

CANNIBAL FEAST

I have loved thee with an everlasting love: therefore with lovingkindness have I drawn thee. Jeremiah 31:3.

Panakaraeo was a fearless Maori chief, the head of a band of fierce warriors in New Zealand.

When Joseph Matthews, an English missionary, visited his camp on Sunday, November 11, 1832, Panakaraeo and his warriors were not very friendly. In fact, they immediately surrounded him and began preparing the fires for a cannibal feast in which Missionary Matthews was to be the main course!

The logs took some time to burn down to the right type of glowing coals over which meat could be roasted. So while the preparations were going on Joseph Matthews said to the chief, "While we are waiting, let me give you my message."

"I don't want your message," said Panakaraeo. "Be quiet."

"But I have come all the way from England to tell it to you," insisted Mr. Matthews. "I will give you my message and then you may cook me!"

So Chief Panakaraeo agreed. "Give it quickly and waste no time," said the chief. "The fires will soon be ready."

Panakaraeo pulled his cloak around him and sat beside the fire. The dancing flames lighted up his handsome face with its many tattoos. He looked intently at his captive and waited to hear the story.

If you had been Joseph Matthews, what would you have told the chief? Would you have talked about the commandment that says, "Thou shalt not kill."? Would you have told of the fires of judgment awaiting those who murder missionaries?

Joseph Matthews told the story of Jesus and His great love. He told how He had come and died on the cross so that Chief Panakaraeo could live forever. He told about the beautiful home Jesus is making for Maoris.

In the light of the glowing embers Joseph Matthews could see tears trickle down the old chief's face. The ovens were ready, but the chief said, "Go on. I want to hear about that Man."

The savage heart of that Maori chief was won by the story of Christ's love. There was no cannibal feast that night. God's love had made the difference.

323

THE NIGHT THE STARS FELL

And the stars of heaven fell unto the earth, even as a fig tree casteth her untimely figs, when she is shaken of a mighty wind. Revelation 6:13.

Young Richard Mauzy, of MaGaheysville, Virginia, was one of thousands who saw the stars fall on November 12, 1833.

The star shower began around nine o'clock and the display increased in brightness until about two o'clock, when it was at its best. It was at this point that Richard woke up and decided to get up and see what was happening outside.

Richard tiptoed out of his room, through the house, to the back door. Quietly he opened it and stepped out into the night. Standing there on the back porch he gazed at the biggest fireworks display he had ever seen. It was as if a giant rocket had burst in the sky and the sparks were coming down and down in a shower without stopping. The whole sky was aglow with the falling balls of fire.

Richard stood there for a long time staring at the beautiful display. Did this happen every night? He decided maybe it did so he wouldn't bother to tell Mom and Dad about it. They might laugh at him.

But at breakfast the falling of the stars was the main subject of conversation. Richard learned that he had witnessed the largest display of shooting stars that had ever been seen. More than 260,000 meteors fell on that one night, an average of about 60,000 an hour. This is a huge number when you consider that on an ordinary night there is an average of one falling star per hour. Imagine seeing one thousand fall in one minute!

Richard heard the falling of the stars discussed a great deal during the next few days. Some people felt that the end of the world was coming. They were afraid and began to pray to God for mercy. Richard was one of those who was unafraid. He was glad the stars had fallen, particularly when his father and mother explained to him that this was one of the signs that Jesus was coming soon. Richard wanted to see Jesus. He wanted to see the angels. He wanted to go to heaven and see the beautiful mansions that Jesus had built.

The memory of that night on the back porch stayed with Richard all his life and helped him to know for certain that Jesus is coming soon.

MONICA'S PRAYER

I love the Lord, because he hath heard my voice and my supplications. Psalm 116:1.

This verse expresses how Monica felt on Easter Sunday, A.D. 387 as she sat in the cathedral at Milan and watched Bishop Ambrose baptize her son, Augustine.

How well she remembered the day he was born, November 13, 354, in the little town of Thagaste, not far from Carthage in North Africa. From the moment of his birth she had been praying that he would become a Christian.

When Augustine was a teen-ager his father sent him to the best schools. The boy did well in his studies, but at the same time he succumbed to the temptations of the city and led a wicked life. Then one night he told his mother that he was going to say goodbye to a friend who was going to Rome. Actually, Augustine was running away from home. Boarding a ship, he sailed away from his family.

The wayward life of her son nearly broke Monica's heart, but she would not give up praying for him. One day she felt so bad about what he had done that she talked to a Christian teacher about him. When she had finished her story, tears were streaming down her cheeks.

"Go thy way," the teacher said. "God will help thee. It is not possible that the child of these tears should perish."

God answered Monica's prayers in a remarkable way. By chance Augustine went to Milan, where he met Bishop Ambrose. He told the bishop about the emptiness of his life and the restlessness he felt. He told how he had traveled many miles to many places, where he had done wild and wicked things, but he could not escape his mother's prayers.

After studying with Bishop Ambrose for some time, Augustine gave his heart to Jesus and decided to be baptized. Of course, he wanted his mother there for such a wonderful day.

Augustine became a great and a good man, both a preacher and a writer. Even today people quote words that he spoke.

Once he wrote, "It was owing to the faithful and daily prayers of my mother that I did not perish."

Do you know someone who, like the teen-aged Augustine, is wayward and foolish? You can do for your friend what Monica did for her son. You can pray and pray and never give up.

CHILDREN'S DAY

Suffer little children, and forbid them not, to come unto me: for of such is the kingdom of heaven. Matthew 19:14.

Children in India are not likely to forget their country's first Prime Minister, Jawaharlal Nehru, nor his birthday, November 14, 1889, for on this day they are honored in Children's Day celebrations.

Schoolchildren from kindergarten through high school receive treats and have a holiday. The poor children are remembered, too. Kind people go to their homes and distribute candy and food. The crippled, blind, and deaf children also receive special attention on this day.

Newspapers publish articles about the needs of children for food, education, medical treatment, and love. Magazines publish stories about people who help children. For one day everyone is interested in children, and then it seems they are more or less forgotten.

However, with God every day is Children's Day. He is always concerned about the happiness of children and youth. In the Bible He has given much instruction about how teachers and parents should treat children.

"Don't make your children angry," God tells them. In another place He says, "It is better for a person to have a millstone put around his neck and for him to be drowned in the depth of the sea than it is for him to hurt one of the children that believes in Me."

"Love your children and care for them," He instructs the mothers. "Teach your children about Me," He tells the fathers.

God promises a special reward to those who give a drink of water to a child. See how very much God cares for children?

When Jesus was living on this earth, the children loved to be with Him. He did not push them aside as unimportant. He did not make them feel that they were in the way. He did not scold them. He gathered them close about Him so that they could see and hear all that was going on. He told them stories that they could never forget. Once He even used a little boy's lunch to feed more than five thousand people. To Jesus, children were always very important.

Jesus still loves the children. He still loves the youth. To you He says, "Come unto me." Will you come today?

326

JOHN LEE'S ESCAPE

There is therefore now no condemnation to them which are in Christ Jesus. Romans 8:1.

John Lee, an Englishman, was condemned to die for a murder he insisted he did not commit. Circumstances, however, pointed to his guilt, and he was sentenced to die by hanging on November 15, 1884.

On that day, James Berry, the executioner, made his routine check of the rope and trapdoor. Everything was in working order. The prison bell tolled, and John Lee was led to the execution platform.

John Lee stood quietly while the rope was adjusted around his neck. We can only imagine the agony of those moments while he waited for the executioner to take the few steps to the lever that would release the trapdoor under his feet.

John Berry pulled the lever, but nothing happened! Puzzled, the executioner examined the trapdoor. There was no reason why it should not work. He stepped back and pulled the lever again. Nothing happened!

By this time John Lee was wishing the trapdoor would open and end his misery. The sweat was pouring from his face. He felt he could not endure the agony of suspense any longer.

The executioner inspected the trapdoor and the lever mechanism a second time. All was in order. Again he stepped back and pulled the lever. Again the trapdoor did not open!

The executioner removed the noose from around John Lee's neck and ordered the guard to take him back to his cell. He was the first man in British history to survive three attempts to be hanged. John Lee was later released and went to the United States, where he married and lived a rather ordinary life.

You and I are in a similar position. We too are condemned to die. Unlike John Lee, we deserve our punishment. We have all sinned "and come short of the glory of God." "The wages of sin is death." We stand, as it were, on the execution platform with the noose around our necks. In that moment we breathe a prayer for forgiveness and mercy through the blood of Jesus. Because of that prayer, the trapdoor will not open. The noose is now removed from our necks. We are set free! Praise God, we do not have to die!

THE GLOOMY EMPEROR

The life is more than meat, and the body is more than raiment.
Luke 12:23.

Have you heard statements such as the following?

"If only I had pizza instead of peas, I'd be happy."

"How happy I'd be if I had a ten-speed bike instead of this old beat-up one."

"If only I could have a new dress for the party, I'd be so happy."

What if you had everything you ever wanted? Would you then be happy?

The answer is found in the lives of two men who lived about two thousand years ago.

Tiberius Caesar, whose birthday is today, was the Roman Emperor when Jesus was living in Galilee. He was one of the richest men in the world. There seemed to be no limit to his wealth. He could have anything his heart desired.

The Emperor's ponies had shoes made of gold. He had a luxurious marble castle on an island in the Mediterranean Sea. He dressed in velvet, silk, satin, and jewels. A multitude of servants waited upon him, bringing him whatever he wished.

Was Tiberius Caesar happy? No. In fact he was a most unhappy man. History books say that he was never known to smile. His nickname, whispered behind his back, was "The Gloomy Emperor." All his possessions could not bring him happiness.

By contrast, Jesus was poor. His father was a carpenter who could not afford to take a lamb or a bull as an offering to the Temple, but could present only a pair of doves and two young pigeons. Jesus had no home. He owned only the clothes on His back and possessed very little money. He ate simply of good food, and sometimes there wasn't much.

Jesus had scarcely anything of this world's goods, but He was happy. He knew that happiness does not come from having peanut butter and jam on your bread. Life is more than boats and bicycles. Dolls and dresses cannot bring us real joy.

Jesus was happy because He lived close to God, His Father, and did not have guilt for wrongs He had done. Jesus was happy because He spent so much of His time helping others.

SHORTCUTS

No man cometh unto the Father, but by me. John 14:6.

Remember when you got up late and had to rush to get to class on time? You ignored the "Keep Off the Grass" signs in your effort to get to school by the most direct route possible. You took a shortcut.

The next time you go to a city park, keep your eyes open for the shortcuts, paths worn into the grass by people in a hurry. The park builders put in sidewalks, but here and there people have made their own paths because they were looking for the shortest way to get where they wanted to go.

For centuries people in Europe knew that traveling around Africa was not the shortest route to reach India. Many dreamed of a shortcut through the Isthmus of Suez.

On November 17, 1869, this dream was realized when the Suez Canal was opened. On that day thousands of people gathered at Port Said, Egypt, to view the fireworks, hear the speeches, and see the visiting royalty from several European nations. The crowd watched as sixty-eight ships entered the new canal.

This geographical shortcut has made a tremendous difference in world trade. Today ships can reach the Indian Ocean from the Mediterranean Sea in a matter of a few hours where before the trip took weeks and months. Because of the Suez Canal, Europe and Asia are 6,700 miles closer together by sea.

Shortcuts such as the Suez Canal and paths across the vacant lot are helpful. Sometimes it is necessary to walk across the grass. It makes sense to find the shortest route when you are traveling from New York to San Francisco.

There is one area of our lives, however, where shortcuts are not needed. There is only one path that leads to God. Jesus is the only way. We cannot know our heavenly Father, or reach our eternal home, except as we follow Jesus. He is the Way, the Truth, and the Life.

There are many other paths that people have made. They may look like shortcuts to peace, happiness, and eternal life, but they will lead you away from your goal.

The shortest distance between us and God is outlined in today's verse. No shortcuts are necessary.

329

SHOOTING THE APPLE

O my God, I trust in thee. Psalm 25:2.

Forty-six miles south of Zurich, Switzerland, in the little town of Altdorf, stands a bronze statue of William Tell. Legend says it was on this very spot that he shot the apple from his son's head on November 18, 1307.

According to the story, the king of Austria sent governors to Switzerland to rule over the people, but all were not good men. The man stationed in Altdorf was proud and cruel. He had a pole erected in the center of town and on it he put his hat. All who passed by were supposed to bow. This made the people angry, but they were afraid to disobey.

One day a man came into town from a country village. William Tell was not afraid. "I will not bow to the hat!" he said.

"If you don't you will surely be punished," he was told.

In spite of the warning, William Tell strode up the street and walked right past the pole with his head held high in the air. People gasped. Immediately soldiers surrounded him and led him to the governor.

"As your punishment you must shoot an apple that we will place on the head of your son," said the governor.

Imagine yourself as William Tell's son. How would you have felt? Would you have tried to run away? Would you have been able to hold your head steady? Would you have ducked when you saw the arrow coming?

William Tell's son did not duck. He stood like a statue, not crying, not flinching. The apple stayed in its place until the arrow split it in two.

That story tells us something about this boy's faith in his father. He knew his father loved him and would not harm him. He had seen William's arrows hit their target hundreds of times. He knew he could trust his father to hit the apple instead of his head.

Isn't that the kind of faith that you and I need to have in our heavenly Father? We do not always understand why certain experiences, like arrows, come our way. However, we need not be afraid. God is our Father. He loves us. We can trust Him.

NO MORE HOPE

Who will have all men to be saved, and to come unto the knowledge of the truth. 1 Timothy 2:4.

At midnight on Tuesday, November 19, 1968, ninety-nine men went to work in the underground caverns of Farmington No. 9 coal mine near Monongah, West Virginia.

At 5:25 A.M. there was a terrific explosion that was felt more than ten miles away. Smoke from the entrance shaft billowed nearly 150 feet into the sky. The mine quickly became a raging furnace, and ninety-nine men were inside.

By noon only twenty-one men had come out. What about the other seventy-eight trapped somewhere in the mine tunnels? Were they still alive? Could they be rescued?

In order to keep the entire mine from burning up it was necessary to seal off the entrances. However, the company president John Corcoran was reluctant to do so as it was possible the men inside might still be alive.

For ten days rescue teams worked with all the latest equipment trying to locate the missing miners. Finally, on November 29, the president announced, "We have to seal off the mine."

A minister began to pray, but he couldn't finish, because the sound of weeping was so great. The end had come. The openings to the mine were shut off. There was no more hope.

That is what it will be like someday for Planet Earth. One day soon, God only knows how soon, the day will come when no one else can be saved.

All will have heard about Jesus. All will have decided for or against Him. Christ will stand up and say, "It is done!" And time will stop. The world will come to an end. The door of salvation will be forever shut. There will be no more hope. We call this the close of probation.

When that day comes it will be too late to decide to follow Jesus. It will then be too late to talk to anyone about the Lord. It will be too late to help those who are lost.

Did it ever occur to you that Jesus has not come back yet for the same reason President Corcoran kept the mines open so long after the explosion? Jesus loves the people of this world so much that He wants to make sure everyone has had a chance to be saved. Could He be waiting for you?

BIG WASH JOB

Unto him that loved us, and washed us from our sins in his own blood. Revelation 1:5.

Sin is deadly. It is a poison that can kill. It is even worse than plutonium.

On Friday, November 20, 1959, there was an explosion in one of the rooms of the Oakridge Laboratory of the Atomic Energy Commission. One fiftieth of an ounce of plutonium escaped into the air. You wouldn't think anyone would be concerned about such a little bit.

Actually, the men who worked at the Atomic Energy Commission were very much concerned. They began a cleansing operation that cost about $350,000.

Everyone who was within four miles of the explosion had to exchange their clothes for new outfits that had not been contaminated. These people were then watched very carefully to make sure they had not inhaled any of the plutonium.

The buildings were washed inside and out with powerful detergents. They were then repainted. The top layer of sod was dug up and hauled away to a remote place for burial. The asphalt around the explosion area was broken up and removed and a new roadway was put down. New roofs were put on the buildings.

Everything possible was done to make sure that every speck of plutonium was removed so that the area would be safe for people to live and work in.

If people are so careful to get rid of a tiny bit of an element that could destroy present life, then how much more concerned they should be about the poison of sin, which can destroy hope of eternal life.

You and I need a cleansing more thorough than that given the Oakridge Laboratory and its surroundings. Washing with soap will not do the job. Detergents cannot cleanse us from evil. Bleach cannot remove the stains of sin. We need something that will get rid of the sin that is stamped upon every cell of our bodies from the time we were born.

In fact, there is nothing we can do to cleanse ourselves. We cannot wash away our sins. Only Jesus can do that through His blood. Will you let Him do it for you today?

RESCUE FROM THE SKY

For yet a little while, and he that shall come will come, and will not tarry. Hebrews 10:37.

On November 21, 1979, an angry mob stormed the United States embassy in Islamabad, Pakistan, and set fire to the building. Ninety members of the staff were trapped inside the burning embassy for six hours while they awaited rescue.

Will we get out alive? the Americans wondered. Why are they taking so long to reach us?

Meanwhile the Pakistani Government was trying to find a way to save the trapped people. The large crowd made it almost impossible to reach the building. Besides, the intense heat would make it a risky venture to enter the embassy from the ground level. The only possible way was to fly in by helicopter and land on the roof. The smoke and rising currents from the blaze made even this a difficult task.

Imagine the joy of the trapped men and women when they saw the first helicopter land safely on the roof and they knew that at last their rescuers had come. Can you picture the scene as the Americans embraced one another, laughing and crying at the same time? What must it have been like to have been so close to death and then to have been saved! The long hours of waiting and wondering were over. They could go home.

Don't you think it will be something like that when Jesus comes at last? We humans have waited so long on this old planet for our Lord to come. It has not been six hours as it was in Islamabad, but six thousand years since the fires of sin were ignited in this world. To Adam and Eve God promised deliverance, and every generation has expected that they would be the fortunate ones to witness the coming of Jesus.

As in the case of those waiting Americans four years ago today, our deliverance will come from the sky. We will look up beyond the rubble of a burning world to see King Jesus come with a multitude of angels. I want to be part of that rescue, don't you?

DO IT NOW

Remember how short my time is. Psalm 89:47.

One o'clock in the afternoon of Thursday, November 22, 1963, John F. Kennedy, thirty-fifth President of the United States, died.

Half an hour earlier he had been smiling and waving to enthusiastic crowds in Dallas, Texas. Suddenly, the cheers were interrupted by the sound of a gun and the President slumped forward, blood spurting from his wounds.

Three days later the leaders of more than ninety nations attended John Kennedy's funeral. More than a million people lined the streets to watch the horse-drawn caisson take the body to the church.

Millions more watched on television as the procession halted on a slope in Arlington National Cemetery. They saw the casket lowered into the ground. They heard the 21-gun salute and saw the fifty Air Force jets roar overhead. They watched Mrs. Kennedy light the eternal flame that was to mark her husband's grave.

John F. Kennedy was the fourth President of the United States to be killed by an assassin's bullet. He was the youngest man ever elected to that office, and people couldn't believe that someone so youthful, so vibrant, so full of plans for his country, could actually be dead. Kennedy had counted on at least one four-year term and possibly a second. Instead it was all over in a thousand days. How short his time was!

Death is no respecter of persons. It snatches away people at 8 or 80. It takes Presidents and paupers alike. For most, it comes at an unexpected moment.

Life is precious. Today is yours to live to the full. There is no certainty about tomorrow. Even if you live to be 99, life will be too short to accomplish all that you need to do.

You may not have another fifty years to give your heart to the Lord. Do it now! You may not have another thirty years to let your mother know how much you love her. Tell her now! You may not have another twenty years to tell your friend about Jesus. Do it today! You may not have another year to make things right with your dad. Talk to him today! You may not have another week to confess your sins. Do it now!

WAIT A WHILE

The eyes of the Lord are upon the righteous, and his ears are open unto their cry. Psalm 34:15.

"Oh, God, help me!"

Simas Kudirka tried to dodge the pounding fists of the sailors. Surrounded by six angry men, there seemed no escape unless God intervened. The savage beating continued. Where was God? Couldn't He see? Didn't He hear? Didn't He care what was happening?

At last the ordeal ended. The men bound Simas and took him back to the ship from which he had tried to escape. He was guilty of treason and would be sent to prison. Why didn't God answer his prayer?

On the evening of November 23, 1970, a fishing ship from another country was tied up beside a United States Coast Guard cutter off the coast of New England. The two vessels were barely three meters apart. Simas waited until the deck of his ship was clear and then climbed over the railing and made a lunge for the American ship. He felt sure that they would protect him. Instead, he was handed back to his ship's officers—to beatings, torture, slave labor, a prison sentence, and no hope. He had done his best. He had cried to God for help. Why was there no answer? Didn't God care?

Yes, God cared. Yes, He saw and heard. And in His own way and for purposes we may not understand He did not answer immediately. But God was nevertheless at work.

Two American women became interested in the case of Simas. In their investigation they learned that Simas' mother had been born in Brooklyn. They located her birth certificate, which proved that she was a United States citizen and this made her son a citizen of the United States also. Four years after Simas cried to God, his prayer was answered. On August 23, 1974, he was released from prison and given tickets for him and his family to fly to New York to begin a new life.

God always hears our prayers. Sometimes He answers with an immediate Yes. Other times in His wisdom He says No. And there are times when, as in the case of Simas, He says, "Wait a while. I will work it out in My own good time for the good of all."

After this, when it seems God doesn't hear your prayers, remember Simas. Perhaps God is saying, "Wait a while."

THANKSGIVING GAME

Enter into his gates with thanksgiving, and into his courts with praise: be thankful unto him, and bless his name. Psalm 100:4.

Today is Thanksgiving in the United States. Many families will celebrate with a family get-together around a heavily-laden table. It will be a time to enjoy one another and to recount God's blessings of the past year.

Here is a game for today. Any number can play and if you have enough people you could even divide up into teams. The person who fails to make a contribution when his turn comes drops out. The object is to stay in the game as long as possible.

The person who begins the game must name something for which he is truly thankful. The next person must name something he is thankful for that begins with the last letter of the word that was just mentioned.

I'll make a start and you can keep it going. I am thankful for my *mother*. The last letter is *r* so now we must think of a word that begins with that letter. Let's see. How about *roof*? I'm thankful for a roof over my head, aren't you? There are millions who don't have even the simplest house with a roof where they can sleep tonight.

The next letter is *f*. I am thankful for *food* and its last letter makes me think of *doughnuts* fresh from the kitchen. Of course I am grateful for *soap* and my *parents*. I wouldn't have gotten very far in life without their guidance and help.

School is something else for which we can be thankful. And what about *love*? Isn't that the best gift of all? That's what makes the world go round.

Everything around us should stir within our hearts a spirit of thankfulness. Take for instance the *garden* and *neighbors, soft ice cream* and *memories,* a *song* and *Grandma.* Wouldn't life be rather dull without these things? What about *air* and *rain* gently falling on our windowpane?

We can be thankful for the *night* and *tears.* How terrible it would be if we could never cry. And there is *sunshine* and *energy.* What about *youth* and *hope* in the coming of the Lord?

You can be thankful for *ears* and a *star,* your *room,* and ... Go on now! See how far you can take the game.

STEREOSCOPIC VISION

Anoint thine eyes with eyesalve, that thou mayest see. Revelation 3:18.

It is important to have good eyesight, particularly if you are a baseball player. No one ever became a top-notch hitter without good vision.

It was Babe Ruth's eyes that made him such a fantastic home run hitter. When duck hunting he could spot birds long before they were visible to anyone else, including the guide. He could read the license number of a car so far away that the ordinary person couldn't even tell the color of the plate.

Ted Williams, another extraordinary hitter, had exceptional eyesight. During his time in naval aviation he broke many records in vision tests used to examine air cadets.

Rogers Hornsby considered vision so important to his batting that he never watched a movie for the twenty years he was in professional baseball. He avoided any use of his eyes that was not absolutely necessary.

Joe DiMaggio, whose birthday is today, was the idol of baseball fans forty years ago. For sixteen years he played center field for the New York Yankees. Joe hit .325 in eleven out of the thirteen seasons he played. One year he hit in fifty-six games straight, setting an all-time record. Three times he was named the American League's most valuable player.

"On my list, keen vision is the first requirement for good hitting," Joe DiMaggio said. "If you can't see it, you can't hit it!"

This kind of vision is more than just seeing the ball; it is a perception of depth and the ability to judge position in space. This is known as stereoscopic vision. A good hitter can sense where the ball will come and how long it will take to get there. Thus he is ready for it at the precise moment it passes over the plate.

You and I are batters in a game much more important than baseball. We also must know when to swing and when to stand still. We must be able to see whether an experience coming our way is a temptation or an opportunity.

That is why Jesus invites us to use His eyesalve so that we may see. We need to pray for the Holy Spirit to be with us every day to anoint our eyes so that we can see and thus make right decisions.

337

THERE IS A FOUNTAIN

The blood of Jesus Christ his Son cleanseth us from all sin. 1 John 1:7.

"There is a fountain filled with blood,
Drawn from Immanuel's veins;
And sinners plunged beneath that flood,
Lose all their guilty stains."

Why not sing this hymn for worship this morning? It is number 163 in *The Church Hymnal* and was written by William Cowper, an English poet who was born on November 26, 1731.

For many years William was a sick man. He became so discouraged with life that he tried several times to commit suicide. At last he had to go to a mental hospital.

It seemed to William Cowper that his sins were so bad that they could never be forgiven. He pictured God as an angry judge who was just waiting for the chance to punish him in the fires of hell. He dreamed about the judgment and awoke in terror. There seemed no hope of peace or salvation.

Thinking it might help, the superintendent of the hospital gave William a Bible. One day while reading in Romans, he came across these words: "Whom God hath set forth to be a propitiation through faith in his blood, to declare his righteousness for the remission of sins that are past, through the forbearance of God" (Rom. 3:25).

Immediately William's sadness left him. It was as though the dark clouds were lifted, and the sun came shining through. It was as if the chains that had been binding him were broken, and he felt like a free man.

Wonder of wonders! God did love him! His sins were forgiven! There was hope!

From that moment William Cowper began to recover from his mental illness. He was released from the hospital and afterward wrote many poems of praise to God. Six of these are in *The Church Hymnal.* Like William Cowper, do you have a burden of guilt for sins you have committed? Do you feel there is no hope for you? Look to Jesus hanging on the cross. See the crown of thorns and the blood trickling down His face. See the hands that were pierced for you. The moment He died He paid the penalty for your sins. He died to show how much He loves you.

SEVENTY YEARS' DIFFERENCE

Even so, come, Lord Jesus. Revelation 22:20.

There was a lot of excitement in New York City on this day in 1910 when the Pennsylvania Railway Station was opened. The beautiful, white-pillared building occupied a whole city block. People marveled at the number of travelers who passed through its doors each day. The fastest trains in the world sped out from that station.

Today the station seems small compared to Kennedy International Airport, Chicago's O'Hare, and London's Heath Row. These complexes take up acres of land, and millions of people from all over the world walk their corridors.

O'Hare is the busiest of them all. A plane takes off there every two minutes.

What a difference seventy years can make! When Pennsylvania Station was the talk of the town, most people had never heard of airplanes, which at that point were just an interesting experiment. The longest recorded flight was just a little over an hour. Who could have imagined then the giant jets and supersonic planes that are now commonplace? No one then would have even dreamed of satellites, rockets, and space shuttles.

Go back seventy years before the Pennsylvania Station was opened, when trains were just coming into use. Cars hadn't been invented, and the horse and buggy were the general mode of transportation.

Now project yourself seventy years into the future. If time should last, what kind of transportation will we have in 2053? Will airports then be as out of date as the Pennsylvania Railway Station is today? Will your children have their private sun-powered rockets to roam around the solar system? Or is something even better in store for our little planet?

Why should we be confined to this small solar system when the entire universe is waiting? The second coming of Jesus will open up new methods of travel to us, new galaxies to explore.

I can't even imagine what it is going to be like. I hope Jesus comes soon so that we can find out.

THE DOOR

I am the door: by me if any man enter in, he shall be saved.
John 10:9.

Four hundred and ninety-two people died on the night of November 28, 1942, because they could not find the door.

It was Saturday night. More than one thousand people were packed into the Cocoanut Grove, a nightclub in Boston. Soldiers were there from a nearby Army camp. A wedding party had come to dance. Hundreds more had come for a football victory celebration. Someone was playing jazz tunes on a piano. The dance floor was crowded with couples. The room, blue with smoke, was filled with music and laughter.

About ten-fifteen a girl rushed into the room screaming, "Fire! Fire!" Someone had struck a match too close to the artificial coconut palms, and within moments the place was ablaze.

The crowd rushed toward a revolving door, the only exit that was open. Nearly five hundred people made it to safety before the crowd became uncontrollable. People pushed, shoved, fought, fell to the floor, and were trampled to death. The doorway became jammed with dead bodies. The remaining people were trapped. The lights went out, and the place was lighted by the roaring flames. There was no more escape.

This story can give us some idea of what is going to happen at the end of this world's history. Because of sin, our planet is doomed to a fiery destruction. The only ones who will be saved are those who have found the Door of salvation, Jesus Christ.

Jesus died on the cross of Calvary to make a way of escape for you and me. We pass over the threshold of that door when we accept Him as our Saviour and the Lord of our lives. When we enter that Door we are safe. The apostle Paul says, "We shall be saved from wrath through him" (Rom. 5:9).

To reject Jesus means to turn away from the only Door of escape. To reject Jesus means destruction in the lake of fire that will destroy this earth. To reject Jesus means death.

To accept Him means eternal life. Won't you walk through the Door of salvation today?

JUMPING TO CONCLUSIONS

Judge not, that ye be not judged. Matthew 7:1.

In order to judge correctly, one must know all of the facts. There is so much about others that we can never know. Therefore, God tells us that it is wiser to leave the judging to Him. Jumping to conclusions is not a good type of exercise.

History is full of examples of wrong decisions made when people jumped to conclusions without knowing all the facts. Take for instance the massacre that took place near Walla Walla, Washington, on November 29, 1847.

At Waiilatpu, Marcus and Narcissa Whitman established a mission station to work among the Cayuse, Walla Walla, and Umatilla Indians. Here they established a school, treated the sick, and gave instruction in religion and farming.

Now it so happened that Waiilatpu was on the Oregon Trail and thousands of white settlers passed through that spot every year on their way west, using it as a rest stop. Unfortunately, these people from the East brought with them diseases unknown to the native Indians.

In 1847 the migration carried a severe measles epidemic. Whites and Indians alike caught the disease. Marcus and Narcissa Whitman worked day and night to try and save the lives of everyone. Unfortunately, the whites all seemed to get well while many of the Indians died.

The Indians jumped to a conclusion on the basis of the facts as they saw them. Whites were living and Indians were dying. They could think of only one reason for this: the Whitmans must be poisoning the Indians. On that false conclusion they acted, attacking the mission and killing fourteen persons, including Marcus and Narcissa Whitman.

What the Indians did made sense to them with their limited knowledge of what had happened. We might have felt the same in similar circumstances. However, they had judged and they were judged in return. Eventually those who had jumped to the wrong conclusion were hanged at Oregon City by officials of the United States Government.

Do you need exercise? Try jogging, swimming, or backpacking. Anything is better than jumping to conclusions!

LIGHTING THE DARKNESS

In the midst of a crooked and perverse nation . . . ye shine as lights in the world. Philippians 2:15.

How many kinds of lights can you name? There are street lights, traffic lights, flashlights, and night lights. There are searchlights, neon lights, floodlights, and stage lights. There are headlights, taillights, signal lights, and ordinary house lights.

One of the most interesting types of light is the beacon used in lighthouses. In ancient days fires were kindled each night to warn the ships at sea. Later gaslights were used and, of course, today we use electricity.

There is another type of light used in some of the wildest and remotest areas of earth where there is no electricity. This is the aga lamp invented by Nils Gustaf Dalén, of Stockholm, Sweden, whose birthday is today.

These lights use dissolved acetylene gas, which is contained under pressure in cylinders. Sun-operated valves control the flow by contracting in darkness, allowing the gas to pass to the burner and expanding when daylight comes, shutting off the flow.

These remarkable lights have made it possible to operate lighthouses in places where people cannot live. No doubt thousands of lives have been saved from shipwreck by these lights.

Do you think that Paul might have had lighthouses in mind when he talked about Christians shining as lights in a dark and wicked world? It is possible for our lives to respond automatically to the darkness of sin and despair around us by sending forth a glowing testimonial of God's love, goodness, and power.

You see, when it gets dark, the lighthouse doesn't stand there and complain. It doesn't give up hope, nor does it worry about ships that might be wrecked and storms that might come. Instead, it turns on its light to show the way.

That is what God expects of us, too. It is of no use to curse the darkness; turn on your light instead. The blacker the situation around you, the more brightly your light will shine. The darker the night, the more your light is needed.

Will you be a light for Jesus today?

THE CHRISTMAS TREE

Bring ye all the tithes into the storehouse, that there may be meat in mine house, and prove me now herewith, saith the Lord. Malachi 3:10.

On December 1, Margaret Young counted out the money for the household bills. She filled each envelope: tithe, rent, food, utilities, clothing.

Mr. Young did not have steady employment. Even his present job was temporary. There were so many things the family needed. To add to the problem, it was almost Christmas. They could, of course, make gifts for one another, and the mother and father were already working on a snowsuit and a rocking horse for their small son.

If only we had enough money for a Christmas tree, Margaret thought to herself as she stared at the tithe envelope she held in her hand. Perhaps God wouldn't mind if she kept back just enough for a tree. Surely He knew how much she wanted it, how much their little boy would enjoy it.

Then the words of Malachi came to her mind: "Prove me now herewith, saith the Lord of hosts, if I will not open you the windows of heaven, and pour you out a blessing, that there shall not be room enough to receive it" (chap. 3:10).

No! Margaret said to herself as she hastily put the tithe money into the envelope. This money is God's. I will not use it. We will do without the Christmas tree.

Margaret used the money that remained very carefully, but no matter how hard she tried, she couldn't save enough for a tree. Then, before she realized it, Christmas Eve had come.

That evening she left her son with a friend and walked to the store where her husband was working.

After he finished, they walked hand in hand down the street toward home. As they neared their corner, they heard a truck coming very fast. It screeched around the corner in front of them, skidding on the icy street. Something flew through the air and landed almost at their feet. It was a Christmas tree!

"Hey—you dropped something!" Mr. Young shouted, but the driver didn't stop. As the Youngs looked down at the lovely fir, they began to realize that this was one of God's special blessings to them. They would have a Christmas tree after all! Happily, they picked it up and ran all the way home.

343

WHEN THE DAM BROKE

He which converteth the sinner from the error of his way, shall save a soul from death. James 5:20.

Do your friends know Jesus? Do they know that He loves them and wants to make them happy? Do they know that He died for their sins? Do they know that He is coming back again soon? Will they be ready to meet Him when He comes?

Is it possible that some of your friends might be lost because you failed to do your part to save them?

It is only natural to try to rescue those whom we love when they are in danger. Disasters show what people will do for their friends and loved ones. Take for instance the night the Malpasset Dam broke in southern France.

The clock in the old church in Frejus struck nine-thirty on the night of December 2, 1959. Moments later, 395 people were dead and 1,850 were homeless. Some six miles away, the dam had burst, sending down the valley a wall of water that destroyed everything in its path.

Eleven-year-old Viviane Olivieri and her two younger brothers were home alone when the water entered the house. Viviane swam to the boys' bedroom and snatched them from their beds. She put them onto an overturned wardrobe and climbed up there herself. All three were saved.

Policeman Blazy went from house to house by helicopter picking up stranded people. He was able to save thirty persons.

At the Kohlstedt home, four children were playing on the ground floor when the wave hit town. The oldest one herded the younger ones upstairs to the attic. As their home floated away they grabbed the branches of a cyprus tree and were able to cling there until help came the next morning.

If you had been in Frejus that day, wouldn't you have done your best to save someone?

There is coming upon this world of ours a destruction much worse than what happened that day when the dam broke. There will be earthquakes, fires, and floods. The earth will be shaken and the mountains and islands will be moved out of their places. Only those who love Jesus and obey His commandments will be saved.

What are you doing to help your friends be ready for that day?

HEART TRANSPLANT

A new heart also will I give you, and a new spirit will I put within you. Ezekiel 36:26.

At two-fifteen in the morning of Sunday, December 3, 1967, Dr. Christian Barnard performed the first human heart transplant. The operation took place in Capetown, South Africa.

The patient was 54-year-old Louis Washkansky, who had suffered two severe heart attacks and was expected to die. There was a chance that a transplant might help him live longer. The problem was where to get a new heart?

Late on the afternoon of December 2, 24-year-old Denise Ann Darvall was hit by a speeding car as she crossed the street. Her head was so badly crushed that there was no hope for recovery. Her father agreed that her heart could be given to Louis Washkansky.

"Dear God, help me in this operation," Dr. Barnard prayed on the way to the hospital. He was naturally a bit apprehensive. The operation had been done many times on animals, but never before on a human being.

The surgery began by opening up Mr. Washkansky's chest, exposing the damaged heart to full view. After Denise's death, the surgeons opened her chest and hooked up her heart to the heart-lung machine. Very carefully Dr. Barnard removed Denise's heart.

Next he took the scalpel and cut out Mr. Washkansky's bad heart. Into this cavity he placed Denise's young heart and then went about the delicate job of sewing it into place, connecting the many blood vessels and nerves. The operation took nearly five hours.

"Pump off," Dr. Barnard ordered as soon as the stitching was complete. Everyone held his breath as they waited to see if the heart would begin to work on its own. It did. The operation was a success.

You and I need a different kind of heart surgery. According to the Bible our hearts are "deceitful" and "desperately wicked." With such, it is not possible for us to be saved. However, Jesus can take away the old heart in an instant and give us a new one that loves Him. Are you willing to have the operation today?

ABANDONED SHIP

Therefore is my spirit overwhelmed within me; my heart within me is desolate. Psalm 143:4.

"Look at that ship over there," said one of the crew on the *Dei Gratia.* "Doesn't something seem strange about it?"

"Yes," answered another. "It seems to be drifting without direction."

"I can't believe it," said a third. "There just wouldn't be a ship out here in the middle of the Atlantic Ocean without a captain and a crew. Something must be wrong."

"Oliver, go over and investigate!" Capt. David Morehouse ordered the mate. "Find out what's going on."

As the investigating party neared the ship they noticed that it was the *Mary Celeste.* She had been docked in New York at the same time as *Dei Gratia.* They called out, but no one answered. Drawing alongside, the men climbed aboard. They found no one there.

They discovered plenty of food and water in the galley. There was no evidence that waves had swamped the ship, washing the passengers overboard. A woman's clothes and a child's toys lay about as if their owners had left in a hurry. A half finished letter lay on the desk in the mate's cabin. The lifeboats were gone, but the ten people who were on the ship when it left New York were never found. What happened is still a mystery.

The crew of the *Dei Gratia* sailed the deserted ship to Gibraltar and gave it into the hands of the British Vice-Admiralty court. The ship was returned to the owners, and the crew of the *Dei Gratia* received $3,500 as a reward.

That desolate ship, left alone to drift unguided across the wide expanse of the Atlantic Ocean is something like people who don't know Jesus. Their lives are empty. They have no goal. There seems to be no captain for their ship of life. They are just drifting along toward destruction.

A heart without Christ is always desolate. A life without Him is always empty and meaningless. After all, without Him what can we do? Without Him where can we go? We are doomed to failure without His blessing in our lives. Without His guidance we are like a ship at sea without a captain or a crew. Without Him we are lost.

GEORGE MUELLER'S PRAYER

Open thy mouth wide, and I will fill it. Psalm 81:10.

George Mueller wanted to start an orphanage, but he was a poor man. He knew that there were six thousand orphans being kept in the prisons of England because there was no place else to put them, but what could he do? He had no house and no money.

On Saturday, December 5, 1835, George was reading in the Psalms when he came across today's verse: "Open thy mouth wide, and I will fill it." He read the verse over and over again and each time he read it he became more excited.

George Mueller had never thought of asking God for an orphanage. Now he fell to his knees and asked the Lord for three things: a building to house the orphans, one thousand pounds of money, and suitable helpers to care for the children.

Two days later George received his first gift, one shilling. From that day forward he determined to never ask man for anything. He would depend completely on prayer to demonstrate to the world that God is faithful. The results were astounding.

On one occasion a woman donated all of her jewels to the orphanage. Among them was a large diamond ring that George Mueller used to scratch the words, "Jehovah Jireh" upon the windowpane of his room. "The Lord Will Provide" became the motto by which he lived.

During his lifetime George Mueller cared for ten thousand orphans, and never once did he ask anyone but God for a penny.

On one occasion there was only seven pence left in the fund to buy the next meal. Eight pence was needed. George Mueller prayed and a gift box arrived. At the bottom of the box was the one pence he had requested.

A 10-year-old boy read about George Mueller's experiences and began to pray daily, "God, teach me to pray like George Mueller." He wanted to become a printer, but he didn't seem bright enough to even get into grammar school. His mother laughed at his ambition, but the boy replied: "I will pray. God helped George Mueller and He will help me." Soon he passed his exam and was accepted.

That boy's prayer is a good one for all of us today: "God, teach me to pray like George Mueller."

347

LIKE A FLINT

Therefore have I set my face like a flint, and I know that I shall not be ashamed. Isaiah 50:7.

More than 200 years ago a 7-year-old boy lay on the bank of a river that flowed through the lovely English countryside. His gaze was fixed on the beautiful house and gardens of Daylesford on the opposite shore. The estate had once belonged to his ancestors, but they had sold it during bad times.

"I am going to own that house someday!" the boy said to himself. "I will work hard and buy it back for my family."

That boy was Warren Hastings who was born on this day in 1732. Although he grew up to become the governor general of India, he never forgot his boyhood dream. Often he thought of Daylesford and saved his money that he might keep his resolve. When he retired he purchased the home and lived there for the rest of his life.

Warren Hastings had the same determination that Isaiah expresses in today's verse. When he was 7 years old he set his face "like a flint." Hastings could not be moved from his goal to own that house.

Daniel was another man of great determination. He purposed in his heart that he was not going to eat the king's meat nor drink the king's wine. He did not waver from his purpose.

Solomon also had a goal. He determined to carry out David's dream of building a temple in Jerusalem. He made up his mind to let nothing interfere with that goal, and he accomplished his purpose.

Jesus was another person with great determination. He came into this world with one purpose in mind, to die for our sins. When the time came to go to Calvary, He set His face like a flint to go to Jerusalem and carry out His plan. He did what He set out to do.

People who accomplish something in life are those who have a definite goal. They know what they want and they go about getting it.

Do you have a goal in life? Have you caught a glimpse of God's purpose for your existence? If you haven't, ask Him to show you what He would have you do, then hold on to that goal and never leave it until it is accomplished.

SURPRISE ATTACK

Therefore let us not sleep, as do others; but let us watch and be sober. 1 Thessalonians 5:6.

Almost everyone in Hawaii was asleep at six o'clock Sunday morning, December 7, 1941, when more than two hundred Japanese planes loaded with bombs destined for Pearl Harbor took off from their carriers.

Many of the United States military officers were still in bed when the unidentified planes appeared on the radar screen. The inexperienced man on duty thought they must be American planes. After all, thousands of miles of ocean lay between Hawaii and Japan. It couldn't be an enemy.

Many still slept and all were unconcerned when the bombs began to fall. Then it was too late to do much. Wave after wave of bombers dropped their deadly loads, destroying a good portion of the United States fleet and most of the military planes parked in close, neat rows at the airbase. During the raid 3,581 people were killed and hundreds of others were wounded.

The Japanese assault was successful because it was a total surprise. No one expected it at Pearl Harbor. American officials were rather expecting an attack somewhere in Asia, far away from home.

The American officials felt so safe that they saw no need to place the Army and Navy units in Hawaii on wartime alert. They were sleeping when they should have been awake.

Pearl Harbor has a lesson to teach Christians today, for we also are engaged in a war that has been in progress for thousands of years between the good and evil powers of the universe. We are coming to the end of the controversy between Christ and Satan that began long ago in heaven, before this world began.

In this war we must each fight our personal battles with the enemy of souls. He is a clever soldier. He knows that surprise is an important part of his success. He's not about to let you know what his next moves will be.

Now is no time to be sleeping. It is time for us to place our senses on wartime alert. We must never underestimate the ability of our enemy.

TOTAL SURRENDER

Yield yourselves unto the Lord. 2 Chronicles 30:8.

To yield yourself means to surrender yourself. It means to give up all your plans and everything you have and are into the hands of Christ. That is not so easy to do.

It is possible to go to church every Sabbath and still keep part of your heart for yourself. It is possible to read your Bible every day and yet to refuse to allow God to control all of your mind.

How often we give God only a part but not *all* of ourselves. Mr. and Mrs. John Stam knew what complete surrender meant. On December 8, 1934, they were massacred in Central China.

Two days before this happened John Stam wrote the following: "My wife, baby, and myself are today in the hands of [the enemy]. . . . All our possessions and stores they have taken, but we praise God for peace in our hearts—and a meal tonight. God grant you wisdom and us fortitude, courage, and peace of heart. He is able and is wonderful, a Friend in such a time. . . . The Lord bless and guide you. And as for us, may God be glorified whether by life or death."

If you were in such a position, imprisoned by the enemy, would you be able to say to God, "Here I am, God. You can free me or let me die, according to Your will. I am Yours"?

A good many of us would pray something more like this: "Oh, God, please help me. Get me out of this. Let me get home safe and I will do anything for You." We like to bargain with God to get what we want. This is not yielding to God.

Mrs. Stam's Bible was found later and mailed to her father. In it were these words: "Lord, I give up my purposes and plans, all of my desires, hopes, and ambitions, and accept Thy will for my life. I give myself, my life, my all, utterly to Thee to be Thine forever. I hand over to Thy keeping all my friendships, my love. All the people whom I love are to take second place in my heart. Fill me and seal me with Thy Holy Spirit. Work out Thy whole life in my life at any cost now and forever. 'For me to live is Christ, and to die is gain.'"

It takes a lot of courage to make that kind of surrender to the Lord.

REJOICE IN HANDICAPS

Most gladly therefore will I rather glory in my infirmities, that the power of Christ may rest upon me. 2 Corinthians 12:9.

Think for a moment about the Christian people whom you know. Are there any who are sick, crippled, blind, or deaf? Why doesn't God heal all of those people? Many have prayed for years to be made well; but still they suffer. Why haven't their prayers been answered?

Paul had that kind of experience. Three times he begged the Lord to remove his handicap, but the answer was No.

Instead the Lord said to him, "My grace is sufficient for thee: for my strength is made perfect in weakness" (Rom. 12:9).

And Paul answered: "Most gladly therefore will I rather glory in my infirmities, that the power of Christ may rest upon me" (verse 9).

Sometimes it may be that through our handicap God can be glorified in a manner that He could not be were we well. Often, because of our needs, God allows us to be put on our backs, so that we can look up and see Him.

Take, for instance, the experience of John Milton, who was born on December 9, 1608. He had weak eyesight as a youth and became blind at the age of 44. Two of his greatest poems, "Paradise Lost" and "Paradise Regained" were written after this tragedy. It is as if in his blindness, his spiritual eyesight became clearer. In a sense, he could "see" better after he became blind.

Beethoven became deaf at age 32. Elizabeth Barrett Browning became an invalid when a teen-ager. Robert Louis Stevenson wrote poetry from his sickbed. Francis Parkman, who has been called the greatest of American historians, was in pain all of his life. Sir Walter Scott was a cripple. President Franklin Roosevelt was confined to a wheelchair most of the time.

We could list scores of famous men and women who accomplished much in spite of sickness and handicaps. For all of these, and hundreds of ordinary Christians who have suffered, Christ's grace has been sufficient.

Do you have a handicap? Then perhaps God wants to reveal His glory in a very special way through you.

351

NEVER A HARD WORD

I will take heed to my ways, that I sin not with my tongue.
Psalm 39:1.

Abraham Lincoln was 9 years old when his mother died. He watched as his father took a log left over from building their cabin and made it into planks for her coffin. With a jackknife, little Abe whittled pinewood pegs. Then he held the planks while his father bored holes in them and stuck in the pegs, making a box in which to bury Nancy Hanks Lincoln.

The next few months were terribly lonely for Abe and his sister, Sarah. Tom Lincoln did his best to care for his children, but the food didn't taste right somehow, and the cabin seemed so bare and drear without Mother. There was no one to see to their clothing, and the children were soon running around dirty and in rags.

Then one day happiness returned to the little cabin in the Indiana woods. Tom Lincoln came home with a new mother for his children. She brought with her nice furniture, warm bedding, new clothes, but most of all love. Soon all was warm and comfortable, and the cabin was a home once more.

Abe found a very special place in his new mother's heart. She recognized right away that he had many talents and encouraged him to read and learn all he could. She was sympathetic with his desire to be something more than a backwoods farmer. She believed in him.

When Abraham Lincoln became a great man he said, "All that I am I owe to my angel mother." He was talking about Sarah Bush Lincoln, his stepmother who did so much to light up his life after his real mother died. He sometimes called her, "My saintly mother."

Mrs. Lincoln lived long enough to see Abe become President of the United States. She was living when he was shot. No one in the nation mourned his death more than she. Although she was sad, she was thankful for the happy memories that consoled her until she died on December 10, 1869.

"I can say what not one mother in a thousand can say," Mrs. Lincoln declared. "Abraham never gave me one hard word."

Isn't that a beautiful thing for a mother to say about her child? Can your mother say that about you?

THE BOLL WEEVIL

He that handleth a matter wisely shall find good. Proverbs 16:20.

Everything that happens is not good. Bad experiences come into the lives of all. It is not the circumstances that are important, but rather how to handle the circumstances that counts. It is possible that out of evil, good may come.

Take, for instance, the story of the boll weevil. One hundred years ago there were no boll weevils in the United States. In 1892 the first ones arrived from Mexico, invading the crops near Brownsville, Texas. Every year after that the insects traveled farther across the country.

Even today, with all the insecticides available, the boll weevil destroys 30 percent of the cotton crop each year, causing more than $200 million in damage.

We can't blame the Southern farmers of eighty years ago if they could see no good to come from such a pest. This little three-centimeter beetle caused many a farmer sleepless nights. Farm families depended on the success of the cotton crop in order to live. When the crop failed, people went hungry. Farms and fortunes were lost.

People prayed. They tried everything possible to get rid of the pests. Still the boll weevils thrived. Then the farmers took the only other course that seemed open. They stopped planting all their land in cotton. They began to raise cattle, chickens, peanuts, corn, and soybeans.

As we look back, we can see that this was the best thing that could have happened to those farmers. That part of the country is much better off now because they grow a wide variety of crops.

On December 11, 1919, the citizens of Enterprise, Alabama, dedicated a monument to the boll weevil.

"We are doing this," the city leaders said, "in profound appreciation of the boll weevil and what it has done as the herald of prosperity." The farmers recognized that because of their change of methods, their income was three times what it would have been had the boll weevil never come.

Sooner or later a bad experience will come to you. Do not be discouraged. Remember the story of the boll weevil. If you face your problem with prayer and understanding some good will surely come of it.

SIGNAL HILL

The Lord will hear when I call unto him. Psalm 4:3.

Dot. Dot. Dot. Pause. Dot. Dot. Dot. Pause.

The operator of the wireless transmitter on the coast of England sent out the letter *S* in Morse Code according to the plan. Over and over he punched the key in rhythm every ten minutes. Would anyone hear it 2,170 miles away across the Atlantic Ocean?

Dot. Dot. Dot. Pause. Dot. Dot. Dot. Pause.

That Thursday afternoon Gugliemo Marconi sat at the receiving set in a small, dark room on Signal Hill, Newfoundland. A storm was in progress, and the icy wind howled around the little cabin where he sat with the single earphone, listening.

Would the signal come through? After many years of experimentation, Marconi was putting his idea of sending messages by airwaves to the test. Scientists said it was impossible because of the curvature of the earth. They said that the waves would continue to travel in a straight line and be lost in space. Marconi had set out to prove the opposite. Was he correct?

Dot. Dot. Dot. Pause. Dot. Dot. Dot. Pause.

The answer came at 12:30 P.M. Newfoundland time. There were the sharp clicks of the tapper on the receiving set. Marconi listened intently. Yes, there it was. Three sharp clicks through the earphone.

With those clicks a new age of communication began. Radio, television, space communication—all became possible because of what happened at Signal Hill on December 12, 1901.

On another day and another hill something happened that made possible communication between earth and the throne of God. Because of what Jesus did on the cross of Calvary we can be sure that our prayers reach heaven.

How is it possible? Does prayer travel on magnetic waves? Is there some type of star waves that scientists have not yet discovered, which are amplified by galaxies, and that take our whispered prayers faster than the speed of light to the center of the universe?

We may not know how prayer reaches God so quickly, but like David, we can believe that it does.

FIFTH AVENUE ESCAPE

It is of the Lord's mercies that we are not consumed, because his compassions fail not. They are new every morning: great is thy faithfulness. Lamentations 3:22, 23.

The man standing on the curb of Fifth Avenue in New York City seemed to be lost in thought. He was an individual who had traveled widely and knew much of the world's difficulties. Perhaps he had those problems on his mind when he stepped from the curb directly into the path of an oncoming taxi on December 13, 1931.

The driver of the cab, Mario Constasino, slammed on the brakes, but couldn't avoid hitting the pedestrian. The blow the man received was equivalent to a fall of thirty feet onto cement.

The taxi driver was relieved to find the man still alive. Police were soon on the spot. An ambulance came and took Winston Churchill to the hospital.

"I ought to have been broken like an eggshell or smashed like a gooseberry," Mr. Churchill said later.

Once, when talking about the number of miraculous escapes he had experienced, Churchill remarked: "These hazards swoop on me out of a cloudless sky and that I have hitherto come unscathed through them, while it fills my heart with thankfulness to God for His mercies, makes me wonder why I must so often be thrust to the brink and then withdrawn."

There is no doubt but that God kept Sir Winston Churchill alive for the very definite part he had to play in the history of this world. God also spares our lives for a reason.

However, few of us are as quick as Winston Churchill to realize that it is not luck, but the mercies of God that keep us alive from day to day.

Most of us are not aware of the many close calls we have each day. If only our eyes could be opened to see the myriad escapes of our everyday lives, how thankful we would be.

Because of God's unfailing love our hearts are still beating this morning. Because of His mercies we can see the sun peeping in our window today. Because of His faithfulness there is food on our table for breakfast. Because of Him we can run out into the wind and shout to the world: "I am alive! God has a purpose for my life!"

A PAINTING AND A POEM

Who gave himself for our sins, that he might deliver us from this present evil world. Galatians 1:4.

"I gave My life for thee,
   My precious blood I shed,
That thou might'st ransomed be
   And quickened from the dead."

Frances scribbled the words quickly on the back of an old circular. She tried to express what she had just seen in the face of Christ in the painting, "Behold the Man," which hung in the art gallery in Düsseldorf, Germany.

"I gave, I gave My life for thee,
   What hast thou given for Me?"

As Frances gazed at the crown of thorns and the blood trickling down Jesus' brow, she wished she might wipe His forehead and comfort Him. Somehow she must put into words the loneliness she saw in that face.

"My Father's house of light,
   My glory-circled throne,
I left for earthly night,
   For wanderings sad and lone.
I left, I left it all for thee,
   Hast thou left aught for Me?"

As Frances stared at that painting it was as if Christ were trying to get her to understand the terrible agony He endured.

"I suffered much for thee,
   More than thy tongue can tell,
Of bitterest agony,
   To rescue thee from hell;
I've borne, I've borne it all for thee,
   What hast thou borne for Me?"

It was done. But as she read the words over she felt that it wasn't very good. She put the paper into her pocket.

This poem is number 230 in *The Church Hymnal*. It was written by Frances Ridley Havergal who was born on December 14, 1836.

Six more of her poems appear as hymns in the book. Number 273, "Take My Life and Let It Be" is another that you probably know. Why not sing these two hymns for worship this morning? Let the first ask the question, and the second be your response.

SPACE MUSIC

Glory to God in the highest, and on earth peace, good will toward men. Luke 2:14.

On December 15, 1965, Astronaut Walter Shirra, on board Gemini VI, took out his harmonica and played "Jingle Bells." Millions on earth heard what was the first music from outer space. Or was it? What about the song the angels sang above the hills of Judea that night so long ago?

Glory: Think of those things that you could describe as having glory, beauty, majesty, and honor. A sunrise. A craggy mountain peak. An eagle soaring high above the plain. The crown jewels of England. A Beethoven symphony.

The glory of God outshines a thousand suns. His beauty is greater than a million symphonies. His strength and power are far above anything we can imagine.

To God in the highest: Our Father, the King of the Universe, the Creator of suns and systems, galaxies and glaciers, shell fish and stars. The Master Designer of a butterfly's wings and a mountain mist. The all powerful, eternal, everywhere present, all knowing God. The Supreme Ruler whose throne is in the heaven of heavens, where there is no need of the sun by day or moon by night.

And on earth: This tiny speck of dust somewhere out on the edges of the universe in the great creation of God. This one dark planet that rebelled against a wise and good Creator. This little part of the universe that is marred by sin. This planet, which is the stage on which the plan of salvation is being acted out. This earth that is filled with grief, greed, violence, and hate. This earth that will one day be destroyed by fire and recreated to be the home of the redeemed.

Peace: The absence of strife. The end of wars, feuds, strikes, and riots. The end of divorce, heartache, sorrow, and insanity. The feeling of well-being that comes from knowing our sins are forgiven. The happiness that comes from knowing God. The experience of being right with God and man.

Good will toward men: Happiness and hope brought to men: sinful, deceitful, impure men who have lost their way. To you and to me, bringing us the loving favor of God because we are now His sons and His daughters through the sacrifice of that Babe in the manger.

DEAF MUSICIAN

Then the eyes of the blind shall be opened, and the ears of the deaf shall be unstopped. Isaiah 35:5.

Imagine what it would be like to sit at a baseball game and not be able to hear the umpire shout, "Batter up!"

Or to be unable to hear the first chirps of the robins in the spring?

What if you couldn't hear your mother call you for breakfast?

Imagine what it would be like to put your favorite record on the turntable and not hear a single note.

What if you walked by the seashore and couldn't hear the pounding of the waves on the rocks?

What if all the television programs were like silent movies to you?

Imagine being in a thunderstorm and not being able to hear the thunder.

Or being at a symphony concert and not being able to hear the violins. Then, what if you were the conductor and couldn't tell whether or not the flutes were playing?

What if you sat down to practice the piano and though you hit the keys with all your strength, no sound came out?

What if your friend was left standing in the cold because you couldn't hear the doorbell ring?

That's how it was with Ludwig van Beethoven, who was born on this day in 1770. Imagine what it must have been like for him, a composer, concert pianist, and conductor, to begin to lose his hearing at the age of 25. Every year he heard less and less until at last he was stone deaf.

In spite of this he continued to compose music until he died. In an attempt to hear the notes when playing the piano, he would bend his body over the keyboard until his ears nearly touched his fingers.

For years Beethoven refused to acknowledge his deafness and continued conducting his orchestra, though it was painful for the players. In order not to hurt his feelings, they kept playing, but watched the first violinist instead of the conductor because his gestures were not in time with the music.

Beethoven died in the midst of a violent thunderstorm which he could not hear. His last words were, "I shall be able to hear in heaven!"

BOSTON TEA PARTY

Neither give place to the devil. Ephesians 4:27.

When it comes to dealing with the devil, we need to have the same determination to resist that the American colonists had in 1773.

At that time they were ruled by the king of England. To show his authority, troops were sent to the New World to carry out his orders. Heavy taxes were charged to the colonists, and the money went to England. After a series of protests, the taxes were all removed except for the one on tea.

"All right," the colonists agreed among themselves, "then we will not buy English tea."

Soon 18 million pounds of tea were rotting in the warehouses. Still the English kept sending shiploads of tea to the colonies.

On the night of December 16 and the early morning hours of December 17, a group of men, led by Samuel Adams, painted their faces, dressed as Indians, and crept down to the docks in Boston. At a given signal they swarmed over the ships that contained the tea. They opened the holds and tossed the wooden chests into the bay.

"Bravo! Bravo!" they shouted to one another as they dumped more than three hundred chests overboard.

Word of the Boston Tea Party soon reached England, and King George III realized that he had a rebellion on his hands.

It might not be a bad idea for Christian young people to take a cue from the rebellious colonists. Perhaps a family "party" would be in order in which we threw out of our homes the devil's products. After all, why should we pay taxes to Lucifer?

Cigarettes, drugs, alcoholic drinks, and yes, perhaps even tea, coffee, and cola drinks are some of the items that need to be thrown out. Novels of crime, violence, and sin surely need to go. There might be some impure pictures that ought to be discarded. Perhaps we need to sort through the records and cassettes as well. Surely there are some television programs that should go.

Getting rid of the devil's products is one way of telling him that we are tired of his tyranny and want to be free. Let's make sure there is no place for the devil in our homes today.

WILL TO LIVE

I have set before you life and death, blessing and cursing: therefore choose life, that both thou and thy seed may live. Deuteronomy 30:19.

"You don't realize how much life means until you come close to losing it," said Wayne Lindblom.

Wayne ought to know, for he is a man the doctors did not expect to live.

The accident happened on December 18, 1971, when Wayne, 27, was crushed by a piece of earth-moving equipment. The skin was torn from his back. Several ribs were broken. His spine was injured. His left kidney was torn and his large intestine mangled. His spleen and pancreas were ruptured and he was bleeding profusely.

"I have never seen such a bad case," his doctor said. Then things went from bad to worse. Wayne's one good kidney failed and his liver stopped working. He developed a bleeding ulcer in his stomach.

Wayne stayed in the hospital for seven months.. When the doctor tried to explain to the injured man's wife the near certainty of his death she refused to believe it. "Wayne is *not* going to die," she insisted.

"God is with us," she told Wayne the first time she saw him after the accident.

God certainly helped them. He gave Wayne the courage to face his pain. He gave wisdom to the sixty-five doctors who worked to save his life. He gave Wayne the will to live so that he could be with his wife and little boy again.

Perhaps one of the greatest factors in Wayne's recovery was this will to live, his inner determination to submit to all that the doctors would do, to cooperate in every way possible, that he might live. People with less serious injuries have died in spite of all that was done to save their lives because they did not possess that will to live.

You and I are in a similar situation as was Wayne Lindblom. We are also casualty cases, sin casualties. But there is hope. Christ, the heavenly Physician, can help us, but we must have the will to live eternally. We must choose life rather than death. We must say, "Yes, Lord, do what is necessary so that I might live." Will you choose life today?

PENKNIFE REMINDER

Obey the voice of the Lord your God. Jeremiah 26:13.

On Friday, December 19, 1777, the weary, defeated Continental Army were in Valley Forge, Pennsylvania, where they had set up camp.

There were eleven thousand soldiers under the command of George Washington. Three thousand of these were unfit for duty because they were half naked and had no shoes. Many were sick.

General Washington requested Congress for supplies but none came. The men had to make their own crude log shelters to keep out the icy winds. Food was scarce and medical supplies were inadequate. A smallpox epidemic broke out and thousands died.

Other thousands wanted to desert the army and return to their families. Even General Washington decided to leave. He wrote out his resignation and showed it to General Knox. Disheartened, Washington took out his penknife and toyed with it idly as he explained his reasons for calling it quits.

"That penknife is the best argument against your resignation," General Knox said.

At first Washington was puzzled. Then he remembered. The penknife was a present from his mother. He had wanted to enlist in the Navy when he was 15 years old, but his mother persuaded him to stay at home. As a reward she ordered a fine penknife from England. When it arrived she handed it to him with these words: "Always obey your superiors."

Washington had often told that story to his friends around army campfires. Now, when he was about to resign, General Knox reminded him of this symbol of his duty. "Always obey your superiors."

"Your orders are to lead this army," said General Knox. "No one has told you to lay down this leadership."

"You are right," responded General Washington. "I will obey my orders." He tore his resignation into shreds.

Obedience is just as important for God's soldiers. Our duty is clearly written across the pages of the Bible: "Obey the voice of the Lord your God."

Will you obey Him today?

BURIED ALIVE

Then they cried unto the Lord in their trouble, and he saved them out of their distresses. Psalm 107:13.

In the early morning hours of December 17, 1968, Barbara Jane Mackle, 20-year-old daughter of a Florida millionaire, was kidnapped and held for a $500,000 ransom.

Barbara was taken to a lonely spot in the woods outside of Atlanta, Georgia, where she was forced into a coffinlike box that was set into the ground. The lid was screwed tight and she heard the dirt being shoveled onto the lid of the box. She was buried alive!

"We'll let you out when we get the money," one of the kidnappers said. But would the money come in time?

The box where Barbara was lying was not big enough to sit up in. Neither could she stretch out her full length. There was a light in one corner and switches for a pump and ventilation fan. Everything was hooked up to a battery in a compartment behind her head. Printed instructions said that the battery would last for seven days if she didn't use the light.

At first she struggled to lift the lid, to shout, to do something about her situation, but at last she gave up. There was nothing she could do but try and control her fears.

Water dripped into the box, making her cold and damp. The light bulb flickered and went out. The darkness terrified her.

She thought about dying. What if the kidnappers didn't reveal her whereabouts, even after they got the money? What if they left her there forever? What if the police couldn't find her?

Barbara hadn't thought much about God before. She was too busy having fun to pray. But now that she was buried alive she began to pray. She talked to God as if He were right there beside her.

She said, "God, I know You are not going to let me die. Even if no one else knows where I am, You know."

God heard Barbara's prayer. At 12:47 P.M. on Friday, December 20, the kidnappers called the FBI and gave directions to her location. Four hours later she was found alive and well.

God is just as willing to hear your prayers.

BOLD REQUEST

Whatsoever ye shall ask the Father in my name, he will give it you. John 16:23.

In November of 1875, the Suez Canal was up for sale. The ruler of Egypt was willing to part with his half of the shares, but he wanted the money right away.

The prime minister of England saw this as a marvelous opportunity. After all, most of the ships using the canal belonged to his country. If there should be a war, England would suffer. It was important that this opportunity not be lost.

The prime minister instructed the British representative in Cairo to sign the contract. Four million pounds had to be paid Egypt within a few hours. How could the Government of England get that much money in such a short time?

There was no time to call Parliament. An application to the Bank of England for a loan would take weeks of board meetings, investigations, and talks. The delay might lose them the opportunity. Someone else would surely buy the canal if they hesitated.

The prime minister decided on a more direct plan of action. He told his secretary to remain just outside the Cabinet room; and when the decision to obtain a loan had been reached, he would put his head out of the door and say one word, Yes. The secretary was then to go directly to Mr. Rothschild, the richest man in Europe, and ask for the money.

In due time the prime minister opened the door. "Yes," he said. And the secretary hurried to Mr. Rothschild.

"The prime minister wants 4 million pounds by tomorrow," he said. "It is very important."

"What is your security?" Mr. Rothschild asked.

"The British Government," the secretary answered.

"You shall have it," said Mr. Rothschild. And the payment was made on time.

The prime minister who was so bold as to go to Mr. Rothschild directly, in the name of the British Government, was Benjamin Disraeli, Earl of Beaconsfield, whose birthday is today.

We need to have that same boldness in bringing our requests before the King of the Universe. Jesus Christ is our security. Whatever we ask in His name we will receive.

MISJUDGED

Blessed are ye, when men shall revile you, and persecute you and shall say all manner of evil against you falsely, for my sake. Matthew 5:11.

Someone in France gave secret military documents into the hands of the Germans. A search was made and evidence pointed to Alfred Dreyfus.

"I am innocent," Dreyfus declared, but the government proceeded with a secret military trial on December 22, 1894. He was found guilty of treason and sentenced to deportation for life to a lonely prison on Devil's Island off the coast of South America.

When Mr. Dreyfus heard the verdict he was overcome with despair. "Give me a revolver," he begged a friend. "I will kill myself and end this horror."

"You must not accept defeat," his friend replied. "To commit suicide would be to acknowledge your guilt. You are innocent, and we will prove it. You must stay alive and await justice."

Two days later Dreyfus was publicly humiliated when his military badges and buttons were removed.

"Alfred Dreyfus, you are unworthy to bear arms," the officials declared. "In the name of the French people we degrade you!"

Dreyfus shouted in reply, "An innocent man is being degraded. An innocent is dishonored!"

A few years later the real traitor was discovered and Alfred Dreyfus was released. He was reinstated in the army and later became a member of the Legion of Honor.

We cannot always expect justice in this world. Men make mistakes. Sometimes we are blamed for things we did not do. Such an experience is very frustrating.

Jesus knows how you feel in such a situation. He went through it during His trial. He suffered for crimes He did not commit and through it all He never said a word. In His love and patience under false accusations He gave us an example as to how we should behave when we are misjudged.

When we are falsely accused we are to be happy and rejoice. We are not to fight back or become despondent, but are to sing and praise the Lord. Someday the truth will be revealed.

ESCAPE FROM RANGOON

Thou shalt not be afraid for the terror by night; nor for the arrow that flieth by day. Psalm 91:5.

On December 23, 1941, Pastor I. Subushanam was helping Evangelist A. E. Rawson catalog slides at the Burma Union headquarters in Rangoon when the air raid sirens began to wail.

Pastor Subushanam was concerned about his wife and 1-year-old daughter, who were home alone. He was determined to be with them. The bombs were already beginning to fall as he made his way by bicycle across town. Crowds of people were rushing to the outskirts while he was trying to push through them into the city.

At last he reached the street where he and his family lived. It was completely empty. When he reached home he found his wife on her knees beside the baby, praying for safety.

Pastor Subushanam knelt beside his little family and pleaded with the Lord to deliver them from destruction. As he said Amen there was a terrific blast, and the house shook.

After a while, they cautiously opened the door to look outside. No one was in sight. A few minutes later the all-clear signal was given, and Pastor Subushanam went outside and found that a Japanese bomber, brought down by antiaircraft guns, had fallen just a few yards from their house.

During the day the city was bombed two more times. The Subushanams were uninjured, but how long could they stay in the burning city? They must find some way of escape. That evening they were able to get tickets on a boat to India, and Pastor Subushanam sent his wife and child ahead to the ship while he stayed to pack up their belongings. When he arrived at the boat he was refused entrance. The gang-plank had already been removed. The ship was about to leave.

Again Pastor Subushanam cried out to God for help. Frantically he ran up and down the jetty looking for a way to board the ship. Then he noticed an open porthole. Looking inside he saw that the hold was full of bags that had not been unloaded. Squeezing into the porthole he crawled over the cargo and made his way to the passenger decks, where he found his family.

Standing there in the confusion of the refugee-crowded deck, Pastor and Mrs. Subushanam held their little one close and thanked God for His marvelous deliverance.

CHRISTMAS IN THE JUNGLE

The righteous cry, and the Lord heareth, and delivereth them out of all their troubles. Psalm 34:17.

Just before noon on December 24, 1971, Juliane Koepcke boarded Lansa airlines flight 508 from Lima to Pucallpa, a jungle town 760 miles northeast across the Andes. She had just finished high school and was going to be with her father for Christmas.

Juliane looked out the window at the loveliness of the snow-covered mountains. Then the white turned to green as they reached the jungle.

Without warning the air grew turbulent. Rain beat against the windows, and the plane was tossed like a kite in the wind. There was a blinding flash of lightning. The plane rocked and luggage fell from the racks. There was a tremendous shudder as the plane broke apart. Juliane felt herself tumbling over and over in the air before she became unconscious.

When she awoke she was lying on the ground with a section of three airplane seats over her. It was still raining. She knew she was hurt, but she couldn't move.

The girl felt better the next morning and crawled out to survey the situation. Dense foliage grew all around. Ferns, trees, and vines seemed to form an impenetrable wall. She couldn't just stay there to die. She had to find a way out.

"God, help me," she cried.

Juliane began walking. Soon she came to a little brook. She knew that this would take her eventually to a river and perhaps to civilization. For days she followed the stream.

Late one afternoon, when Juliane felt she could go no further, she came around a bend in the river to see a boat tied to the bank and a path which led to a small cabin in the jungle. No one was around, but the next day the owners of the boat came and discovered her. Immediately, they took her to a town where she could get medical help.

Do you think it was a mere coincidence that Juliane found the cabin when she did? Was it only by chance that the men arrived on that particular day? They came only once in three weeks. Was it only luck that it was raining so hard that she stayed in the cabin for a day instead of pushing on through the jungle? What do you think?

CHRISTMAS GIFT

I am come that they might have life, and that they might have it more abundantly. John 10:10.

It was Christmas Day, 1809. Mrs. Thomas Crawford lay on a bed in the log cabin of Dr. Ephraim McDowell in Danville, Kentucky.

Beside her stood the doctor. Nearby waited his wife and nephew, ready to assist in the first abdominal surgery performed in America. The boiled instruments sat in a kettle on the table. The operation would be without anesthetic. It was time to begin.

Inside of Mrs. Crawford there was a tumor that was growing larger everyday. "In this condition you will certainly die within a few weeks," Dr. McDowell had explained. "However, there is a slim chance that we can help you by removing the tumor. If we fail, then you die a little sooner. If we succeed, you can expect to live for many more years."

"I'm putting my faith in God," Mrs. Crawford told Dr. McDowell as she looked up into his kindly eyes. "I'm ready now. I will be praying and thinking of Him as you do what you have to do. If He wants me to live, if it's His will, everything will come out all right."

The operation lasted about twenty-five minutes. The pain was terrible, but Mrs. Crawford gripped the sides of the bed and sang hymns.

Outside the cabin a large mob gathered. Word had spread of what was happening, and the people felt that the doctor was going against the laws of God. Who had ever heard of opening up a person's stomach? The doctor must be in league with the devil. "If she dies, we'll hang him," they agreed.

Just then the door of the cabin opened and there stood the doctor. "A life has been saved," he said quietly. "It's Christmas. You should all be home with your families."

As they turned to leave, the crisp winter air carried the sound of Mrs. Crawford singing a Christmas carol. She had just been given the best Christmas gift ever—her life.

But Mrs. Crawford's gift of life did not last forever. She died at the age of 79. Today Christ offers life to you that will never end—glorious, beautiful, abundant, eternal life. What better Christmas present could there be?

CHRISTMAS SURPRISE

Behold, I come as a thief. Blessed is he that watcheth.
Revelation 16:15.

If the Hessian sentries had been watching, George Washington's troops would not have captured a thousand troops at Trenton, New Jersey, on December 26, 1776.

The Hessians were expecting an attack from the Continental Army. They were not very happy with the thought of it being on Christmas Day. They had special festivities planned, but instead they were ordered to watch.

To make matters worse the weather was foul. An icy wind blew snow out of the north. In the afternoon it turned to sleet and then to a freezing rain that penetrated to the very bones.

An attack came just as dusk had fallen. A group of Americans ran out of the woods and raced toward the sentries, killing three of them. The drummers beat out the call to arms, and the Germans responded with fire. The Americans fled into the darkness.

To this day no one knows who those soldiers were. They were definitely not part of Washington's army, which at that time was on the other side of the Delaware River, several miles away, just beginning to load the boats for the crossing.

In any case, the Hessians believed it to be Washington's army and were relieved that there had been so few soldiers and that they had retreated so quickly.

"Do we have to stand duty any longer?" a guard asked.

"They won't be back. No one can fight in this rain," someone else argued.

"We can't even keep the powder dry for our muskets," another said.

"You are released from duty," replied Colonel Rahl. "Go back to your festivities. Enjoy Christmas as though you were safe at home in Germany."

So the men ate, talked, sang, and drank far into the night.

When Washington's men arrived about eight o'clock the next morning, the town was silent. Even the sentries were asleep at their posts. Victory was easy.

That is how Christ's coming is going to be for those who are not watching—sudden, unexpected, frightening.

MAD DOG!

A man can receive nothing, except it be given him from heaven. John 3:27.

One sunny autumn day in France about one hundred years ago, six boys were watching their cows among the hills of Jura. Suddenly, along a lonely road, a dog came racing toward them, foam dripping from its open mouth.

"Mad dog!" the boys screamed and ran.

Fourteen-year-old Jupille did not run. He was the oldest, and felt responsibility for the younger boys. He faced the raging animal. As it neared him, he lashed out at it with his whip. The dog lunged, sinking its teeth into the boy's left arm.

It was a heroic deed Jupille had done at the risk of his own life. He had been bitten by a rabid dog, and in due time he would get rabies and die a most horrible death. People in the village talked and cried and wished they could do something to save their hero.

It so happened that the mayor had heard of a scientist in Paris who was working on a cure. That man was Louis Pasteur, whose birthday is today.

Jupille went to Paris where he received fourteen injections, and his life was saved. So new was the cure that had the boy been bitten one year earlier he would surely have died.

How thankful Jupille and his family were for what Louis Pasteur had discovered! The whole town rejoiced that their hero was saved!

There is another whom they should also have thanked. After all, who gave the wisdom to Mr. Pasteur so that he could make the discovery? Who set in motion the laws by which scientists work? Who guides them to all good and noble inventions? Who knows better than the Creator of the world how to counteract the results of sin that we see in sickness, pain, suffering, and death?

For every discovery that makes this world a happier place let us say, "Thank You, God."

TOMMY'S CONSTITUTION

I delight to do thy will, O my God: yea, thy law is within my heart. Psalm 40:8.

Tommy Wilson walked to the vacant lot where the neighborhood boys were playing baseball. Especially today he wanted to play with them because he had a new ball and bat. He stood by a tree and looked wistfully at the players. Then he leaned his shiny bat against the tree trunk and began to play catch with himself.

"Where'd you get the ball and bat?" someone yelled.

"My father gave them to me," Tommy answered.

The game stopped, and the boys gathered around to see the bat of polished hickory wood and the real baseball. They could do with a new boy on their team, they decided, particularly since he had such a neat ball and bat!

Tommy really wasn't much good at baseball, but he was good at making rules and organizing things. So the boys made him president of a club they called The Lightfoots.

One day Tom called the club together and said, "I have made a constitution."

"What's a constitution?" someone asked.

"The constitution gives the name of our club and states all the rules we are going to follow," explained Tommy.

After reading the rules to the boys, he said, "Will someone please move that the constitution be adopted?"

The boys remained quiet. They didn't know what Tommy meant.

"If you like the rules one of you must say, 'I move that the constitution be accepted.' Then someone else has to say, 'I second the motion.' Then we will vote on it."

So the motion was made and seconded and the constitution became the law of The Lightfoots. Thomas Woodrow Wilson, whose birthdate is today, and who later became the twenty-eighth President of the United States, had learned an important lesson. A government must have rules, and the people must be willing to follow them.

God's government also has rules. They are found in the Ten Commandments.

Would someone like to move that we accept them as our constitution? Who will second the motion? All in favor, please say, "Aye."

SHORTSIGHTED PEOPLE

Esteeming the reproach of Christ greater riches than the treasures in Egypt: for he had respect unto the recompence of the reward. Hebrews 11:26.

Some people are shortsighted. They can see only what is near to them, the *now*. They are not able to take the long view and see what is important in the light of the future. They do not reckon with eternity.

Moses, who is described in today's verse, was not short-sighted. He thought life through and realized that if he wanted the reward of Christ in the future, he would have to sacrifice some things in the present.

One time a shortsighted young man approached William Gladstone, prime minister of Great Britain, whose birthday is today, and asked him for advice about his future.

"I want to study law," the youth said.

"Yes," said Mr. Gladstone, "and what then?"

"Then, sir, I expect to be admitted to the bar."

"Yes, and what then?"

"I hope to get a place in Parliament."

"Yes, and what then?"

"I will do great things for my country."

"Yes, young man, and what then?"

"I suppose I will retire and take life easy."

"And what then?" Mr. Gladstone persisted.

"Of course I will die," answered the young man.

"Yes, and what then?"

"I had never thought any further than that," he replied.

"Then you are a fool," said Mr. Gladstone. "Go home and think life through."

Have you thought life through? Have you taken the long look and thought about your final reward? If not, then today is a good time to do something about your shortsightedness. Stop a moment and take a look at your life.

What is a hockey game when compared to eternity? What does a little misunderstanding with a friend count when you think about heaven? What is a motorbike compared to a mansion in glory? How do your friends look in the light shining from the New Jerusalem? How much will clothes mean when you see Jesus come? Is sin really worth it when you consider eternity?

FIGHTING FEAR

Fear thou not; for I am with thee: be not dismayed; for I am thy God. Isaiah 41:10.

Fear is a terrible thing. It can cause people to behave in a stupid, irrational manner. Take, for example, what happened at the Iroquois Theater in Chicago on December 30, 1903.

It was an icy 8 degrees below zero in the windy city, but in spite of the miserable weather, a crowd of 2,400 mothers and children attended the afternoon performance of *Mr. Bluebeard.*

The beginning of the second act featured a musical number called "In the Pale Moonlight." Special high-temperature lamps were used to create the appearance of a moonlight night. During this particular performance, the operator was careless and one of the lights touched a painted backdrop. Immediately the stage was ablaze.

The heavy asbestos fire curtain was lowered on the stage, thus keeping the fire away from the audience and giving them plenty of time to leave the building.

Some of the thirty exits were frozen shut and the people panicked. They lost control of the situation as they screamed and pushed to try to get out. Fear made them indifferent to the lives of others. As people fainted, others walked right over them.

Five hundred and eighty-nine people perished. Very few of these died because of the fire or smoke. They were trampled to death by a fear-crazed throng.

What frightens you? Are you afraid of high places or dark alleys? Do new faces or spiders send chills down your spine? Are you afraid of doing something to cause your friends to laugh at you? Are you frightened that you might fail?

Do your hands break out in a cold sweat when you have to do something in Sabbath school? Does your heart beat faster when you are all alone at night in the house? Do you feel like running when you see a mouse?

It might be helpful to make a list of all your fears on a piece of paper. Study your list. Do you really want to hang on to your fears? Why not make a New Year's resolution to get rid of them? Ask the Lord to take them all away. We really have nothing to be frightened about since Jesus has promised to always be with us.

INVENTORY TIME

So then every one of us shall give an account of himself to God. Romans 14:12.

Some businesses shut down for a few days this time of year to take inventory. Armed with clipboards and merchandise lists, employees take stock of the assets of the company. Every piece of furniture and equipment is listed. A tally is made of the supplies and merchandise on hand.

Now might be a good time to do a personal inventory. For this you will need paper, pencil, and a quiet place. No distractions should be permitted. You will need time to take a good look at yourself and give an account to God. I'll show you part of my inventory to give you an idea of how to go about doing it.

Health: Ears, eyes, hands, feet, and all systems of the body are in good working order. Weight, however, is twenty pounds more than it should be.

Interests and hobbies: This year I identified 152 birds and have more than 200 wildflowers on my list. We made a rock garden in the corner of the front lawn, and I learned a dozen new recipes. Cycling has been a growing interest and reading has taken up much of my spare time. I have read about sixty books, most of them biographies.

Bad habits: Chewing my fingernails when I am nervous or bored. Leaving my clothes lying around the house. Eating more than I need to at meals. Blaming my husband when something goes wrong.

Personality strengths: Cheerfulness, sense of humor, high sense of duty and responsibility, thoughtfulness of others, ability to give and receive love.

Personality weaknesses: Sensitive, too easily hurt, shy in the presence of strangers, too independent.

Of course, this is only a beginning. Other headings might be: Personal appearance, spiritual life, intellectual development, personal relationships, debts, ambitions, material possessions.

There are several benefits from this type of activity. It can show us where we are in a rut. We can see those areas of our lives where improvement is needed. It will help us to set specific goals to work on in the New Year.

SCRIPTURE INDEX